Company Confessions

Company Confessions

Secrets, Memoirs, and the CIA

CHRISTOPHER MORAN

Thomas Dunne Books
St. Martin's Press
New York

THOMAS DUNNE BOOKS.
An imprint of St. Martin's Press.

www.thomasdunnebooks.com
www.stmartins.com

Library of Congress Cataloging-in-Publication Data

Names: Moran, Christopher R., author.
Title: Company confessions : secrets, memoirs, and the CIA / Christopher R. Moran ; foreword by Tony Mendez.
Description: First U.S. edition. | New York : Thomas Dunne Books/St. Martin's Press, 2016.
Identifiers: LCCN 2016003324| ISBN 9781250047137 (hardcover) | ISBN 9781466847491 (e-book)
Subjects: LCSH: United States. Central Intelligence Agency—Officials and employees—Biography. | Intelligence officers—United States—Biography. | United States. Central Intelligence Agency. Publications Review Board. | BISAC: POLITICAL SCIENCE / Political Freedom & Security / Intelligence. | HISTORY / United States / 21st Century.
Classification: LCC JK468.I6 M656 2016 | DDC 327.1273—dc23
LC record available at https://lccn.loc.gov/2016003324

Our books may be purchased in bulk for promotional, educational, or business use. Please contact your local bookseller or the Macmillan Corporate and Premium Sales Department at 1-800-221-7945, extension 5442, or by e-mail at MacmillanSpecialMarkets@macmillan.com.

First published in Great Britain by Biteback Publishing Ltd

First U.S. Edition: August 2016

10 9 8 7 6 5 4 3 2 1

Contents

Foreword

by Tony Mendez and Jonna Mendez

British scholar Christopher Moran's absorbing new book is a fascinating look at a subject very much on the mind of many former and current employees of the Central Intelligence Agency. The infamous Publications Review Board (PRB) is an unpredictable speed bump on a CIA author's road to the publication of any written work, whether a fully-fledged book or a letter to the editor. Anything else in between these two points, for that matter, written for public consumption by an agency professional, is required to run the gauntlet of the PRB. And that can be quite a difficult and capricious experience for an author. In fact, this is one of the basic premises of Moran's detailed study of the intelligence memoirist.

Dr Moran's approach is freshened by the fact that he comes to the subject as an outsider; not as a CIA officer or even a member of the intelligence community, but as a serious student of national security and the very process of collecting intelligence. As such, he is well-equipped to lift the exquisite veil of secrecy surrounding the CIA's review board and examine the machinery lying behind it. And what a machine he describes – reminiscent of the giant Wurlitzer at the heart of *The Wizard of Oz*; one that proceeds by fits and starts, then runs smoothly for a time, years perhaps, before it begins to cough and splutter again as a new CIA director takes the controls. The resulting chaos that repeatedly ensues is an amazing read. *Company Confessions* is a serious enquiry into the process of how successfully and appropriately the CIA has, through the machinations of the PRB, balanced national security with the American public's right to know.

Those CIA directors, and the chairmen of the PRB, have a very direct impact on the ability of a CIA officer to write a book, while the Agency maintains control of its information. Another key element of *Company Confessions* takes a penetrating look at the politics behind the PRB policies. While many in the intelligence community will recognise general trends emanating from the White House and filtering down into their agencies, Moran is able to form a much more direct cause-and-effect relationship regarding censorship and takes considerable pains to demonstrate this point with detailed descriptions of the way different authors and books have been dealt with. The results themselves frame the Agency's mixed feelings about its image, its story and even secrecy itself.

CIA director George H. W. Bush established the PRB in June 1977. Less than a year later new CIA director Stansfield Turner's appointment by the Carter administration and his desire to usher in a new era of openness are discussed at length, not only Turner's desire to 'make the public one of the direct beneficiaries of our efforts' but his establishment of a Speaker's Bureau at the CIA. To the Agency's old guard this was tantamount to a betrayal from the top; they feared that, by opening that vein, even a little, the control over secrecy, the life-blood of the Agency, would bleed away.

The case of former CIA officer Frank Snepp and his unauthorised publication of *Decent Interval*, an insider's unflattering book about Snepp's CIA experience in the Vietnam War, illustrates the other side of the coin. Under Turner's military-centric control, the PRB would not, could not, tolerate this insubordination. The CIA's cold fury rained down on Snepp, who published without PRB review and then suffered the retribution that this precedent-setting case deserved, bluntly drawing a line in the sand. Future publication without PRB approval would result in prosecution and, in this case, forfeiture of all profits from the book. Case made.

The final irony, of course, is the story of DCI Stansfield Turner himself and his attempts to publish his own memoir, *Secrecy and Democracy: The CIA in Transition*. Upon stepping down as head of the CIA, he was hoist on his own petard. Turner agonised through a hostile PRB review of his manuscript that lasted two years. Moran's detailed documentation of Turner's journey as CIA director is a fascinating behind-the-scenes look at the politics and policies of the PRB as they evolved during his tenure.

There are a multitude of stories, some of almost urban legend fame in the intelligence community. Even though the stories may be familiar to insiders, Moran brings a level of detail and a story-telling ability to each that will keep readers turning the pages, or swiping their screens.

Moran's approach to his subject reads as fair and even-handed. There are plenty of examples that will cause a new evaluation of what those in the intelligence community would consider an old story; the author clearly does not have a dog in this fight. He does, however, deliver his research with fresh eyes and with a bent for balance. Perhaps it is this ultimately unbiased approach that brings him to a philosophical discussion of the well-regarded head of the CIA's Publications Review Board, John Hollister Hedley.

From 1996 to 1998, the PRB functioned under the chairmanship of Hedley. A thoughtful officer who described his role as that of an 'honest broker', he set out to find solutions, not create new problems. Attempting to set a new course, Hedley stressed that new realities required new thoughts. Redefining the role of the PRB, Hedley presented a new formula for the Board to consider in performing its duties: he emphasised not what had to be taken out, but what could be left in. The rules were relaxed, and the publication of Dewey Clarridge's book *A Spy for All Seasons* and Richard Helms's memoir *A Look Over My*

Shoulder followed. It was Helms, in fact, who began to advocate against the once-common adage that revealing the history of intelligence was unwise.

Christopher Moran calls out the Hedley era as a false dawn in terms of PRB process, with many of the old habits subsequently returning after Hedley's departure: too long to review the material, hostility toward unflattering material, inconsistent definitions of what is deemed classified. Additionally, discreet support has been lent to friendly treatment of classified material.

As the CIA's Chief of Disguise, when working with a surveillance team in a zone around Washington, DC, we had code names for use in our radio transmissions. The CIA's headquarters building in Langley, with a new addition cloaked in copper screening that appeared to be green glass, was christened 'The Emerald City'. We always knew that there was a wizard inside, the Great and Powerful Oz, pulling the strings and levers, controlling the secrets. Christopher Moran provides a wealth of information documenting the CIA's internal battles over disclosure versus the right to secrecy. It is a revelatory read.

Acknowledgements

One of the pleasures of completing a book is taking a moment to thank the various people who helped it come into being. Andrew Lownie is perhaps the most good-natured and tirelessly attentive agent into whose hands a young author could hope to fall, and I count myself exceptionally fortunate in having him to represent my literary interests. From Biteback, I should like to thank Michael Smith for seeing the book's potential, and Victoria Godden, for copyediting the manuscript to the highest professional standards and much more besides. From St Martin's, deepest thanks to Thomas Dunne and Will Anderson. I am especially grateful to Will, the soul of patience, for guiding me step by step through the publishing process. Help has also flowed in liberally from many other corners of the press, and I can only add my praise to the long list of authors appreciative of their efforts.

For historians, there is nothing more exhilarating than the paper chase, travelling from archive to archive, immersing oneself in documents, in the hope of discovering some hidden nugget or gem. However, without the help of archivists and librarians, the historian would be lost – ultimately high on enthusiasm, but low on end product. This one is no different. Without the assistance of staff at the following repositories, this book could never have come into existence: Arthur and Elizabeth Schlesinger Library on the History of Women in America, Harvard University; Bancroft Library, University of Berkeley; Churchill College, Cambridge University (UK); Davidson

Library, University of California, Santa Barbara; Edward L. Doheny Jr Memorial Library, University of Southern California; Eisenhower Presidential Library, Abilene, KS; George C. Marshall Research Library, Lexington, VA; Georgetown University Special Collections Research Center, Georgetown University; Harry Ransom Center, University of Texas, Austin; Hoover Institution, Stanford University; Howard Gotlieb Archival Research Center, Boston University; Houghton Library, Harvard University; Library of Congress, Washington, DC; Margaret Herrick Library, Academy of Motion Picture Arts and Sciences, Los Angeles, CA; Milne Special Collections and Archives, University of New Hampshire; National Archives II, College Park, MD; National Archives of Japan, Tokyo; Rare Book and Manuscript Library, Columbia University; Rauner Special Collections Library, Dartmouth College; Seeley G. Mudd Manuscript Library, Princeton University; State Historical Society of Wisconsin, Madison, WI; Tamiment Library and Robert F. Wagner Labor Archives, New York University; US Army Military History Institute, Carlisle, PA; Wendell H. Ford Public Policy Research Center, University of Kentucky; and Yale University Library, Yale University. I am also grateful to these institutions for giving me permission to quote from their collections.

The completion of this work was made possible by several grants and fellowships. Between 2008 and 2011, I had the good fortune to work as a research assistant on the AHRC-funded project, 'Landscapes of Secrecy: The CIA and the Contested Record of US Foreign Policy, 1947–2001'. Coming so soon after finishing my PhD, the 'Landscapes' project was a godsend, and I am thankful beyond words to the two principal investigators, Matthew Jones and Richard J. Aldrich, for putting their faith in me. Richard and Matthew are both outstanding scholars, and their work has been instrumental in shaping my understanding of the CIA, intelligence and US foreign policy. As part of the project, I was lucky to work alongside a number of talented early career researchers, all of whom have since gone on to secure permanent academic posts. Now at the University of East Anglia, Kaeten Mistry is the author of a pioneering book on the CIA, Italy and the early Cold War. Based at the University of Hull, Simon Willmetts is an expert on the relationship between the CIA and Hollywood, and has an extremely bright future ahead of him. At the University of Nottingham, Paul McGarr has established himself as one of the world's leading authorities on re-lations between the United States, Great Britain and the developing world. Paul and Matthew also deserve credit for putting together our end of project conference, held at the East Midlands Conference Centre in April 2011.

As the finishing line came into sight, the British Academy gave a welcome injection of funds, under the auspices of a Postdoctoral Fellowship. At least a quarter of the book was written at the Rothermere American Institute at the University of Oxford, a highly stimulating en-vironment where students and scholars consider 'all things American'. For making me feel at home during my time there, I am grateful to Huw David, Jay Sexton, Sebastian Cody, Ursula Hackett and, above all, the Director of the Institute, Nigel Bowles. I am extremely fortunate to have held a six-month postdoctoral fellowship at the John W. Kluge Center at the Library of Congress, which gave me access to a vibrant community of scholars, plus key archival holdings. Since 2008, I have enjoyed working with Peter Earnest, Anna Slafer, Vince Houghton, and Alexis Albion as a part-time consultant at the International Spy Museum in Washington, DC. This book would be a poor shadow of itself had it not been for frequent pilgrimages to the nation's capital, at the invitation of the museum.

My reflections on CIA memoirs have developed in dialogue with many friends, colleagues and interviewees, though they bear no re-sponsibility for any errors of fact or interpretation, which are mine alone. It would be impossible for me to thank them all, but I feel obli-gated to mention a handful of standout individuals: Adam Svendsen, Andres Vaart, Arthur Hulnick, the late Cameron LaClair, Christopher

Andrew, Christopher Hughes, Christopher Murphy, Cynthia Helms, David Gioe, David Kahn, Eric Pullin, Frank Snepp, Frederick Hitz, Hayden Peake, Hugh Wilford, Jonathan Nashel, John Hollister Hedley, John Prados, Joseph Wippl, Jonna Mendez, Mark Phythian, Mark Zaid, Michael Goodman, Mike VanBlaricum, Nicholas Reynolds, Nick Vaughan-Williams, Nigel West, Oz Hassan, Patrick Major, Paul Maddrell, Philip Murphy, Rhodri Jeffreys-Jones, Richard H. Immerman, Robert Johnson, Scott Lucas, Tony Mendez, Tracey Rich and Wesley Wark. My heartfelt thanks are due to those close friends who read the text in full: Andrew Hammond, Christopher Read, Mark Stout and William Rupp. My debt to these individuals is impossible to repay. Acknowledgement is also due to several writers on US intelligence who sadly I have never met, but whose pioneering works have paved the way for a generation of authors like myself: Amy Zegart, Evan Thomas, James Bamford, Kathryn Olmsted, Ronald Kessler, Seymour Hersh, Steve Coll, Thomas Powers and Tim Weiner.

I am grateful to Peter Martland and the organisers of the Cambridge Intelligence Seminar, the finest of its kind anywhere in the world, for twice inviting me to test my arguments before such a discerning and insightful audience. I would also like to thank the CIA History Staff for their encouragement and wise counsel, in particular David Robarge and Nicholas Dujmovic. Keep up the good work.

Despite time spent 'on the road', this is fundamentally a University of Warwick book. The Department of Politics and International Studies at Warwick is my scholarly home, and I have benefited beyond measure from the advice and questions of staff and students, both past and present. For nearly ten years, Richard J. Aldrich has been my closest colleague, mentor, and dear friend. A constant source of encouragement and wisdom, Richard remains as devoted as ever to answering the distressed early-morning email, for which I am grateful. Invaluable support has also come from Trevor McCrisken and my four PhD students, Jules Gaspard, Melina Dobson, Nikita Shah and Dee

Dutta. As this book progressed from inception to realisation, I had the good fortune to enjoy the company of many talented students. I owe a special debt to those who have taken my Tuesday afternoon class on the history of the CIA. My thinking has been greatly enriched by their lively and astute contributions. It has been a privilege to learn with them and from them.

Finally, it would be remiss of me if I did not thank my parents and especially my fiancée, Ioanna. Their unflagging support and encouragement has benefited me in ways too numerous to enumerate. Quite simply, this book would not have been possible without Ioanna's love and companionship.

List Of Abbreviations

Used in the Text

ACLU	American Civil Liberties Union
AFIO	Association of Former Intelligence Officers
AHRC	Arts and Humanities Research Council
CIA	Central Intelligence Agency
DCI	Director of Central Intelligence
DD/CIA	Deputy Director of the Central Intelligence Agency
DGI	Dirección General De Inteligencia
DNI	Director of National Intelligence
DO	Directorate of Operations
HUMINT	Human Intelligence
ICBM	Intercontinental Ballistic Missile
ISCAP	Interagency Security Classification Appeals Panel
JIC	Joint Intelligence Committee [UK]
KGB	Komitet gosudarstvennoy bezopasnosti
MID	Military Intelligence Division
MI5	Security Service [UK]
MI6	Secret Intelligence Service [UK]
MSU	Michigan State University
NASA	National Aeronautics and Space Administration
NCS	National Clandestine Service
NSA	National Security Agency

NSC	National Security Council
OGC	Office of the General Counsel
OPC	Office of Policy Coordination
OSS	Office of Strategic Services
OTS	Office of Technical Service
PRB	Publications Review Board
RAF	Royal Air Force [UK]
SIGINT	Signals Intelligence
WMD	Weapons of Mass Destruction

Locations

AES	Arthur and Elizabeth Schlesinger Library on the History of Women in America, Harvard University, Cambridge, MA.
AMHI	US Army Military History Institute, Carlisle, PA.
AMPAS	Margaret Herrick Library, Academy of Motion Picture Arts and Sciences, Los Angeles, CA.
BL	Bancroft Library, University of Berkeley, CA.
CCC	Churchill College, Cambridge University, UK.
DL	Davidson Library, Department of Special Collections, University of California, Santa Barbara, CA.
ELD	Edward L. Doheny Jr Memorial Library, University of Southern California, Los Angeles, CA.
EPL	Eisenhower Presidential Library, Abilene, KS.
GCMF	George C. Marshall Foundation, Lexington, VA.
GFPL	Gerald R. Ford Presidential Library, University of Michigan, Ann Arbor, MI.
GUSC	Georgetown University Special Collections Research Center, Georgetown University, Washington, DC.
HGARC	Howard Gotlieb Archival Research Center, Boston University, MS.

HI	Hoover Institution, Stanford University, CA.
HL	Houghton Library, Harvard University, Cambridge, MA.
HRC	Harry Ransom Center, University of Texas, Austin, TX.
JFK	John F. Kennedy Presidential Library and Museum, Boston, MA.
LOC	Library of Congress, Washington, DC.
MSC	Milne Special Collections and Archives, University of New Hampshire Library, Durham, NH.
MSU	Michigan State University.
NAJ	National Archives of Japan, Tokyo, Japan.
NARA	National Archives and Records Administration, College Park, MD.
RBML	Rare Book and Manuscript Library, Columbia University, NY.
RSC	Rauner Special Collections Library, Dartmouth College, NH.
SGM	Seeley G. Mudd Manuscript Library, Princeton University, NJ.
TAM	Tamiment Library and Robert F. Wagner Labor Archives, New York University, NY.
USAHEC	US Army Heritage and Education Center, Carlisle, PA.
WHF	Wendell H. Ford Public Policy Research Center, University of Kentucky, Lexington, KY.
YUL	Yale University Library, Yale University, New Haven, CT.

Collections

AD	Allen W. Dulles Papers
AK	Arthur Krock Papers
BAR	James O. Brown Associates Records
BS	Bayard Stockton Papers
CF	Corey Ford Papers

CM   Cord Meyer Papers

CREST   CIA Records Search Tool

DAP   David Atlee Phillips Papers

DPM   Daniel P. Moynihan Papers

FBI   FBI Files

HNS   H. N. Swanson Agency Records

JM   John A. McCone Papers

JRF   James Russell Forgan Papers, 1945–73

LF   Ladislas Farago Papers

LK   Lyman B. Kirkpatrick Papers

LWC   Lawrence Weingarten Collection

MB   Mary Bancroft Papers

MGM   Turner/MGM Scripts

PA   Philip Agee Papers

RC   Ray Cline Papers

RH   Richard Helms Papers

RLEW   Ronald Lewin Papers

RW   Robert Wear Collection

SB   Scott Breckinridge Papers

SK   Sherman Kent Papers

WC   William Casey Papers

WCE   Wilbur Crane Eveland Papers

WCP   William Colby Papers

WFF   William F. Friedman Collection

WH   William Hood Papers

WJD   William J. Donovan Papers

WRC   William R. Castle Diaries

WRD   Wallace Rankin Deuel Papers

Company Confessions

Introduction

I. If Walls Could Talk

The secret of our success is the secret of our success.
CIA Proverb.[1]

In autumn 1973, the Central Intelligence Agency approached a man named Harold Vogel for a special assignment. Vogel was not a spy, but possessed a particular set of skills required by the Agency. Born in Detroit, Michigan, he had been raised in the Bavarian town of Ansbach during the period of the Great Depression, where his grandfather, a restoration sculptor, taught him everything he knew about a hammer and chisel. Inspired by his elder's teachings, Vogel studied for a stone carving apprenticeship in Nuremberg, before eventually returning to the United States, settling in Northern Virginia, as a Master Carver, where he found his talents in high demand. His various projects included restoring the Senate Chamber in the US Capitol, working on the National Cathedral, and fashioning a new wooden frame for the Declaration of Independence at the National Archives. Alerted to his craftsmanship by the US Commission of Fine Arts, the CIA asked him to build a wall, a memorial wall to be more precise, only ever to be seen by CIA employees and approved visitors.

Earlier that year, several CIA officers had recommended that a plaque of remembrance be installed at CIA headquarters at Langley to honour comrades who had died in the jungles of Vietnam and Laos. It was subsequently suggested that the Board be a tribute to all CIA men and women who had fallen in the line of duty, provided they satisfied Agency-defined criteria of a 'heroic' death. Inspired by an aesthetic of elegant minimalism and simple geometric forms, Vogel's concept was a memorial wall designed to evoke a sense of pride and loss in everyone walking by it. This was approved by Director William Colby in November 1973.

Unveiled without ceremony in July 1974, Vogel's design is one of the first things visitors to Langley will see, located on the north wall in the grand foyer of the Original Headquarters Building. Made out of smooth, white, Vermont marble, and flanked by 'Old Glory' on the left and a flag with the CIA's seal on the right, it currently bears 111 stars, each signifying a fallen hero, a solemn constellation that has increased from thirty-one since the wall was erected. Measuring precisely 2.25 inches tall by 2.25 inches wide and half an inch deep, each star is painstakingly produced, first drawn by hand, following a stencil, before a pneumatic air hammer and chisel are used to carve out the traced pattern. The star is then cleaned and sprayed black, which, with age, fades to grey.

Above the stars is an inscription that reads: 'In honor of those members of the Central Intelligence Agency who gave their lives in the service of their country'. Below them on a marble shelf is a Book of Honor, made from Moroccan Levant leather, locked in a stainless-steel and inch-thick bulletproof glass case. Inside, some of the names of the fallen are neatly inscribed, penned by a professional calligrapher, using a dip pen and black sumi ink for a lustrous finish. Next to these names is the year they died and a hand-etched, 23-carat gold-leaf star, no bigger than the size of an asterisk. In recent years, the job of making new stars for the wall has passed to Tim Johnston, a little-known tradesman out of Manassas, Virginia, who ordinarily makes bespoke bathrooms and kitchen surfaces. Like Vogel, his mentor, he derives no pleasure in carving new stars, but recognises that it must be done and is thankful that he is the one entrusted with the responsibility.[2]

The CIA prides itself on quiet patriotism. A CIA officer, it is said, puts his country first, the Agency second, and then himself. The Memorial Wall is a silent and lasting reminder of the men and women who paid the highest price for this pledge. It is a poignant symbol of the dangers associated with intelligence work – dangers that most people, thankfully, will never experience. Every year, since 1987, the CIA holds a commemoration ceremony in which the names of the fallen are read aloud by representatives of each of the four directorates. Family members of the deceased are invited to attend and, since 2009, are given a keepsake replica of their loved one's star. The National Anthem is observed, prayers are read, and an all-white floral wreath is placed before the wall. Finally, a trumpeter concludes the occasion with a playing of 'Taps', the bugle call sounded at US flag ceremonies and funerals.

What are the stories that lie behind the Memorial Wall? Ironically, more is known about the building of this edifice, thanks to a glossy 23-page brochure produced by the CIA's Office of Public Affairs, than many of the people it venerates. As much as it is a shrine to the CIA's heroes, it is also a testament to what is arguably the Agency's operative virtue – secrecy. The Book of Honor is essentially censored. One hundred and eleven stars are inscribed on its pages, but only eighty have names next to them. For security reasons, the identities of thirty-one employees honoured on the wall are not contained in the book. Nor are the omitted thirty-one known to the men who carved their stars. Anonymity – even in death. The book contains no information about what position any of the officers held, what missions they were on, or how or where their lives were tragically cut short. The year of death is recorded, but not the day or month. Because of compartmentalisation within the organisation, the stories behind the wall are just as much of a mystery to most CIA officers as they are to the public. Retired CIA field operative Melissa Boyle Mahle has written that, 'The identity of most were clouded in secrecy even to me, and I did not dare inquire because I did not have the need to know.'[3] Remarkably, Richard Helms, whose career in US intelligence spanned more than three decades, including over seven years as CIA Director, has said that: 'Most of the names didn't have any resonance with me … I didn't know who they were.'[4]

The annual commemoration ceremony sheds no extra light on the careers of any of the 111 heroes. Indeed, it too is a monument to the culture of secrecy. Guests, who are instructed to leave cameras, video recorders and mobile phones at home, arrive at the visitor's centre from Route 123, where they are greeted by guards carrying pistols or, in times of high alert, assault rifles. After presenting their ID and Social Security Number, they are issued with a badge and directed to the compound proper, where there is a VIP parking lot. Many of the grieving parents, widows and widowers arriving that day have no clue about the circumstances in which their spouses or children died; some may have even been fed falsehoods. Entering into the cavernous lobby through a set of turnstiles, visitors might take a moment to step on the granite inlaid CIA seal, sixteen feet across, made famous by countless Hollywood movies, or observe, even genuflect, at the statue of William Donovan, Director of the wartime Office of Strategic Services (OSS). Undercover CIA officers are told long in advance to stay away. Eventually, everyone takes his or her assigned seat, arranged in a horseshoe pattern, looking directly at the Memorial Wall. There is no press. The incumbent CIA Director says a few words about sacrifice, but that is it. This contrasts starkly with Medal of Honor ceremonies, where a citation is given outlining an individual's achievements. If they are lucky, guests might receive a vetted transcript of the proceedings, containing only the sparse remarks made about their loved ones.[5]

Ever since it was created in 1947, the CIA has worried about people wanting to tell its stories – not just the stories that lie behind each of the 111 stars, but many more besides. An oft-quoted CIA proverb is: 'The secret of our success is the secret of our success.' In common with all intelligence services – worldwide – the CIA is keen to protect stories that, if disclosed, would endanger the lives of sources, jeopardise operations or expose to the nation's enemies the methods by which vital information is collected and analysed. President Gerald Ford once said that he would gladly share all the CIA's secrets to every American, at the time estimated to be 214 million people, if he could guarantee that Moscow wasn't listening. The CIA's anxiety about the revelation of sources and methods is long ingrained in American history, dating to the foundation of the Republic. George Washington was adamant that such information was sacrosanct. On 26 July 1777, at the height of the American Revolutionary War, he wrote to Colonel Elias Dayton, who ran a spy ring in Staten Island, urging secrecy: 'The necessity of procuring good Intelligence, is apparent and need not be further urged. All that remains for me to add is, that you keep the whole matter as secret as possible. For upon secrecy, success depends in most Enterprises of this kind.' So apposite were these words that, some 200 years later, the CIA hung a framed reproduction of Washington's letter on a wall at Langley for employees to see. At least one CIA Director has taken it with him when testifying on the Hill.[6]

The CIA has a justifiable argument that it needs to prevent the disclosure of stories that would undermine its ability to carry out its mission. Even in a free democratic society, there is a need for intelligence secrets, just as there is a need to protect the secrets exchanged between doctor and patient, or attorney and client.

The danger of not having a veil of secrecy for sources and methods should not be underestimated. The CIA's effectiveness hinges to a large degree on whether it can protect this body of information. Foreign intelligence services, whose cooperation is often crucial, will not enter into liaison relationships if they cannot trust the CIA to protect basic secrets. When secrecy about unique and sometimes fragile techniques is compromised, enemies will develop countermeasures, potentially denying policymakers with intelligence essential to national security. CIA Director Admiral Stansfield Turner (1977–81) was committed to opening up the CIA, but remained acutely aware that transparency about methods was a line he could not cross. 'If we tip the other side off to just how we are collecting our data', he said sternly at a meeting of the Commonwealth Club of California in August 1977, 'the flow of information will end and cost money, men and time to turn it on again in some way.'[7]

The CIA will struggle to recruit personnel and sources if it cannot guarantee that their identity will remain secret. In some cases, the life of an intelligence officer or source hinges on that guarantee being preserved. Indeed, at least one of the stars on the Memorial Wall – that of Richard Welch (more about him later) – is there because someone told a story the CIA failed to stop.

It is generally accepted – or at least it should be – that there is a public interest in the CIA protecting stories that impinge directly on sources and methods, even if the most compelling evidence to demonstrate the actual harm caused by disclosure is only available in the classified domain. The real controversy starts when the CIA is perceived as wanting to withhold stories where it is not obviously apparent that national security concerns are at stake. In the United States, where the political health of the nation stems from the ability of citizens to know and criticise policies carried out in their name, people have a right to be angry when it appears that the CIA is suppressing stories that might cause embarrassment, because they contain evidence of failure, ineptitude, wrongdoing or violations of law. That anger is intensified if the CIA is seen to be seizing upon the leverage of 'national security' – traditionally a sure-fire way to strike fear into people who do not know any better – to throw indiscriminately a blanket over a multitude of sins. It has long been claimed by critics that secrecy is a largely mindless reflex at the CIA, with the Agency keeping secrets for secrecy's sake, irrespective of whether there is a legitimate national security reason for doing so. Steven Aftergood, a political activist who directs the Federation of American Scientists Project on Government Secrecy, has argued that the bureaucratic instinct to avoid embarrassment is so powerful at Langley that the guiding mantra is not simply 'If in doubt, classify,' it is just 'classify'.[8]

Every story requires a storyteller. This book examines how the CIA, with varying degrees of success, has attempted to control one particular type of storyteller. Investigating what tales this breed of storyteller wants to tell, and why, and exploring how much or how little the CIA has allowed them to say, provides a fascinating vantage point from which to assess the depth of secrecy at Langley (the secrets of secrecy, so to speak), and for thinking about whether the Agency has struck a fair and appropriate balance between its need to protect sources and methods and the core American value of openness.

Meet the intelligence-officer-turned-memoir-writer.[9]

II. What Would Walter Say?

Exposed intelligence agents are either dead, 'turned',
or retired – and writing their memoirs.
Warren F. Kimball, historian and former Chair of the State
Department Historical Advisory Committee.[10]

Walter Pforzheimer owned two apartments at the Watergate complex in Washington, DC. Purchased in 1966, six years before a 'third-rate burglary' made the site infamous, the two apartments served different purposes. One was Pforzheimer's living quarters. The other, overlooking the Potomac River, and fortified by a locked steel gate, was home to the largest private collection of intelligence books in the world. The son of a rare book dealer, Pforzheimer was a bibliophile all his life, but his particular love for spy stories began in 1942 when he joined the OSS and wanted to read all about his new trade, the so-called 'second-oldest profession'. That passion grew in 1956 when he was asked by CIA Director Allen Dulles to found and curate the Historical Intelligence Collection at the CIA, intended to help the Agency keep on top of what had been published and what was still secret. Acquiring the title of 'Dean of Intelligence Literature', Pforzheimer purchased two copies of every book – one for the CIA, and one for himself. As his obituaries noted, he was the custodian and keeper of the CIA's institutional memory. Those lucky to have seen his private library with their own eyes will remember books in every room, even the lavatory, spilling off ceiling-high shelves, tables and chairs, and out of liquor boxes and fruit crates cannibalised for storage. As a personal touch, tacked onto one shelf was a bumper sticker with the words: 'The world is at peace, 'cause the CIA is at war'.[11]

A lifelong bachelor, known by his friends as a loveable curmudgeon, outspoken to a fault, Pforzheimer was never happier than when he was at home, surrounded by his literary possessions, with a bottle of whisky and a fellow 'old boy' for company, musing about Yale, his beloved alma mater, his days at the CIA or the latest spy book. Were he alive today, he would need a third apartment to accommodate the staggering volume of books now being written about US intelligence, especially by CIA veterans. In recent years, it has become almost obligatory for senior retirees of the CIA to publish a memoir. In the words of one journalist, 'The spies are coming in from the cold – and heading straight to Amazon.com'.[12] In the words of another, 'At retired spooks' conventions, the card tables in the lobbies must be creaking under the weight of them all'.[13] In 1998, the Chairman of the Publications Review Board (PRB), the body at the CIA responsible for vetting and clearing publications by CIA personnel, reported that the Board was being called into action more than 300 times a year.[14] This was just the start of it. In 2004, the PRB reviewed no fewer than 30,000 pages.[15] By 2007, some 100 prospective authors were contacting the Board every month.[16] In 2010, it reviewed more than 1,800 manuscripts. In March 2011, the Board set a new one-month record by reviewing more than 300 manuscripts – the equivalent of what was reviewed in an entire year only a decade earlier.[17]

Memoir writing by ex-CIA officers is big business. Six-figure advances are relatively common, while intelligence officers of the first rank, such as former Directors, can command a lot more. Published in 2014, *Worthy Fights*, the memoir of CIA chief Leon Panetta, reportedly earned its author a lofty $3 million.[18] Memoirs by particularly controversial or high-profile individuals will often become bestsellers, in some cases overnight, and draw the attention of a broad range of national and international presses. Published in 2007, the memoir of George Tenet, CIA Director at the time of 9/11, climbed as high as No. 2 on the Amazon bestseller list, beaten to the top spot only by the seventh and final Harry Potter novel.[19]

If large promotional tours, television appearances and the sound of ringing cash registers are not enough, some authors have even seen their memoirs become major motion pictures. Ben Affleck's film adaptation of *Argo*, the true story of how CIA disguise and exfiltration expert Tony Mendez rescued six American diplomats from post-revolutionary Iran under the guise of being a Canadian film crew, pulled in a cool $136 million in domestic box office receipts and won Best Picture at the Oscars. The only down side, Mendez has joked, was not being played by George Clooney.[20]

The popularity of CIA memoirs should not come as a great surprise. They offer a special window into a realm of human activity that has long attracted public curiosity and concern, but which has also been obscured by secrecy and contorted by fantasy. While often eliciting hostility for what critics perceive as dubious literary quality, in many cases they provide the first draft of history, containing insights that one simply cannot get from other sources and which might otherwise remain hidden from the scrutiny of posterity. Indeed, since the CIA's approach to declassification can at times leave a lot to be desired, memoirs might be the only place that certain information will ever be found.

Authors and publishers are keen to entice readers with the promise of a privileged and expert peek inside the secret world. Dust-jacket hyperbole will give the impression of an all-knowing spy, in the autumn of their life, making one final dead drop that will leave the reader infinitely better informed. In 1976, Ballantine Books raised reader expectations by claiming that Joseph Burkholder Smith's *Portrait of a Cold Warrior* was 'one of the most vivid, honest and revealing looks ever at the CIA by a man who was inside during the hottest decades of the Cold War.'[21] In 1989, Berkeley Books boasted: 'Former CIA Deputy Director Russell Jack Smith takes you on a thrilling behind-the-scenes tour of the intelligence community – for a rare glimpse of the everyday inner working of the *real* CIA.'[22] Eye-catching titles like *The Unknown CIA*, *Need to Know* and *Blowing My Cover* are cleverly designed to invite the reader to pick at forbidden fruit.[23] Moreover, publishers sometimes cannot resist giving a book a more titillating title than it deserves, or its content can actually sustain. For example, Praeger insisted that CIA veteran Arthur Hulnick call his book *Fixing the Spy Machine*, against his better judgement.[24] As a result, Hulnick spent a large part of the book explaining that intelligence is not a machine, is not in fact broken, and, ergo, doesn't need to be fixed.[25]

Given the abundance and popularity of CIA memoirs, it is surprising that scant effort has been made to study them or explore their historical development. Naturally, whenever a new title is released, journalists are quick to pen reviews. The CIA also provides engaging and informed critiques of recent memoirs in its in-house journal, *Studies in Intelligence*, written by the heir to Pforzheimer's bibliographic throne, Hayden Peake. Yet, the frame of investigation for book reviews is understandably narrow, focused on whether the work in question constitutes 'good history'. The absence of any serious or book-length enquiry into this body of literature can be traced to a broader reluctance among historians to study 'official memoirs' of any kind. The acid of envy has played its part. As George Egerton explained in a perceptive article in 1988, many historians are uncomfortable with the harsh reality that their painstakingly researched monographs seldom match the excitement and earnings generated by an official memoir promising secrets, scabrous details and high-class gossip.[26] Jealousy, however, tells only half the story. Historians have long been sceptical about official memoirs, which they regard as self-serving and selective, irrespective of claims by the author to 'tell it how it was'. Every memoirist, they believe, to justify and vindicate their actions, will resort to *suggestio falsi* and *suppressio veri*. Indeed, as Egerton remarks, 'Are not [officials] uniquely disqualified, by years of habit-forming professional obfuscation, from telling the truth about what they have done and why they did it?'[27] With good reason, concerns about factual contamination and mendacity are increased in the case of spy memoirs. Why, after all, should anyone believe a word of what a spy has to say? They are trained to lie, deceive and dissemble; that is their business. The historian's frustration is compounded by the fact that it is often impossible to verify the author's version of events because the documents necessary to do so are not available in the public domain.

Moreover, the older the memoirist, and the further the distance from the events described, the greater the likelihood of memory being eroded by the encrustations of time. At Langley, there is an old story about two elderly spies, a husband and wife. One evening, the wife announces that she would like a big fat sundae before going to bed, with vanilla ice cream, chocolate sauce, whipped cream and a cherry on top. She asks her husband to write the order down, knowing he would forget, but he repeats the ingredients verbatim and leaves the house. Sometime later, he returns with a brown paper bag and a satisfied grin on his face. After opening the bag and pulling out a ham sandwich, his wife says to him: 'See. I told you to write it down. You forgot the mustard.'[28]

The time has come, however, to think about CIA memoirs in a new light and not simply dismiss them because of their questionable objectivity. Whether historians like it or not, they play a significant role in shaping public perceptions of the CIA. By the time they have been serialised and reviewed in mass circulation newspapers, displayed in the windows of bookstores, attracted the attention of talk shows, been reborn in paperback and, in some cases, made the journey to the silver screen, they have left a powerful cumulative imprint on modern political culture and collective social memory. Egerton refers to this as the 'latent function' of the memoir.[29] In the case of CIA memoirs, this latent function is even greater because they exist in a world where information about intelligence and intelligence agencies is extremely limited. Quite simply, our knowledge of many aspects of intelligence history would be greatly diminished without them.

The ubiquity of CIA memoirs, coupled with their latent function in framing popular perceptions, represent compelling reasons to subject them to in-depth analysis. By sheer dint of numbers, they are important. From the perspective of this study, what makes them particularly worthy of detailed investigation is that they provide a window onto a bigger subject: secrecy. By looking at the development of CIA memoirs – why they have been written; what they have revealed; what the CIA has allowed to be revealed; and the battles the CIA has fought and the strategies it has adopted to try to prevent certain disclosures – we learn a great deal about how the Agency has approached the age-old puzzle of secrecy in an open society. In short, an examination of CIA memoirs is highly revealing of how successfully and appropriately the Agency has managed the high-wire act of balancing national security concerns with the founding principles of the American Republic.

III. Blood Sport

On the Agency's scale of preferential occupations for ex-employees,
a second career in writing is a cut above double agents and
a shade below gunrunners.
CIA Officer David Atlee Phillips, 1975.[30]

This book makes three major claims.

One: for most of its history, the CIA has regarded memoirs with outright hostility. 'There used to be a feeling of "Don't even think about writing a book", and I shared that feeling,' recollected CIA officer Floyd

L. Paseman, who retired in 2001 and published *A Spy's Journey* in 2004.[31] As we shall see, intelligence officers have had a range of motivations for wanting to write memoirs, some more noble than others. No author is exactly the same, but common factors include a desire to expose wrongdoing, settle scores, correct popular misconceptions, seek self-glorification and obtain money. Unsurprisingly, money looms large in many cases, and is perhaps the common denominator. Whatever the motive, the CIA's default position was for a long time clear and simple: spies should not write books. If intelligence officers saw something they did not like, they should speak with their superiors, report to the CIA's Inspector General or go to the President's Intelligence Oversight Board – not write a book. If they feel their reputation or actions have been un-fairly impugned, they should resolve the conflict in-house – not write a book. If they are fed up with the distorted and lurid fantasies spun by certain journalists and spy novelists, they should suck it up and get on with their job – not write a book. If they feel underpaid, they should start a new career on Wall Street – not write a book. And finally, if they find it maddening to have saved the world and have no one know about it, they should polish their medal or see a therapist – not write a book.

Memoir writing is fundamentally antithetical to the Agency's most cherished code: never celebrate successes or explain failures. Spies are meant to be inveterate 'hiders' of things, expected neither to confirm nor deny. The principles of silence and discretion are ingrained in staff from the moment they walk through the door at Langley. Accordingly, when someone produced a book, the Agency's natural instinct was, for many years, to regard this as improper at best, traitorous at worst. James E. Flannery, who joined the CIA in 1952 and was later deputy chief of the Latin American division, encapsulated this uncompromis-ing attitude in a letter to fellow CIA man Scott Breckinridge:

Every CIA employee is required to sign a secrecy oath as a condition of employment; he is not released from that oath in leaving. He was not forced to work for the CIA, and it is clear to him at the time he enters its employ that he is obligating himself to observe unusual restrictions and rules of conduct.[32]

The CIA's deep-seated dislike of intelligence officers writing books can be discerned from a myriad of declassified documents. In May 1947, a few months before the CIA came into being, Lawrence R. Houston, who became the first general counsel of the CIA and who built the statutory foundation on which it rests, agreed with his superiors that a British-style Official Secrets Act, which enjoined any intelligence officer from saying anything in public (even the colour of the office wallpaper), was highly desirable. However, he lamented that the timing to introduce it was wrong, with congressmen still adjusting to the idea of a permanent foreign intelligence service, and wondered anyway if it might contravene the First Amendment.[33] Six years later, the desire at the CIA for a draconian Secrets Act was still very much alive, but again the legal obstacles were judged to be too great. Pforzheimer, the CIA's man on the Hill at the time, concluded that Congress would never pass such an act because it 'appeared to run counter to our prohibition against internal security functions'.[34] In 1981, an internal CIA investigation was set up to 'find ways to discourage former officers from writing books'.[35] Proposals ranged from tougher exit briefings, warning departing officers of the damage caused by books to operations and other equities, to lectures by senior management giving employees the third degree about publishing.[36] It should be emphasised that the CIA's basic aversion to intelligence officers 'treading the boards' is not anomalous in US history. 'I do not mean to protect or countenance them in any manner of trade, should they attempt to carry it on,' wrote a decidedly unforgiving George Washington.[37] Indeed, Washington punished offenders with the lash!

Two: the CIA's core belief that it is unbecoming of an intelligence officer to write a book has ensured that, in many cases, memoir writing is a blood sport. To put this argument into some context, as a condition of employment, every CIA employee must sign a secrecy agreement vowing, subject to civil and criminal sanctions, not to disclose classified information. Contained in this agreement is a pre-publication review clause, mandating submission of all writings that bear relation to the officer's career or the CIA – memoirs, speeches, articles, editorials, book reviews, dissertations, even movie scripts. This requirement extends beyond employment, into perpetuity. According to the PRB, the 'sole purpose' of pre-publication review is to safeguard classified information, which, if disclosed, would harm the Agency or the country.[38] In April 2014, the PRB Chairman described the Board as 'another set of eyes', there in case an author fails to spot something, 'either because of an oversight or because they were not even aware that the information is classified'.[39] This second set of eyes, he continued, is not intended to 'interfere with people wanting to tell their stories'.[40] Permission to publish cannot be refused because the material is either embarrassing to the CIA, critical of it, or inaccurate. Authors, even CIA officers, have a constitutional right to free speech under the First Amendment – albeit that right is curtailed for the sake of national security. The late CIA stalwart William Hood, author of several books, once said: 'We could write that everyone is dead drunk at eleven o'clock in the morning and they couldn't say no.'[41] If the drunkards were named, that would be a different matter.

For the majority of authors, however, even loyalists, the pre-publication review process is exhausting and infuriating. Bitter and lengthy disputes over what can be disclosed are commonplace, with authors, not the guardians of secrecy, invariably the ones to make the greatest sacrifices. The net result: books littered with lines and sections 'blacked out', sometimes for pages on end. Frustrations with the PRB have extended all the way to the CIA's seventh-floor executive offices. For example, in 1991, former CIA Director Stansfield Turner was aghast when the PRB refused him permission to mention, in an article for the journal *Foreign Affairs*, the National Reconnaissance Office – an organisation acknowledged in a Senate committee report in October 1973 and extensively reported by the press. Required to refer to a completely fictitious organisation known as the Satellite Reconnaissance Agency, Turner wrote mockingly in a footnote: 'For reasons that are difficult to comprehend, the true name of this agency is classified.'[42]

Captain Nathan Hale, a martyr soldier of the American Revolution, executed for spying by the British, famously described espionage as a 'peculiar service'. Peculiar is probably the kindest word one can use to describe the decision-making of the PRB. Examples abound of the PRB exceeding its mandate, using redactions to silence critics and shelter the CIA from embarrassment. Yet, this is not its biggest fault. Time and again, the evidence suggests that it fails to pass what Warren Kimball, speaking in the context of CIA declassification, has called the 'common sense test'.[43] Plain old common sense dictates that as human sources die, as technologies become obsolete, and as governments and liaison arrangements change, there comes a time when secrecy is no longer needed. This might take thirty years to be the case; but eventually, as Kimball observed, the risk surely dies with the ageing. Alas, the PRB has seldom thought in these terms, making author disputes inevitable.

To illustrate this, take the experiences of CIA alumni Scott Breckinridge and Joseph Wippl, both dyed-in-the-wool patriots and Agency men, with no desire whatsoever to hurt the country. Breckinridge's exchanges with the PRB were, in his own words, 'painful' – so painful, in fact, that he protested to the CIA's Inspector General, Frederick Hitz.[44] 'This is a complaint ... about the Publications Review Board,' he wrote:

> My complaint is not just that they have caused me problems, but they seem to have a narrow and unthinkable adherence to some set of rules that so often stem from either a lack of knowledge of what is in the public domain, or that reflect a bizarre sense of human judgment.[45]

Breckinridge's main grievance was that he had been prevented from saying that he had served in Australia for three years, despite the fact that this was well known. To expose what he perceived to be the absurdity of the Board's decision, he showed them a postcard he had received from CIA colleagues wishing him 'Good Luck Down Under'. The postcard, which appealed to his love of bladed-weapon combat sports with a picture of a kangaroo, in full fencing garb, poised to launch a sabre attack, had been sent through normal postal channels.[46] If his Australian assignment was so sensitive, he remonstrated, why had the Agency sent a postcard and had it delivered by an ordinary mailman? Moreover, it was now 1995 and his Australian tour had ended in 1959. Surely enough time had elapsed for such a disclosure not to damage national security?

As a former operations officer who spent thirty years in the National Clandestine Service (NCS), Wippl is as qualified as anyone to know what secrets need protection. Like Breckinridge, he has found the PRB to be overly conservative in its approach, wedded to the notion that the world will end unless it errs on the side of extreme caution. Nowhere more evident is this than the PRB's long-standing refusal to allow authors to use the word 'station'. 'The whole world knows that there are [CIA] stations in embassies,' Wippl said in a recent interview, 'but I had one person in the PRB say that if we admitted there was a station in the Japanese embassy, they would break off relations with the United States. And I said, "Are you kidding me? Are you crazy?"'[47]

The justification the PRB commonly provides for redacting this sort of material is that, while it may be common knowledge, it is not something that has been *officially* acknowledged by the CIA or the US government. Accordingly, if a book containing this information were sanctioned, it would be tantamount to an official acknowledgement. Let me be clear: there *is* logic to this argument. For example, it would not have been in America's interests to acknowledge openly, in real time, that the CIA was arming mujahedeen rebels in Afghanistan with man-portable Stinger missiles to destroy Soviet helicopter gunships. Similarly, during the Iran hostage crisis, it would have been highly ill-advised to acknowledge that six diplomats were secretly fleeing the country the moment their plane left Iranian airspace and Tony Mendez ordered a Bloody Mary to celebrate. But, as the Breckinridge and Wippl examples highlight, surely there comes a moment when it just becomes plain silly to keep up the fiction? According to Wippl, the Board's inability to recognise that definitions of 'national security' and 'harm' are neither absolute nor constant stems from the fact that the real power in the Board has long resided with its members from the NCS and its predecessors, the Directorate of Plans and the Directorate of Operations (DO). In his words: 'They understand operations, but they don't really understand international affairs … Spending a lifetime in operational intelligence, for some people it screws them up, it warps their minds. They get really funny.'[48] Historically, one adverse vote is all it takes to block publication of a manuscript. Ergo, the DO representatives hold enormous power, and can literally make or break an author's fortunes.

Being pushed through the meat grinder of the PRB is nevertheless only one part of what has made memoir writing a blood sport. For some authors, especially those who have sought to embarrass the Agency, the endless haggling and arbitrary decision-making of the Board represent the least of their worries. If the CIA really dislikes a book, the author in question will face an almighty struggle to get into print, and may even have their name dragged through the mud. In these cases, the rule is not simply 'If in doubt, classify', or even just 'classify'; it is, as Wippl puts it, 'If in doubt, take 'em out!'[49]

The CIA has had numerous authors placed under physical surveillance, causing emotional distress. It has made staff take lie-detector tests to determine if they are writing a book, or whether they have contacted a publisher. It has used informants in the publishing world to acquire proposals by intelligence officers and has sent threatening letters to editors in the hope that they knuckle under the pressure and desist from publishing. On at least one occasion, it has used an *agent provocateur* to learn an author's secrets and entice him into breaking the law. It has dragged its heels during the pre-publication review process in the hope that authors will lose interest, and there is evidence to suggest that it has tried to render works unpublishable through excessive, nit-picking redactions. It has dragooned several ex-officers off to court, and, in one instance, legally sequestered an author's revenues, leaving him in penury. Moreover, in the case of particularly contumacious memoirists who have not played by its rules, it has taken revenge by asking its friends, including contacts in the media, to write devastating reviews. These have often included attacks on the author's character, the logic being that if the messenger's reputation is tarnished, the message is lost. In short, like a boxer unable to secure a knockout blow, the CIA will look to win on points.

The third claim made in this book is that the CIA has gradually come to realise that certain memoirs, at certain times, by certain people, are beneficial. Richard Helms once famously said, in a speech before the Council of Foreign Relations on 17 April 1967, that: 'The Nation must to a degree take it on faith that we too are honourable men.'[50] During the early years of the Cold War – the era that Helms doubtless remembered with affection when uttering these words – this was generally the case. Today, however, the CIA operates in a world where people do not take intelligence matters on faith, and where popular discourse is awash with negative headlines and stereotypes about the Agency – some deserved and some not. It has been this way for some time. Lyman Kirkpatrick, who served as Inspector General and Executive Director of the CIA, remarked in a private letter in July 1966 that he was 'astounded' and 'dismayed' by what he saw and heard about the CIA in the 'outside world', writing:

> Some see CIA behind every plot and coup throughout the world, and want to blame it for all failures of American foreign policy. CIA

is practically a dirty word on some university campuses. Even repu-
table members of the United States Congress show a deplorable lack
of knowledge and an unwillingness to learn about CIA.[51]

In December 1969, in a radio interview, he claimed that a 'popular mythology' had developed about 'CIA men under every bed'.[52]

Lack of public trust in the CIA is a problem that cannot be ignored.
Without public support, the CIA will struggle to recruit the most talented people or obtain the resources necessary to keep the country
safe, while the policymaking community it is designed to serve will
question its judgements.[53] Moreover, as CIA Director William Casey
explained to the Senate Select Committee on Intelligence in January
1981, poor public perception and understanding of the value of the
CIA reduces the self-worth of intelligence officers and generates institutional self-doubt.[54] In this context, the lesson that more enlightened
figures at Langley have learned is that the right memoir can help, and
that the old attitude of 'the less written about the CIA the better' is
not necessarily the best course to follow. One-time PRB Chairman
John Hollister Hedley, a rare example of someone with a progressive
outlook occupying that position, has written persuasively about the
meaningful contribution that certain memoirs can play. 'Evidence
abounds', he claims,

> that former CIA officers can offer pertinent and valuable insights
> without damaging national security in the slightest. Indeed, they can
> enhance it. Memoirs can help clear the air. They can illuminate and
> inform. They can correct misconceptions. They can contribute expert
> opinions on current issues. They provide insight into what kind of
> people work for the CIA – people with intellect and integrity.[55]

Historically, individuals like Hedley have been the exception rather
than the norm, but there is evidence that their influence is growing. In

the twenty-first century, the CIA is trying to have it both ways when it comes to memoirs by continuing to create roadblocks for many authors, but no longer instinctively opposing the publication of stories that might enhance the Agency's reputation and build faith in its mission. The adage – 'an intelligence success revealed is an intelligence failure' – is breaking down, as evidenced by the CIA's decision to allow Tony Mendez to tell the 'Argo' story. However, as will be shown, this two-pronged strategy has made the Agency vulnerable to the accusation of having a two-tier or class-based system, with one law for senior personnel and those who toe the 'company line', but another for the regular rank-and-file and critics.

Chapter 1

Herbert Yardley: Playing for High Stakes

I. A 'Magnificent Book'

The truth never hurts. There is too much secrecy in the world.
Governments are run by a small clique. They connive and scheme and
when they get in trouble they ask the rest of us to settle their disputes by
warfare. If a publisher in each country would do what Bobbs-Merrill are
doing, a big step would be taken for international peace. Let the people
know what is going on. Let them see how governments are conducted.
Herbert Yardley, 4 March 1931.[1]

In December 1930, with the United States slipping deeper into the worst economic depression of the twentieth century, a former star high school quarterback, starved for money, and with a wife, mistress and young child to support, began writing a memoir of his time in government service. Billeted in a dingy, small second-floor apartment in New York's Greenwich Village, the man, in his early forties, was not an accomplished writer and utterly detested spending his days camped inside, tapping away at a rented typewriter. He later recalled: 'I could do no more than stare into space. For days I pecked out a few lines and threw them into the fire ... I wanted to weep for words.'[2] Adding to his feelings of frustration and foreboding, Manhattan's literary and journalistic heavy-hitters' poured cold water on the project, telling him, 'You might have a story; I doubt it.'[3]

Scrambling for a living, the man persevered and eventually the words started to flow. After seven weeks of hard graft, working through the night, the man ('dead on my feet and hollow-eyed') delivered his manuscript to George T. Bye, New York's premier literary agent, whose list of clients included such personages as the future First Lady Eleanor Roosevelt and the legendary aviator Charles Lindbergh.[4] To the man's astonishment, Bye considered it a 'magnificent book' – 'ten times better than my most optimistic expectations.'[5] Not long after, a deal was successfully brokered with Bobbs-Merrill, a publishing house from Indiana. George Shively, a senior editor at the publisher, believed that the book had all the hallmarks of a bestseller; indeed, he even predicted that it should 'make the front page of every paper in the world.'[6] The excitement, however, was tempered by anxiety, for publication would represent the biggest leak of classified information in US history. There was a real danger, suggested Shively, that everyone associated with the book would 'be charged with treason and shot at sunrise.'[7]

The book in question was *The American Black Chamber* by Herbert Yardley, a colourful and controversial character who, in two decades, went from being a precocious small-town boy from the Midwest to head America's first professional and permanent cryptography bureau, funded jointly by the State Department and the US Army. Published on 1 June 1931, the book detailed the inner workings of the 'Cipher Bureau', which Yardley led from its creation in 1917 until its dissolution in 1929.[8] Among the secrets disclosed was the startling revelation that Yardley's codebreakers had intercepted and deciphered Japanese diplomatic traffic during the Washington Naval Conference of 1921–22, meaning that the US diplomatic delegation knew exactly how far they could push Japanese representatives on the critical issue of naval ratios. More broadly, the book revealed that the US had read the communications of some twenty-one countries, including friendly nations such as Great Britain, over the course of the bureau's twelve-year existence. Generally praised by the press, it outraged the cryptanalytic community and ensured that its author would never work for the US government again, a sad demise for a man whose talents and experience would surely have benefited his country in the future cryptographic conflict against Japan during World War Two. In consolation, the book made Yardley a national celebrity, something he relished. When he was not on the radio or lecturing, he was socialising with actors and actresses, famous authors, even Nobel Prize winners and future presidential candidates.[9] A far cry indeed from the cloistered world of a cryptographer.

The story of *The American Black Chamber*, scarcely remembered today, is hugely significant in the context of US spy memoirs. First, it confirmed that knowledge of intelligence work was a profitable commodity and, by extension, established money as a key motivating factor as to why spies might be tempted to publish. Finding himself in hard times, in the midst of the Great Depression, Yardley exploited his secret knowledge out of financial necessity; although he did not make a fortune, the rewards were plain to see. Second, it showed that there was an enormous global market for recollections by former intelligence officers. *The American Black Chamber* was a bestseller not only in the United States, but overseas, especially in countries where the hidden hand of US espionage was felt. Third, Yardley's pioneering book established many of the qualities of the spy memoir genre. It followed a quasi-historical narrative, arranging its material in a chronologically sequential order and anchoring the content behind a single, clear story. It included 'revelations'. It gloried in technical detail, yet contained moments of high-drama and adventure. Fourth, it triggered a fevered discussion about whether the book had harmed national security, with critics arguing that the disclosures had prompted Japan to improve the security of its cryptosystems. Debates about the potential damage inflicted by spy books would be commonplace in the years to come.

Finally, for all the positives of *The American Black Chamber* in establishing the embryonic form of the nascent spy memoir genre, it
might also be said to have had a chilling effect on memoir production
in the short term. For the rest of his life, Yardley became a 'watched'
man and an outcast. The authorities impounded the manuscript of a
further volume of reminiscences and scrupulously examined for classified information the trashy spy fiction stories he produced to make
ends meet. In its hour of need after Pearl Harbor, the US government
refused his services and then, suspecting him of harbouring pro-Axis
sympathisers, watched his movements and staked out a restaurant
he opened in Washington. Legislation was also passed, triggered
by Yardley's writings, to criminalise the unauthorised disclosure of
cryptographic material. In short, he became a cautionary tale for any
aspiring memoirist looking to follow suit.[10]

II. Codebreaker

I knew that I had one of the most dramatic stories in American history.
Herbert Yardley, 14 June 1931.[11]

Being a pariah in intelligence circles was not the life that Yardley
had imagined for himself when, in late 1912, at the age of twenty-
four, fresh out of college, he became a code clerk and telegrapher in the
State Department's code room in Washington, DC. Yardley came to
the nation's capital burning with ambition. His formative years growing up in Middle America had given him the taste of success. He had
been a high-achiever in the classroom, especially at mathematics, and
was an outstanding sportsman. He earned good money on the side by
playing poker in the smoke-filled saloons and dive bars in the small
frontier town of Worthington, Indiana, and, to the envy of his male
friends, was unerringly successful at chasing members of the opposite

sex. At State, Yardley became fascinated with the magic and mystery of cryptography. In his spare time, he became interested in the construction of US diplomatic codes, and tried to solve them. The White House was horrified and amazed when, in less than two hours, he translated an encoded message from Colonel Edward House to President Woodrow Wilson. He then embarrassed the State Department by penetrating its system of secret communications. As a direct result of this cryptographic stunt, a new method of encoding State Department messages was introduced. Leveraging his unique talents, he charmed his way to an army commission and a pay rise to $1,000 a year.[12]

US entry into the war in April 1917 gave Yardley the perfect platform to use his cryptographic expertise. His apprenticeship complete, he was promptly made head of MI-8, the covert and deniable cryptologic branch of the newly created Military Intelligence Section in the Army War College Division. As the historian David Kahn has argued, although MI-8's creation was a secret, 'it marked one of the most significant steps in American intelligence'.[13] For the first time in its history, the US had an official agency to break foreign codes. From humble beginnings, with just two civilian clerks on its books, it grew to an organisation of 151 men and women at its peak.[14]

After the armistice was signed in 1918, Yardley was given a Distinguished Service Medal and then used his considerable powers of persuasion to convince the army to extend the life of his unit into peacetime, with himself remaining as chief. He supported his case by proudly declaring that, in eighteen months, his staff had read nearly 11,000 messages of eight foreign governments.[15] An unexceptional brownstone three-storey building just off Fifth Avenue in New York was selected as the organisation's new home, renamed the 'American Black Chamber' after the secret letter-opening service of King Henry IV of France, the *cabinet noir* (or 'black room'). $100,000 of annual funding from the army and state allowed for the employment of twenty-five code and cipher experts.[16] Yardley, the consummate 'wheeler-dealer', talked his superiors into giving him a salary of $6,000 – a sum exceeding that of the principal assistant secretary of state.[17]

The cipher bureau worked in conditions of absolute secrecy. Personnel were remunerated in cash from a secret payroll, and were instructed, if questioned about their job, to say that they worked for the War Department's Translation Division.[18] Mail was delivered to a numbered post box at Grand Central Station. The bureau itself took the cover of a private business, the Code Compiling Company, which produced commercial codes. To add to the verisimilitude of the cover, Yardley served as a consultant to commercial firms in code matters. He was also a licensed real estate broker. His colleague William Friedman later claimed (possibly out of spite, for they were no longer friends) that Yardley had a 'field day' at the government's expense by spending most of his time on private enterprises.[19] In terms of actual government work, commented Friedman, Yardley devoted 'two or three hours a week'.[20]

The highpoint for Yardley came with the Washington Naval Conference of 1921–22, where, at the invitation of President Warren Harding, the world's largest naval powers had gathered to discuss disarmament and ways to relieve rising tensions in East Asia. The key issue was to determine the relative allowable tonnages of capital ships for the major powers. Concerned about growing Japanese militarism, the US desired a favourable ratio of ten to six over Japan; Japan, which was looking to build its navy to realise its ambitions in the Pacific, insisted on a ten to seven ratio. However, a week before the conference commenced, the bureau deciphered what Yardley later described as 'the most important and far-reaching telegram ever to pass through the Black Chamber's doors'.[21] The telegram in question was addressed from Tokyo to Admiral Baron Kato, head of the Japanese delegation. In it, Tokyo told Kato that, if pressed, he was authorised to accept the 10:6 ratio as a final compromise. Armed with the knowledge of Japan's bottom line, US negotiators, led by Secretary of State Charles

Evans Hughes, only had to stand firm until the Japanese caved in, which they did. In Yardley's words, 'Stud poker is not a very difficult game after you see your opponent's card.'[22] The bureau thus helped the US achieve a major diplomatic victory. Knowing this, Yardley asked for – and got – a salary of $7,500, equivalent to the Under Secretary of State.[23]

By the end of the decade, however, the bureau had fallen on hard times. At the start of 1929, its budget stood at one-third of what it had been eight years before. Cryptographic coups had dried up. Indeed, as David Kahn has written, it did not contribute any decisive information about any of the major events of the decade: not the Rapallo Pact in 1922, when Germany accorded the Soviet Union *de jure* recognition; not the Ruhr Crisis in 1923, when French and Belgian forces occupied Germany's premier industrial district; and not the breaking of diplomatic relations between Britain and Russia in 1927.[24] On 31 October 1929, it closed its doors for good, its fate sealed a few months prior when Henry Stimson, President Herbert Hoover's new Secretary of State, terminated its chief source of income, the State Department's disbursement.

Stimson's decision to close the Black Chamber was based on several factors. Firstly, in what with hindsight seems to have been undue optimism, he believed that the world was entering a new era of lasting peace. He could point to the fact that most major countries now had peace agreements to preserve, such as the Kellogg-Briand Pact, ratified in summer 1928, in which signatories promised not to use war as a way of settling disputes. In this context, influenced by the open government idealism of Woodrow Wilson, it was his opinion that spying, secret diplomacy and cryptography could make way for mutual trust and frankness between nations. Secondly, Stimson was uncomfortable with the idea of the State Department taking the lead when it came to codebreaking, believing that the War Department was the natural home for this sort of activity. When biographer McGeorge Bundy interviewed him in 1946, Stimson said that it was 'highly unethical' for the State Department, in its capacity as the lead US foreign affairs agency, to be reading the messages of officials it had invited to the country as guests.[25] Finally, Stimson, by most accounts a man of high moral value, possessed a squeamishness about the whole enterprise of spying. His famous and quaint pronouncement – 'Gentlemen do not read other gentlemen's mail' – is testament to this.[26] As he saw it, the Black Chamber went against the puritanical principles on which the Republic had been founded, principles that set the United States apart from every nation on earth. In short, it was un-American.

The idea that honour counted for more in geopolitics than the benefits of codebreaking was anathema to Yardley. In his view, Stimson was ignorant to the realities of the anarchic international system, where gentlemen in the traditional sense were in short supply. Other nations were intensifying, not reducing, their cryptographic efforts. Stalin was certainly no gentleman. In Yardley's eyes, the consequences of not being vigilant were severe. History had taught him that if you cannot see an enemy, it is necessary to acquire stronger binoculars. His pleas nevertheless fell on deaf ears. In late 1929, the US Army Signals Corps offered him a job on half his normal salary, almost certainly knowing that he would turn it down, which he did. A slightly improved second offer was forthcoming in spring 1930, but this too was rejected, with Yardley believing that he could make a handsome living out of real estate and private consultancy. However, with the stock market crash and resultant Great Depression, Yardley, like many of his generation, found work hard to come by. Casting about for an income, he served briefly as forensic cryptologist at the Scientific Crime Detection Laboratory of Chicago, created to put an end to the city's violent criminal element, but generally found that his esoteric expertise was in low demand.[27] A spendthrift all his life, constantly frittering away his money in hard-drinking male company, he had no savings put aside for a rainy day. 'Out of a clear blue sky', Friedman later wrote, 'the bottom fell out of his affairs.'[28] In desperation, with a family to support, plus a bibulous lifestyle made particularly costly by prohibition, he decided to become a writer.

III. Outcast

Lies! Lies! Lies!

William Friedman, annotated remarks in his personal copy of
The American Black Chamber.[29]

F ew could have predicted that Yardley would spill the beans about the Black Chamber. His reputation in official circles was that of a staunchly closed-mouth civil servant, fully aware of the need to be security conscious for the sake of operations. In October 1924, he wrote to a colleague and declared: 'Ever since the war I have consciously fought against disclosing anything about codes and ciphers. My reason is obvious: it warns other governments of our skill and makes our work more difficult.'[30] He regularly impressed upon his staff the importance of secrecy. Giant posters adorned the walls of his Manhattan workplace, emblazoned with warnings like: 'SECRET! If enemies learn that we can decipher their present codes, they will try to devise more difficult forms.'[31] On his watch, nothing ever leaked to the press, although it is interesting to note that Captain (later Admiral) Reginald Hall, head of British Naval Intelligence from 1914 to 1919, refused Yardley permission to visit Room 40, Britain's codebreaking nerve-centre, citing his garrulous manner.[32] However, one should not read too much into this; the British were not only notoriously secretive about their intelligence services, but also very protective of their patch, even with allies like the US.

It thus came as a shock to senior officials when word reached them of Yardley's intention to write a book. The alarm bell first sounded in spring 1930 when Viking Press contacted Colonel Stanley Ford, the assistant chief of staff for intelligence, about a proposal it had received from a certain Mr Yardley. Ford convinced Viking not to publish on the grounds of protecting national security, but it was only a matter of time before someone else took the bait. Confirmation of this arrived in January 1931 when the cryptologist tendered his resignation as a major in the Military Intelligence Reserve. Yardley claimed that he no longer desired to associate himself with the policies of the Military Intelligence Division (MID), but it was obvious to the authorities that his real motivation was to avert the possibility of being prosecuted in a military court for revealing secrets. With this, Lieutenant Colonel Owen Albright of MID spoke to Yardley and cautioned him about the damaging effect publication could have on US diplomatic relations. Albright also underlined that, if Yardley published before his resignation had been approved, he risked being court-martialled. This was an empty threat. The army's Judge Advocate General had already established that Yardley could not be prosecuted because, as a reservist, he was not on active duty and was regarded as a civilian. He had concluded: 'There is no law known to this office which would render this individual liable to any prosecution or penalty as a Reserve Officer for any disclosure.'[33]

Yardley dug his heels in. He justified the book by claiming that since the Black Chamber was no more, there were no secrets to protect. 'The episode in American history that I deal with is past,' he wrote in a memo to his publisher.[34] 'I doubt if we will receive any protest from the present administration,' he continued, 'for they washed their hands of my bureau.'[35] Famous last words. Nor did he anticipate any complaints from overseas, since, he argued, there was a 'gentleman's agreement' between nations that codebreaking was par for the course in international relations.[36] Officials saw it differently and desperately searched for a way to block publication. Eventually, however, they were forced to accept that there was nothing in US law that allowed them to do so.

Keen to be better safe than sorry, Yardley's publisher, Bobbs-Merrill, still hired an army of lawyers to scrutinise every word of the manuscript. By daring to reveal intelligence secrets, the book was the first of a kind in the US, and Bobbs-Merrill was acutely aware that it was sailing into uncharted legal waters. To quote one of the publisher's senior editors: 'some careful manoeuvring' was required.[37] Close attention was paid to potential infringements of laws relating to espionage, sedition and treason. Outside counsel also read the text to detect possible libel. Legal advice led Yardley to make several alterations. For example, it was seen as inflammatory to put on record that the Black Chamber's job was to 'break federal laws'. This was reworded to the less prickly statement that it had 'used embarrassing means'.[38] Lawyers also recommended that Yardley remove any personal asides he had made about eminent individuals. Experience had shown that powerful people had sensitive egos and, with deep pockets, would not think twice about bringing a civil suit for defamation of character. As a result, Yardley deleted the quip about the various undersecretaries of state he had known who seldom, if ever, got to work before nine o'clock in the morning.[39] With these changes, the legal team concluded that publication could go ahead. From Yardley's perspective, this came not a moment too soon. He was broke, and his advance of $500 was payable only when the book went into production.

The American Black Chamber was published on 1 June, preceded by three serial extracts in the *Saturday Evening Post*, which, with a readership of 2.8 million, was one of the most popular magazines in the country. Chronicling Yardley's involvement with code and cipher work from 1913 to 1929, and running to 375 pages, the book had something for everyone. For the cryptographic cognoscenti, there was highly technical subject matter, including thick descriptions of how Yardley's team had analysed and broken complex codes. According to intelligence veteran Hayden Peake, a former member of the CIA's Directorate of Science and Technology: 'No book written since has revealed as many technical secrets as Yardley's did.'[40] For the general readership, there were exciting tales of how MI-8 played cat and mouse with German spies during World War One, including the story of how the organisation facilitated the arrest of the beautiful conspirator Madame Maria de Victorica by reading messages written in invisible ink. In describing these episodes, Yardley demonstrated the qualities of a novelist. He would later claim: 'To write saleable stuff one must dramatise. Things don't happen in dramatic fashion. There is nothing to do but either dramatise or write nothing at all.'[41] In the years to come, writing spy fact in the style of spy fiction would become a hallmark of many US spy memoirs.

The book was packed with revelations. Yardley listed twenty-one countries, including some of the United States' closest friends, whose codes had been successfully broken. Controversially, Yardley revealed some of the 'extra-legal' ways in which his Bureau had acquired private communications, including the infiltration of foreign embassies, both at home and abroad. Moreover, the book embarrassed Western Union by revealing how its telegraph offices had given the Bureau access to foreign governments' coded messages.

The most explosive chapters dealt with the breaking of Japanese Foreign Ministry codes, and the intelligence about Tokyo's negotiating stance during the Washington Naval Conference. Perhaps the most startling revelation was that Yardley had deciphered a message reporting that the Allies, in a horrendous plot, had planned to assassinate President Woodrow Wilson during the Versailles peace talks either by administering slow poison or by giving him influenza in ice. Disclosures like this, while not necessarily accurate, ensured skyrocketing sales. Two weeks after publication, the book was in its third printing.[42] By the end of the year, it had sold 17,931 copies. Chinese, French, Swedish and Japanese translations appeared, contributing to worldwide sales of approximately 60,000 copies.[43]

The authorities knew nothing about the contents of the book until it was published. Yardley had refused to submit his manuscript to Military Intelligence for security screening. He also failed to mention to his former bosses that parts of the manuscript were based on documents he had taken, illicitly, from the office of the Cipher Bureau upon its closure. The first instinct of officials was to deny everything. General Douglas MacArthur, then Army Chief of Staff, announced that he had never heard of any such unit as the Black Chamber. A spokesman for the State Department flatly rejected that US codebreakers had broken Japanese codes during the naval summit of 1921–22.

Eventually, however, the denials were replaced by open condemnations, and the simmering resentment of the cryptographic community, military professionals and the US government more broadly, boiled over into public view. Outraged officials gave statements to the press deploring Yardley's betrayal of trust, suggesting that the book would cause grave damage to US diplomatic relations. Nations, they argued, would hardly be thrilled to discover that Washington had been eavesdropping on their conversations. There was concern that Yardley's actions would starve the United States of future cryptographic successes, as countries would surely look to tighten up the security of their cryptosystems. Despite Stimson, the closure of the Black Chamber had not signalled the end of US codebreaking; far from it. Packed with mathematicians, gifted linguists and crossword puzzle whizzes, the Signal Intelligence Service, within the US Army Signal Corps, was busy training the next generation of codebreakers in the event of a future conflict. Yardley shrugged off the criticism. The book, he argued, highlighted what a terrible mistake Stimson had made. By extension, it alerted the American public to the country's defensive vulnerabilities, and thus put pressure on Washington's slumbering statesmen to reverse the decision.

One person who felt particularly aggrieved was Friedman, the head of the Signal Intelligence Service who, in the late 1930s, led the team that broke the supposedly unbreakable Japanese cipher system 'Purple'. In his opinion, the book was a 'terrible blow'.[44] Friedman's personal copy of *The American Black Chamber*, available to read at the George C. Marshall Foundation Research Library, is highly revealing of his disdain for the book since it includes marginalia penned by Friedman, as well as other eminent cryptologists of the time. Friedman's complaint was twofold. One, that Yardley had revealed important state secrets. In the book, Yardley had claimed that because the Black Chamber had been destroyed, 'there is no reason for withholding its secrets'. This appalled Friedman; by the same logic, he remarked, a lawyer would be 'justified in violating the confidences entrusted to him by his ex-client!'[45] Two, Friedman believed that Yardley had exaggerated and dramatised his own role in the decipherment of codes, and had made serious factual inaccuracies. Scribbled in the margins of the text were comments including: 'This appears to me as pure bunk'; 'Yardley was a good executive – not a real cryptographer'; 'I have never heard of this and believe all of it a fish story'; 'It's a damned lie'; and 'This is a patch-work of misstatement, exaggeration, and falsehood'.[46] Interestingly, on the title page, Friedman wrote that he doubted whether Yardley actually wrote the book at all. 'Sometime in 1942', he recalled, '[John] McGrail [head of MI-8's secret ink section] told me that he had it on most excel-lent authority that this book was actually "ghostwritten" by an AT&T Co engineer named Clem Koukul, who received $1,000 for his work. I don't know Koukul but feel sure Y[ardley] had much help in writing, from somebody'.[47]

Outrage was by no means limited to the federal government. There was strong protest from sections of the US media. The *New York Evening Post* regarded Yardley's actions as highly improper, bordering on treason, and suggested that if President Theodore Roosevelt were alive he would give the author a 'lecture on betraying the secrets of one's country'.[48] The *Boston Globe* declared that Yardley's behaviour amount-ed to treachery, and that he should be stripped of his Distinguished Service Medal. In Japan, where sales of the book were almost quad-ruple those in the US, there was widespread anger that Yardley's unit had cracked Tokyo's codes and used the information to force a conces-sion from Japanese negotiators at the Washington Naval Conference.

For such a proud nation, this was a bitter pill to swallow. 'Betrayal of International Trust', headlined one Japanese newspaper.[49]

Assessing the exact harm caused by Yardley's book is fraught with difficulty, and has attracted competing theories. There is no doubting that the disclosures served as a wakeup call to Japanese cryptographers, setting in motion a series of improvements to code security. We know from a declassified National Security Agency (NSA) report that the communications department of the Japanese Foreign Ministry sent 138 copies of the book to its various embassies and legations around the world to warn them that their codes might be compromised.[50] We know that Japan increased research spending into communications security, and that this led to its manual code-cryptology system being replaced by a machine-generated cipher known as 'Purple', the most challenging encryption process the US had ever encountered. What is less certain is how quickly these changes took effect. Some sources suggest a fast-paced conversion, leaving US codebreakers floundering. In December 1931, Friedman stated that: 'Every nation had spent time since the publication of the book in revising its codes.'[51] A US Navy report of 1931 hinted at an immediate blackout, claiming that the navy's ability to read traffic of a certain 'foreign power' – namely, Japan – had collapsed because 'the systems [that] convey this information have undergone a complete change'.[52] In contrast, the eminent codebreaking authority David Kahn has argued that it would have been impossible for nations to improve their security overnight. According to Kahn, replacement systems take time to devise, test, distribute and teach before they can be used. Moreover, nations typically do not have reserve cryptosystems ready to put into immediate effect because they are costly to maintain and risk becoming obsolete.[53]

Kahn also makes the thought-provoking case that, in the long run, Yardley's indiscretions proved advantageous to US security. Japan, he claims, was forced by the book's publication to change its codes and embrace automated encryption much sooner than it might otherwise have done. Because of this, American codebreakers, in the lead-up to World

War Two, gained invaluable experience in solving these systems. Had the book not been published, the Japanese would probably have persisted with their old methods for much of the 1930s, meaning that Friedman and his staff would have been caught cold when the improvements finally were made at a much more critical moment in US history. According to Kahn, this is why the cryptologic pioneer Frank Rowlett, who played a major role in solving 'Purple', believed that Yardley 'did us a favour' and called the book a 'terrific' thing.[54] Predictably, attempts to exonerate the cryptologist on these grounds do not wash with most intelligence professionals. For them, Yardley had committed the ultimate sin – betrayal.[55] Moreover, there is a case to be made that Yardley contributed to rising anti-Americanism in Japan, thereby accelerating the eventual road to war. In the weeks following publication, Foreign Minister Kijūrō Shidehara, who had promoted cooperative diplomacy with Euro-American powers, was pilloried by Japan's militarist elements for capitulating to deceitful Americans when he was a Japanese delegate to the Washington Naval Conference. Shidehara and other moderates were forced from office by military expansionists in December, bringing to an end the restraining hand of civilian government and, with it, liberal foreign policy.[56]

IV. Traitor?

You must think me dead, or back in China or somewhere. At the moment, George, it is ABSOLUTELY necessary for me to avoid any publicity because of the work I am doing ... it is really important that at this time – for a while at least – I keep myself buried.
Herbert Yardley to George T. Bye, 11 December 1940.[57]

It did not take long for the profligate spender Yardley to burn through the money he earned from *The American Black Chamber*. Royalties of approximately $10,000 were squandered on a licentious lifestyle of liquor, laying bets and ladies of easy virtue.[58] Blacklisted by the US government and desperately chasing a buck, he pursued a series of suitably exotic get-rich-quick endeavours, from dabbling in real estate speculation and selling commercial invisible ink concoctions, to attempting to make 'de-alcoholised alcohol tonic for reformed drunkards'.[59] None were successful; indeed, his experiments with secret ink cost him a finger. Once again, therefore, he looked to make money by publicising his knowledge of the secret world. He lectured college students, clubs and service organisations, touting US cryptographic successes and warning of a bleak future without them. The honorariums were modest, while he was often left footing the bill for travel expenses. Whenever he felt short-changed by his host, he would write to Bye in anger. 'This god damn Jew would run me nuts', he complained in one letter, after someone had apparently 'forgot' to pay him for a lecture at South Bend.[60] He also sold cryptographic puzzles – nicknamed 'Yardleygrams' – to *Liberty* magazine for bi-weekly publication. He knew, however, that the real money was to be gained by writing another book. Accordingly, in late 1931, despite his close brush with the law earlier that year, he began planning a new project, entitled 'Japanese Diplomatic Secrets', which would divulge every twist and turn of his greatest and most famous achievement: the breaking of Japanese codes at the Washington Naval Conference.

With unhappy memories of how he had laboured day and night to write his first book, Yardley scraped together just enough money to employ a ghostwriter, Marie Stuart Klooz, a freelance journalist known for her speed. By summer 1932, she had produced a 1,000-page manuscript. The end product, to quote Kahn, was 'suffocatingly dull' – made up of hundreds of intercepted dispatches stitched together with weak and insipid text.[61] Unsurprisingly, there was no bidding war to contract it. Bobbs-Merrill showed no interest. Macmillan eventually picked it up, but at a fraction of the amount Yardley was hoping for.

Word of the book filtered through to the State Department and set pulses racing. The early 1930s had seen a major deterioration in

US–Japanese relations. To Tokyo's umbrage, the US had continued to close its door to Japanese emigrants, and had refused to recognise Japan's conquest of the Chinese province of Manchuria in September 1931. Understanding that there was no will on the part of either the administration or the American public to fight a war in East Asia, the State Department was anxious not to generate further antagonism. On 12 September, therefore, Stanley Hornbeck, State's senior expert on Japan, informed the undersecretary that: 'In view of the state of excitement which apparently prevails in Japanese public opinion now, characterised by fear or enmity towards the United States, every possible effort should be made to prevent the appearance of this book'.[62] State also feared that the book would tarnish the reputation of Charles Evans Hughes, Chief Justice of the US Supreme Court. In 1922, Hughes had been Secretary of State and had led the US delegation to the conference. Yardley's book made the serious allegation that Hughes had been the 'moving spirit in all this business of securing and decoding cables'.[63] Stimson was horrified by the charge: 'He [Hughes] stands too high to be touched by slander'.[64] Hughes himself was 'profoundly disturbed'.[65] Although there was no truth to the claim, it would be necessary to deny it, and this in turn might trigger more sticky questions about the whole enterprise.

In September 1932, a pair of army captains visited Yardley at his home in Worthington and requested that he surrender the documents he had 'made and obtained … while connected with the US government'.[66] William Richards Castle Jr, the Under Secretary of State, wrote in his diary that officials did not seriously expect to retrieve the documents from Yardley, but hoped that the sight of armed service personnel turning up on his doorstep 'might frighten him'.[67] Yardley refused but the authorities discovered the priceless detail that the typescript was due to be submitted to the New York offices of Macmillan early the next year. On 22 February 1933, with the help of a federal prosecutor in New York named Thomas E. Dewey (a future presidential candidate), US marshals seized the manuscript and impounded it under the Espionage Act of 1917, which prohibited the appropriation and retention of classified documents.[68] The confiscation was of dubious legality, since the statute required hard evidence that the person was intent on injuring US interests. Yet Macmillan's president, a former military intelligence officer, had no desire to risk the government's ire. Interestingly, Yardley did not protest. He too was of the opinion that the book was dry and commercially non-viable. In a meeting with Friedman on 25 February, he doubted whether 2,000 copies would be sold.[69] Moreover, ever the impulsive, by this point his head had been turned by the far more lucrative prospect of script writing in Hollywood. The manuscript would remain in federal custody for forty-seven years.

Federal authorities moved to erect a legal barrier against Yardley, and others similarly inclined. 'Are we so helpless that we cannot stop a book which may endanger the country?' lamented Castle in his diary entry of 20 February 1933.[70] On 10 June 1933, officials successfully pushed through Congress the 'Protection of Government Records' Bill, which criminalised the publication of codes and coded material, punishable by up to ten years in prison and a $10,000 fine. The 'Yardley Act', as it became popularly known, demonstrated how seriously the government took the issue of unauthorised disclosure. The message was clear and simple: people looking to follow Yardley's lead should think twice before attempting to cash in on their spying experiences.

In May 1934, Yardley excitedly informed Bye that he had been offered a 'VERY VERY SECRET' job, worth $12,000, that would 're-quire him to disappear for a year' and which would give him 'enough material to write for the rest of my life'.[71] Whatever this opportunity was, it never materialised, so he tried cutting his teeth as a script writer in Hollywood, where spy stories were very much in vogue. In 1932, the legendary Greta Garbo had achieved commercial success with her screen portrayal of Mata Hari, an exotic dancer and courtesan, shot by the French for espionage during World War One. The film caused a minor storm, as the Swedish actress performed sensuous dances and turned the lights off during two love scenes with Latin lothario Ramon Novarro. Films such as *Mata Hari*, but also Fritz Lang's *Spione* (1928) and Alfred Hitchcock's *The Man Who Knew Too Much* (1934), established many elements of later spy cinema. *Spione*, for example, featured a numbered secret agent (*à la* 007); secret headquarters; and a fetching female who falls in love with a good-looking lead. With Yardley, filmmakers wanted to capitalise on the craze for spy fiction, but also move it in a new direction. The contribution of codebreakers represented original and fertile territory for Hollywood, albeit any film would need to avoid focusing on the tedium of cryptanalytic methods. Seeing the potential, MGM paid Yardley $7,500 for the rights to his published writings, which included *The American Black Chamber* and a mildly successful recent work of fiction, *The Blonde Countess*, hastily ghosted by English professor Carl Henry Grabo in early 1934 to help Yardley with his grocery bills.[72]

Yardley moved to Los Angeles for ten weeks starting in late April 1934, employed by MGM at $250 per week.[73] There, he experienced mixed emotions. On the one hand, he enjoyed the frivolous sensibility of it all, which was a welcome escape from the realities of being perpetually a poor and washed-up codebreaker with no career to speak of. 'What a hell of a way to make a living – motion pictures,' he enthused in a letter to Bye.[74] On the other hand, there was something quite demeaning about one of the founding fathers of American cryptography reading film scripts. In the words of Robin Denniston, the son of Bletchley Park Director Alastair Denniston: 'This was small beer after the heights of secret diplomacy.'[75] Yardley's feeling that his talents were wasted on Hollywood was confirmed when the film he assisted on, *Rendezvous*, was developed by the filmmakers into something that bore no resemblance to his books or the scripts he had written. Indeed, his contribution was ultimately limited to checking artefacts and ensuring that all the little details were right. For example, he advised the director to change the colour of the fluid in the bottle of secret ink from 'pink' to 'fairly pink' to better reflect the reality that secret ink is, of course, absolutely colourless.[76] He also pointed out that officials 'say "government printing office" instead of "house"'.[77]

Released in 1935, *Rendezvous* was a humorous and rousing spy melodrama, marking Rosalind Russell's first star billing in a film. The story centred on Bill Gordon, played by William Powell (of *The Thin Man* fame), a puzzle specialist tasked with staying one step ahead of a German spy ring, intent on reading American codes to help U-boats destroy American troop ships on their way across the Atlantic to the front. The film received universally positive reviews. The *New York Post* described it as a 'boisterously entertaining picture … a sure-fire antidote to boredom'.[78] *Variety* magazine called it 'Hollywood storytelling at its best'.[79] Powell was singled out for praise, with critics adoring his blend of sleek banter, bored nonchalance and razored shrewdness. Advertising for the film played on the idea that women, not cryptography, were life's greatest mystery. Radio slots remarked that Powell 'could solve the most intricate puzzles … unless they were dressed in skirts'.[80] Advertisers also took advantage of Yardley's reputation. 'Do not hesitate to use Major Yardley's name in your publicity,' emphasised MGM bosses. 'Yardley is known to millions. Capitalise on this angle to the fullest extent.'[81]

Yardley was open to another Hollywood assignment, but despite the efforts of his new agent, Harold N. Swanson, offers never materialised. In March 1938, 'Swannie' (as he was known) wrote to over two dozen studio executives, producers, screenwriters and directors singing the praises of his client. 'This country,' he declared, 'is becoming spy conscious and with this in mind we offer you the services and material of Major H. O. Yardley.'[82] Swanson underlined that Yardley had a 'wealth of material at his fingertips, material which could be developed into an amazing and exciting story of peacetime spy activities'.[83] But no one was interested. Later in the year, Swanson informed the German director Fritz Lang that Yardley was available to provide an 'authentic flavour' to the screenplay of Paramount's 'Man Without a Country', a yarn about German espionage.[84] Lang declined the offer and, in any event, the film was never made.

After Hollywood proved to be something of a busted flush, Yardley wandered from job to job, none of which lasted more than a couple of years. He dabbled in the hospitality business by opening a restaurant, the Rideaux, in downtown Washington, DC. Despite being confident that it would net him 'close to $10,000 a year', he sold the joint after only a few months, amid spiralling costs and tired of having to deal with thirteen squabbling employees.[85] From September 1938 to July 1940, he worked in Chongqing, the provisional capital of the Republic of China, where he helped to establish a cryptological bureau for the nationalist forces of Generalissimo Chiang Kai-shek.[86] Using the alias 'Herbert Osborn', he earned a reputation as someone who knew his way around a Chinese whorehouse; indeed, he boasted about hosting an orgy for a young visiting journalist so that he could be blooded as a man. During his time in China, he kept a journal of his activities that he later turned into a book manuscript, but never submitted for publication. (The manuscript was later discovered gathering dust in a closet by the bestselling author James Bamford, who wrote an introduction and escorted the work into print in 1983 as *The Chinese Black Chamber*.)[87] Back in North America, Yardley repeatedly tried to find a way back into government service, but to no avail. On 5 December 1941, Bye even wrote to the First Lady, Eleanor Roosevelt, suggesting that the nation was 'suffering a great handicap' in letting his client's unique talents go to waste.[88] Two days later, the Japanese attacked Pearl Harbor.

Yardley was eventually hired by the Canadian authorities to develop a cryptanalytic agency called the 'Examination Unit of the Department of External Affairs'. His time in Ottawa was nevertheless short-lived. In January 1942, he was shown the door after the Americans and the British threatened to sever all cryptographic ties with the Canadians unless Yardley was removed. Neither country trusted him, certainly not enough to jeopardise their achievements against the Purple and Enigma codes. Alastair Denniston, Director of Britain's Government Code and Cypher School (GC&CS) at Bletchley Park, personally flew to Ottawa to tell the Canadians that they would receive no cooperation from Bletchley so long as Yardley was employed.[89] General Dawson Olmstead, the US Army's Chief Signal Officer, said he 'would have nothing to do with this man'.[90] Even more forcefully, Rear Admiral Leigh Noyes, Director of Naval Communications in Washington, ruled that the navy would 'not touch [him] with a ten foot pole' and emphasised that, if it were his decision, Yardley would be rotting in jail.[91]

The pursuit of simple masculine pleasures dominated the latter part of Yardley's life. He hunted ducks at the crack of dawn, shot a good round of golf and played poker at every level, from nickel-and-dime neighbourhood games to large tournaments. His skill at poker led him to write an enchanting little book on the subject called *The Education of a Poker Player*. Published in 1957, the book was a masterwork in the art of bluff, selling over 100,000 copies. Part instruction manual, part autobiography, it included practical tips on how players could raise their game and provided stories of epic matchups across the green baize. The final third of the book, which narrated the author's poker-playing days in China and Hong Kong, had a strong feel of spy fiction to it, blending the worlds of cards and international espionage. Yardley casually claimed that poker had led to the capture of a secret agent whose mission was to assassinate Chiang Kai-Shek. To boost sales, the UK edition by Jonathan Cape featured an introduction by James Bond creator Ian Fleming, himself no stranger to the gambling tables, who recommended it to 'every consenting adult card player in Great Britain'.

Yardley died of a cerebral haemorrhage on 7 August 1958. Despite his clashes with the authorities, he was buried in Arlington National Cemetery, with full military honours. His biggest frustration was that he never again broke codes for his country. He had hoped that Pearl Harbor would herald a reversal in his fortunes, as America searched desperately for cryptographers of his calibre. He made applications to the army, Federal Bureau of Investigations (FBI), navy and State Department; all were rejected.[92] In early 1942, he was reported to have been chosen by William Donovan, who was setting up the OSS, to direct a cipher bureau. However, according to a declassified memorandum to FBI Director J. Edgar Hoover, someone had Yardley's appointment 'killed'.[93] As a result, he spent the war shuffling paperwork on meat inspections for the Office of Price Administration. His failed attempts to return to high-level government service led him to believe that he was on a black-list. In his eyes, the surprise attack on Pearl Harbor had proved him right in all his forebodings about the stupidity of closing his bureau. 'I can at least console myself', he wrote later in life, 'that so long as I ran the show there were no Pearl Harbors!!!!!'[94] He simply could not understand why, in a moment of national crisis, he was not asked to resurrect his good work. He nevertheless remained ostracised. He had broken a moral code with *The American Black Chamber* that no one was prepared to forgive.

There might, however, be a more disturbing explanation as to why Yardley was continually snubbed from sensitive work – was he a traitor? In his 1967 book *The Broken Seal*, the espionage writer Ladislas Farago made the startling charge that, during the summer of 1928, Yardley betrayed his country and committed high treason by selling the secrets of the Black Chamber to the Japanese for $7,000.[95] According to Farago, Yardley needed the money to support his extravagant lifestyle. Moreover, he was upset that the government was not fully recognising his efforts. Farago's account claimed that Yardley, through a Japanese reporter in New York, was put in contact with Setsuzo Sawada, a counsellor in the Japanese embassy. A meeting between the two men reportedly followed in a discreet location off Connecticut Avenue in Washington, DC, where Yardley offered to hand over decrypted Japanese diplomatic messages, the techniques used in their solution, copies of his worksheets and information about the cipher systems of other countries, including Great Britain. The exchange was agreed, but only after Counsellor Sawada had two Japanese cryptographic experts, flown in from Tokyo under assumed names on diplomatic passports, to check the material.[96] The main source for Farago's allegation was a memorandum by Shin Sakuma, chief of Japan's Foreign Ministry Telegraph Section, to the Japanese Foreign Minister Shidehara. Available to inspect in microfilm at the Library of Congress, it mentions a telegram, *Document No. 105*, sent from the Japanese ambassador in Washington seeking guarantees that Yardley will deliver the material as promised.[97]

Was Yardley guilty? Not according to Kahn. In his richly researched 2004 biography of Yardley, Kahn claims that the cryptologist was a scoundrel, not a traitor: 'I believe that Yardley never sold any documents to the Japanese.'[98] Like other researchers before him, Kahn found no evidence in Japanese archives of dispatch No. 105, leading him to conclude that the Sakuma Memorandum was probably fabricated by the Japanese Foreign Ministry to blacken Yardley's name and save Japanese face in the wake of the embarrassment caused by *The American Black Chamber*. Kahn supports his conclusion by pointing out that the Sakuma Memorandum was written on 10 June 1931, ten days after publication of the book. Surely not a coincidence? Doubts about Farago's thesis are compounded by the fact that he was notoriously unreliable as a researcher. His books were frequently criticised for their inaccuracies. In February 1972, for example, the renowned English historian A. J. P. Taylor wrote a savage review of Farago's *The Game of Foxes* in the *New York Review of Books*, calling it 'undiluted nonsense'.[99] Looking to put the matter of Yardley's alleged treachery to rest once and for all, John Dooley, in a 2010 article for the journal *Cryptologia*, reviewed all the available literature and evidence. His conclusion: 'There does not seem to be any hard evidence that he was a traitor.'[100] Case closed then.

Perhaps not though. During the course of researching this book, the NSA declassified a report into Yardley's alleged treachery, completed in

1981 by Theodore Hannah, a writer for the NSA publication *Cryptologic Spectrum*. After examining Japanese Foreign Ministry records 'not once, but several times', Hannah concluded that the evidence 'tends strongly to substantiate Farago's basic claims'.[101]

Another document to recently enter the public domain is a report carried out by CIA man Fred C. Woodrough Jr, a Japanese linguist, just a few months after *The Broken Seal* was published in 1967. After extensive research in the Japanese Foreign Ministry microfilm collection, studying close to 400,000 pages, Woodrough determined that Yardley 'was personally and directly involved in a transaction', albeit his main source for this deduction was the problematic Sakuma Memorandum.[102]

We now also have access to the findings of a third investigation, conducted by the highly respected Walter Pforzheimer, submitted to Deputy Director of Central Intelligence Vice Admiral Rufus Taylor on 12 December 1967, six months after *The Broken Seal* had been published. Pforzheimer's report is nothing short of explosive. 'In the light of the charges that Yardley collaborated with the Japanese in cryptographic matters', wrote Pforzheimer, 'I have tried to ascertain whether Yardley was ever actually in Japan from the time that he ceased working for the State Department until the end of World War II.'[103] On the question of whether Yardley had hawked secrets, the report wholeheartedly agreed with Farago, albeit Pforzheimer put the date of the exchange as 1930, not 1928: 'There seems to be no question that, in June 1930, Yardley sold certain information to the Japanese for the sum of $7,000, but this transaction appears to have taken place in Washington.'[104] The report then explained that the deal had been made through the Japanese embassy in Washington, DC, and that the Japanese 'sought Yardley's assurance that he would not make this [information] available to others'.[105] According to the report, as of June 1931, Tokyo was 'still reading the material which they had purchased', although there was no evidence of further contact with Yardley himself.

In the penultimate paragraph of the report, Pforzheimer dropped an even bigger bombshell, stating that contained in the files of the Japanese Foreign Ministry was a decrypted cable from the British ambassador in Tokyo, Sir Robert Craigie, to Foreign Secretary Anthony Eden in London (copied to Washington). According to Pforzheimer, the cable was dated 30 September 1941 at 4.20 a.m., with the decryption by the Japanese taking place a few days later, on 3 October 1941. The existence of this document within Japanese Foreign Ministry files is quite spectacular, since it suggests that the Japanese, in the critical months before Pearl Harbor on 7 December 1941, were successfully intercepting British or American messages, perhaps even both. Amazingly, Pforzheimer then revealed that attached to the cable is a handwritten note, in Japanese, which, when translated, reads: 'A message decrypted (Kaidoku) by Yardley'.[106]

What are we to make of this? Is Pforzheimer's report really proof that Yardley – buried in hallowed ground at Arlington, the resting place for fallen heroes, humble soldiers, even commanders-in-chief – sold his country down the river on the eve of the worst moment in American history? The Craigie telegram exists. A copy is available in the Library of Congress, while the original – with the handwritten note[107] – can be found in the National Archives of Japan, in Tokyo.[108]

If the Americans had any suspicion that Yardley was a traitor, it would certainly help to better explain why officials went out of their way to make life difficult for him, right up until his death in 1958. *The American Black Chamber* ruffled feathers, no doubt; but did it really warrant punishing him for the rest of his life, unless something more sinister was lurking in the background? It would also help to explain why the authorities felt it necessary to keep a close eye on him long after he dropped off the radar of public interest. The NSA long kept a dossier on him, which included recollections of his childhood friends.[109] Declassified FBI files reveal that, in August 1942, when Yardley was running his restaurant, he was subject to surveillance by the US Army Counterintelligence Corps. Surveillance commenced on 6 August after

information was received from a 'reliable source' that the eatery was a
'hang-out' for Axis sympathisers. For three weeks, agents watched the
restaurant, chatted with patrons and employees, and eavesdropped on
conversations. From a neighbouring building, equipped with a pair of
army-strength binoculars, they twice spied on the second-floor apartment above the restaurant where Yardley lived.[110] Agents even visited
Yardley's bank to view deposits and withdrawals dating back to August
1940.[111] Although the investigation found no proof that the restaurant
was a meeting place for enemies of the state, Special Agent Frederick
A. Tehaan produced a five-page report in which he expressed major
doubts about Yardley: 'This agent feels that Yardley is a very shrewd
man and that he is capable of performing subversive acts against the
Government if he desired.'[112] Fuelling further suspicion, he then remarked: 'It seems difficult to believe that this man ... is satisfied to
remain inactive during the present world crisis.'[113]

The debate about Yardley's alleged treachery is likely to run and
run, and it is quite possible that the truth will never come out. Ever
the shrewd poker player, Yardley took his cards with him to the grave.
Such is the nature of the intelligence world, with its smoke and mir-
rors, even when 'smoking guns' are discovered, there will always be
people who refuse to believe them. Rightfully, though, the search
goes on and who knows what might be found. One of the pleasures of
truffle-hunting in the archives is that a researcher will often go in search
of one thing and stumble upon an item of equal or greater interest. And
so it was with Dooley's recent research. At the Library of Congress,
rummaging through Japanese Foreign Ministry papers in search of the
tell-tale document about Yardley, he uncovered the following telegram
sent from Isaboru Yoshida, the counsellor to the Japanese embassy, to
Foreign Minister Shidehara on 10 March 1925:

Mr. W. Friedman, an American, from Cornell University seems very
skilled in breaking codes ... When he came to see me recently he

mentioned that the US Army had no difficulty breaking codes. In order to prevent this, we have no choice but change our codes very frequently.[114]

As Dooley explains, if the telegram is correct, it is potentially 'more of a blockbuster' than the alleged Yardley betrayal.[115] In 1925, at the time of the reported tête-à-tête with Yoshida, Friedman was the War Department's chief cryptanalyst. For his success against the Japanese Purple code in World War Two, he is considered by some to be the greatest cryptologist of all time. After the war, he was inducted into the Military Intelligence Hall of Fame, and even has a building named after him at the NSA's present-day facility at Fort Meade, Maryland. What – one might ask – was he doing in 1925 talking to a Japanese diplomat and bragging about the US ability to break codes? In death, as in life, it seems that every codebreaker likes to keep us guessing.

Chapter 2

Limited Hangout

I. Care of Devils

The average man in the street really doesn't know
what it does, what it stands for, and who's who.
Patty Cavin, WRC Radio, 15 January 1962.[1]

Sylvia Press had joined the New York Office of the OSS as a counter-intelligence analyst in 1942. After the war, she remained in the intelligence game with the newly formed CIA. In 1954, she came under suspicion as a possible subversive and was dismissed. At the time, the CIA was under the gun to discover 'Reds' within their ranks and fire them. The charges against her were flimsy. A lengthy grilling at the hands of Robert Bannerman, CIA Director of Security, suggested that she had taken one too many holidays to Mexico during the 'Red Scare', while subtle hints were made as to the appropriateness of an ex-lover. The fact that she had known Francis Kalnay, a Hungarian-born professor, who had angered OSS headquarters by recruiting Yugoslavs allied to the communist revolutionary and statesman Josip Tito, was also used against her.[2] She appealed directly to CIA Director Allen Dulles, but to no avail. Discharged without any real evidence of wrongdoing, she believed herself to be a sacrificial lamb served to appease Senator Joseph McCarthy, then whipping up public hysteria with accusations that communists had infiltrated every part of American government, including the CIA. As a woman with an absence of friends in high places, she was expendable.

Press refused to take her sacking lying down and penned a fiction-alised autobiography, *The Care of Devils*, published in hardback by Beacon Press in 1958.[3] The book was unmistakably based on her career. Only people's names were changed. Press became the heroine, Ellen Simon. The novel starts out with Simon working at the Washington, DC headquarters of an unspecified intelligence agency, clearly the CIA, during the McCarthy witch-hunts. It is not long before she is summoned to the security office and told to pack her bags. A fruitless meeting with Clarence Rommel (a.k.a. Dulles) follows. The book con-cludes with her being thrown as a bone to McCarthy, who was threat-ening to launch a full-scale investigation of the Agency. Clearly, the last thing the CIA wanted was the demagogue Senator digging into its files.

Press has the distinction of being the first CIA memoirist, albeit through the medium of fiction. However, to her enormous disap-pointment, the book flopped. Although it had a healthy print run, only a handful of copies actually appeared in bookstores. Despite its revelatory subject matter, it fell stillborn from the press. The fate of the book, together with the reasons for its weak reception, remains a mystery, although evidence points to CIA involvement. In May 1966, writing for *Esquire* magazine, the well-connected former MI6 officer and journalist Malcolm Muggeridge claimed that the CIA had spent between $50,000 and $100,000 buying up all the copies, including intervention at the distribution level.[4] Press's friends at the CIA told her that library copies would be borrowed by CIA officials and never returned. Reportedly, there was even an unwritten directive for anyone who came across the book to seize it and turn it over to security.[5] In his stellar biography of CIA Director Richard Helms, Pulitzer Prize-winning journalist Thomas Powers learned from intelligence sources that, in 1967, Press wrote to Helms to ask why she had been denied a pension for her years of service with OSS and CIA. Granted a meeting with Howard Osborn, head of the CIA's Security Office, she pleaded: 'Why am I having so much trouble?'

'The thing is, Sylvia,' he replied, 'if only you hadn't written *that book!*'[6]

If the CIA was responsible for the plight of Press's novelised memoir, we should not be surprised. In the two decades or so following its establishment in 1947, the CIA was passionately, some might say obsessively, secretive. As we shall see in this chapter, it was firmly against anyone discussing it, whether in books, in the newspapers, on the silver screen, or on the floor of Congress. Its favoured strategy was that of 'limited hangout'; hiding as much as possible but occasionally allowing for a carefully controlled blast of publicity executed by its Director. Speaking at Santa Clara University on 3 May 1976, a year after he was compelled to resign as CIA Director, William Colby said of the Agency's formative years: 'It was all secret. We weren't allowed to say anything about it and we pretended that it didn't exist.'[7]

Secrecy stemmed as much from a desire to maintain a mystique about the CIA as it did from a requirement to protect sources and methods. In the two years leading to its formation in September 1947, there had been much earnest salesmanship of the CIA to a sceptical American public. The CIA was presented as an almost quasi-celestial body – powerful, omnipresent, and all-seeing.[8] Staff were portrayed as honourable 'can-do' types who worked on the side of the angels. Anxious to avoid another Pearl Harbor, people accepted this message. Few have written about this secular mythology of the CIA better than the American writer Don DeLillo.[9] In his novel *Libra* (1988), one of the characters describes the CIA as 'the best organised church in the Christian world, [with] a mission to collect and store everything that everyone has ever said and then reduce it to a microdot and call it God'.[10] After its creation, the CIA recognised that much of its power came not from what it did, but what people believed it did. As long as the public believed it to be successful and (to quote a British expression) run by 'good chaps', the policy was to say as little as possible.

The figure chiefly responsible for the CIA's mythical status was Allen Welsh Dulles, CIA Director from 1953 to 1961. Dulles oversaw a legendary period of CIA secrecy. Staffing rolls were classified. Like members of Freemasonry, employees were instructed not to reveal the nature of their work, even, in many cases, to other members of the Agency. Robert Wear, a recruiter for the CIA in the early 1950s, recollected that he and his team were:

> strictly forbidden to talk with anyone about any of the people we had interviewed. If by accident we bumped into an interviewee at a later date on the bus or train, we were not permitted to ask him or her what part of the CIA organisation they were connected with.[11]

Under Dulles, the CIA had a press office, but the job of the press spokesman was to say 'no comment' to virtually every question. The only person afforded any freedom to discuss the CIA was the man at the top – Dulles. A gifted raconteur and self-promoter, he was the exception to an otherwise completely secret and mute organisation. While everyone else around him was bound to a code of silence, he sought the public spotlight when it suited, proselytising the cause of intelligence.

By the early 1960s, it will be shown that the CIA's bunkered strategy of limited hangout had become a source of some of its woes. Secrecy had begun to cut both ways. While it guaranteed that the CIA had been able to operate successfully overseas in places like Iran and Guatemala without scrutiny and interference, it eventually created a news void that was filled with speculation, distortion and even outright fantasy. Nature abhors a vacuum: since the CIA was not prepared to talk about itself, journalists, historians and Soviet propagandists filled that vacuum. In the wake of the U-2 incident and then the Bay of Pigs fiasco in April 1961, when Fidel Castro's army defeated approximately 1,400 CIA-backed exiles, there came a wave of hostile writing on the CIA, including *dezinformatsiya* of the KGB's creation. The myth, so diligently policed by Dulles throughout the 1950s, came apart at the seams. Almost overnight, the CIA went from being a source of wonder to an object of distrust. In his retirement and with his own reputation sullied, Dulles tried to rehabilitate the myth by taking pen in hand, speaking to the press and cultivating friendships with people happy to say nice things about the CIA. He did this with no support from his old employer, meaning that as the 1970s came into view, the CIA was as secretive as it had ever been.

II. The Rebirth of the US Spy Memoir

The cloak-and-dagger boys of 'Wild Bill' Donovan's Office of Strategic
Services waged a successful war behind enemy lines and have demon-
strated the need for a coordinated intelligence office for the US.
John Chamberlain, *Life* magazine, 19 December 1945.[12]

Yardley had simultaneously given birth to the US spy memoir and suffocated its early development. The passage of the so-called 'Yardley Act' in June 1933 created an expectation that any intelligence officer writing about their trade would be summarily dealt with. The Japanese attack on Pearl Harbor and the advent of war with the Axis powers in December 1941 killed off any chance of the genre resurfacing, as everyone was sworn to secrecy. Accordingly, a number of years elapsed before anyone with first-hand knowledge of American intelligence came forward with a story to tell.

The process of resurrection for the US spy memoir did not happen naturally. Instead, it was forced. What's more, it was forced by senior US intelligence professionals. For most of World War Two, the OSS was extremely secret and received minimal public credit for its work. Unable to remove its light from beneath the bushel, it suffered from the jibes of columnists who suggested that OSS stood for 'Oh Shush Shush',

'Oh So Secret' and 'Oh So Social'. As the war came to an end, however, OSS head General William Joseph Donovan (nicknamed 'Wild
Bill' for his aggression on the college football field and for his courage
under fire in combat during World War One) launched a major public
relations crusade to showcase the achievements of his service and promote the cause of a permanent intelligence agency. Since the surprise
attack on Pearl Harbor, a national debate had raged on whether the
United States possessed an adequate intelligence apparatus to protect
itself. From the summer of 1945, passions on the subject began to run
particularly high with the emergence of the Soviet threat and the reality that a war-torn Western Europe was in no position to fight back.
Although public opinion was moving steadily in favour of the creation
of a peacetime intelligence agency, Donovan was keen to get it over the
line. Furthermore, he longed to see the OSS as that agency, with him
at the helm. Accordingly, he encouraged his clandestine warriors to
return from the field and publish exciting tales of derring-do, showing
how OSS had 'made a difference'. The battle for the future of US intelligence was to be waged by recounting the past.

Donovan enlisted the help of Wallace Deuel. Not cut out for clandestine work overseas, Deuel had been Donovan's special assistant
and had a particular flair for propaganda. Indeed, for the OSS, he
collaborated with Walt Disney on a cartoon propaganda project.[13] On
4 August 1945, he issued a memorandum to key OSS staff emphasising
the importance of a comprehensive public information programme.
In the absence of such an initiative, he explained that the OSS might
appear to people as a 'sort of Flash Gordon series of operations', costing
the lives of many men, at high expenditure, without actually helping to
win the war.[14] Allowing this to happen, he asserted, would be 'tragic'.
Not only would it do enormous disservice to the 'men who have done
such great things', but it would 'discredit the whole idea of having
any such agency in the future'.[15] Moreover, it would 'play directly into
the hands' of government rivals with ideas and pretensions of their

own on the subject. OSS was not the only horse in the race to lead America's post-war intelligence effort. The 'feuding fiefdoms' of the army, navy and State all had aspirations of extending their empires by leading a 'super-spy system'.[16] Deuel therefore called on old OSS hands to communicate their silent and significant deeds to the press. These stories, he underlined, would 'demonstrate that some such agency … is an absolute necessity in the future'.[17] Deuel also saw this as a good way for the OSS to endear itself to the press. The majority of journalists had for four years conscientiously respected Donovan's requests for secrecy. Providing them with stories, therefore, would be seen as rewarding them for their silence.

With good reason, Deuel was very particular about what sort of recollections he wanted published. The OSS had engaged in several activities that, in his words, 'would not be approved in Sunday school'.[18] Donovan had been of the view that, 'in a global and totalitarian war, intelligence must be global and totalitarian', meaning that nothing was off limits, including assassination.[19] Although the American public was not naïve to believe that OSS had behaved like 'goody-goodies', it was important not to give the impression that the service had fought fire with fire, by copying the 'worst methods [of] our enemies'.[20]

Deuel was also particular about *who* should be allowed to publish reminiscences. As a recruiter, Donovan had not paid much attention to background checks; if he saw talent, he hired it. Consequently, the OSS had employed a range of ex-convicts and criminal types. Individuals like this were at odds with the image Deuel was looking to sell to the public. Spying was still seen in certain circles as unsavoury, ungentlemanly and un-American – a view encapsulated by Stimson's now immortal admonition that 'gentlemen do not read other gentlemen's mail'. Moreover, leaks to the press by bureaucratic enemies of OSS had sought to conjure up the image of an 'American Gestapo'. To allay these concerns, Deuel was keen to present the OSS as an 'honourable' organisation, comprising men who had kept the game honest and who had known where to draw the line. The officers he wanted to publish ideally had to conform to the cliché of the 'all-American boy' – modest almost to a fault, dedicated to his family, class president, good at sports, thoroughly a team-player, and red-blooded. The American public might always regard espionage with distaste; but they could take comfort in the fact that at least American spies were honourable men.

In the weeks following Japan's surrender on 15 August 1945, the number of OSS stories hitting the press turned into a flood. Every day, newspapers were filled with tales of brave agents jumping behind enemy lines, blowing up bridges and railway lines, running guns and plotting against the Nazis. Headlines read: 'OSS Part in Victory is Disclosed' and 'OSS Played Major Role in Allied Victory'.[21] To stimulate further publicity, Deuel organised a press conference where reporters were given declassified summaries of more than 100 Top Secret operations – many of which included code names and the identities of agents.[22] To avoid giving the misleading impression that operations amounted to a 'helter-skelter conglomeration of unrelated stunts that had no basic logic or plan', additional information was provided outlining the general nature and purposes of the service, as well as details about organisation and personnel.[23] At the conference, Donovan thanked the press for helping to preserve OSS security during the war, even when this meant passing up good stories. Through their cooperation, he emphasised, they had saved many lives and made possible many valuable operations.[24] Boldly, he explained that the American people 'have a right to be told as much as possible about an agency they have supported with their money and the energies and lives of their sons'.[25] In a manner unprecedented in the history of nations, the creation of the United States' foreign intelligence service was unfolding in full public view. The British intelligence community was horrified by events taking place across the pond. With agencies such as MI5 and MI6 not even on the statute book, there was concern in London that the Americans, in touting their espionage achievements, would be responsible for generating unwelcome public interest in British secret services.[26]

Many of the insider stories centred on Donovan. This is unsurprising, as he had overall editorial control of what was published. But it also reflected the fact that this brave old soldier, a recipient of the Medal of Honor for heroism in the trenches during World War One, commanded enormous respect from his men. People loved to serve under him. With a 'leave no man behind' mentality, he had sanctioned daring rescue missions of downed pilots in Nazi-occupied territory. For example, between 19 June and 19 September 1944, 1,880 American airmen were rescued by OSS from the Balkans. In a letter to Donovan, Henry Arnold, Commanding General of the US Army Air Forces, rhapsodised, 'This is an achievement in which the OSS should have much justifiable pride.'[27]

Deuel, who left OSS to join the *Chicago Daily News*, wrote a series of articles lionising his former boss. In one article, he raved:

> Donovan is one of the trickiest open-field runners who ever carried the ball in the great game of politics either at home or abroad. Once in motion – and he is seldom still – there is no telling where or when he will stop or what he will be up to in the meantime.[28]

He credited Donovan as being a master of psychological warfare, suggesting that he 'acted more effectively on it than any other American, perhaps more than any other human being'.[29] He praised Donovan for 'waging a one-man psychological warfare campaign in the Balkans and Middle East to strengthen the will to resist [Hitler]'.[30] To show that Donovan had always put his men first, he gave the story of how the general, true to his sobriquet of 'Wild Bill', had ignored orders from his superiors in Washington and joined the invasion armada that landed at Normandy in June 1944. Donovan's presence in the combat zone had been strictly forbidden by General George C. Marshall, US Army Chief of Staff, for fear that he might be captured and forced to reveal secrets to the enemy. Not a man to take no for an answer, he hitched a ride across the English Channel on a heavy cruiser, boarded a landing craft and went ashore with American forces on Utah Beach. At one point, bleeding copiously and hiding in a hedgerow to evade German fighter planes, he turned to his commander of covert operations in Europe, Colonel David Bruce, to ask if the latter had packed any suicide capsules. When Bruce confessed that he had not, Donovan announced that in the event of capture, 'As your commanding officer, I'll shoot you first and then myself.'[31]

Sadly for Donovan, the promotional hype could not save him or his agency. On 20 September 1945, President Truman ordered the OSS to disband in ten days and dismissed its head with scarcely an acknowledgement of gratitude for services rendered, a ghastly snub for someone who had created the OSS *ex nihilo*. All the publicity in the world could not change one incontrovertible fact: Donovan was a hugely divisive figure. While his men in OSS stood in awe of him, he was much-maligned where it really mattered, in the post-war scramble for power, in Washington. Indeed, he was quoted as saying that his 'greatest enemies were in Washington, not in Europe.'[32]

In senior military circles, there was scarcely anyone with a good word to say about him. Dogmatic, scheming and obsessed with gaining power, he had run roughshod over many leading figures in the army and navy. According to Deuel's private notes, Major General George V. Strong, US Army Deputy Chief of Staff for Intelligence (G-2), 'hated WJD as violently as any human being probably hated any other. He turned purple and the vein in his forehead swelled and pumped.'[33] Added to this, career professionals in the armed forces loathed the thought of a permanent spy agency being created out of what they saw as a motley band of amateurs. Donovan had recruited all sorts, including: con-artists, safe-crackers, circus stars, paroled convicts, remittance men, hustlers, Ivy League boffins, horse breeders and Wall Street bankers. A number of operatives would later become household names. They included Julia Child, the beloved doyenne of US television cookery shows; Moe Berg, a major league baseball player; and Sterling Hayden, the actor who played the crazy general in *Dr Strangelove*. Such was the determination of the military establishment to drive Donovan and his amateurs out of Washington, several figures in the US Army passed to Truman, through a White House military aide, a devastating 59-page memo characterising the OSS as a rogue outfit, bedevilled by failures, poor leadership and all manner of scandal.[34]

Donovan was not helped by the equally ambitious J. Edgar Hoover, Director of the FBI, who looked to undermine the OSS at every opportunity. Hoover was violently opposed to Donovan on both a personal and professional level. As a bachelor who lived at home with his mother and who had wormed a draft exemption from the army, he had little in common with Donovan, a man of action with mud on his boots. Hoover, who had Donovan watched and kept a dossier on him filled with incriminating information, resented the General's close ties with British Intelligence and what he saw as the encroachment of OSS and Anglophile influence onto his turf. Keen to get the brazen interloper out of his hair, and cement his own position as US spy czar, he spread the ugly rumour that Donovan was sleeping with Truman's daughter-in-law, Mary, a blatant lie but one that carried some traction given Donovan's notorious womanising and string of extramarital affairs.[35] Hoover may also have been behind leaks to the press exposing bungled OSS operations, including instances where brave young men had paid the ultimate price for Donovan's over-exuberance. With such powerful constituencies conspiring against him, Donovan's vision of heading an all-powerful US intelligence service was extinguished. The newly sworn-in Truman, never a fan of 'Wild Bill' in any case, was looking to downsize government after the war. Moreover, as one retired intelligence officer has put it, he had advisers in his ear saying,

'You've got enough problems with Hoover. One troublemaker is more than enough.'[36]

Donovan's disappointment at losing the OSS did not quell his enthusiasm for publicity. It was not in his nature to go quietly into the night; but, more importantly, he remained hopeful of returning to public life and having a piece of whatever intelligence pie was finally agreed upon. Moreover, with an eye on posterity, he was determined to ensure that the first draft of OSS history was a positive one.

To complement the reminiscences coming out in the press and being developed into books, he called on OSS veterans to go westward, to Hollywood, to assist filmmakers racing to be the first in theatres with a World War Two spy movie. In a memorandum written not long after the dissolution of OSS, on 1 October 1945, he explained that 'there are former members of the OSS organisation, thoroughly familiar with its affairs, who will shortly return to their civilian occupations, upon whom the motion picture companies may, if they so desire, call for such advice and assistance as these men care to furnish'.[37] To coordinate the effort, he set up a committee comprised of several senior OSS staff, including John Shaheen (chief of Special Projects); David Bruce (commander of OSS in European Theatre of Operations); Russell Forgan (Bruce's successor as head of OSS in Europe); Edward Buxton (Assistant Director of OSS); and Allen Dulles (wartime Station Chief in Switzerland). Its primary purpose was to 'meet with any or all of the companies which have approached OSS and requested assistance in recording its activities'.[38] Between late 1945 and summer 1946, the committee was on hand to provide stories, check the accuracy of scripts, and even loan artefacts, such as film footage shot by the OSS Field Photographic Branch. Moreover, there is some evidence to suggest that the committee even gave filmmakers an opportunity to inspect OSS files.[39] If true, they would have been the only 'outsiders' to see these files for more than three decades, since OSS records remained closed until 1980.

Thanks to Donovan, Los Angeles became a new home for scores of

'OSSers' after the war. Richard Maibaum, who produced the film *OSS* for Paramount and who later wrote most of the screenplays for the James Bond films between 1962 and 1989, recollected: 'We had literally about ten technical agents all telling us marvellous stories of what happened to them all over the world which we incorporated into the plot.'[40] In the press releases for the film, the studio inflated this figure, bragging that 'Thirty or more real-life be-medalled heroes of the OSS have actively contributed to the realism of the picture as technical advisers or bit players or in both functions.'[41] Twentieth Century Fox, working on *13 Rue Madeleine*, benefited from the technical assistance of Aubrey Wayne Nelson, a recipient of the Bronze Star who had worked as a personal assistant to Donovan at OSS administrative headquarters in Washington before serving overseas in North Africa, Sicily and Sardinia. Twentieth Century Fox could even boast OSS people among their permanent staff, such as special effects supremo Ray Kellogg who had been deputy chief of the Field Photographic Branch.[42]

OSS veterans working as technical advisers earned good money. Former covert operations officer Michael Burke, a University of Pennsylvania football star who went on to become President and co-owner of the New York Yankees, picked up $300 per week for his work on the Warner Bros production *Cloak and Dagger*.[43] After the hardship of war, it is safe to say that the veterans enjoyed the West Coast lifestyle. In a letter to a friend on the East Coast, dated 5 November 1945, Burke teased: 'Swimming yesterday – Temp 93°. How's the snow in Washington?'[44] As well as sharing their expertise and experiences with filmmakers, the veterans loaned an array of 'special devices'. These ranged from knives and blades to more outlandish items, such as a pipe that doubled as a gun and a foul-smelling odour, akin to flatulence, that OSS agents used to spray on people they wished to discredit, causing them to be socially humiliated.[45]

In 1946, therefore, with the idea of the CIA being discussed at the highest levels of government, three high-grossing films came out celebrating the achievements of US intelligence. The first of these was *OSS*, released on 26 May 1946. Starring Alan Ladd and Geraldine Fitzgerald, the film openly acknowledged its connection to the now defunct agency, listing half a dozen OSS people in the credits. Donovan gave his seal of approval by providing a signed statement, featured in the opening sequence. That Paramount received a degree of special treatment is unsurprising. During the war, the studio had provided foreign currency for espionage operations in Finland and Sweden. Logistical help for this had come from Stanton Griffis, a top Paramount executive who had been a special agent in Finland. A film of high suspense, *OSS* was explicit in agitating for the creation of a peacetime intelligence service that carried out covert action, as well as traditional intelligence work. In one scene, an OSS instructor announces to a band of hearty new operatives:

> We can't waste too much time with you. We're late. Four hundred years. That's how long ago the other major powers started their OSS. We've only got months to build the first central intelligence agency in our history – a worldwide organisation that will beat the enemy at its own game.

The second film into theatres was *Cloak and Dagger*, which opened on 4 October 1946 and was derived from a book of the same name. Written by OSS veterans Lieutenant Colonel Corey Ford and Major Alastair MacBain, *Cloak and Dagger: The Secret Story of the OSS* (1945) had been one of the first insider histories of the organisation.[46] However, in true Hollywood fashion, the film had little in common with the book, save the title. Starring Gary Cooper as a nuclear physicist who joins OSS to help with the rescue of a scientist captured by the Nazis, it borrowed more heavily from the adventures of Michael Burke, one of the film's technical advisers. A winner of the Navy Cross and Silver Star, the urbane and matinee-idol handsome Burke had worked closely with the French Resistance. Between missions, he had bar-hopped in Paris with Ernest Hemingway, who called him 'kid'. His most daring assignment had been to smuggle Eugenio Minisini and other anti-Nazi scientists out of Italy and into the US, where they would lend their expertise to weapons development. Burke had wanted legendary filmmaker John Ford, head of the OSS Field Photographic Branch, to direct the film, but contractual issues meant German émigré director Fritz Lang took the helm.[47] Obsessive about historical accuracy, Lang spent many hours with Burke and fellow veteran Andries Deinum. Anxious to bring realism to a scene in which Cooper's character kills a man with his bare hands, he invited them both to his home one evening and got them to perform a bare-handed brawl. As the two former spies rolled around on the floor, he hovered over them (in Deinum's words) 'making a square with his fingers'.[48]

The final film in the OSS trilogy was *13 Rue Madeleine*. Released in December, it starred James Cagney, the quintessential movie tough guy, and one of Hollywood's highest-paid actors, as a hard-boiled spy instructor tasked with finding a German agent among his trainees. The film is essentially divided into two parts. It begins in the US, with Cagney adopting an intellectual persona, grooming his neophyte spies and overseeing their training. It then switches to overseas, with Cagney being parachuted into Nazi-occupied France, at which point the screen hoodlum takes over and the fists start flying.

Donovan had been heavily involved in the film's initial development. Early scripts featured an opening-credit sequence paying homage to OSS. The main character, Bob Sharkey (Cagney), was an attorney, just as 'Wild Bill' had been.[49] However, Donovan's support did not last. In spring 1946, he received alarming reports from the committee he had set up to help scriptwriters that the picture was riddled with inaccuracies and too far-fetched. 'This script is not an authentic OSS story,' considered the committee. 'The basic plot and most of the details are not only highly fictionalised but fantastic.'[50] Ultimately, it was 'unfair to the thousands of hard-working, clear-thinking men and women who made the success of OSS possible.[51] Many of the objections related to historical accuracy. The committee considered it 'ridiculous in the extreme' that, on the eve of the Normandy landings, one man, even one as heroic as Cagney, would parachute behind enemy lines and successfully survey every potential sabotage target. 'All sabotage targets had been carefully thought out and laid on by OSS before D-Day,' protested committee member Russell Forgan.[52] The committee rejected the idea that Cagney's character, first of all, would have been made privy to the date and place of the invasion, and then, with such priceless knowledge in his possession, have been sent into action in advance of the expeditionary forces: 'We would never have allowed any individual who knew all the plans for Overlord to have gone into France prior to D-Day.'[53] It was felt that in trying to give the British some credit, too much emphasis had been given to the air cover provided by the Royal Air Force (RAF). 'Our own air force', the committee remarked, 'would have done most of the air support required by OSS.'[54] Also troubling was a theme running throughout the film that the OSS, for the sake of ultimate victory, had played dirty. In one of his pep talks to recruits, Cagney had stated: 'No secret agent is a hero or a good sport. That is, no living agent. You are going to be taught to kill, to cheat, to rob, to lie ... Fair play, that's out. Years of decency and honest living, forget all about them.' Such a portrayal was at odds with Donovan's desire to make the idea of a permanent intelligence agency more palatable by presenting espionage as a game of cops and robbers, with US spies behaving like gentlemen. In short, it was OK for Cagney to kick a man, but not when he was down.

Most troubling of all, however, was the film's key plot twist, in which an OSS trainee was in fact a German spy. 'It seems little short of ridiculous', remonstrated the committee, 'to have OSS admit a known Gestapo agent into its ranks.'[55] Any suggestion that OSS had been vulnerable to Nazi infiltration would hardly inspire public confidence.

Pressure was put on the studio to make changes, but largely to no avail. 'This is Hollywood', emphasised a senior studio executive, 'and, in obeisance to local tradition, no doubt our picture will not avoid entirely certain creative license.'[56] Donovan was furious, and even threatened to organise a boycott of the film unless the script was changed. In a letter to the film's producer, Louis de Rochemont, he labelled the picture a 'phony'. 'With all the excellent authentic material which we have sought to make available to you it seems absurd that your company would persist in making a picture that not only lacks reality but plausibility,' he protested.[57] He made it clear that he would not approve of the studio branding the film an 'authentic, or even a typical, story of OSS operations'.[58] 'It would clearly be unfair', he argued, 'to OSS agents who voluntarily jeopardised their lives to engage in valuable clandestine operations to couple their names and experiences with the events pictured in the script'.[59] Rather than rewrite the script, the studio simply deleted all references to OSS and to Donovan. The spy agency in the film was renamed '077', while Cagney's character was no longer a lawyer and was instead described as a 'scholar and soldier of fortune'. Whatever the faults of 13 Rue Madeleine, like OSS and Cloak and Dagger, it raised public awareness about the importance of US spies. All three films made the Top 50 highest-grossing films of the year, each earning in excess of $2.5 million in domestic rentals.[60]

In spring 1947, with Congress still debating the pros and cons of a new intelligence establishment, a further blast of spy hype was achieved with the publication of two OSS memoirs. The first represented something of a breakthrough for the US spy memoir, since it was penned by a woman. Until this point, women had barely featured in the postwar publicity, save the sight of Cagney grabbing a hysterical 'dame' by the lower lip, and then giving her a resounding slap across the face. Undercover Girl by Elizabeth MacDonald, which included a two-page preface by Donovan, changed this.[61] Born in Washington, DC, but raised in Hawaii, where she had learned Japanese, MacDonald was recruited by the OSS in 1943 for her language skills. She was assigned to the service's Morale Operations (MO) Branch, involved in distributing 'black propaganda' to demoralise the enemy. Sent to the Pacific Theatre, she was among the rarest breed of operative, a woman based overseas in an operational capacity. As Donovan acknowledged in his foreword, 'Only a small percentage of the women ever went overseas, and a still smaller percentage was assigned to actual operational jobs behind enemy lines.'[62]

MacDonald prepared her manuscript in close conjunction with Donovan's committee, which gave her privileged access to documents from every theatre of OSS activity.[63] The end product contained an important message, one shrewdly designed to resonate with contemporary discussions about US intelligence – OSS propaganda had shattered the morale of the enemy and prepared him for the final kill. How exactly had this been achieved? MacDonald revealed that her unit had intercepted postcards that the emperor's soldiers were mailing home, before substituting the reassuring messages with complaints about lack of ammunition and food. Moreover, letters to wives and girlfriends were changed to say that the soldier had fallen in love with a Burmese sweetheart and would not be coming home. Similar tactics, she emphasised, would be invaluable in the struggle against the USSR.

The second memoir was *Germany's Underground* by Allen Dulles.[64] Dulles was no ordinary public servant. As Robin Winks has written, he came from a world of 'privilege and high personal expectation'.[65] A scion of a politically connected family, with a strong tradition of public service, he was the grandson of one Secretary of State, John Watson Foster, who served President Benjamin Harrison, and the nephew of another, Robert Lansing, who worked with President Woodrow Wilson. The son of a Presbyterian minister, he grew up in Watertown, New York, with his ambitious elder brother, John Foster, who went on to become President Dwight D. Eisenhower's immensely powerful Secretary of State. Like Donovan, he was a born publicist. As

OSS Station Chief in Bern, Switzerland, he had put a sign on his door specifying his name and position, a form of exhibitionism that would have been unthinkable to publicity-shy European secret services like the British.[66] In the history of US intelligence, there will never be a better after-dinner speaker. His favourite story stemmed from his time in the Foreign Service in World War One, where he was attached to the American legation, again in Bern. There, in Easter 1917, he turned down a request for an urgent meeting from a then unknown brusque Russian émigré, opting instead to keep a tennis date with a girlfriend. This, he would tell listeners, was a mistake since the man in question was none other than Vladimir Lenin, who days later was ferried to St Petersburg to begin the Russian Revolution. With everybody spellbound, Dulles would then explain that this episode taught him two rules in life. One, a good case officer should always take time to listen to a walk-in source, however unpromising that person might seem. And two, the game of intelligence always takes priority over the game between men and women.[67] Then came the punch line: to the first rule, he adhered religiously; the second, not so much.

The storied Dulles jumped at the chance to answer Donovan's call to acquaint the public with the history of American espionage. A national bestseller, published at the precise moment when the proposal for the CIA was on the verge of being approved, *Germany's Underground* looked at Dulles's time as head of OSS operations in Switzerland (1942–45). The book showed that, from a rented flat in Bern, he was responsible for gathering intelligence on the Nazi enemy and supporting resistance groups under the rule of Hitler or Mussolini. It revealed how he had built a sprawling network of contacts spanning a dozen European countries. From these refugees, exiles, resistance fighters and anti-Nazi intelligence officers, he received valuable information about the Axis powers, including the V-1 and V-2 rocket programmes and the development of the Messerschmitt Me 262 jet fighter. Just as Macdonald emphasised the usefulness of psychological operations in combating future enemies, Dulles underscored the importance of not letting his wartime experiences go to waste in trying to deal with the Soviet Union, writing: 'Here we have an unprecedented opportunity to study the totalitarian technique and to learn lessons for our own defence.'[68]

On 26 July 1947, Truman signed into law the National Security Act establishing the CIA, the nation's first peacetime foreign intelligence agency.[69] Donovan had good reason to be pleased. In key respects, the new organisation resembled the proposal he had been kicking around Washington since the war. It was an independent agency controlled by the White House, although it would report to a newly created National Security Council (NSC) and not, as Donovan had desired, directly to the President. As he had hoped, it was tasked with conducting both clandestine activities abroad and the analysis of intelligence centralised in one organisation, but with no policymaking authority or law-enforcement powers.

However, his vision of him leading this agency did not materialise. When the CIA officially opened for business on 18 September, he was conspicuous by his absence, with a reluctant Admiral Roscoe Hillenkoetter put in charge. The political elite simply could not bring themselves to trust him. There was no room in the new, disciplined national security state for someone predisposed to freewheeling and in-fighting, and whose approach to life was to act first and pick up the pieces later. In what Donovan saw as the final insult, Truman made him chairman of a trivial committee investigating the nation's firefighters.[70] After the 1952 presidential race, in which he campaigned hard for the successful Republican candidate Dwight D. Eisenhower, Donovan hoped that he might at last get the job he craved. Again, he would be passed over, this time in favour of his protégé, Dulles. Instead of taking pride from this appointment as a sign that the spirit of OSS would live on, he chose to be bitter at losing out to an underling.

Although Donovan failed to realise his dream of running a peacetime intelligence agency, his role in bringing that agency into being cannot be underestimated. The exigencies of the Cold War and the fear of another Pearl Harbor, especially the nuclear kind, had created a need for a spy service. But, there had also been a powerful desire not to introduce anything that would undermine American core values. By resurrecting the US spy memoir and encouraging real flesh-and-blood secret agents to tell hearty tales, Donovan helped to create a landscape in which Americans did not simply tolerate the creation of the CIA, but welcomed it. His PR campaign established a mystique about American spying. It appropriated brilliant operational successes from the war to demonstrate just how valuable American espionage could be in the future. It promoted the idea that American spies were decent people, committed to playing the game of espionage the right way. Donovan's skill and legacy was to make the figure of the American spy appear less like a dealer of dirty tricks and more like a folk hero, righteous and committed to protecting the very freedoms upon which the US was founded. As we shall now see, the need to keep aggressively pushing this message ended with the CIA's creation. The time for openness about spying was over.

III. The Golden Age

There was some kind of thing out there
but no one really knew what it was.
Joseph Wippl, 35-year CIA operations officer.[71]

After the blaze of publicity that had accompanied and helped to facilitate the CIA's creation, the focus shifted to keeping contact with the outside world to a bare minimum. Having entertained the public for nearly two years with countless stories of spies and saboteurs, the press was suddenly confronted with an organisation that adopted a 'no comment' policy. Overnight, the situation went from feast to famine.

In its first four years, the CIA had no officer formally designated to deal with queries from the press. In spring 1951, Colonel B. Hansen, a former public relations aide to General Omar Bradley, was appointed the first 'CIA Spokesman', but he and his successors were encouraged to say as little as possible to reporters.[72] According to Walter N. Elder, a press spokesman in the 1950s: 'People badgered the Agency, and most of the time, the assistant had nothing to say.'[73] In testament to how low key the job of press liaison was, one spokesman even went back undercover![74]

The period of American spies working with Hollywood ended.[75] Filmmakers and television networks were legally required to receive permission from the CIA to use its name. In June 1951, the chief censor of NBC wrote a memorandum informing staff: 'Management advises us that any reference to the Central Intelligence Agency or the Secret Service in script material requires clearance with these bodies.'[76] Permission was never forthcoming, as the CIA was firmly against filmic representations. In February 1952, a senior figure in Warner Brothers was given extremely short shrift by CIA officials when he proposed that the Agency give the studio technical assistance in the making of a spy movie set in the present day. The CIA brusquely wrote to him that it would 'not only be unable to afford such guidance, but that we would take every step to discourage the production of a picture which purported to represent current US espionage.'[77] Meanwhile, former intelligence officers were no longer given the freedom to publicise their careers. In the summer of 1954, for example, Robert Wear, who served overseas in the Mariana Islands, retired from the Agency to undertake graduate work at the University of Michigan. He was forbidden in his dissertation from mentioning anything about his time in the CIA or from using recreational photographs he had taken of the South Pacific – 'No names, no faces, locations or source materials were permitted.'[78]

There were many reasons why the CIA made such a determined effort to preserve secrecy about itself. Firstly, like any spy service, it held secrecy to be an essential element of successful operations and was committed to protecting its sources and methods. As the NSC ruled on 6 January 1950, 'Any publicity, factual or fictional, concerning intelligence is potentially detrimental to the effectiveness of an intelligence activity and to the national security.'[79] Secondly, the CIA followed an 'Alice in Wonderland' logic. The reasoning went that if the CIA publicly denied a charge, people would interpret its silence on other charges as evidence that they were true.[80] Third, the CIA recognised that without a reputation for keeping secrets, other intelligence services would be reluctant to share information. Liaison was and remains a central element of the intelligence business. No spy service can achieve perfect or even near-perfect coverage of the world. Nations, even ones as wealthy as the United States, are limited by finite resources. Accordingly, as Michael Herman has argued, cooperation with allies shares the burden of cost and allows nations to 'get better views of the world at cut prices'.[81] For the CIA, it was critical to start earning the trust of allies. The agency was in its infancy and ill-equipped for its mission. Until congressionally appropriated funds were secured in 1949, it had to survive on a subsistence allowance maintained by a handful of friendly congressmen. It would take time to develop the necessary skills to run effective human intelligence (HUMINT) operations. Moreover, the CIA knew that allies could provide training and access to facilities, as well as support joint operations. To ensure therefore that valuable liaison opportunities were not lost, showing a commitment to secrecy was essential.

However, the chief reason for being secretive was to maintain the CIA's mystique. An indefatigable publicist of clandestine efforts, Donovan had been so successful at magnifying OSS's achievements that the public were completely in awe of the CIA, even though they had no real clue what it was or what it was doing. For most Americans, the CIA was simply 'out there'. It was a magical organisation that existed to save the world. It was led by the tough young veterans of the last good war – plucky amateurs who carried out deadly hush-hush escapades in the spirit of Donovan's OSS. With good reason, the CIA wanted to keep this myth alive for as long as possible. The myth stopped both Congress and the public from asking too many questions, and deflected attention away from what the Agency was really up to, including activities that went beyond its charter (see Chapter 3). As the new kid on the bureaucratic block, the myth also gave the CIA a voice in a cut-throat lobbying environment where, in the words of Rhodri Jeffreys-Jones, 'He who hypes best wins the appropriation.'[82] In short, the money would continue to roll in so long as the myth remained intact.

In the early years of the Cold War, there was no large or sustained challenge to CIA secrecy. Quite the opposite: as the Soviet Union became more imposing, especially after it tested its first atomic bomb in 1949, the 'duck and cover' generation in America respected government institutions and saw secrecy as more of a virtue than a vice.

Congress was happy to look the other way. Mirroring the reluctance of MPs in the United Kingdom at this time to discuss MI5 and MI6 in Parliament, Congressmen declined to debate the CIA in either house. They rarely asked for or received intelligence briefings. There was no formal mechanism of congressional oversight. Instead, oversight was delegated to small sub-panels of the Appropriations and Armed Services Committees, which met only a handful of times a year, possessed nominal authority, and benignly wrote cheques with no questions asked.[83] In 1951, the CIA subcommittee of the Senate Armed Services Committee had one meeting.[84] The Senate Appropriations Committee's CIA panel convened once in 1956 and not at all in 1957.[85] On the rare occasion when a CIA official was required to testify on the Hill, that person would say next to nothing, especially when it came to operations. During one of the McCarthy hearings, CIA Director Walter Bedell Smith, a master of self-control, muttered only two words – 'Yes' or 'No' – and sat in complete silence in between the questions. ''Twas absolutely marvellous to watch,' recollected one intelligence veteran.[86] Dulles once remarked that he would 'fudge the truth' when speaking to oversight committees. Occasionally, he would come clean with the chairman, but strictly in private and only 'if he wants to know'.[87] John Warner, who served as CIA Legislative Counsel from 1957 to 1968, later gave an interview in which he described a meeting he and Dulles had with subcommittee chairman Clarence Cannon in the late 1950s, worthy of repeating in full since it perfectly encapsulates how undemanding Congress was during the early years:

> [We were asked to give] a budget briefing, Sunday afternoon, in the House Office Building in the Capitol at 1 p.m. ... It was sort of a crowded room and Clarence Cannon greets Dulles, 'Oh, it's good to see you again Mr. Secretary.' He refers to [Secretary of State John Foster Dulles rather than DCI Allen Dulles] but he knows it is the CIA budget. [Allen] Dulles is a great raconteur. He can tell story after story. He reminds Cannon of this, and Cannon reminds him of that, and they swap stories for two hours. And, in the end: 'Well, Mr. Secretary, have you got enough money in your budget for this year, the coming year?' 'Well, I think we are all right, Mr. Chairman. Thank you very much.' That was the budget hearing.[88]

Truly, see no evil, hear no evil!

Lack of oversight was not a reflection of lack of CIA activity. The 1950s have been characterised as a 'golden age' for the CIA, a period when an all-male, largely Ivy League band of adventurers dropped agents into Eastern Europe to foster insurgencies, and discreetly engineered the defeat of leftist insurgents in the Philippines and overthrew popular governments in Iran and Guatemala.[89] Rather, lack of oversight reflected a congressional belief that CIA activities 'had to be taken on faith', as Senator Richard Russell had said in 1956, because of the need for ruthlessness in the battle against the Soviet Union. In the context of a dangerous Cold War environment, and with presidential control over foreign affairs approaching its zenith (this was the era of Arthur Schlesinger Jr's famous 'imperial presidency' thesis), the CIA was respected as a vital tool of the executive branch in confronting the communist threat. Senator Leverett Saltonstall, who sat on both the Senate Appropriations and Armed Services Committees in the 1950s, spoke for his colleagues when he said: 'It is not a question of reluctance on the part of the CIA officials to speak to us. Instead it is a question of our reluctance, if you will, to seek information and knowledge on subjects which I personally, as a Member of Congress and as a citizen, would rather not have.'[90] According to Walter Pforzheimer, the CIA's first legislative counsel and liaison on Capitol Hill, Congress simply did not want to know: 'There were very loose reins on us at the time because the Congress believed in what we were doing. It wasn't that we were attempting to hide anything. Our main problem was we couldn't get them to sit still and listen.'[91] 'No, no, my boy, don't tell me,' was the response Dulles typically got from the chairman.

Despite the First Amendment of the Bill of Rights granting the press broad constitutional protection to write about sensitive matters of state, journalists seldom broke stories about the CIA. When the CIA helped to oust Mohammad Mossadegh from power in Iran in 1953, the American media said nothing about the Agency's involvement. In 1954, Arthur Hays Sulzberger, chairman and chief executive of the *New York Times*, acquiesced to the CIA's request that the newspaper pull an overly inquisitive reporter, Sydney Gruson, out of Guatemala to protect CIA operations in the country.[92]

In fact, many journalists worked 'hand-in-glove' with the CIA at this time. In 1976, investigative reporter Carl Bernstein calculated that as many as 400 US journalists had secretly been employed by the CIA since 1952 (the CIA itself puts the figure at 'some three dozen').[93] With the appointment of OSS veteran Frank Wisner as director of the CIA's Office of Policy Coordination (OPC) in September 1948, sections of the media became a vehicle for covert propaganda. CIA luminaries such as Thomas Braden and Cord Meyer co-opted respected members of the mainstream media. Leading journalists such as the brothers Joseph and Stewart Alsop were tasked with publishing anti-communist screeds and stories that painted US foreign policy in a favourable light. (Later, although not necessarily at the CIA's behest, Joseph issued shrill warnings about the catastrophic damage to American power if the US 'ducked' out of Vietnam, a position that came back to haunt him and eroded his professional standing.) False information was planted in foreign newspapers to try to win the 'hearts and minds' of people vulnerable to communist indoctrination. At the same time, journalists with CIA connections were required to remain silent about things the CIA did not want revealed.[94] The Alsops, for example, knew about Iran and Guatemala but did not print a word.

The obedience of the press can be explained on several levels. On one level, there were patriotic people who genuinely wanted to do their bit for their country. As World War Two evolved into an uneasy peace with the Soviet Union, the lion's share of mainstream reporters were deferential to America's clandestine soldiers, and accepted officially defined parameters of what was 'in the public interest'. Many journalists had served in the Pacific Theatre and in Europe, and therefore had ingrained in them mottos like 'Loose lips sinks ships'. According to his wife, *Washington Post* editor Alfred Friendly 'never told secrets', a rule he had learned while serving as an intelligence officer in the Army Air Forces during World War Two.[95] On another level, journalists knew that their loyalty would be rewarded with access to a steady stream of newsworthy material. Any reporter who dared to cross the national security establishment ran the risk of being cut off. When columnist Drew Pearson wrote a negative piece about Paul Nitze, the principal author of NSC-68, which shaped US foreign policy for many years by calling for containment to stop the Kremlin's drive for world hegemony, he was struck off the guest list for an exclusive gala dinner and dance at the 1925 F Street Club.[96]

Importantly, there was a remarkable homogeneity between the CIA's top brass and those who headed cultural institutions, including the press. In the early years of the Cold War, many publishers, editors and journalists of east coast newspapers had the same WASP background, had gone to the same Ivy League schools and attended the same cocktail parties and clubs as the leading lights in the CIA. Family networks, dating back to when DC was just cow pasture, meant that they all lived in close proximity, in mansions along Massachusetts Avenue or the city's landmark traffic circles. The distinction between 'insiders' and 'outsiders' was completely blurred. The Sulzbergers were social acquaintances of CIA Directors Dulles, John McCone and Helms. Joseph Alsop and CIA Deputy Director for Plans Richard Bissell had been best friends since childhood. Everyone was in ideological sync. They were all committed to the same heady Cold War mission of defeating the godless proletarian hordes from behind the Iron Curtain, which they regarded as the defining struggle of the age, analogous to Rome's struggle against Carthage or Greece against Persia. They all held the same unapologetic view of the US taking a leading role in world affairs, especially in areas where communism threatened to establish a beachhead. They all liked the idea of running the universe from their Georgetown dinner tables. 'It was a social thing, my dear fellow,' said Joseph Alsop, the quintessential WASP, in 1976: 'I never received a dollar. I never signed a secrecy agreement. I didn't have to … I've done things for them when I thought they were the right thing to do. I call it my duty as a citizen.'[97]

For most of its early history, the CIA did not have to worry about its employees divulging secrets. Lyman Kirkpatrick, who joined when it was created in 1947, and enjoyed a successful 23-year career (despite contracting polio in 1952 which left him paralysed from the waist down), has claimed that during its formative years the CIA could rely on staff to keep secrets 'from inception to eternity'.[98] True to their Skull and Bones pedigree, which prized discretion above all other qualities,

CIA men were loath to admit they worked for the Agency, much less disclose what they did or, heaven forbid, write books. The temptation to appear wise or important at a cocktail party was firmly resisted. When asked in a recent interview to explain why the first generation of CIA officers was so tight-lipped, Frederick Hitz, the first statutory Inspector General of the CIA, acknowledged that the Ivy League upbringing was important, but so too was the Cold War mission: 'Everybody knew what the mission was, and that secrecy was essential to that mission. In the 1947 to 1960 period, the Soviets were ahead of us. They were better placed in Eastern Europe. They had more reporting assets. We were fighting to get a foothold.'[99] Even OSS memoirs ground largely to a halt. A survey conducted by the CIA Library in July 1958 identified less than half a dozen OSS autobiographies published since 1947.[100] In short, almost every intelligence officer, serving or retired, was a deep believer in absolute secrecy.

Of the few OSS memoirs that were written, two deserve special mention. The first is *You're Stepping on My Cloak and Dagger* by Roger Hall, published by Norton in 1957. Achieving critical and popular acclaim, the book was noteworthy for its author's comedic approach to the subject, something that was (and remains) largely without progeny in the realm of spy memoir writing. Critic Charles Poore, writing for the *New York Times* in 1957, called it 'the funniest (unofficial, that is) record of rugged adventure in the OSS'.[101] Now regarded as something of a cult classic in intelligence circles, the book follows Hall as he completes quirky OSS training rituals before going on to reveal his exploits in the field, where he worked alongside a number of rising stars including Colby. (He would later be an usher at Colby's first wedding.) OSS is presented as the perfect fit for Hall, who found the buccaneering spirit of the service more agreeable to his maverick temperament than the regular army. Indeed, he joked that a formal military posting would have led to him being executed by firing squad. One of the best stories in the book involved an OSS officer being sent to Axis-occupied France to destroy a German tank, impervious to grenades, positioned at a key intersection. Using his wits, the officer approached the tank dressed like a French peasant and shouted, in his best German, 'You've got mail'. With this, the vehicle's hatch opened and in went two grenades.

It is easy to see why the book has attracted a cult following among the intelligence cognoscenti; scarcely a page goes by without Hall juxtaposing the craft and innovation of Donovan's enthusiastic amateurs with either lockstep military thinking or bureaucratic fumbling back home in Washington. With a wry wit, and in a manner redolent of Joseph Heller's *Catch-22*, it is suggested that Hall's biggest battles were with bumbling and pompous superiors in the military, not the Axis enemy. For example, there was the time when he parachuted into France to coordinate resistance operations, only to discover after the jump that lackadaisical military staff had not informed him that General George S. Patton had pushed the Germans back, meaning that he had landed in Allied territory! There was also the time when a cocksure colonel, holding a cigar in his hand, casually pointed to a map protected by celluloid. 'The map didn't burn,' recalled Hall, 'it simply vanished in a sheet of flame.'

Hall's account is also important for being one of the first US spy memoirs to poke fun at the British. Hall recognised the enormous value of working with British intelligence officers, but could not resist taunting their customs and eccentricities, whether the cut of their clothes ('Savile Row all the way'), their wobbly chins, or their unnecessarily cultured apologies ('Forgive my rudeness, old boy'). In the years to come, it would not be uncommon to see a US spy memoir gently mock British spies, who until recently belonged, by reasons of birth, connections and inherited wealth, to an extremely narrow section of elite society, alien, if not anathema, to most Americans. CIA alumnus Chester Cooper, who did a tour of duty in London in the 1950s, brilliantly evoked and satirised the club-like atmosphere of British intelligence in his 1978 memoir *The Lion's Last Roar*:

I found myself sitting between two giants wearing identical black suits (Savile Row), identical blue-striped ties (Eton) and identical spectacles (National Health). The man on my right passed a paper to the one on my left. It looked like something from Sanskrit Vedas (I later found out it was Greek Pentameter). A chap stuck his head round the door and bellowed, 'South Africa, fourteen for three!' All groaned. (I made a surreptitious note in the event this was code for some crisis in Commonwealth affairs.) 'Cricket test match y'know', someone shouted to me. All laughed. I smiled weakly.[102]

Wallace Deuel had similar things to say, albeit in private, about what he called 'British intelligence types'. He wrote ironically that members of MI6 were 'gilded youths who generally concealed a title (or at least a double-barrelled name) behind some silly little-boy nickname like Billy or Teddy or Pongo'. (Deuel was clearly a fan of English author P. G. Wodehouse and his character Reginald 'Pongo' Twistleton.) He commented drolly that he suspected the reason British spies wore monocles was so that they could tell languid tales of 'nearly swallowing the damned thing when the 'chute failed to open last time over Normandy'. Moreover, he wrote of his bemusement at the fact that the British never got badly wounded, but rather 'had a little trouble with one leg, old boy'.[103]

The other OSS memoir to warrant a few words is *The Scarlet Thread* (1953) by Donald Downes.[104] A schoolteacher in Cape Cod before the war, Downes had worked first for British intelligence and then OSS between 1940 and 1945, serving in every continent except Australasia. On one level, Downes remained true to the memoir formula established after 1945, showering praise on Donovan and showing how intrepid individuals had found innovative ways, in sticky situations, to win the war. He said of Donovan: 'I do not think there was another American in 1941 capable of creating a functioning secret intelligence organ overnight … He's a great guy and he did an extraordinary job … he loves the country more than any man I know'.[105] On another level, however, Downes was outspoken in his criticism of aspects of the intelligence business. As Wesley Wark has argued, the book took the US spy memoir in a direction never dreamed of by either Yardley or the post-war publicists by conveying the author's distaste for the unpleasant methods of espionage.[106] Downes, who recalled being a 'secret intelligence virgin' in 1940, perhaps unsuited to the job, looked back on his time with OSS as a 'career of paralegal crime' and expressed his unease at certain actions, such as burgling the Spanish embassy in Washington, DC.[107] The description of espionage as a 'crime' was a far cry from the virtuous associations conjured up by Donovan and his publicity machine. Downes also accused the US government of breaking promises and thus failing to live by its own high ethical standards.[108] Particularly upsetting to him was the decision, in many cases, not to honour the salaries and life-insurance policies that were promised to agents overseas who had risked their lives by working with the US against the Nazis. 'The Russians may bump off their ex-agents who know too much,' he remonstrated, 'but they aren't dumb enough to cheat them and then leave them in circulation to talk badly.'[109] By lifting the cloak to reveal the dagger, and questioning the morals of policymakers, *The Scarlet Thread* was ahead of its time, presaging, as we shall see, the dissident memoirs of the 1970s.

The one person at CIA who had the luxury of being able to stick his head above the parapet was Dulles. It is important to emphasise here that Dulles was still a staunch advocate of secrecy. Sherman Kent, who headed the CIA's Office of National Estimates from 1952 to 1967, wrote in an unpublished memoir that, 'There is no question about Allen being a close lipped and cautious man.'[110] Dulles felt, however, that it was important from time to time to give the myth a gentle helping hand by letting the public know in general terms about the dangers of communism and the role performed by the CIA in combating this threat. He also believed that only *he* should have the authority to do this. In a meeting of senior CIA colleagues on 29 July 1954, he declared:

'I know perfectly well this "shop" is run by the case officers, but by God I'm going to run the public relations.'[111] As he saw it, the job of public outreach had to be done by someone who could appear affable and affectionate; hard men returning from the field were out of the question, as were humourless bureaucrats. Following in Donovan's footsteps, he wanted the public to be comforted by the fact that, while the US was dirtying its hands in the espionage business, at least those involved were men of kindly, patrician manners. Dulles certainly fitted the bill. With his bristling closely cropped white brush moustache, baggy tweeds, briar pipe, and wholehearted 'ho-ho-ho' laugh, he evoked the spirit of a college professor.[112] Unlike his brother John – who is often held as being cold and distant, and who was afflicted with chronic bad breath, which made people around him feel uncomfortable – Allen's demeanour was convivial and avuncular.[113] 'He had a gay outlook on life,' recalled Kent, 'laughed a great deal, joked and kidded, and was a marvellously warm and attractive fellow human.'[114]

Dulles's approach to public relations was to be seen and occasionally heard. He was happy to be photographed and enjoyed the busy social scene of the nation's capital. 'My father was very, very extroverted,' noted his daughter Joan some years later. 'He would work hard and then he wanted to go to a party, or to give a party.'[115] When his schedule allowed, he would speak about the CIA's mission to war colleges, business councils and volunteer groups.[116] In 1954, for example, he lectured the Women's Forum on National Security on the need to be vigilant against Soviet propagandists.[117] As a public speaker, he was charming in his delivery and exuded a calm, philosophic air. He also endeared himself to audiences with his wit and sense of humour. Kent could only remember one occasion when Dulles fluffed his lines and told an off-colour story. 'That was a story which hinged on the word "fuck" – Allen simply couldn't bring himself to use that word, and spoiled the story by using the elegant "fornicate" in the places where it should have occurred.'[118] And who says CIA officers do not possess a sense of humour!

Dulles used the press to the CIA's advantage. Every so often, when he considered it necessary to remind the American public that there was an organisation working day and night to defeat the Red Menace, he would invite selected journalists to his home in Georgetown for a tennis match, lunch, dinner or cocktail party, during which he would give circumscribed briefings. 'The dinner with the correspondents was a magnificent success,' reported Deuel, the day after one particular banquet in January 1954. 'I don't think I've ever heard newspapermen speak so admiringly of anyone as they spoke of you. Nor has there been a single breach of security, so far as I can tell.'[119]

With Dulles calling the tune, the press publicised the CIA the way it wanted to be seen – an effective and benign body operating according to the law, and doing nothing controversial. There was no mention of covert action, and no stories, like there had been in OSS memoirs, of derring-do. The job of the CIA was to cogitate quietly on the Soviet threat, much in the same way that a university studies the world, and provide accurate and timely intelligence to policymakers. In this vein, on 8 August 1954, the Associated Press asserted that the 'very survival of the free world could one day depend on how well this man [Dulles] and his colleagues gauge Russia's intentions and capabilities – and calculate the reactions to diplomatic and military moves.'[120] Dulles was presented by journalists as a man of worldliness, refinement and intimidating intellect; in effect, someone Americans could trust. In a glowing 1953 profile, the *New York Times* wrote approvingly of his 'intellectual forehead surmounted by a tidy thatch of sparse grey hair.'[121] Press photographs, which typically showed Dulles sucking ruminatively on his pipe and leaning back in his chair, reinforced the image of the CIA as contemplative rather than action-oriented. On 3 August 1953, *Time* magazine even put him on its front cover. In the fawning portrayal that followed, it was claimed that Dulles, with 'the cheery manner of a New England prep-school teacher', was shouldering 'the most important mission in the long, heroic and colourful history of the intelligence services.'[122]

By the late 1950s, Dulles was not alone among US intelligence officers in wanting to promote the CIA. However, he steadfastly refused to allow anyone but himself to do it. One person who wanted to help was Mary Bancroft. A glamorous and dynamic woman of the world from Beacon Hill in Boston, Bancroft had been with the OSS in Switzerland, where she worked for Dulles as an analyst and translator. Her looks and high-society credentials soon caught the wandering eye of her boss, a pathological womaniser, and the two became romantically involved. (Dulles's affairs of the heart are legendary and are said to have included Countess Wally Toscanini Castelbarco; Ambassador Clare Boothe Luce, the wife of Henry Luce, the owner of *Time*; and Queen Frederica of Greece, whose charms he allegedly enjoyed in a dressing room adjacent to his office at CIA. He once demanded that he and Bancroft, herself married, make love hurriedly on a sofa 'to clear his head' before a meeting.)[123] After the war, the romance cooled but they remained on good terms. Surprisingly, Bancroft became close friends with Dulles's long-suffering wife, Clover, who knew all about her husband's extramarital dalliances and approved of him having a mistress.[124]

Bancroft's idea, which she pitched to Dulles in spring 1957, was a ten-part educational television series – called *Above the Call* – looking at American intelligence during and after World War Two. Bancroft admired the skill with which the FBI, Air Force and Department of Defense employed liaison officers to boost their public image in radio programmes, films and television shows, yet still maintain security. 'This shows that such things can be done,' she wrote.[125] To be made in conjunction with Figaro, an independent production company, the series would:

> show how the various intelligence services of the United States help our government in much the same way that personal intelligence helps the individual … and demonstrate the many Americans who have served their country most devotedly but have done so without any thought of recognition or hope of reward.[126]

Robert Lantz, Figaro's vice president, was happy for the series to be (in his own words) a 'propaganda arm of the CIA, entirely disguised as pure entertainment'.[127]

Dulles, together with CIA Inspector General Lyman Kirkpatrick and press spokesman Colonel Stanley Grogan, met with Bancroft on several occasions. In these meetings, Dulles's old flame explained that the series would do wonders for recruitment, as college graduates would be captivated by images of agents in exotic locations, and realise that 'it is not necessary to join the navy to see the world'.[128] Nonetheless, Dulles blocked the project, concerned that it would establish a precedent for officials to go off on freewheeling PR initiatives. Moreover, as he saw it, the situation did not demand the kind of all-out publicity Bancroft had in mind. The CIA's stock was at an all-time high. Through a mixture of impenetrable secrecy and sporadic spin, Dulles had made the CIA respectable and respected. However, as we shall now see, it would not be long before its stock started to tumble.

IV. Secrecy Interrupted

The past year has contained enough operational unpleasantness and 'wild blue yonder' thinking to last most of the Old Hands for a long time.
Richard Helms, Deputy Director for Plans, 15 November 1961.[129]

At 6.26 a.m. on 1 May 1960, Francis Gary Powers, in a full-body pressure suit and helmet, commenced 'Operation Grand Slam' – the longest and most daring mission yet attempted by the CIA's U-2 spy plane, with a flight plan of 3,800 miles stretching across the whole of the Soviet Union from Peshawar in Pakistan to Bodö in Norway. His mission was to reconnoitre the suspected construction of an ICBM base at Plesetsk near the Arctic Circle. Keeping tabs on Soviet missile development was a national security priority. A few days before the flight, the CIA had sent a report to the White House stating: 'The Soviets claim that the power balance vis-à-vis the United States is changing. We believe that if this is true the missile factor is the key.'[130]

The Top Secret U-2 reconnaissance aircraft was a marvel of modern technology. Capable of flying as high as 70,000 feet, it possessed a high-resolution camera that could photograph a strip of land 125 miles wide and 3,000 miles long. Reportedly, in order to demonstrate the capability of the aircraft to President Eisenhower, the CIA presented him with a U-2 photograph, taken at 55,000 feet, showing him playing golf at his favourite course in Augusta, Georgia. Amazingly, the golf-mad president was even able to pick out his ball on the putting green.[131] For four years, the U-2 had provided vital intelligence on the Soviet bomber force, missile programme, atomic energy programme, and submarine programme.[132] Yet, the risks were considerable – even for the experienced Powers, a veteran of some twenty-seven missions. Because of the rarefied atmosphere in which the plane had to travel, there was the risk of a flameout or other malfunction. From the first flight over the Soviet Union in 1956, Russian radar had tracked the planes and it was feared that they would soon develop a surface-to-air missile capable of reaching the U-2's altitude. Richard Bissell, who ran the programme, had also failed to consider that Soviet airspace would be virtually empty on 1 May, a public holiday, meaning that the plane would be relatively easy to trace.

Almost exactly four hours into the ambitious sortie, Powers was knocked back into his seat as a missile detonated close to and behind his aircraft.[133] 'Suddenly, there was a dull "thump",' he later recalled, 'the aircraft jerked forward, and a tremendous orange flash lit the cockpit and sky.'[134] The Soviets had been tracking him the moment he had crossed the border. Determined to stop the aircraft, they had fired fourteen newly designed S-75 missiles, even accidentally destroying one of their own MiG-19s, which had been in hot pursuit.[135] Powers frantically tried to regain control but couldn't. The blast wave had dismembered the aircraft, first tearing off its tail section and then its wings. With the plane in a flat spin, spiralling down towards the ground, he released the canopy and prepared to bail out. Before he could arm the self-destruct mechanism, the centrifugal force threw him out of the aircraft, leaving him dangling by his oxygen hose. He tried to clamber back in to activate the destruct switch, but the g-forces were too great and he was forced to sever the hose. With this, his parachute opened automatically and he drifted down to earth, miraculously unhurt, where he was greeted by two Russian farmers.[136]

When Powers failed to return home, Bissell had a cover story on hand, prepared years before, declaring that NASA had lost a test plane engaged in meteorological research.[137] Both the State Department and White House put out press releases to this effect.[138] To support the charade, a U-2 was painted with NASA livery, with a fictitious serial number, and displayed to the press at the NASA Flight Research Center. The CIA assured Eisenhower that it was highly unlikely that the pilot, the plane or its precious cargo would have survived the crash. Moreover, if by some miracle Powers had come through unscathed, he knew the dangers of being captured alive and carried cyanide pills.

The Soviet premier Nikita Khrushchev shrewdly waited a few days to allow the Americans to keep peddling their bogus story. On 7 May, the cover story blew up in Washington's face when Khrushchev, clearly enjoying himself, rose to the podium in the Supreme Soviet and revealed that he possessed the wreckage of the plane and had rolls and rolls of high-altitude surveillance film. 'The whole world knows that Allen Dulles is no great weatherman,' he boasted.[139] As for the pilot: Khrushchev had him too, an American, 'quite alive and kicking'. Having survived the ordeal unscathed, Powers was in custody in Lubyanka Prison, headquarters of the KGB, a prized possession in the superpower game. Wrongly led to believe that he had plausible deniability, Eisenhower had fallen into Khrushchev's political trap and been caught lying to the American public.

Historians have long recognised the disastrous diplomatic consequences of the U-2 affair for the US. The incident was a propaganda
coup for the Soviet Union of which Khrushchev took full advantage.
Parts of the downed plane, including the charred engine, were put
on display in Gorki Square in Moscow, drawing large crowds of curious Muscovites. After sixty-one consecutive days of interrogation by
the KGB, Powers was charged with espionage offences and was subjected to a televised show trial. He was convicted and sentenced to
three years' imprisonment, followed by seven years of hard labour.
(He was eventually freed on 19 February 1962 in a well-publicised spy
swap across the Berlin Wall with captured KGB officer Rudolf Abel.)
The affair doomed the already precarious, but much hoped-for, four-
nation Paris peace summit designed to usher in a period of 'peaceful
coexistence' between the two superpowers. Beginning on 16 May, the
summit never went beyond preliminary meetings. On the first day,
the belligerent Khrushchev wasted no time in tearing into the US,
condemning its 'inadmissible, provocative actions' and threatening to
'take the American aggressors by the scruff of the neck and give them
a little shaking'.[140] In a devastating public dressing-down of the US, he
insisted that Eisenhower apologise and promise never to violate Soviet
airspace again. When Eisenhower refused, he went home in a huff. On
the second day, the summit was abandoned and key issues such as disarmament, a potential Test Ban Treaty and the problem of Berlin were
left unresolved.[141]

As much as the U-2 incident was a seminal moment for Cold War
relations, it was also a watershed for the CIA. As we have seen, since
its creation the CIA had enjoyed not only a 'golden', but 'gilded' age.[142]
Congress gave the money and asked for no explanation in return; journalists regarded it as their patriotic duty either to stay silent or lend a
hand; and Dulles provided a further layer of protection from public
scrutiny with carefully managed PR. The U-2 shoot-down brought
this halcyon era crashing to a close. Congress suddenly awoke from its

slumber. On 10 May, with Eisenhower yet to comment on Khrushchev's speech, the previously carefree House Appropriations Chair Clarence Cannon took the remarkable step of revealing the true nature of the mission. In an open session of the House of Representatives, he announced that the 'plane was on an espionage mission' and had been 'operated ... under the direction and control of the US Central Intelligence Agency'.[143] No one tried to stop him; there were no howls of disapproval as he revealed to the American people and the world the hidden hand of the CIA. At the end of his speech, Democrats and Republicans even rose to their feet to applaud. The Agency's role in the affair was widely reported in the press, with particularly critical coverage coming from Drew Pearson and Jack Anderson.[144] One of the few journalists who refused to condemn the CIA was, unsurprisingly, Joseph Alsop. In a column entitled 'Wonderful News', Alsop tried to put a positive spin on things by arguing that at least the US was concerned about Soviet ICBM development. However, there was no escaping the new reality that the CIA was now in the public spotlight.

That new reality was underscored by the Bay of Pigs debacle. The episode ranks among the greatest PR disasters in CIA history, an epic blunder for which the myth of the Agency suffered a fatal blow, and which would inspire a culture of conspiracy about the CIA, linking it to every plot and coup, that exists to this day. Truly, nothing would ever be the same again.

In April 1961, some 1,400 Cuban exiles trained and equipped by the CIA landed on the south-eastern shore of Cuba in what was planned as a surprise attack. The purpose was to establish a beachhead and then to move into the interior, in anticipation of inciting a spontaneous popular uprising against communist leader Fidel Castro, a perennial thorn in the US's side. Within seventy-two hours, however, the mission was defeated. Without adequate air support, the invasion force was easily picked off by the Cuban air force. The majority of the brigade were captured and imprisoned; more than 100 were killed. The botched landing became headline news around the world; President Kennedy was humiliated. CIA involvement was impossible to hide. Indeed, it had been apparent even before the invasion had begun.[145] In January 1961, the *New York Times* had revealed that the US had been training anti-Castro forces in guerrilla warfare at 'secret' camps in Guatemala; the article even came with a map pinpointing the facility. The likelihood of a US-sponsored amphibious or airborne assault against Castro had been the talk of the Cuban exile community in Miami for months. By April, the *Washington Post*, *Miami Herald*, *Wall Street Journal*, *Time*, and *St Louis Post-Dispatch* were running pieces on the coming invasion. The essence of covert action is that it must be secret and, above all, hide the presidential hand that sponsors it: on both counts the CIA had failed.

A post-mortem followed in which the CIA was heavily scrutinised and its reputation plummeted. 'Last week the CIA was back in the news in a big way – and will probably stay there for some time,' declared *Time* magazine.[146] Although Kennedy publicly assumed sole responsibility for the failure, criticism of the CIA was staggering, fuelled in part by leaks from the White House designed to make the Agency the scapegoat in the court of public opinion. Dulles would later criticise White House aides Theodore Sorensen and Arthur M. Schlesinger for abusing their position to write books filled with incriminating classified information intended to exonerate Kennedy and shift the blame onto the CIA.[147] The complaints against the CIA were manifold. The Agency was upbraided for not calling off the invasion when it was clear that operational security had been compromised. Bissell, the architect of the project, was said to have kept important details from the President such as the fact that, days before the small army had blundered ashore, two of the operation's key planners had predicted a 'terrible disaster' owing to not only the absence of secrecy, but also the landing beach being too secluded, with no local population to support the invaders.[148] It was also claimed that the CIA, buoyed by its successes in the 1950s, had grown arrogant and overestimated the chances of a successful landing and insurrection. More generally, in the eyes of many writers, the Agency was now a symbol of US neo-imperialism.[149] The Bay of Pigs was the first time that it had been unmasked as an organisation that meddled in the domestic affairs of foreign states. The 'spin' of the Dulles years had made no mention of the covert-action side of the business.

Like the proverbial pebble cast into the water, the dual crisis of the U-2 and the Bay of Pigs would have a rippling effect. Both blunders were the catalyst for people to start writing full-length populist histories of the CIA. In the 1950s, as historian Richard J. Aldrich has shown, an embryonic historiography of CIA misdemeanours had emerged in the Global South. Most works were funded by Moscow and its satellites as propaganda pieces, designed to make life difficult for American diplomats seeking to make friends in developing countries.[150] But the events of the early 1960s brought historical writing about the subject to US soil for the first time.

Out of the traps quickest was syndicated columnist Andrew Tully with the *New York Times* bestseller *CIA: The Inside Story* (1962).[151] The book was lauded by the press as a remarkable piece of investigative journalism. A survey of the Agency's first fifteen years, it contained startling insights into episodes of CIA activity hitherto hidden from public view, including the CIA's role in the revolt that ousted the pro-communist Arbenz regime in Guatemala in 1954. William Stringer of the *Christian Science Monitor* was hugely impressed: 'How Washington newsman Andrew Tully managed to penetrate as far as he did … one doesn't know.'[152] Unbeknown to people at the time, Tully had in fact drawn heavily on the Moscow-inspired political tracts that had been published in the Third World.[153] The CIA refused to comment, save a passing remark by Dulles on the weekly television show *Meet the Press* that it represented an 'upside-down' story.[154] Behind closed doors, however, it was furious. Sherman Kent, chairman and founder of the CIA's in-house journal *Studies in Intelligence*, wrote a damning review consisting of no fewer than forty-nine pages. 'It is a bad book, a shoddy piece of goods,' he declared.[155] 'From the purely technical point of view', he went on, 'it is by all odds the worst bad book that this reviewer has ever encountered.'[156] Kent recognised immediately that the material for the book had come from propagandistic texts penned by Soviet writers or communist fellow travellers, claiming that 'Tully repeats communist canards which have no relation whatsoever to the truth.'[157] Kent accused Tully of larding the text with references to his apparent 'sources' in Washington in a disingenuous attempt to convince the reader that the revelations had stemmed from knowledgeable 'insiders'. Tully's central thesis that the CIA was an insulated pocket of power and irresponsibility, hiding behind a screen of secrecy, naturally stuck in Kent's craw. But by far Kent's biggest grievance was that the author had had the nerve to write the book in the first place. In his eyes, it was not just harmful to national security for people to probe the CIA; it was unpatriotic.

Two years later, Kent would again find himself penning a lengthy, negative review of a bestselling spy book. Written by two hard-nosed reporters, David Wise of the *New York Herald Tribune* and Thomas Ross of the *Chicago Sun Times*, *The Invisible Government* (1964) was a fully-fledged attack on the myth of the CIA and sent shockwaves through Washington. Its core contention was that the US intelligence community, with the CIA at its core, had grown so vast and powerful that it threatened the very democratic principles it was designed to defend.[158] Cloaked in a veil of secrecy, the CIA was presented as a free-wheeling organisation, subject to grossly inadequate control by either the White House or Congress. As well as adding further flesh to the bones of the U-2 and Cuba fiascos, Wise and Ross gave details of how the Agency had operated outside of the remit of proclaimed US policy in places like Vietnam, Laos and Burma.

CIA officer John Bross acquired the galley proofs through a friend of a family member who worked for Random House.[159] He and his superiors were horrified. Wise and Ross had insisted that the book contained only the names of officers 'considered to be already in the public domain', but this did not square with an internal study that identified eight individuals being named for the first time, three of whom were serving in particularly sensitive posts in the clandestine services.[160] More broadly, the CIA feared that the book would undermine its integrity around the world, especially in underdeveloped areas of Africa and Asia. A further concern was that the book would hand Soviet propagandists valuable ammunition to attack the CIA and the overall thrust of US foreign policy. Wise and Ross's discussion of 'gringo' interventions in Latin America might be used to prejudice Latin attitudes towards the US by making a mockery of American pretensions to world moral primacy and its rhetoric about self-determination of peoples and rule of law. 'Had the authors chosen to offer their manuscript to the Soviet embassy', remarked Kent, 'they might have fared better financially. The latter are getting a real bargain at $5.95 a copy.'[161]

Once again, however, what most angered the CIA was that someone had dared to investigate it. 'That it should have been written is a mark of their and their informants' stunning immaturity', protested Kent, 'that it should be printed and sold, a mark of grave irresponsibility on the part of an established publisher.'[162] So disturbed were they, CIA Director John McCone and his deputy, Lieutenant General Marshall Carter, both personally telephoned Wise and Ross's publisher, Random House, to ask for changes to the text.[163] Rebuffed, the Agency then threatened to buy up the entire first print run of 20,000 copies, a course of action described by Random House's president, Bennett Cerf, as 'laughable'.[164] According to Wise, 'Cerf responded that he would be delighted to sell the first printing to the CIA, but then immediately added that he would then order another printing for the public, and another, and another.'[165] With this, the CIA resorted to commissioning a handful of unfavourable reviews, including a particularly savage hatchet job from William F. Buckley, who claimed that the authors had done a 'disservice to their country' and 'verged close to unpatriotic'.[166]

The combination of 'operational unpleasantness', to quote Helms, and the flurry of critical histories saw morale at the CIA plummet. John McCone, who replaced Dulles as DCI after the Bay of Pigs, recollected that during this period: 'Men were in despair and on the verge of seeking other careers and the interest of young men to join the organisation was nil.'[167] The indomitable optimism and self-confidence that energised the 'golden' age was gone. It was bad enough that people were criticising the CIA's operational record; but even more troubling was that larger philosophical and ethical questions were now being asked about the constitutional dangers posed by the CIA. It was now obvious that the CIA was far more than a normal intelligence-gathering organisation; the cat of covert action was out of the bag. With this, a debate broke out about whether 'special operations' have a place in the policies of a democratic nation. There was an understandable anxiety about whether this 'action-agency' was sufficiently accountable and whether elected officials were kept suitably informed of its programmes to make sensible decisions. Moreover, many people were left wondering whether the catalogue of recent failures really warranted the moral ambiguities of the work. The media was on the cusp of entering a new activist phase in its history and many journalists wrote stories castigating the Agency's overseas intrusions, which they argued were born of misguided zeal and overheated enthusiasm. Alarmingly, as one journalist from Freeport, Illinois, put it, 'Since the invasion-fiasco, people are just about ready to believe anything they're told about the CIA.'[168] How the mighty had fallen.

Despite the bad press, CIA policy under McCone was to be as secretive as possible and refuse to comment on any charges levelled against the organisation. One person who disagreed with this approach was the recently retired Dulles. As he saw it, the only way to boost morale and, by extension, efficiency at the CIA was to remind the public, as he and Donovan had done in the past, of the vital role that spies play in the defence of US national security. 'It is impossible to erect a wall around the whole business of intelligence', he went on record as saying, '[and] nor do I suggest that this be done.'[169]

Whereas McCone believed that the Agency should not 'lower itself' to responding to sensational headlines, seeing this as indecent, Dulles felt that too much secrecy was self-defeating because – like it or not – people were influenced by what they read in the newspapers and in books. 'It is hardly reasonable to expect proper understanding and support for intelligence work in this country if it is only the insiders … who know anything whatsoever about the CIA,' he wrote.[170] He went on: 'Certain information must be given out if public confidence in the intelligence mission is to be strengthened and if the profession of the intelligence officer is to be properly understood.'[171]

Dulles had an added incentive to open up. The recent troubles had been personally traumatic, and sent his stock tumbling. Robert Kennedy recollected that, after the Bay of Pigs, Dulles 'looked like living death … had the gout and had trouble walking, and was always putting his head in his hands'.[172] CIA alumnus Ray Cline has described Dulles as being 'wiped out'.[173] After the humiliation of being fired by Kennedy, he endured further ignominy as authors and journalists took it in turns to portray him as ruthless and deceitful, never stopping to consider the righteousness or human cost of his actions. As David Wise has argued, he came to symbolise the 'split American psyche' of the era, which projected the highest moral principles of freedom and liberty but at the same time sanctioned covert interventions to advance US interests.[174] For Dulles, therefore, opening up was vital to restoring his reputation.

Right up until his death in January 1969, Dulles was rarely out of the news, writing articles and book reviews, giving talks and appearing on television at a rate that rivalled the most prolific of commentators.[175] (His private papers at Princeton University include twenty-one boxes of writings and a further twelve boxes of speech material.) In Jonathan Nashel's words, he became an 'American Cold War celebrity'.[176] With the press now awash with as many critics as supporters of the CIA, he went looking for new sources amenable to putting a positive spin on the CIA's work, this time from the field of popular culture. One person to whom he turned was Ian Fleming, creator of the hugely popular super-spy, James Bond.[177] To the anguish of more serious spy fiction writers such as John le Carré and Graham Greene, Dulles rhapsodised about 007 in the press and at after-dinner speeches, doing wonders for Fleming's book sales. For example, at the annual conference of the American Booksellers Association in 1963, he declared that the CIA could do with half a dozen or so James Bonds, an announcement that led Fleming to refer to Dulles in the British press as 'Agent 008'.[178] 'The organisation and staff have always cooperated so willingly with James Bond,' Fleming cooed in a private note in July 1961.[179] In exchange for the free publicity, he acquiesced to including positive references to the CIA in his novels, especially those published after the Bay of Pigs when the Agency most needed them. Dulles himself is even the object of several honourable mentions, including a line in *You Only Live Twice* (1964) where he is referred to affectionately as the 'old fox'.[180]

Dulles's experiment with spy fiction did not end here. Envious of British success with the genre, he persuaded CIA propaganda specialist E. Howard Hunt, a gifted novelist in his youth, to funnel his literary talent into creating the Agency's answer to 007. Using the very British pseudonym David St John (also the name of his son), Hunt produced eight spy novels between 1965 and 1969, all written on company time, glorifying the CIA. Sadly for Dulles, readers did not warm to the fictional protagonist, Peter Ward, like they did Bond. Moreover, it was not long before Hunt was making headlines for the wrong reasons, not as a writer of hardboiled thrillers, but as one of the organisers of the Watergate break-in.

Dulles's determination to change attitudes towards the CIA led him to produce what is still held among the intelligence cognoscenti as perhaps the definitive textbook on his chosen trade – *The Craft of Intelligence*. Without McCone's knowledge or approval, it was in fact largely ghost-written by Howard Hunt and another CIA veteran Howard Roman.[181] Published in late 1963, the book was a primer on the art and profession of intelligence. While not a memoir, it was abundantly illustrated with cases and anecdotes drawn from the author's own experience. After a brief glimpse at espionage through the ages and its early history in the US, the bulk of the book dealt with the discipline and techniques of intelligence – its tradecraft – as practised by the US, its allies and the Soviet Union. Unsurprisingly, it did not lay bare any secrets or contain startling revelations; it was more cloak than dagger. 'Any Soviet agents who have been lurking around bookstores waiting for the appearance of this work … have been wasting their time; bad luck, comrades,' declared the *New York Herald*.[182] Scarcely a word was spoken about the controversial subject of covert action, with Dulles at pains to emphasise that the CIA was overwhelmingly about analysis, not action. 'In terms of space', lamented the *Washington Post*, 'this important topic hardly receives a balanced share of the book.'[183] As far as the ill-fated Bay of Pigs adventure was concerned, he rejected the popular belief that he and his colleagues had given the White House poor advice, but refused to be drawn on the sensitive issue of whether he felt Kennedy had lost his nerve, and doomed the would-be liberators by calling off promised air support. Despite all the vitriol that had been thrown at him, Dulles never wavered from his belief that the relationship between DCI and President should remain a 'very private one'.[184]

The Craft of Intelligence, which became a bestseller and was crowned the Encyclopaedia Britannica Book of the Year, won many admirers in the Western intelligence community. Lyman Kirkpatrick, then executive director at the CIA, called it a 'magnificent job'.[185] Dulles's idea of dispelling misunderstandings about intelligence and answering, if only by inference, the attacks upon the CIA was warmly welcomed by a number of senior intelligence professionals. Kirkpatrick claimed that the book would 'help us a great deal in portraying the image of the profession', and 'be of inestimable help in recruiting young professionals'.[186] Roger Hollis, Director-General of Britain's publicity-shy MI5, commended Dulles for 'helping to train the new generation … in our difficult business'.[187] Dick White, the Chief of Britain's even more secretive MI6, was hugely impressed and told Dulles that the book was now 'required reading' for his subordinates. Moreover, White hoped that one day he too would be able to embark on a similar public discussion about the role of intelligence in a free society, from the British standpoint.[188]

The warm reception for the book from respected intelligence professionals nevertheless did nothing to change McCone's mind about how the CIA should interact with the public. Throughout the 1960s, openness remained anathema not only to McCone but also his successors, William Raborn and Richard Helms, who took the view that it would lead the CIA to ruin. In spring 1965, Raborn wrote that he was committed to 'keeping the CIA profile as low as possible, and our public relations posture fundamentally defensive'.[189] He also rejected a proposal to turn *The Craft of Intelligence* into a feature film, much to Dulles's annoyance.[190]

The reluctance of the Agency's top brass to entertain even a scintilla of self-promotion is puzzling when we consider that negative publicity about the CIA had failed to subside. In September 1965, Raborn wrote to Clark Clifford, Chairman of the President's Foreign Intelligence Advisory Board, to express his concern about the damaging impact of growing Soviet disinformation efforts not only overseas (where it had the potential to disrupt the CIA's liaison relationships with other Western agencies), but in the US – against the American people.[191] One recent example of KGB-manufactured lies was Joachim Joesten's *Oswald: Assassin or Fall Guy* (1964), the first book to appear in the

US to claim that Kennedy's death was the result of a deep right-wing conspiracy involving the FBI, Dallas Police and the CIA. A naturalised US citizen, living in New York, Joesten was according to later released documents a paid Soviet agent; his publisher was a KGB front.[192]

The CIA's decision to stay quiet as its dirty laundry flooded the marketplace partly stemmed from the traditional fear that as soon as it started commenting on one thing, it would have to comment on everything, or people would interpret silences as evidence of guilt. Moreover, CIA officials probably thought that the worst PR disasters were behind them. That, however, was not the case.

Chapter 3

Renegades and
Whistle-blowers

I. Time of Troubles

As the sign on Jimmy Hoffa's desk said, ILLEGITIMI
NON CARBORUNDUM. Or, freely translated,
'Don't let the bastards wear you down.'
Mr Jeff Rosenzweig to DCI William Colby.[1]

The 1970s rank as the most turbulent decade in the CIA's history. It is often referred to as the 'Time of Troubles' or 'Decade of Horrors'. During this time, startling revelations emerged suggesting that the Agency had violated its charter responsibilities, including, most controversially of all, claims of domestic espionage operations. The level of scrutiny from a decreasingly deferential media and an increasingly inquisitorial Congress was totally alien to an organisation that historically had been accustomed to limited accountability and oversight. Public confidence in the CIA was shattered. In 1973, the public opinion pollster Gallup published a survey in which only 23 per cent of Americans gave the CIA a positive rating. In 1975, the figure dropped to 14 per cent. Among college students, the CIA was favoured by a damning 7 per cent.[2] The transformation in the CIA's fortunes is perfectly captured in two strikingly different front covers from *Time* magazine, one published on 3 August 1953, the other on 30 September 1974. The first has DCI Allen Dulles, looking cheerful and avuncular, grey hair parted in the middle, puffing away at a crusty old pipe that was as much his trademark as his professorial bow tie. By contrast, the 1974 cover featured DCI William Colby staring menacingly through blackened spectacles, which contained the ominous words: 'The CIA – Has It Gone Too Far?'

A portent of troubles came in April 1966, when the gleefully incendiary radical magazine *Ramparts*, with a peak circulation of 250,000, making it by far the bestselling leftist publication of its era, exposed how the CIA had infiltrated a Michigan State University (MSU) Vietnam Advisory Group as a front for covert operations.[3] Academics across the country protested at what they perceived as an assault on scholarly freedoms. 'It is not right for a university to provide cover for intelligence work or to have people on its staff involved in undercover work,' remonstrated Professor Ralph Smuckler, dean of international programmes at MSU.[4] Anxious to prevent further disclosures about front organisations, DCI William Raborn ordered his director of security, Howard Osborn, as a matter of 'high priority', to provide him with a 'rundown' on the San Francisco-based magazine.[5] Two months later, he asked Osborn to persuade the FBI to investigate its members as a 'subversive unit' and to search for material of a 'derogatory nature'. As the award-winning journalist Angus Mackenzie has written, 'To "rundown" a news publication because it had exposed questionable practices, the CIA was clearly in violation of the 1947 National Security Act's prohibition on domestic operations.'[6]

Attempts to find dirt on *Ramparts* were unsuccessful. Its staff consisted of moderate hippies and liberal Catholics, no more subversive than any other freedom-loving American who lived in the San Francisco Bay area at that time. Yet Agency fears about what *Ramparts* might unearth next were realised in February 1967 when the underground magazine revealed the CIA's illegal secret financing of the National Student

Association as a front group in the battle to win Cold War 'hearts and minds'. Filtered through various foundations, CIA annual subsidies of approximately $20,000 had paid for delegations to attend international student conferences, where they were required to promote the Western viewpoint and influence decision-making. CIA meddling in the nation's largest and oldest student body sparked outrage. The *New York Times* denounced 'the corruption of youthful idealism'.[7] In a speech at Stanford University, Vice President Hubert Humphrey said that CIA funding of the Association represented 'one of the saddest times our government has had in terms of public policy'.[8] In response, the CIA tried to destabilise the magazine. Edgar Applewhite, assigned by the Directorate of Plans to coordinate the effort, later told author Evan Thomas that he 'had all sorts of dirty tricks to hurt their circulation and financing. The people running *Ramparts* were vulnerable to blackmail. We had awful things in mind, some of which we carried off'.[9]

Ultimately, *Ramparts* died of its own accord, folding in 1975 owing to mounting debts. It nevertheless left an important legacy. Its gutsy revelations ushered in a new era of journalism, one that re-established the faded institution of muckraking, and put showmanship back into reporting. In the weeks following the story about student financing and secret dollars, the mainstream media picked up the scent and discovered a trail of hot CIA money running through a host of independent, private organisations. Stories revealed Agency links with think tanks, labour unions, universities, student and women's groups. The gritty, relentless reporter Mike Wallace, best known for his hard-hitting interviews on *60 Minutes*, moderated an hour-long CBS documentary entitled 'In the Pay of the CIA' in which he interviewed apologetic liberals, including the feminist heroine Gloria Steinem, who had been involved in CIA-backed organisations. The storm of protest was deafening. Critics on Capitol Hill lambasted the CIA for suborning innocent US citizens. Newspaper headlines focused on the threat to civil liberties of the CIA operating at home. Behind the scenes, the

CIA was left to lament that its entire system of anti-communist fronts in Europe, Asia and Latin America had been compromised.

There was to be no respite for the Agency. In May 1973, it came under heavy fire when it emerged that several of the so-called 'Plumbers' who had broken into the headquarters of the Democratic National Committee at the Watergate hotel, to wiretap phones and steal documents, had traceable ties to the CIA. Embarrassing stories about the doomed burglars thrust the CIA into the spotlight like never before. E. Howard Hunt, the acerbic and tweedy former high-ranking CIA officer who had masterminded the break-in, was the object of particular fascination for press sleuths like young *Washington Post* reporters Bob Woodward and Carl Bernstein. Writing to a friend on 16 August 1972, DCI Richard Helms remarked:

> I feel like a GI creeping through a mine field. There is no predicting what is going to blow apart next. Not the least of my problems has been to distance the Agency from those scallywags who indulged in the Watergate caper. I wish their previous employer had been the Salvation Army.[10]

The CIA was soon submerged under a tide of scandal. In 1975, it was the main subject in no fewer than 227 newspaper editorials with an aggregate circulation of 28 million, compared with none in 1970.[11] Speaking at the Associated Press annual meeting in April of that year, CIA Director Colby suggested that the CIA had earned the 'status as the nation's number one sensational lead'.[12] With Vietnam and Watergate engendering a healthy distrust of official statements, watchdog journalists like Seymour Hersh and Daniel Schorr sought to perform a quasi-constitutional function by peering under the curtain of the intelligence community, although the line between reasonable investigative reporting and partisan witch-hunting and sensationalism was often a fine one. Hersh was already a household name by the time he started to publish headline-grabbing stories about the CIA. He had won a Pulitzer Prize as a young freelance journalist for his exposure of the My Lai massacre in 1969, in which an American platoon had stormed a village in South Vietnam and killed as many as 500 unarmed civilians in cold blood. Recruited by the *New York Times* to chase the tail of Watergate, a story broken by its fiercest rival, the *Washington Post*, he cemented his reputation as an extraordinary investigative journalist with his reporting of the CIA. In September 1974, the high-flying journalist disclosed that the Agency had been involved in destabilisation efforts in Chile in the run-up to the overthrow of democratically elected President Salvador Allende in 1973, which led to the brutal military dictatorship of General Pinochet. Later that year, he published a stunning front-page article exposing parts of the CIA's 'Family Jewels' – a Top Secret record of illegal activity. This included the shocking detail that the CIA had spied on opponents of the Vietnam War in a special operation designated as 'CHAOS'. The *New York Times* called the scoop the 'son of Watergate'. Not to be outdone, the combative broadcast reporter Schorr, who had the dubious honour of being on President Nixon's 'Enemies List', alleged that the CIA might have 'literal' skeletons in its closet by revealing that the CIA had run assassination plots abroad, including hare-brained attempts against Cuban leader Fidel Castro – poisoned pens and handkerchiefs, contaminated frogman suits and exploding cigars and sea shells. 'What had been an anti-CIA frenzy became hysteria,' wrote future CIA Director Robert Gates (1991–93) some years later.[13]

Suggestions that the CIA had spied on US citizens, the inference being that it had become a Gestapo, compelled legislators to act. Already in the midst of an activist phase in its history, triggered by a confluence of events like Watergate and Vietnam, in 1975 Congress launched sweeping investigations into the CIA. The most famous of these was headed by Senator Frank Church of Idaho, who, with aspirations of securing the Democratic presidential nomination in 1976, hoped to ride the wave of anti-CIA feeling to national prominence.

His investigation lasted fifteen months, held 126 formal hearings, and carried out more than 800 interviews. Dozens of officers were dragged from Langley to testify under the glare of television lights, almost for public sport.[14] After the season of inquiry was over, a host of dirty tricks had been revealed, from drug experimentation on unwitting human guinea pigs, assassination attempts and poison caches, to the infiltration and disruption of dissident groups – whose 'crimes' had been to campaign for civil rights and oppose the war in Vietnam.

In a bid to stop such abuses from happening again, both the House of Representatives and the Senate established permanent select committees, in March 1976 and July 1977 respectively, to watch the CIA's budget and programmes. John Greene, biographer of President Ford, described this as an example of a 'Power Earthquake'.[15] Relations between the Legislative Branch and the CIA would no longer be *ad hoc* and relaxed. Oversight replaced overlook. Moreover, Congress was given the power to challenge the President's authority to launch covert action without legislative approval. President Nixon would later call the congressional handcuffing of the CIA a 'national tragedy'.[16]

Blazing newspaper headlines and high-profile investigations shattered Agency morale. David Atlee Phillips, a former Division Chief, said that the controversy 'changed my life'.[17] Stansfield Turner, who headed the Agency during the Carter administration, recalled that the oversight revolution had made staff 'nervous'.[18] Looking back at the events of 1975 – 'the worst year in CIA's history' – Gates claimed in his memoir that the CIA's pride 'took a blow from which [it] never recovered'. 'We would all go home at night', he remembered,

and face spouses and children who had watched news of poison dart guns and assassination attempts … and question whether that was a place they wanted a spouse or father to work. Some colleagues became estranged from their college-age children, who couldn't understand how a parent could work in a place like CIA.[19]

It is the chief contention of this chapter, however, that while the CIA was undoubtedly wounded by revelations that came out of the press and on Capitol Hill, the greatest trauma and pain came from another source. In the 1970s, for the first time in its history, the CIA was forced to deal with renegades and whistle-blowers.

II. Breaking the Brotherhood of Spies

We expect that the unusual legal complications around the book – The CIA and the Cult of Intelligence – *will make for very large sales indeed.*
Eleanor French (Alfred Knopf), 19 April 1974.[20]

As we have seen, the CIA had never really had to worry about employees wanting to tell tales out of school. In the 1960s, a handful of intelligence officers had gone into print, but only to say good things about the Agency and defend the organisation in the wake of scandals like the Bay of Pigs. In the 1970s, everything changed. Memoirs exploded. Moreover, the majority of them were written by apostates, keen to expose perceived abuses and blunders. Some of these people might be regarded as 'true' whistle-blowers, in the sense that they revealed illegal, immoral or illegitimate practices, but others might be more accurately described as renegades since they exhibited a distinct lack of measured responsibility over what they released into the public domain. Ultimately, it depends on who is asked. One person's whistle-blower is another person's traitor.

Dissident veterans, whether motivated by dollars or dogma, hurt the CIA like a knife to the heart. When a person joins the CIA, he chooses more than just a career, and enters into what French sociologist Pierre Bourdieu calls a 'habitus' with socialised norms that guide behaviour and thinking. At the heart of the CIA's habitus is a code: never celebrate our successes; never explain our failures. Every officer is expected to

abide by this code. They are made aware of it from the moment they
walk through the doors at CIA headquarters, when they are escorted
into a room and required to sign a secrecy agreement. Signed irrespective of whether the officer is based in the antiseptic offices at Langley,
the boondocks of Eastern Europe or the bazaars of the Middle East, the
agreement is a symbol that the officer is giving his word that he will
not reveal the secrets of the 'Company', in perpetuity. As a reporter for
the *Washington Post* put it in June 1972, the officer 'enters a Trappist
monastery for the remainder of his natural life'.[21] When a person breaks
this agreement, therefore, he is rejecting not just a job, but an entire
belief system. While this might appear strange or baffling to outsiders, inside the hallowed walls of Langley it is the worst crime a person
can commit.

Accordingly, disclosures by apostates hurt the CIA on a deeper,
emotional level than the revelations of journalists and congressmen.
In a speech delivered to the Association of Former Intelligence Officers
(AFIO) annual convention in October 1978, former CIA Director John
McCone perfectly encapsulated the anguish:

> The most serious [development] is the creation of a climate that has
> given licence to the Victor Marchettis and the Philip Agees to set
> aside their vows to their country, and to preserve secrecy, to unveil
> – in books written for modest profit – information more damaging
> than that of most serious defectors.[22]

'No violation of trust,' he continued,

> no defection to the other side, no damage from the acts of the [Kim]
> Philbys, the [Donald] Macleans or the Klaus Fuchses has been more
> damaging to our national interest and our security than the work
> of these men who prostitute their principles and make disclosures
> which places their close associates of many years in mortal danger.[23]

For Herbert Hetu, who headed the CIA's Public Affairs Office under Director Stansfield Turner, officers who vented their spleens in public had no honour. 'It's a matter of honor,' he declared in a 1978 interview. 'There's some sort of personal moral obligations – you either have personal integrity or you don't.'[24] Atlee Phillips has argued that nothing 'gnaws more voraciously at the fabric of the CIA' – its habitus – than renegades and whistle-blowers.[25]

This chapter will explore two intelligence officers who 'turned against the CIA' in the 1970s – Marchetti and Agee. Three themes emerge from the analysis. One, for the CIA, the learning curve was steep. As dissident authors arrived on the scene, the Agency hit the panic button and mistakes were made. Foolhardy attempts were made to spy on authors, steal manuscripts and intimidate publishers. When these tactics became known, they fed into the broader narrative circulating in political discourse that the CIA was unethical, lawless, and an enemy of free speech. The CIA eventually sought refuge in the panacea of the law, but again this only served to fuel suspicion that it disrespected freedom of expression. The First Amendment to the US Constitution protects the right of every American, even disillusioned CIA officers, to speak their mind – irrespective of what that message might be. Benjamin Cardozo, the distinguished depression-era Supreme Court Justice, famously described this freedom as the indispensable condition of nearly every other form of freedom. By taking authors to court, especially when it is not obvious that national security had been harmed, the CIA was castigated by many respected voices for pursuing a course of action that was antithetical to American values. In short, it was seen as asking people to renounce their birthright.

Two, being someone who speaks out against the Agency is a brutal experience. The official backlash against the individuals studied in this chapter was such a ferocious orgy of overkill that they were left devastated. As we shall see, Marchetti was thrust into a psychological and financial tailspin that left him a shadow of his former self; Agee was, quite literally, cast into the wilderness. The sad moral of their story was: publish at your peril.

Three, memoirs by renegades and whistle-blowers fundamentally challenged the celebratory story of US Cold War foreign policy, and provided further grist to the mill of nascent revisionism in this area. For much of the 1950s and 1960s, the dominant interpretation of the Cold War in the West was that it had been caused and kept alive by Soviet expansion in Eastern Europe and then into other parts of the world. The major dissenting voice to this model had been William Appleman Williams, whose landmark 1959 work, *The Tragedy of American Diplomacy*, represented an iconoclastic assault upon conventional wisdom.[26] Contra the traditionalists, and focusing on the US rather than the Soviet Union, Williams argued that the main driver of the East–West dispute was not Soviet aggression, but the unquenchable requirements of US capitalism, dating from when the original thirteen states drove westwards to claim the rest of the continent. Specifically, he pointed to the US pursuit of an 'Open Door' world in which all countries and peoples would buy into free-market principles laid down by Washington. As a result of American involvement in the quagmire of Vietnam, Williams's thesis achieved greater traction and a host of works were published excoriating the inherently imperialist tendencies of US capital and power.[27] Memoirs by disaffected CIA officers contributed to this new way of seeing US foreign policy. At the heart of these works was the argument that the primary objective of US policymakers was expansion, both territorial and economic, with the CIA as an obedient servant of this policy. Agee, in particular, showed that the engine of foreign policy was fuelled not by any devotion to morality or democratic values, but by a desire to make the world hospitable for globalisation, led by American multinational corporations. Renegades and whistle-blowers also revealed the forgotten victims of US strategy abroad, such as the people who suffered under the authoritarian Shah of Iran, installed by the CIA (and MI6) in 1953. In sum, they held up a mirror to the face of the nation; few liked the reflection staring back.

Victor Marchetti came from a working-class family in a small Pennsylvania mining town. After graduating from Penn State University with a degree in Soviet Studies, he was recruited by the CIA in 1955. The approach came in a hotel room; one of the two men that recruited him that day was missing a finger, an injury that impressed Marchetti, who was looking for adventure. He later recalled: 'If they had said, "Here's your gun, Khrushchev is over there in Moscow. Go get him," I would have done it.'[28] Marchetti went on to enjoy a successful fourteen-year career with the Agency. Starting at the bottom as a trainee, he climbed the escarpments to become executive assistant to the Deputy Director, Admiral Rufus Taylor, in 1966. In this role, he mingled with the CIA's senior bureaucrats, who resided on the seventh floor of its Langley headquarters, otherwise known as the Executive Suite, and learned much about the Agency's covert actions. Indeed, he was one of the privileged few who had morning coffee with Director Helms.[29] 'This is where I got the big picture,' he later claimed in a radio interview. Hitherto, because of compartmentalisation, his knowledge of CIA activities had been narrowly focused.[30] For a long time, he regarded the CIA like a second family. 'I never loved anything in my life so much as the CIA,' he later asserted. 'I was going to be one of these guys who get special dispensations to keep working past retirement age. I wanted to die with my boots on.'[31]

However, the higher he rose within the organisation, the more disenchanted he became. He eventually arrived at the view that the CIA had abandoned its primary function as a collector and producer of national intelligence, and had instead become obsessed with covert action and indefensible levels of secrecy. The dualism of US foreign policy became clear to him; while politicians at home openly declared their belief in self-determination, the CIA carried out a range of clandestine political and paramilitary operations in the Third World.

Vietnam weighed heavily on his mind. Particularly troubling to him was that while, on the one hand, CIA analysts were reporting that the war was a 'lost cause', on the other hand, the Agency was getting itself in 'deeper and deeper' with the controversial 'Phoenix Program', a campaign aimed at 'neutralising' the political infrastructure and leadership of the Viet Cong.[32] Moreover, Marchetti became angry at what he perceived as the bigoted 'old-boy network' that pervaded the higher echelons of the CIA. 'I was the lone ethnic,' he later told reporters, sneeringly referred to by colleagues as the 'Token Wop'.[33]

Marchetti resigned in September 1969. His first act of rebellion was to publish a spy novel, *The Rope Dancer*. Beforehand, a CIA officer vetted the text at Marchetti's home in Virginia. There was no objection from a security perspective, and publication went ahead in spring 1971.[34] Interviewed by the press, Admiral Taylor called it 'pretty trashy'.[35] Behind the scenes, however, senior CIA officials were vexed. Although the book had been marketed as pure fiction (everyone worked for an imaginary organisation known as the National Intelligence Agency), the plot was clearly based on Marchetti's career. The main protagonists were unflattering *romans à clef* of real CIA officers, including Helms and counterintelligence supremo James Jesus Angleton. In the novel, agents twisted facts to suit the whims of the President and, in a not-so-subtle nod to real CIA activities against Allende in Chile, plotted the downfall of an anonymous South American government.

Helms placed Marchetti under surveillance, had his mail traced and his tax forms reviewed. The operation, known as 'Project Butane', commenced on 23 March 1972 and lasted for about a month.[36] The CIA justified the operation by reporting to the Justice Department that it needed to ascertain if Marchetti was intending to sell secrets to a foreign power. It is unknown whether this was a genuine concern, or whether the CIA simply wanted to establish if he was writing a book. In the Agency's defence, *The Rope Dancer* had given the impression that he might have treacherous intentions. The book's hero, Paul Franklin, modelled on the author, sells to the Soviets every secret he can Xerox, photograph or tape-record before being spirited away to Moscow.

Butane found no evidence linking Marchetti with enemy services. The best it came up with were photographs of him meeting with Ben Welles from the *New York Times*.[37] With this, the CIA turned the surveillance side of the operation over to the FBI. The Bureau agreed, but warned that, 'Under such circumstances he could be the target of a recruitment attempt by the opposition, and it is not entirely inconceivable that he might choose to defect.'[38] Marchetti had no intention of defecting and later told the press that he 'laughed' when he learned that the FBI had even entertained the notion.[39] But he *was* planning to write a book and had circulated a proposal to six New York publishers. The CIA acquired a copy through an informant in the publishing world. Robert Lohman, an officer from one of the Agency's Manhattan offices, later gave a sworn affidavit claiming that this 'confidential source' had 'provided reliable information in the past' about potentially dangerous books.[40] Under the terms of its charter, it was illegal for the CIA to have a spy inside a New York publisher.

At the very moment the CIA had its eyes on Marchetti, Patrick J. McGarvey, a fourteen-year veteran of the Agency, published *CIA: The Myth and the Madness*.[41] The book depicted the CIA as a bureaucratic shambles, with no central direction, and suggested that, if senior officials spent as much energy and time plotting against the Russians as they did each other, the Cold War would be over much sooner. McGarvey claimed that the CIA had grown so unwieldy that the country's intelligence product was inferior to what it had been a decade before, with fewer personnel and less high-tech equipment. The book contained several startling disclosures, including the detail that, in 1958, CIA agents stole a Sputnik satellite while it was on a world tour. It talked about Project 'Fat Fucker', the CIA plan to overthrow Egypt's paunchy and sybaritic King Farouk in 1952. McGarvey reported that the CIA tried to determine the state of Farouk's health by obtaining a sample of his urine from the lavatory of a Monte Carlo casino. Helms came out of the book particularly badly. He was accused of blunting the investigative spirit of the press by dining with journalists and keeping them happy with periodic leaks about other agencies. He was shown to be a ruthless careerist, unafraid to step on others to reach the top. Indeed, McGarvey quoted CIA Director Raborn as saying: 'I thought for a time when I was Director that I might be assassinated by my Deputy [Helms].'[42]

Although the CIA was rankled by the book, no thought was given to taking legal action. McGarvey revealed nothing about illegal domestic operations, while his thesis that the biggest problem with CIA was mismanagement, not excess power or secrecy, was tolerable. 'CIA is not a ten-foot ogre,' acknowledged the author. 'It is merely a human institution badly in need of change.' McGarvey also gave the CIA the chance to vet the manuscript. This led to the 'blacking out' of several items in the final text, including the name of the country where the Sputnik had been snatched.[43] Mischievously, the publisher was not especially diligent in redacting the forbidden passages since it was possible to hold the text up to the light and read through the crossovers.

In Marchetti's case, however, the CIA turned to the law. For Helms, the book was the stuff of nightmares. As well as revealing how the CIA had violated its authority overseas, it was going to discuss how the CIA had broken the law with Operation CHAOS, a domestic spying programme of alleged Orwellian proportions.[44] Whereas McGarvey attributed failures to the bumbledom of bureaucracy and wanted the CIA to reform itself from within, Marchetti, more controversially, targeted excessive levels of secrecy and wanted to open up the Agency to greater congressional and public scrutiny. Helms regarded the situation with such seriousness that he took the matter directly to Nixon; the President's support was essential if Helms was to convince the Justice Department to make the CIA's case in court.[45] As we shall see later in this book, Nixon and Helms rarely saw eye to eye, but on this matter they were in total agreement: Marchetti had to be restrained. Nixon, like Helms, despised leaks. He had long admired the draconian Official Secrets Act in Britain, which allowed the government to prosecute journalists, as well as civil servants, who divulged classified information. His mania about leaks had grown out of all proportion after the Pentagon Papers storm, when, in June 1971, military analyst Daniel Ellsberg leaked to the *New York Times* a Top Secret Department of Defense history of the Vietnam War. Although Nixon revelled in the substance of the leak, which showed the blundering and deceit of his predecessor, Lyndon Johnson, he loathed the leaker, who he feared would inspire people within his own administration to make embarrassing disclosures. Barely a month after the first excerpt appeared in the *Times*, disbelieving that agencies such as the FBI could handle the problem, and seeing enemies all around him, he established a covert action unit among his own staff, the infamous 'Plumbers', to root out leakers and gather political intelligence on perceived threats.

With Nixon's blessing, and cleverly sidestepping the civil libertarian-oriented bench in Washington, DC, the CIA asked Judge Albert V. Bryan Jr of the Federal District Court of Virginia for a court order requiring Marchetti to submit all his writings, 'factual, fiction, or otherwise', to the CIA for pre-publication review. Entering a legal no man's land, the request hinged on the idea that Marchetti had signed a secrecy contract, which might have the same legal weight as a commercial contract that prevented employees from disclosing trade secrets.[46] Nixon was just as interested as the CIA in whether this would be accepted. If the suit was approved, he could consider inserting a similar secrecy clause into the contracts of Executive Branch employees.

On 18 April 1972, Bryan sanctioned the request and issued a temporary injunction. He also ordered Marchetti to return to the CIA any documents he might have taken when he left the Agency. Bryan's order was hugely significant. This was the first occasion in US history that a former government official had been subjected to such a censorship order. Moreover, the injunction had been issued before the author had written a single word. Put another way, Marchetti was being punished for information that existed in his head.

The question raised by the action was whether a US citizen should be required to surrender his or her freedom of conscience, of thought, in the manner prescribed by the CIA. The outcry from the media and civil liberties groups suggested that the CIA would have been better advised to leave the issue well alone. In a leading article entitled 'Free Speech, Security and the CIA', *Washington Post* reporter Alan Birth was indignant: 'It is trying to impose a kind of preventive detention in the realm of ideas.'[47] He continued: 'The expression of ideas cannot be enjoined in America. To imprison ideas is to dam the democratic process.'[48] The popular weekly journal *The Nation* proposed that the case dramatised the 'fact that the CIA is essentially an alien institution – alien to American custom, alien to the Constitution – and incompatible with both the forms and the spirit of democracy.'[49]

Marchetti told reporters that the unprecedented attempt by the CIA to secure prior restraint reflected a 'paranoiac, clandestine mentality, more than I ever thought'.[50] He also rejected the suggestion that he had taken any documents: 'I'm no Ellsberg. I did not walk out with a boxload of stuff. That's not my bag.'[51]

The American Civil Liberties Union (ACLU) agreed to provide free counsel for Marchetti. Together, they demanded that the injunction be lifted, and argued that anything less would represent a breach of the Republic's most cherished right, that of free speech. In the opposite corner, the CIA demanded that the injunction be made permanent in the interests of national security. At stake, the Agency claimed, was nothing less than the sanctity of its contracts and, more generally, its ability to keep secrets. Marchetti later said that he had a friend at Langley who told him that the CIA felt so strongly about the matter that there were people, had they been asked, who would happily have killed him.[52] Before the trial, Rufus Taylor, perhaps out of some sense of personal loyalty to his former assistant, embarrassed the CIA by stating publicly that, having read an article by Marchetti in *The Nation*, he regarded the material as 'inaccurate but not damaging'.[53]

The trial began on 15 May 1972 and lasted less than eight hours. In a ruling of great importance, Bryan agreed with the CIA, claiming that the contract signed by Marchetti amounted to a relinquishment of his First Amendment rights. Marchetti appealed to the Supreme Court, the final arbiter of law, on the grounds that no contract should trump a constitutional right. The Supreme Court declined to hear the case.

This was not to be the last of the struggle. Teaming up with John Marks, a former State Department employee, Marchetti wrote a 400-page book called *The CIA and the Cult of Intelligence*. Contracted with Alfred K. Knopf, it netted the authors a cool $45,000 advance – not spectacular by the standards of presidents and secretaries of state, but a considerable amount for hitherto unknown public servants.[54] After the book was contracted, Marchetti was fairly certain that the CIA attempted to entrap him. Almost every day, he later told the press, a random stranger with a foreign accent would ask him if he would give him an advance copy, in return for cash.[55]

As required by the court, Marchetti and Marks submitted the text for pre-publication review. After thirty days, they were contacted and ordered to remove 339 passages, roughly a quarter of the book, ranging from single words to entire pages.[56] It was immediately clear to them that the CIA had taken a wide interpretation of what had to be safeguarded in the interest of national security. Deleted was the insight that Helms had mispronounced the name of the Malagasy Republic at a National Security Council meeting. Interestingly, no objection was taken to the authors mentioning that, at the same session, Nixon mistakenly called the Chairman of the Joint Chiefs of Staff 'Admiral Mormon'.[57] (As we shall see later in this book, since the CIA had problems with Nixon, this is perhaps not surprising.) Also removed was the remark by Henry Kissinger, US National Security Adviser, that the US could not let Chile fall into communist hands 'just because of the irresponsibility of its people'.[58] Moreover, the CIA deleted the book's discussion of CIA efforts to train a cat, fitted with a bugging device, to eavesdrop on people's conversations. With the best will in the world, it was hard to see how such 'revelations' could damage American security.

Marchetti and Marks struck back by filing a suit to challenge the deletions. Once again, everybody found themselves back in the Virginia courtroom of Judge Bryan. In March 1974, with the Agency being hauled over the coals in the press for its wholesale hatchet job on the book, CIA attorneys agreed to reduce the number of deletions to 168. However, this concession only served to heighten the suspicion that the CIA's classification policy was *ad hoc* and capricious, with no formal or consistently applied standards.

On 20 March, having grown impatient with the CIA's strategy of constantly moving the classification goalposts, Bryan decreed that of the 168 items, only twenty-seven were valid. Embarrassingly for the CIA, he announced that First Amendment rights had to be protected against the 'whim of the reviewing official'.[59] The CIA instantly filed an appeal. But, rather than be dragged through the courts any longer, in June 1974 the authors threw caution to the wind and decided to publish a version with 168 blank spaces. In the opinion of one reviewer, this 'Swiss cheese quality curiously reinforced rather than diminished the book's credibility'.[60] Doubly embarrassingly for the CIA, the publisher also set in bold typeface the reinstated 141 passages the CIA had originally cut. Readers, therefore, knew exactly what information the CIA had regarded as a threat to national security, if disclosed. Among the reinstated items was the perfectly innocuous disclosure that Director McCone had had his office 'enlarged, panelled in wood, and impressively furnished' – hardly a disclosure that was likely to cost lives. Also in bold typeface was the detail that, between 1950 and 1955, the CIA grew from 5,000 to 15,000 staff – again, not exactly earth-shattering stuff.[61]

The book resonated with disillusionment at home about Vietnam and more broadly America's ill-fated and morally questionable attempts to remake the world in its own image. Increasingly, in books and articles, the US was being presented as a cross between a greedy colossus and schoolyard bully – its foreign policy, far from being benign, being dictated instead by a determination to acquire foreign markets under the auspices of a new international economic order. Marchetti and Marks contributed to this. The central contention of the book was that, despite the United States' rhetorical devotion to the self-determination of nations, it had been violating the sovereignty of foreign states. As a result, the CIA's authorised mission to coordinate and process intelligence had been supplanted by an obsession with covert action. This obsession, the book argued, had led the CIA, without approval by Congress, to fuel the Cold War and destabilise the international system. The authors recalled the CIA's early 'back-alley' struggles against communism, including the successful putsch against Iranian premier Mohammed Mossadegh in 1953 and its abortive attempt five years later to overthrow Indonesian President Sukarno. They discussed the CIA's programme to train Tibetan rebels to fight Chinese communists. They also suggested that the CIA worked for 'corporate America'. For example, they revealed the CIA's ownership and management of proprietary organisations, including Air America.

Colby, who became CIA Director in September 1973, later admitted that the CIA should have backed down much earlier than it had done.[62] Media coverage of the case gave unprecedented publicity to a book that might have sunk without a trace. The liberal magazine, *The New Republic*, ironically suggested that the CIA merited a nod of gratitude for having unwittingly launched the book in the direction of the bestseller list.[63]

With legal expenses of nearly $125,000, Knopf had its profits from the book wiped out.[64] Bloodied and bruised, the publishing giant had no inclination to contract any more CIA memoirs. For Marchetti, there was no happy ending either. Chief Judge Clement Haynsworth of the Fourth Judicial Circuit eventually threw out Bryan's ruling. The courts, he argued, had no authority to determine what constituted a genuine secret, announcing that information was 'secret' the moment the CIA official affixed the legend to the document.[65] A CIA officer, he underlined, sacrifices his First Amendment rights when he signs a secrecy agreement. Marchetti was mortified and spent a week in bed licking his wounds: 'I didn't shave or bathe or even turn on a light.'[66] Marchetti's fifteen minutes of fame soon came to an end and he slipped into oblivion. The two-year legal tussle left him on the brink of bankruptcy – with 'nothing but his house and a prayer'.[67] It also came at an enormous emotional cost to him and his family; his drinking worsened, belying his description of himself many years later as a 'functional alcoholic', while his children were subject to taunts of 'Your old man's a traitor.'[68] He later confessed that 'I shoulda kept my mouth shut [and] never taken on the CIA.'[69] When future whistle-blower Frank Snepp (Chapter 5) met Marchetti for the first time in 1978, it was clear that events had taken a huge toll: 'The potbellied munchkin with the double chin and Buddy Holly glasses who greeted me was so unrelentingly pathetic that I found myself mumbling apologies for even disturbing his evening.'[70] Before the two parted company, Marchetti embraced Snepp and said, with tears welling up in his eyes, 'From now on you're gonna be an outlaw, a gunslinger all by yourself. And every time you walk down the street there's gonna be somebody waitin' to take a shot at you.'[71]

III. 'The Agency's No. 1 Nemesis'

If I can get him with my bare hands, I'll kill, I'll kill him.
An unnamed CIA official, speaking to the
United Press Association, 1980.[72]

A conservative Catholic from an upwardly mobile, white family in Tampa, Florida, Philip Agee was prime CIA material. He served as staff officer from July 1957 to November 1968. Eight of those years were spent undercover in Ecuador, Uruguay and Mexico. As a case officer on the streets in South America, he was more familiar with intelligence work overseas than the desk-bound Marchetti.

The circumstances behind his resignation have long been disputed. According to Agee, he resigned because his Roman Catholic social conscience had made him uneasy with US foreign policy. The CIA, he came to believe, had become the 'secret policeman of capitalism', wielded by presidents at the request of big business to facilitate the optimal conditions for multinational corporate investment.[73] Specifically, he was distressed with the CIA's support for anti-communist, authoritarian regimes across Latin America. He later told the British journalist Duncan Campbell: 'It was a time when the worst imaginable horrors were going on … Argentina, Brazil, Chile, Uruguay, Paraguay, Guatemala, El Salvador – they were military dictatorships with death squads, all with the backing of the CIA and the US government.'[74] Agee has written that there was no bad blood between him and the Agency for leaving. Indeed, his boss was reportedly 'startled' since he had been lining Agee up for another promotion.[75]

The more likely scenario, however, is that Agee was pushed. CIA evaluations of his performance and character were extremely negative. One report suggested that he 'showed himself to be an egotistical, superficially intelligent, but essentially shallow young man'.[76] Another report stated that his 'financial accountings were constantly in a poor state', and that he was 'always borrowing money'.[77] Moreover, he was frequently in trouble for heavy drinking, as well as the vulgar propositioning of wives of US embassy staff.[78] Any one of these indiscretions could have been grounds to dismiss him; intelligence officers need to be free from controversy to avoid being blackmailed. Agee's 'family difficulties' proved the final straw. The trouble originated when Agee separated from his wife, subsequent to a string of extramarital affairs, and, defying a court order, relocated his children to Mexico where he lived with his mistress – 'an American woman deeply involved in leftist activity.'[79] Agee's ex-wife informed the US ambassador in Mexico City that, unless her boys were returned to the US, she would reveal her former husband's CIA work. With this, Agee was asked to leave.

After resigning, Agee studied for a Master's degree in Latin American history at Mexico's largest university, the National Autonomous University of Mexico, a hotbed of leftism. He had high hopes that he would get rich by assisting affluent Mexicans he had met through his work. When, to quote CIA records, his 'grandiose schemes for making money in Mexico did not bear fruit', he seemingly turned to a more sinister trade: treachery.[80] According to several respected accounts, in 1973 he strolled into the KGB station in Mexico City and offered what Oleg Kalugin, a former head of the KGB's Counterintelligence Directorate, described as a 'mound of information' about CIA operations and agents worldwide.[81] The KGB resident wrongly believed him to be a CIA plant and sent him packing. With this, he approached the Cuban Dirección General De Inteligencia (DGI), who accepted his offer with alacrity. Kalugin has gone on record as saying that, while the Cubans shared Agee's information with the KGB, he 'cursed our officers for turning away such a prize asset'.[82]

Agee always denied that he worked with either the KGB or DGI. The charges, he claimed, were CIA smears. 'I am no Cuban agent,' he told Pulitzer Prize-winning journalist James Risen in October 1997.[83] 'The CIA', he continued, 'has used the word "agent" to characterise my relation to the revolution because to them it means "sold out", "controlled", "traitorous" etc.'[84] The evidence, however, tends to suggest otherwise. In 1992, a high-ranking Cuban intelligence defector claimed that Agee had received nearly $1 million from the DGI. In 1999, Vasili Mitrokhin, a former KGB librarian who had been smuggled out of Russia by British intelligence complete with six trunks of classified files, disclosed that Agee was a communist agent with the codename 'PONT'.[85] And, in an interview for this book, CIA alumnus Cameron LaClair, who spent twenty-one years with the Agency before retiring in 1978, claimed that the CIA had amassed 'overwhelming' evidence that Agee was 'in the hands of the Cuban intelligence service'.[86]

Agee revealed himself as a serious critic of the CIA in November 1971 with an article, published in a Montevideo newspaper, accusing the CIA of meddling in Uruguayan elections. In it, he confirmed that he was writing a book. With this, CIA officer Salvatore Ferrera was dispatched to Paris, where Agee was based, with orders to befriend him and earn his trust. Ferrera's cover was that of an 'underground' journalist with close ties to anti-Vietnam War activists organising peace demonstrations in Paris. Exploiting Agee's weakness for women, Ferrera introduced the renegade spy to Leslie Donegan, a blonde, bosomy and wealthy heiress of an American businessman in Venezuela. Donegan, who announced herself as a graduate student at Geneva University, was in fact a CIA officer (real name, Janet Strickland), sent to acquire a copy of his manuscript. Presenting herself as a patroness of the arts, she agreed to finance his research. Additionally, she gifted him use of her modern studio apartment and gave him a portable typewriter. Grateful, he gave her 250 photocopied pages of draft material.[87]

The CIA's attempts to monitor Agee came back to haunt them. Agee discovered that the typewriter was secretly packed with microphones, transmitters and fifty tiny batteries – concealed inside the case. That the CIA believed that Agee, a trained spy, would fail to detect the electronic apparatus hardly inspires confidence in its tradecraft from this period. As we shall see, the renegade spy would publicly embarrass the CIA by including a photograph of the impressively wired typewriter on the front cover of his book. Moreover, Strickland's financial assistance actually facilitated the book's completion. Agee was destitute before she arrived on the scene bearing gifts, compliments of the CIA. The book was the last thing on his mind. 'It is no exaggeration to say that', he later claimed, 'the CIA itself financed me during the most critical period in writing the book.'[88] Upon realising that the typewriter was bugged, he immediately left Paris. The CIA was left to lament a comedy of errors.

He eventually showed up in London in October 1972, where he lived until he finished the book in May 1974. There is every reason to believe that, during this time, he received help from the Russians, the Cubans, or both. Stansfield Turner has written of Agee having been 'brainwashed' by the KGB while writing the book.[89] According to Mitrokhin, whose secret notes were turned into a bestselling book by Professor Christopher Andrew, there is a KGB file that proudly declares that the manuscript was prepared in conjunction with the KGB's 'Service A, together with the Cubans'.[90] Agee's KGB contact in London was said to be Edgar Anatolyevich Cheporov, London correspondent of the Novosti news agency. Mitrokhin did not elaborate on what exactly the KGB or DGI contributed in terms of information, but did claim that, at Service A's insistence, Agee deleted unflattering details about the CIA's successful penetration of communist parties in Latin America. On the lecture circuit, Agee acknowledged the help of the Communist Party of Cuba, and even admitted to conducting interviews with Cuban embassy officials in London, some of whom were DGI intelligence officers.[91]

The CIA made repeated, unsuccessful, efforts to remind Agee of the Agency's contractual right to review the manuscript before its publication. Assistant CIA General Counsel John Greaney visited the spy's father in Tampa, Florida, while letters were sent to potential publishers warning them of the legal implications of publishing the book without pre-publication review. In one letter, Greaney explained that the CIA was 'gravely concerned as to its possible damage to the security of the United States'.[92] According to Agee, out of desperation, Greaney contacted his ex-wife and told her to communicate to him that the CIA was willing to pay him, and even offer him another job, in return for his silence – a deal he refused: 'Money to stop, eh? Another job? Fuck you people.'[93] With this, he claimed, the CIA went after him with no holds barred. The Internal Revenue Service reportedly began harassing his father with audits. In London, he allegedly found himself the object of round-the-clock surveillance by British security services.

'This surveillance', he recollected, 'caused psychological pressures and fears of physical assault.'[94] Moreover, articles started appearing in the press about a drunken and despondent CIA officer, stationed in Latin America, who had given secrets to the KGB. The first to break the story was John M. Crewdson of the *New York Times*, later described by Agee as a CIA patsy chosen to discredit him before his book was even published. 'KGB, eh? Those dirty, fucking bastards.'[95]

To avoid the potential for the kind of arbitrary censorship that had shredded parts of Marchetti and Mark's book, *Inside the Company: CIA Diary* was published by Penguin in London in April 1975. The cover featured the bugged typewriter in all its glory and boasted that, unlike Marchetti and Mark's redacted work, 'There are no blanks in Philip Agee's.' London distributors shipped around 500 copies to Classics Book Store in New York, as well as Sidney Kramer Books in Washington, DC. However, they were on sale for just a few days, before US Customs interceded and seized them.[96]

The book, which took the form of a diary rather than a memoir, represented an uncompromisingly negative assessment of the CIA and US foreign policy. The central thesis was that the US was defending despots in Latin America, while ensuring that its states were kept in peonage to US investors under the ruse of 'development'. At a press conference, Agee said that the CIA's job was to 'plug up leaks in the political dam, night and day, so that shareholders of US companies operating in poor countries can continue enjoying the rip-off'.[97] He accused the CIA of an 'anything goes' mentality. Bugging; blackmail; burglary; the hiring of people to plant bombs; the buying and selling of elected officials, journalists, and union leaders – nothing was reportedly off limits. The *London Evening News* called it a 'frightening picture of corruption, pressure, assassination, and conspiracy'.[98] To expose the ugly side of US intervention around the world, Agee provided gruesome tales of local populations being killed or tortured. For example, he revealed that his superiors forced him to hand over the identities of hundreds of Uruguayan rebels to police officers, even though it was obvious that this would seal their fate. On one occasion, he recalled, in a Montevideo police station, he heard the screams from a nearby cell of a man he had recently turned over to the police. Appallingly, the officers simply turned up the volume of a televised soccer match to drown out the noise.

Horror stories such as these were nevertheless not the most controversial aspect of the book. In an alphabetised appendix, Agee identified some 250 CIA officers working abroad, as well as front companies, foreign agents and collaborators, including high-profile figures such as President José Figueres Ferrer of Costa Rica, President Alfonso López Michelsen of Colombia, and President Luis Álvarez of Mexico. Nothing is more sacred in the intelligence world than the identity of people who agree to work for you in secret. It has always been that way. During the American Revolutionary War, when he realised that the British had penetrated his camps (even corrupting some of his personal bodyguards), George Washington ruled that no names were to be included in the 'Orders of the Day', as was the military custom.[99] In his journal, Washington wrote that he had a moral obligation to protect the identities of men and women who risked their lives in the struggle against the British: 'The names of the persons who are employed within the Enemy's lines or who may fall within their power cannot be inserted.'[100] From the CIA's perspective, keeping the names of agents secret was essential to not only guarantee the safety of the agent and his family, but also ensure that friendly intelligence organisations, with whom it enjoyed productive dealings, did not break off relations for fear of having their own secrets exposed. As Director Turner would later state in a sworn affidavit, 'Foreign intelligence agencies simply will not cooperate with the CIA unless they are confident that the CIA's assurances of confidentiality can be honoured.'[101] Agee, therefore, had taken a huge step. By revealing names, seemingly with reckless abandon, he had crossed the Rubicon from being a whistle-blower into something far more dangerous, since whistle-blowing has defined legal parameters relating to the exposure of illegality and wrongdoing. He seemed to be operating under the overall pretext that everything the Agency does is wrong.

Unsurprisingly, the CIA deplored the book. A review in the Agency's in-house journal, *Studies in Intelligence*, suggested that it was a 'severe body blow' to the organisation.[102] It lamented that, 'A considerable number of CIA personnel must be diverted from their normal duties to undertake the meticulous and time-consuming task of repairing the damage done to its Latin American programme, and to see what can be done to help those injured by the author's revelations.'[103] David Atlee Phillips predicted that the book would lead to the 'unnecessary death of an American intelligence officer abroad', and accused its author of being 'responsible for untold worry and anxiety on the part of CIA families'.[104]

Agee was unrepentant. He declared that his intention was not to endanger the lives of CIA officers, but to 'drive them out of the countries where they are operating'.[105] He emphasised that publishing the names of CIA officers was not an act of espionage on behalf of the Soviet Union, but a political act in the 'long and honourable tradition of dissidence in the United States'.[106] Exhibiting coldness in the extreme, he argued that CIA officers can 'take care of themselves', a view totally insensitive to the fact that wives and children, who had no training, might be targeted. In a rare display of sympathy for the CIA during this time, large corners of the US mainstream media believed that Agee had gone too far. The hugely respected national security reporter Walter Pincus described the book as 'exposure for destruction's sake'.[107]

The CIA then proceeded to shoot itself in the foot once more by failing to heed the lessons of its legal tussle with Marchetti. There was every chance that the book would scarcely have registered on the public's radar. To quote the espionage writer Ladislas Farago, it was 'repetitious, anti-climactic, badly written and confusingly organised'.[108] For six months, the Agency nevertheless tried to block publication of the book in the US, with the press reporting every action that whiffed of being heavy-handed. Legal proceedings were threatened against Agee's US publisher, Stonehill, and the ACLU again became involved in defending an author's right to free speech. At one point, Director Colby told a house appropriations committee that government prosecutors were investigating the possibility of charging Agee with treason.[109] By the time the CIA backed down, its actions had generated enormous public interest in the book, which became an instant bestseller, and intensified the feeling that the CIA was overly secretive. The fact that the nation's enemies could already read the book, from Chairman Mao to General Secretary Brezhnev, undermined the Agency's claim that domestic publication would harm national security and was suggestive of a more sinister desire to keep the American people in the dark. 'The CIA can blame only itself for this mishap,' considered Farago:

> This is what they deserve for hiring an unstable young scout and making him perform some of the dirtiest tricks of the Cold War … The wise men of Langley [should have] let his book die the natural death it so amply deserves by its acute boredom.[110]

Agee saw *Inside the Company* as just one element of a larger campaign against the CIA. He became closely affiliated with the 'Fifth Estate', a watchdog organisation founded by the outspoken writer and gadabout of leftist causes Norman Mailer in February 1973. The Fifth Estate was conceived as a citizens' action committee designed to monitor spy agencies and to investigate their possible complicity in scandals ranging from the assassination of President Kennedy and Martin Luther King to the death of Marilyn Monroe. Mailer called it a 'democratic secret police keeping tabs on Washington's secret police'.[111] At first, the organisation lacked credibility and came close to folding. Much of the blame for this rested with Mailer. Promising an 'announcement of national importance', he threw an elegant bash at the Four Seasons off Park Avenue in New York, which was attended by a veritable 'who's who' of political and cultural life, including Senator Eugene McCarthy, Andy Warhol and Jack Lemmon. Esteemed public intellectual Arthur Schlesinger Jr attended and jokingly suggested that the host was going to announce his vasectomy. Unfortunately, Mailer got outrageously drunk and emptied the room with a series of dirty jokes. He later wrote in the *New York Times Book Review* that it was the 'worst speech' he had ever made. The press corps, already affronted at having to pay to attend the star-studded event, delighted in mocking him and his nascent vigilante group. Sally Quinn of the *Washington Post* said that his speech, which included talk of 'totalitarianism', 'paranoia' and 'plots', was greeted with hissing and catcalls.[112] However, as hair-curling revelations emerged about Watergate, Mailer's fears about secret government and conspiracies began to look less and less foolish. Agee sensed this and found a valuable ally.

Agee worked as an adviser to the Fifth Estate's quarterly magazine, *CounterSpy*, which was edited by a motley band of disaffected intelligence officers. These included Tim Butz and Kenneth Osborn, both with backgrounds in military intelligence, and Perry Fellwock, otherwise known by his pseudonym, Winslow Peck, a former analyst for the NSA. A kid in his mid-twenties, Peck had become the NSA's first whistle-blower when, in 1972, he gave an anonymous interview to *Ramparts* in which he claimed that the NSA administered an automated global interception and relay system capable of breaking Soviet codes, listening to Soviet communications, and keeping track of virtually every missile-carrying plane or submarine around the world.[113] The declared aim of *CounterSpy* was to name CIA officials in the hope that exposure would force the CIA to bring these 'techno-fascists' home. The CIA interpreted this as a declaration of war, analogous to the mission of the KGB. 'In twenty-five years as a professional intelligence officer', announced Atlee Phillips, 'this is first time I have seen a group of citizens urge a covert action plan against its own secret service.'[114] *CounterSpy* perfected a system for identifying CIA operatives that did not require classified documents, aided by the fact that agents had poorly constructed cover. In November 1974, in an article for *Washington Monthly* entitled 'How to Spot a Spook', John Marks explained to readers how it was possible to uncover CIA officers stationed in embassies by consulting government publications such as the *Biographic Register* and the State Department's *Foreign Service Roster*. Marks explained that CIA personnel were referred to as 'Foreign Service Reserve' or 'Foreign Service Staff' and had brief biographical entries with tell-tale gaps in their employment history. The CIA derided this as 'political mischief of the worst sort', only for *CounterSpy* to defend itself by saying that the material was extrapolated from open sources.[115]

CounterSpy made a name for itself with several scoops, including an exposé on the CIA's 'Phoenix Program', a set of operations designed to 'neutralise' the political infrastructure of the Viet Cong in South Vietnam, but later alleged to be an assassination campaign with death squads and secret interrogation centres. Controversially, this printed the name of the CIA's Chief of Station in Saigon, Thomas Polgar.

The magazine's most sensational disclosure came in 1975. According to Fellwock, Agee had long been pressing the editors to publish not just a trickle, but a flood of names. They eventually acquiesced. The winter 1975 issue featured a list of 225 CIA officers around the world under diplomatic cover, with each name accompanied by an address and short biography. Agee was indelibly associated with the list since, in the same issue, he wrote an editorial declaring: 'The most effective and important systematic efforts to combat the CIA that can be undertaken right now are the identification, exposure, and neutralisation of its people working abroad.'[116] One of those named was Richard Welch, Station Chief in Athens. Tragically, on the night of 23 December 1975, as Welch returned from a Christmas party at the American ambassador's residence with his wife, he was ambushed by three masked assailants outside the gate of his fashionable suburban home and shot to death. This was the first assassination of a Station Chief in CIA history. The gunmen, who belonged to a terrorist group called 'November 17', would eventually be caught, tried and imprisoned. The chief assailant was a maths teacher who lived on a Greek island.[117]

Agee's associates rightly predicted that the CIA would 'burn [his] ass and the Fifth Estate's over Welch'.[118] Incoming CIA Director George H. W. Bush laid the blame squarely at their feet. A CIA press release announced: 'We've had an American gunned down by other Americans fingering him – rightly or wrongly – as a CIA agent.'[119] The magazine's editors moved quickly to refute the charge, releasing a statement on 24 December stating: 'If anyone is to blame for Mr Welch's death it is the CIA that sent him there to spy.'[120] They explained that Welch's identity as a CIA man was well known. And they were right. It had first been revealed in 1968 by a small hardbound East German publication called *Who's Who in the CIA*, sponsored by the KGB. In 1974, the Peruvian press had published that he was, then, Station Chief in Lima. A month before he was slain, the newspaper *Athens News* had printed his name, as well as his address in the city and telephone number. It emerged some years later that hundreds of Athenians knew Welch's identity because he lived in a house known to be the residence of the incumbent CIA Station Chief in Athens. Reportedly, local tour guides even pointed out the residence during their bus journeys around the city.[121] Declassified documents also reveal that, before Welch moved in, he had been warned by Langley that he and his wife should live elsewhere because the location had been compromised. Fatally, he wired back that he would take his chances.[122] For these reasons, *CounterSpy* argued that 'the blood of Mr. Welch is on the hands of the CIA.'[123]

Agee nevertheless attracted little sympathy. The *Washington Post*, which ran no fewer than thirteen stories on Welch in the week following his murder, declared that the winter edition of *CounterSpy* was 'tantamount to an open invitation to kill him'.[124] His death, it lamented in another editorial, was 'the entirely predictable result of the disclosable tactics chosen by certain American critics of the Agency'.[125] It did not matter that Welch's name might have been printed elsewhere: what mattered was that Agee was the loudest and most high-profile champion of naming names, and now an American who had served his country with distinction for twenty-two years was coming home in a body bag. Welch was a good man. It was characteristic of his decency that on the fateful night in question it was he – not his chauffeur – who exited the car to open the gate of his home. Not of the generation that had run wars and played court procurer for presidential dirty tricks, he despised violence (indeed, he was blinded in one eye in a childhood accident) and had been appalled by revelations of gung-ho covert operations.

Reeling from congressional investigations and sensing an opportunity to swing the pendulum of popular opinion back in favour of the need for secrecy, the CIA, with the help of the Administration, wasted no time in making Welch a martyr; a symbol not only of the dangers of disclosing names, but of transparency in general. Atlee Phillips and his AFIO old-boy network (more in Chapter 4) wrote press articles imploring Americans to take pride in the way Welch lived his life, but also to learn lessons from his untimely death. Congress and journalists were criticised for exposing intelligence methods and operations, and for whipping up a destructive hysteria about the CIA. In the *Evening Independent*, Mike Ackerman, an operations officer for eleven years, wrote that 'Maybe, just maybe, his death will have some meaning.' 'Maybe', he went on, 'it will at last turn the debate on the future of American intelligence into a constructive dialogue.'[126]

Although a non-combatant, the fallen Welch was buried, by order of President Ford, in Arlington National Cemetery. The plane bearing the hero's coffin was perfectly timed to land at Andrews Air Force Base for live coverage on breakfast television, even circling for fifteen minutes to maximise viewing figures. On arrival, it was welcomed by a 'who's who' of the national security establishment, including Colby, Atlee Phillips and top White House aides. The funeral was handled with the pomp and ceremony typically afforded to the burial of presidents, replete with honour guards and hundreds of fluttering flags. The horse-drawn caisson that carried Welch to his final resting place that chilly winter morning was the one that had been for used for JFK. After the service, President Ford himself escorted the veiled widow to her motorcade. With both House and Senate committees at that very moment drafting their final reports and recommendations for intelligence reform, Senator Church accused the CIA of exploiting the death to frighten would-be reformers and water down their proposals. 'The Welch murder was *the* event,' he later recalled:

> It was stage-managed. There was a big public funeral which the president attended. An attempt was made to lay the responsibility on the congressional investigations ... I sensed the political interests of the administration to close down the investigation as soon as possible and to try to keep control of whatever remedies were sought.[127]

Another critic went so far as to call Welch's funeral a 'Cold War coup d'état'.[128] Even CIA counsel Mitchell Rogovin later acknowledged that the CIA had 'waved [the death] around like a bloody shirt'.[129]

CounterSpy survived the furore, but the backlash left it a pale shadow of its former self. The IRS revoked its tax exemption. East Coast intellectuals, who had been drawn to the magazine because it was chic, pulled their support. So too did many of its closest allies on the left. It was inappropriate – and certainly not cool – to be making donations to an outfit accused of murder. Mailer cut all ties. For someone as pugnacious and provocative as Mailer to abandon the magazine spoke volumes; this, after all, was a man who over the years delighted in courting controversy – whether engaging in public brawls, reciting obscene poetry or crusading against women's liberation. Agee later alleged that members of the Fifth Estate asked for police protection after receiving death threats from former intelligence officers.[130] Tim Butz told a reporter that he started carrying a gun.[131] *CounterSpy* eventually folded in 1984. Its supporters would long accuse the CIA of dancing on Welch's grave, and attack the mainstream national media for 'swallowing the bait' of an official strategy to blame the magazine for the death. Agee would achieve a small measure of revenge in 1995 when he sued former First Lady Barbara Bush for falsely stating in her memoirs that Welch had been killed because 'his cover had been blown by [Agee's] traitorous, tell-all book'.[132] *Inside the Company* had not in fact mentioned Welch. A legal settlement was reached in which Mrs Bush agreed to withdraw the charge from subsequent editions.

His reputation had taken a buffeting, but Agee was determined not to be silenced. After Welch's murder, he can be likened to a sailor, tossed at sea, clinging to a swaying mast. Living in Cambridge, England, he colluded with alternative publications such as *Time Out* and other elements of the underground press. One of his closest associates was the young journalist Mark Hosenball, another American national, with whom he caused a stir by unmasking members of the CIA London station, including the Agency's London chief, Cord Meyer. Press photographers staked out known CIA addresses, while an American theatre group even staged satirical productions outside the homes of CIA officers. Meyer, who was given a vigil outside his Belgravia residence, recollected that he 'felt very much like a sitting duck … in the gun sights of terrorists'.[133] In Parliament, a Commons bill, with thirty-two signatures, demanded the expulsion of CIA spies from the UK.

With powerful enemies on both sides of the Atlantic, it is no surprise that someone decided to clip Agee's wings. On 16 November 1976, the UK Home Secretary Merlyn Rees served deportation orders on Agee, as well as Hosenball, requiring them to leave the country. Rees told MPs that Agee's contacts were 'harmful to the security of the United Kingdom'.

There was almost certainly more to the deportation order than Rees was willing to publicly acknowledge. One possibility was that officials in London, concerned that US-style investigations into intelligence would inspire similar probing into British agencies, wanted to punish Agee as a warning. Another possibility is Agee might have been responsible for the death of two MI6 agents in Poland.[134] Agee strongly believed that Washington was behind efforts to deport him. The CIA's legendary chief of counterintelligence James Jesus Angleton had publicly criticised the UK for providing sanctuary to a declared enemy of the United States.[135] Agee speculated that the CIA wanted him out of the UK, concerned that he was using London as a base to pen a new tell-all book with London-based co-author, Steve Weissman.[136] He also believed that US Secretary of State, Henry Kissinger, had urged the UK to act in retribution for Agee's revelation in September of that year that the CIA was waging a destabilisation campaign in Jamaica in order to swing the forthcoming election against the left-wing ruler Michael Manley.[137]

UK Prime Minister James Callaghan strongly rejected the notion that Britain's hand been forced by the US, but it is hard to imagine that the decision was taken without some consideration of US feelings on the matter. UK–US relations, especially in the intelligence field, were steadily getting back on track after a series of spats in the early 1970s. British officials were particularly aware of the dangers of alienating the powerful Kissinger. In August 1973, vexed by Britain's independent stance regarding troop reduction talks with the USSR, and annoyed with Prime Minister Edward Heath's overtures towards Europe, Kissinger, then National Security Adviser, temporarily cut off privileged UK access to US intelligence in a bold attempt to get the British back in line.[138] The threat worked; the Joint Intelligence Committee (JIC), the UK's senior intelligence assessment body, panicked. Accordingly, if pressure had come from Washington to deport Agee, the likelihood of Her Majesty's Government objecting was slim.

Agee fought the order in what became a cause célèbre. He was supported by dozens of left-wing MPs, union leaders, academics and journalists, while a defence committee organised rallies, petitions and pickets of the UK Home Office. Notes acquired by the KGB defector Mitrokhin indicate that some of Agee's supporters were taking orders from the KGB, which was understandably ecstatic at the 'deeply embarrassing nature of [the] fuss'.[139] The appeal procedure dragged on for over six months, in what must have felt like an eternity for the authorities as Agee used the delay to tour the country, giving endless lectures on CIA abuses and his rough treatment at the hands of the British government.

Agee was forced to leave England on 3 June 1977, setting in motion a lifetime of jumping from country to country in search of asylum, knowing that a return to the US would result in prosecution and jail. From England, he had planned to go to France, only to be denied residency there, so instead travelled to the Netherlands where he lived until March 1978 before being expelled there too. After a brief period in Switzerland, he established residency in Hamburg, West Germany, with the help of a marriage to Giselle Roberge, a German ballet dancer. He also accepted Fidel Castro's hospitality, owning an apartment in Havana.

In 1979, the State Department revoked his US passport on national security grounds after he called for the Iranian hostage crisis to be resolved by exchanging the US hostages for CIA documents on Iran. (A left-wing magazine claimed that a CIA case officer told them he would rather let 500 people die, never mind fifty, before he would ever release these files.)[140] The Supreme Court upheld the passport ruling in 1981. With this, he travelled on passports issued by Maurice Bishop's radical regime in Grenada, and then the Sandinista government in Nicaragua.

Agee claimed to be hounded and harassed by the CIA for the rest of his life. His expulsions, he believed, had to be the result of CIA pressure. He also alleged he had suffered invasions of privacy, injurious falsehood, infliction of mental distress, physical surveillance, a barrage of false newspaper stories and illegal search and seizures.[141] His personal papers, available for inspection at the Tamiment Library in New York, are full of cat-and-mouse tales about being hunted by the

Agency. Recalling one episode, a family holiday to San Sebastián in Spain, he explained that 'several carloads' of Spanish security forces were waiting for him as he disembarked the ferry. Changing number plates when possible, they proceeded to shadow him for most of the day, with two agents even following him into the Cave of Altamira to see the prehistoric paintings.[142] According to Agee, on the day he married Roberge, she was interrogated at Frankfurt airport and 'forced to remove all her clothes'.[143] How much truth there is to all of this is open to question. However, it is interesting to note that, under the Freedom of Information Act, Agee learned that the CIA, by June 1980, had no fewer than 45,000 documents on him – evidence, perhaps, that they were intent on chasing him into the obituaries.[144] One of those documents, now declassified, contained the sensational revelation that in the late 1970s the Civil Rights Division of the Justice Department had conducted a criminal investigation into CIA activities against him. Nothing apparently came of this, although a memorandum was sent to the Attorney General from the lead investigator questioning 'whether to prosecute CIA officials for civil rights violations against Philip Agee'.[145] The allegations against the Agency, therefore, may not be baseless.

Agee did not let his struggles diminish his appetite to attack the CIA. In 1978, he became the leading light of 'Counter-Watch', a new anti-CIA organisation with a bimonthly journal called *Covert Action Information Bulletin*. An offshoot of the tainted *CounterSpy*, operating from a secret office in Washington, DC for fear of harassment, the bulletin urged a worldwide campaign to blow the cover of US spies abroad. Its tone was uncompromising. With a regular 'Naming Names' section, it called on subscribers to send in tips on possible CIA agents, with the editors promising to 'track down all your leads'.[146] Agee encouraged his followers not to stop there, but to organise public demonstrations against those named – 'both at the American embassy and at their homes', and bring pressure on the governments to throw them out.

More sinisterly, he declared that when peaceful protest fails, people should '*find other ways of fighting back* [emphasis added]'.[147] General (Ret.) Richard G. Stilwell, representing AFIO, called the bulletin a 'crime'.[148]

Files acquired by Mitrokhin claim that the bulletin was in fact founded 'on the initiative of the KGB', which set up a task force to provide it with incriminating material about the CIA.[149] With such assistance, Agee also penned two further books – *Dirty Work: The CIA in Western Europe* (1978) and *Dirty Work: The CIA in Africa* (1979) – which, taken together, exposed more than 2,000 personnel. After this, his influence in the public consciousness faded drastically. In 1983, he was left lamenting that his 'call for a continent-wide action front against the CIA's people in Latin America went nowhere. People had other preoccupations and priorities'.[150] Later in the decade, a distinctly unimpressed Oliver Stone rejected the opportunity to make a film of his life, lamenting 'it needs more Hitchcock'.[151] His post-Agency travails were a cautionary tale for anyone who dares to challenge the CIA. He lived in abject fear, had doors constantly slammed in his face and was always 'on the run'.

Calculating the exact cost of Agee's uncontrolled disclosures is difficult. No enemy of the United States has ever publicly admitted to benefiting from his revelations. Moreover, as the storm over *CounterSpy*'s role in Welch's murder underscores, correlation does not imply causation. That said, it is hard to escape the conclusion that the damage done was anything less than severe. A secret CIA investigation estimated the monetary value of Agee's exposures, as of June 1977, to be more than $2 million.[152] This figure took into account that the exposures had led to the retirement of more than 100 intelligence officers. CIA Director Turner informed the editor of the *Washington Post* that Agee had been personally responsible for 'ending the careers of a large number of patriotic and unquestionably dedicated American public servants', with the cost of those retirements picked up by the American taxpayer.[153]

However, the dollar value of the leaks tells only half the story. The aforementioned investigation reported that several CIA officers and their families, especially 'undercovers', were suffering from 'mental anguish' as a result of Agee's actions. Inexcusably, Agee had also named individuals who had no connection to the CIA but who, as a result, now lived in fear. The same investigation reported that there had been 'many instances' where the Agency's liaison contacts had been less cooperative than in the past 'because they feel the US is incapable of compelling its intelligence officers to keep secrets'.[154] Moreover, a number of prospective sources had refused to cooperate because they believed the CIA 'may be unable to protect their identities'.[155] Turner painted a similar picture to the editor of the *Washington Post*: 'The CIA does not operate in a vacuum. American national security is to a significant degree dependent on the goodwill and willing cooperation of other intelligence organisations and individuals.' He went on: 'Many foreign services and individuals will only work with us on the assurance that their efforts and sometimes even their existence be kept absolutely secret. They are becoming increasingly sceptical we can do this.'[156]

Agee had wanted to die in harness, revealing CIA secrets, but his final years were spent running a website in Havana helping US citizens to find legal loopholes to holiday in Cuba.

Chapter 4

Winning Friends and Influencing People

I. Feeling the Heat

This is to let you know that I will be leaving the Agency shortly. It is also to let you know why … We have a serious image and credibility problem with the press, public and Congress. There are a number of reasons why this cannot be corrected from within the Agency. I hope to be able to do something from without by lecturing, writing and apprising a number of key media people of the realities of the clandestine service and its role in service to our society. I also plan to organise ex-employees of the Agency to spread the word and defend you and the intelligence community. In short, I expect that I will be working on your behalf just as many hours a day after retirement as I do now.
Resignation Letter, David Atlee Phillips to all CIA personnel,
May 1975.[1]

By the mid-1970s, the CIA's image had taken a beating from not only congressional committees and crusading journalists but also dissident ex-spies, in what amounted to the closest and harshest public scrutiny of any intelligence service in history. Political discourse was awash with charges that the CIA had violated American rights, and that it was running wild around the globe, only rarely delivering to policymakers a valuable intelligence product. Post-Watergate cynicism was de rigueur – meaning, as future CIA Director Robert Gates has written, that any allegation against the CIA, no matter how far-fetched, was treated as 'automatically credible'.[2]

With three decades of dubious clandestine dealings laid bare, at Langley two distinct camps emerged on how to deal with the huge loss in popular support for the Agency. In one camp were those who believed that the CIA had to ride out the storm through a combination of secrecy and stonewalling. George H. W. Bush, DCI from January 1976 to January 1977, was firmly of this opinion. In March 1976, fresh from a grilling by the press in which a reporter said that the journalistic profession thinks intelligence officers 'all lying bastards', he told President Ford that the best approach would be to 'get the CIA off the front pages and at some point out of the papers altogether'.[3] John McMahon, CIA Deputy Director of Operations from 1978 to 1981 and later Deputy Director of the CIA under William Casey, was of the same mind:

> You have to live with the fact that when it screws up, it's going to get a lot of publicity, and when it does good, you're not going to see it. That's the life of an intelligence officer. If the people can't deal with that, they ought to be Fuller brush salesmen.[4]

Richard Bissell simply could not see any practical alternatives. Asked in an interview if the CIA should explain itself better, he replied: 'I don't know how it would go about that'.[5]

In the other camp were those who held that the embattled CIA had to fight back, even if this meant reneging on the principle of secrecy that had long been a feature of the CIA's culture. For DCIs Colby and Turner, as well as leading operators like Atlee Phillips, the lesson learned from the recent scandals was that it was better to contribute to the public debate about intelligence than to remain silent while it was being contested. Operating in complete silence, they argued, was self-defeating; it bred suspicion and helped to blow mistakes out of proportion. 'The past secrecy', suggested Turner, 'meant that there was no way for the American public to balance past achievements of the intelligence community with alleged abuses.'[6] The intelligence 'flap' had ushered in a brave new world where the public demanded assurances that what intelligence agencies do is ethical, effective and worth the enormous outlay of public funds. As Colby wrote in his memoir *Honorable Men*, 'The CIA must build, not assume, public support, and it can do this only by informing the public of the nature of its activities and accepting the public's control over them.'[7] In short, it was better for the country to know something about the CIA than to imagine the worst.

The danger of inaction was judged to be severe. Firstly, without public support, there was concern that the Agency's very existence was at stake. As AFIO President John Blake warned in a letter to CIA alumnus Scott Breckinridge, 'There are strident voices, some well-intentioned, who would seek to reduce the intelligence community to a discussion group on international affairs.'[8] Acting CIA Director Frank Carlucci later looked back at the mid-1970s as a period when 'the need for a vigorous intelligence organisation in a free society was seriously challenged on many fronts', by not only media pundits, but also future presidential candidates like Fred Harris and Morris Udall.[9] Secondly, it was feared that unless public confidence was restored, the CIA would be subject to further investigations. Moreover, it was hoped that by opening up of its own volition, the Agency would lessen the likelihood of external forces railroading it into more far-reaching transparency initiatives. As Herbert Hetu, Turner's principal public affairs adviser, emphasised: 'Things are not going to go backward, and we'd better do it in our own way and at our own rate.'[10] Thirdly, lack of public support was seen as having a damaging effect on morale, as well as making it harder to attract new recruits. Finally, in failing to promote public understanding, it was felt that the CIA would jeopardise its vital relationships with intelligence allies. Since the CIA had become a public whipping boy, Phillips had observed that 'our friends overseas are saying thanks but no thanks', fearful of working with an organisation that had a bad reputation, but also could not be trusted to keep secrets. Phillips even had 'a friend from another country's intelligence network ask to return the documents he had given us'.[11]

This chapter will explore how the CIA gradually came round to the view that a public relations policy was a gamble worth taking. It will be shown that this was a bumpy ride, with backtracking and considerable resistance. Convincing opponents that PR was a valuable undertaking, and did not amount to the CIA 'blowing its own cover', was never going to be easy. As Hetu explained, 'They are all good Americans, but they've been taught for thirty years to keep their mouth shut'.[12] It will be shown that efforts in the realm of opinion-forming came in three waves. The first was initiated by Colby, but only went so far, prompting a second 'unofficial' wave carried out by loyal CIA veterans like Ray Cline and Phillips. Phillips called this his 'Last Assignment' and it involved writing books and press articles, as well as speaking at universities. He also founded AFIO, recruiting members from across the US intelligence community to organise conferences, workshops and publications that spoke out in favour of US intelligence. His private campaign to mobilise public support was analogous to Scott Lucas's idea that, during the Cold War, there were 'state-private networks' lying behind the more formal institutional structures of the national security state that championed American values and institutions.[13] Although he received no official help from Langley, his crusade to rehabilitate the CIA's image can be seen as an extension of this wider psychological battle. The final wave came from Turner. During his tenure as Director

(March 1977 to January 1981), public relations at CIA were finally put on an institutional footing.

It is important to underline from the outset that CIA public relations certainly did not mean baring all the secrets of the company; nor was it a unilateral reduction of secrecy. It signalled a shift from what political scientist Peter Gill, in the UK context, has described as a defensive approach to information control to an offensive strategy of 'persuasion'.[14] Nothing that came out of the CIA or the public defenders would excite or satisfy the advocates of freedom of information. CIA officers themselves even admitted this. Phillips had no shame in calling himself a 'propagandist' for the Agency.[15] Similarly, speaking at the second annual AFIO conference in Reston, Virginia, in September 1976, CIA veteran Sam Halpern said to a member of the audience that 'he must have rocks in his head if he thought I was going to reveal any secrets'.[16]

What occurred were calculated educative efforts to make the CIA less of a bogeyman, dispel some of the mystery, and defend its record against what Phillips called 'snowballing innuendo'. This was about telling the American public that the security of the US from communism and other threats demanded a permanent foreign intelligence service and that the men and women at the CIA were working, responsibly, with high risk and little reward. It was about convincing people that lessons had been learned, and gone were the days when the CIA violated constitutional rights, invaded privacy and abetted *coup d'états*. It was about emphasising that analysis – not covert action – was the CIA's chief function. As Phillips stated in an interview for the *Dallas Texas Herald*, 'The truth would be better served if the CIA symbol were … a stack of three by five cards and a typewriter'.[17] It was also about raising awareness about the importance of secrecy, something people had perhaps lost sight of during the years of scandal.

II. The Last Assignment

AFIO believes that speaking 'from the outside' can do much to make the job of those still on 'the inside' a lot easier.
John Blake, AFIO President.[18]

As historian Rhodri Jeffreys-Jones has written, between the autumn of 1974, when press reports first surfaced linking the CIA with attempts to destabilise Salvador Allende's democratically elected Marxist regime in Chile, and the start of 1976, when the House counterpart to the Church Committee under Congressman Otis Pike had its report leaked, it was 'open season' on the CIA.[19] The person tasked with steering the Agency through this political storm was William Colby, a career intelligence officer, who had joined the fledgling organisation in 1950 and who, before this, had been a member of the OSS. For the most part, as Thomas Powers has shown, Colby climbed steadily through the ranks, progressing in a way that neither made enemies nor generated much by way of anecdote.[20] This changed when the United States went to war in Vietnam. In 1959, he was thrust into the worsening crisis in South-east Asia as Station Chief in Saigon, before becoming in 1962 head of the CIA's Far East Division, responsible for the doomed cause of trying to win the hearts and minds of the Vietnamese people.

Appointed steward of the CIA in September 1973, he inherited an organisation that had practically no interest in seeking publicity. In 1971, the idea was raised of celebrating the CIA's twenty-fifth anniversary the following year with some television and radio coverage, but was quickly rejected. 'We do not feel the Agency should embark on a public relations programme,' concluded senior officers. 'To do so would open a Pandora's Box so to speak and do us more harm than good.'[21] The reasoning behind this decision was explained in a document entitled 'Should the Agency concern itself with the public understanding of the role of intelligence?'[22] It claimed that the CIA would find it difficult to say anything worthwhile without compromising sources and methods: 'As long as sources and methods must continue to be fully protected, it would seem doubtful that the Agency and its role can ever be credibly presented to the American public.'[23] Recalling the period of the *Ramparts* disclosure, when DCI Helms had stayed quiet, believing 'that the winds of the storm were blowing too strongly to be heard', the report questioned whether public relations could realistically drown out the critical noises coming out of the press. Specifically, it doubted whether anyone would care to listen to the CIA when they were too preoccupied with the Pentagon Papers scandal – a 'wind that [was] blowing just as strongly, but from another direction.'[24]

The report also referred to the American public as a 'curious people' who, because of their individuality, were 'collectively slow learners who only begin to catch on through a process of repetition'. To win them over, therefore, public relations would need to be a rolling programme rather than a one-off project, like honouring the anniversary. The problem with a sustained effort, it was argued, was that the public would come to expect more and more, to the point where it would become impossible for the CIA to stay silent on certain issues. Put another way, the appetite would grow with the eating. For these reasons, the extent of public outreach in the years immediately before Colby was the decision by DCI James Schlesinger in 1973 to erect CIA road signs pointing to Langley headquarters. Amusingly, even this token gesture failed. According to a CIA report, the sign along the southbound of Route 123 disappeared nine times – 'almost overnight' – every time it was put up.[25] Alas, the nation's premier spy agency never caught the offenders and was forced to accept that the signs 'now grace the walls of some local bedrooms or fraternity houses'.[26]

Colby's track record suggested that he too would have little desire to make the CIA more open. With his grey suits, grey slicked-back hair, and grey face, he had the look of an invisible man. Throughout his career, when faced with a question he did not care to answer, his tactic was to tilt his head back so that light reflected off his pastel horn-rimmed glasses, simultaneously blinding the questioner and turning his eyes into steely blank white discs.[27] Colby had been at the centre of the CIA's 'Secret War' in Laos, where thousands of jungle warriors had been hired to fight communist guerrillas on the western fringes of Vietnam, and had directed 'Operation Phoenix', the hugely controversial pacification programme in South Vietnam which, critics charged, led to the indiscriminate arrest, torture and murder of thousands of political cadremen. At Colby's confirmation hearings in July 1973, where he put the body count from Phoenix at 20,000, anti-war activists marched through Washington with 'Wanted' posters featuring his face, a skull and crossbones and the ace of spades, a symbol of death. One of the protesters was Daniel Ellsberg, of Pentagon Papers fame, who took to the streets with a placard that read, 'William Colby Murders Humans and Democracy'.

However, in what came as a shock to many of his colleagues, Colby took a number of steps designed to educate the public about what the intelligence business was all about. In the hope of putting stories about the CIA into proper perspective, and mirroring the strategy employed by Dulles in the 1950s, he gave informal background briefings to certain journalists and arranged lunches with the editorial boards of some leading newspapers and magazines.[28] He fulfilled a number of speaking engagements and organised an 'alumni day' at Langley so that old-timers could reminisce about past adventures, but most importantly receive 'the answers they needed to defend the institution'.[29] He had planned to hold a monthly press conference on world affairs, but reneged on the idea when, during a trial session, he inadvertently revealed how many businessmen ('around two hundred') worked for the CIA abroad or as a cover.[30]

Most controversially, Colby adopted a policy of controlled cooperation with congressional investigators. To the Pike and Church committees, he turned over a mass of confidential documents that confirmed what he called 'bad secrets' – assassination plots, drug testing, etc. His earlier testimony before President Ford's 'blue ribbon' commission, whose purpose was to calm the outcry and thus block full investigation by Congress, was so forthcoming that the chairman, Vice President Nelson Rockefeller, admonished him, 'Bill, do you really have to present all this material to us?' He had even felt it necessary to place before a Senate committee, and the attendant TV cameras, a dart gun and several bottles of deadly shellfish toxin that had been gathering dust in the CIA storeroom. (He later admitted that this was not his smartest move.)

Many at Langley were appalled by Colby's willingness to accede to congressional requests for information, and believed that he should have given only bare-bone answers to the questions put to him by commissioners. To quote Thomas Powers, they considered it a form of 'institutional suicide', because it betrayed agents and officers who had trusted the CIA in good faith, and because it sucked outside forces into the world of intelligence – political careerists like Church, who were arguably more interested in making headlines and political point-scoring than the nation's health.[31] There was also concern that hostile intelligence services, good at nothing if not patiently looking for needles in haystacks, would benefit from the material so readily surrendered by Colby. His reckless candour, they protested, was the 'functional equivalent of giving the KGB a guided tour'.[32] Now ambassador to Iran, Richard Helms was incandescent. On 19 March 1975, he wrote a letter to journalist Charles Murphy in which he fumed:

I must say that Colby has done a startlingly successful job at making a total mess … He may have thought he could become the 'white hat', but that ploy has surely backfired now and he must look to sophisticated Washington like the biggest jerk on the block. It is all terribly sad and he had brought it all on himself by his mumblings and other matters about which he should have kept his mouth shut. The Agency committed no assassination of foreign leaders, but by the time [President] Ford and Colby get through passing their sentences, they leave the worst possible impression.[33]

Elsewhere, Helms wrote that Colby's testimony before Congress was comparable to the Bolshevik's opening up the Tsar's intelligence files after the Russian Revolution, or the Allies ransacking Nazi secret documents after World War Two.[34] Senior officers from the clandestine service – once described by CIA Director Schlesinger as Helms's 'Praetorian Guard' – could never forgive Colby for his role, at least implicit, in suggesting to the Justice Department that Helms, his former colleague and patron, had been untruthful before a Senate Committee in February 1973 when asked about CIA malefactions in Chile. For his mendacity under oath, Helms was subsequently prosecuted by the Justice Department and pleaded *nolo contendere* to a charge of misdemeanour. Outside the courthouse, his supporters gave him a hero's welcome and passed a hat to raise the $2,000 fine. Colby, meanwhile, was considered a snitch. Many years later, when his body was fished out of a river near his home in Rock Point, Maryland, after apparently suffering a heart attack while paddling his canoe on a late-night boating trip, conspiracy theorists suggested that his death was a revenge killing by the CIA's old guard who never forgave his candidness on the witness stand.

Colby's transformation from ruthless controller of the 'Phoenix Program' to confessor of sins owed less to a sudden bout of morality than a pragmatic belief that concessions were necessary to save the organisation he loved. 'The Agency's survival', he later wrote, 'could only come from understanding, not hostility, built on knowledge, not faith.'[35] He went on:

A public informed of the CIA's accomplishments and capabilities will support it. A public aware of its true mission and the limits of its authority will accept it. A public that understands the issues and problems involving intelligence and its role in the American government will debate and decide them. A public convinced of the CIA's value will help protect its true secrets.[36]

In his opinion, the CIA's strategy of trying to distance itself from scandals, hoping they would blow over, had failed. A Columbia Law School graduate, he had been taught that when a defendant tries to suppress evidence, he invariably loses the battle.[37] Watergate, he argued, was proof that the CIA should nip damaging accusations in the bud, rather than allow them to escalate. Ignoring the advice of CIA General Counsel John Warner (who said, 'Dick, no matter what, we've got to respond to this'),[38] Helms's instruction at the time had been: 'Stay cool, volunteer nothing, because it will only be used to involve us. Just stay away from the whole damn thing.'[39] However, by doing so, the CIA was perceived as having something to hide; allowed the White House to spread rumours that the CIA had masterminded the break-in, not Nixon; and raised questions 'about the Agency's good faith and its use – or abuse – of institutionalised secrecy'.[40] Colby also hoped that by volunteering 'bad secrets', there would be less congressional pressure on the CIA to relinquish 'good secrets', such as sources and methods, which deserved absolute protection.

In late 1975, Colby established a task group to assess what more could be done to improve the CIA's image.[41] The group was chaired by Lt General Samuel Vaughan Wilson, Deputy Director of the CIA. 'General Sam', as he was known, was no stranger to public relations. In 1961, then assistant to the Secretary of Defense for Special Operations, he had worked as a technical adviser on *Merrill's Marauders* (1962), a propaganda film celebrating the exploits of a US Army deep-penetration jungle warfare unit that fought in Burma in World War Two; he even appeared in and narrated the film's trailer.

Wilson delivered his report on 30 October, addressing the question

'How can we tell the intelligence story better?' The report opened with the pessimistic, but hardly surprising, observation that: 'Publicity on the CIA in the last year has not resulted in a rounded story.'[42] To correct this, the task group made several recommendations. One, the CIA should adopt a 'more open and forthcoming attitude' with the media. Specifically, it encouraged the CIA to provide more background briefings and collaborate with certain reporters in developing feature articles. Two, it called for more public appearances and presentations by Agency officials, not just the DCI. Three, it advocated approaching 'respected senior statesmen' to make positive statements championing the 'important contribution of intelligence in foreign policy formulation'. And, finally, it recommended giving 'judicious assistance' to 'selected' former employees and retirees who wanted to defend the CIA in books, articles and speeches. 'Judicious and selective', it emphasised, 'were the operative words.'[43] In other words, helping the Agees of the world was out of the question.

Interestingly, despite his desire to change public perceptions of the CIA, Colby did not endorse the suggestions. Like Dulles, he was something of a control freak when it came to public relations and only trusted himself to be the messenger. The idea that potentially dozens of employees would have the freedom to speak their mind in public was anathema to him. Colby also worried that an overly aggressive PR campaign would result in accusations that the Agency was using taxpayers' money for propaganda purposes. Relatively fresh in the memory was the outrage generated by the CBS television documentary *The Selling of the Pentagon*, aired on 23 February 1971. Narrated by Roger Mudd, the programme exposed the enormous expenditure of public funds by the military-industrial complex to win support for the armed forces. Sparking huge controversy, it revealed that the Department of Defense was annually spending $30 million on PR, sponsoring disingenuous promotional films on how the war in Vietnam was being won and even taking VIPs on cruises to Hawaii on board aircraft carriers.[44] Fearful of implicating the CIA in a similar scandal, Colby discarded the report, ruling: 'We're just going to have to take the heat.'[45]

Colby's refusal to intensify the public relations effort appeased the Helms faction at the CIA, but it did not please everyone. One of those who wanted to see more being done was David Atlee Phillips, a decorated 25-year veteran of the Agency, dubbed the 'clandestine granddaddy of Central America'. 'I was shocked because our bureaucracy had failed to fight back against … the campaign being waged against us,' he declared in a press conference.[46] Phillips was concerned about the damage that sensational headlines had on morale. An internal study carried out by John Blake, CIA Deputy Director for Administration, reported in October 1975 that, while most staff had adopted a 'hang in there' attitude, there had been a 'gradually eroding effect on the conscience and morale of employees'.[47] It claimed that many staff now felt a 'sense of embarrassment and shame' in admitting they worked for the CIA, and were mortified that a career of dedicated service was open to criticism. Indeed, there were tragic stories of company families being ripped apart, with children turning against their parents in revulsion at what they read in the news. Blake's study also reported widespread concern about the 'amount of "unproductive time" spent responding to congressional committees at the expense of carrying out basic duties and responsibilities'.[48] Having been at the CIA when it was held as 'the best' in government, Phillips feared that unless pride was restored, efficiency would be lost. He worried about the impact on recruitment of constant stories likening the CIA to cold-blooded imperialist assassins. Moreover, he was anxious that allies would refuse to work with the Agency if the negative publicity was not corrected. He ultimately decided that he had to do something when he confessed to his daughter that he worked for the CIA, not the State Department as she had been led to believe, and she replied: 'But, Daddy, that's dirty.'[49] 'I realised that we had a public relations problem of some magnitude,' he later went on record, 'so we needed a public relations programme of some magnitude.'[50]

In spring 1975, a 52-year-old Phillips boldly turned his back on his $38,000 salary and resigned. This decision was deeply felt at home. His pension of $18,000 was not enough to cover the school fees of his seven children, meaning that his wife Gina was required to get a job. 'We've gone from steak to stew,' he joked to the press.[51] Nevertheless, it was a price he was willing to pay. With Colby's 'gradual' strategy failing to keep up with the rising criticism, and with confidence in and within the CIA at an all-time low, he took it upon himself to refurbish the CIA's image from the outside.

Phillips possessed excellent credentials for what was essentially an exercise in psychological warfare. In the early 1950s, he had run the CIA's propaganda campaign against the left-wing President of Guatemala, Jacob Arbenz, paving the way for a *coup d'état* in 1954. As well as producing anti-communist literature, he organised a hugely successful pirate radio station, 'Voice of Liberation', which aired counter-revolutionary broadcasts from the neighbouring jungles in Honduras and Nicaragua.[52] Most recently, in winter 1970, he had led a special task force in Chile set up to prevent the country from electing Allende as its first socialist president. Millions of dollars were given to Allende's opponents, while newspapers were co-opted to print stories of 'communist atrocities'. The efforts were nevertheless in vain, as Allende won a plurality of the vote.

Within days of resigning, Phillips founded the Association of Retired Intelligence Officers, renamed the Association of Former Intelligence Officers (AFIO) in 1978. Membership was open to anyone who had served in the US intelligence community. The declared aim of the association was to 'defend the community' and 'promote public understanding of the role of intelligence so as to preserve and strengthen the nation's intelligence gathering and evaluation capabilities'.[53] Phillips tried to convince his old friend Ray Cline to be the association's inaugural president – a position for which he was eminently qualified. Cline had been one of the CIA's top analysts of the Soviet Union, before moving in 1969 to head the State Department's Bureau of Intelligence and Research. Like Phillips, he was an Agency 'diehard' and was concerned about the effect that negative publicity was having on the CIA's ability to carry out its mission. 'I am quite sure', he lamented, 'that recruiting agents and securing foreign cooperation is extremely difficult in this atmosphere.'[54] In 1973, he had left government service for the groves of academia, and was now Director of Studies at Georgetown University's Center for Strategic and International Studies. Keen to reach out to the public and explain the function of intelligence, he regularly spoke on television and squared off against critics of the Agency. His appearance on *The Dick Cavett Show* in June 1974, alongside Marchetti and Hersh, was particularly well received by friends of the CIA. Oliver Patton, a retired army Brigadier General, called it a 'shut-out for the lions'.[55] Cord Meyer claimed that the opposition had been made to look 'extremely foolish'.[56] It therefore came as a disappointment to Phillips that Cline turned down the offer. Despite wanting to spread the word about the need for quality intelligence, Cline was eager to cement his reputation as a 'scholarly commentator', rather than as a partisan 'CIAnik'.[57] Rebuffed, Phillips himself became the first president.

From day one, Phillips had to counter accusations that the AFIO was funded and sponsored by the CIA; the fact that its main office was in McLean, Virginia, three miles from Langley, only served to support this belief. In reality, this could not have been further from the truth. Funding came from annual dues of $10, or $200 for lifetime membership, with additional income deriving from speaker honoraria. CIA officials rejected Phillips's request for former employee contact details, meaning that he was required to identify potential members by using an old mailing list he had kept for Christmas cards.[58] Colby ordered that the AFIO receive 'no special help or relationship from the CIA', for fear that the Agency would be 'pilloried for attempting to run a covert operation on the American public'.[59] Declassified documents show that the CIA and the AFIO often did not see eye to eye. In June 1980, for

example, Agency officials were furious when the then AFIO President
Jack Blake took to the airwaves to launch a stinging attack on a PBS
documentary called *The Company*. At Langley, it was believed that
'Blake's efforts could draw too much public attention and run counter
to the Director's advice re. maintaining a low profile at this time.'[60] In
a bid to stop further statements from Blake, a CIA officer met with the
AFIO Board of Directors but – in the words of an internal CIA memo –
was 'treated with polite hostility'. The officer was sent packing with his
tail between his legs, told, in no uncertain terms, that the AFIO were
'the good guys' and would not tolerate interference from the Agency.

Despite being left to his own devices, Phillips succeeded in turning
the AFIO into a large, well-financed organisation. From humble beginnings (for the first few months AFIO HQ was Phillips's living room),
by late 1975 it had 1,000 members; by summer 1978 it had grown to
2,500 members.[61] Today, it boasts over 5,000 members, with twenty-four
active chapters across the country. Members received subscription to a
bi-monthly newsletter, *Periscope*, as well as a directory with the names
and telephone numbers of fellow members. Keen to reconnect with
colleagues from the 'old days', former DCI John McCone claimed that
the 'Membership Directory alone was worth the price'.[62] With a healthy
income, the AFIO organised annual conventions, some of which were
held in particularly luxurious settings. In 1978, for example, members
descended on the iconic Hotel Del Coronado in San Diego, a beachfront
resort famed for its signature red turrets and a setting for the classic
comedy *Some Like It Hot*, starring Marilyn Monroe. At the conventions,
members welcomed interviews from the press, held open sessions under
the lights of television cameras and gave public lectures on the need for
a strong intelligence community. Reporting on the 1976 symposium, a
journalist from the *Washington Post* wrote that he was astonished to see
more than 200 retired spooks, each 'wearing a boldly lettered name tag'.[63]

To 'get the word out', Phillips established an AFIO Speaker's Bureau
to arrange for members to talk to journalists, students, teachers, as well

as civic and professional groups. Periodic luncheons were scheduled with the press. As scholar Kathryn Olmsted has remarked, Phillips 'guaranteed that pithy, pro-CIA quotes were just a phone call away'.[64] An actor by avocation, Phillips was much more comfortable in the limelight than the quiet and retiring Colby. Accordingly, he relished speaking in front of audiences and prized the fact that some of the students who heard him speak went on to work for the CIA ('in spite of their teacher's better career advice').[65] Sneakily, if he learned in advance that Agee was speaking at a university, he would feed professors loyal to the CIA questions designed to 'make Agee squirm'.[66]

Phillips's mission to clean up the CIA's image led him to write a memoir of his quarter of a century in the clandestine services. Published in 1977, *The Night Watch* was the definitive pro-CIA book. It rejected the humanist position that covert action was undemocratic and should be outlawed, arguing instead that it was a much safer policy option than engaging the Soviet Union overtly and was a cold-blooded necessity in the era of the Cold War. British Prime Minister Winston Churchill had famously given a similar defence of unethical methods, claiming that even the noblest man, when he falls into a river of crocodiles, must smile back. A major theme of the book was that the threat of the Soviet Union had not abated, an unfortunate reality that made a secret intelligence service – and secrets – a necessity. To reinforce the importance of secrets, Phillips dedicated the book to murdered CIA Station Chief Richard Welch, and even derived the book's title from Welch's comment to a new recruit that doing 'the night watch' was a lonely but essential business.[67] Another recurring theme was that the CIA was not, as Senator Church had provocatively charged to capture the public imagination, a 'rogue elephant'. It was and always would be a servant of decisions taken in the White House. Thus, if there was blame to be apportioned, it was with the elephant rider – the President. Phillips also responded to the accusation that the CIA was not an equal-opportunities employer, and was only interested in flamboyant Ivy League graduates, preferably white, male and wealthy. To emphasise diversity in the workplace, he pointed out that he appointed the first female head of station.[68]

As well as keeping its distance from the AFIO, the CIA gave Phillips no support whatsoever with *The Night Watch*. The Agency was obstructionist – dragging its feet when it came to vetting the manuscript and insisting on arbitrary deletions of text that had no bearing on national security. In a private correspondence, Phillips commented 'that on the Agency's scale of preferential occupations for ex-employees a second career in writing has plummeted to a cut above double agents and a shade below gunrunners'.[69] His experience of the clearance process was, in his words, 'entirely consistent with the CIA's public image: murky and at times disconcerting'.[70] Endless meetings were held, spread over many months, 'wrangling over what is secret and what is not'. By the time the book went into print, he was utterly demoralised. There is a case to be made that the CIA missed a trick in not helping Phillips. The memoir genre was a powerful social force. Regularly appearing on bestseller lists, memoirs had the capacity to shape public opinion either for or against the CIA. Marchetti, McGarvey and Agee all realised this and had used books to do much damage to the Agency's reputation. The CIA was behind the curve.

III. The American Model of Intelligence

We are trying to be more open … not publicity gimmicks, but sincere attempts to level with the American people without damaging that ongoing work which must be kept secret to succeed.
CIA Director Admiral Stansfield Turner.[71]

When Admiral Stansfield Turner became DCI in March 1977, he carried with him a clear directive from President Jimmy Carter, a fellow Naval Academy classmate, to better acquaint the public with the

CIA. Both he and the President had been hugely impressed by the campaigning of the loyal veterans, and could not understand why the CIA had not given them more support. 'We operate well when the public is informed,' he told *Time* magazine in June 1977.[72] Like Atlee Phillips, he had observed a seismic shift in the relationship between the CIA and the public that could not be wished away. The recent exposures and investigations had confirmed to him that public trust in the Agency could not be taken for granted; it had to be earned. Since trust was an essential buffer against further congressional probing of the CIA, and since secrecy was believed only to breed suspicion, it was of paramount importance, so Turner felt, to interact with the public and address their concerns. Forged in the crucible of public examination, the new reality was that the CIA's very existence relied on its ability, within the constraints of national security interests, to tell the American people and Congress that it was 'back on track'; had learned from its mistakes; and was functioning within the law and in a responsible and effective manner. 'You will be hearing from the intelligence community,' Turner declared at a gathering of the Commonwealth Club of California in summer 1977. 'I intend to make the public one of the direct beneficiaries of our efforts to a degree which has never been attempted before.'[73]

At Langley, many old Agency hands were aghast at Turner's promise to usher in a new era of openness. If the door was opened even slightly, they feared, it would soon be forced open completely; more questions would be raised than answered; and the day-to-day practice of intelligence would be left a demoralised shambles. Worries also remained that a more outward-reaching CIA would be accused of running a domestic operation to brainwash the American people. Winning over the sceptics was not going to be easy; indeed, *Detroit News* called it 'Mission Impossible'.[74] Turner, however, was not prepared to take 'no' for an answer. Ignoring the hallway murmurings of discontent, he emphasised in one of his first internal communications as Director that his openness strategy was to be no 'passing fancy'. 'Can we ride out the current efforts by the public and the press to uncover every secret operation in the expectation that this will pass and, when it does, we will be able to return to the traditional secrecy we once enjoyed?' he asked rhetorically – 'The answer is a simple but unequivocal, no.'[75] The effects of whistle-blowers and renegades, he claimed, would have been 'far less severe' if the public had had a better understanding of how the CIA benefited the national well-being. Turner also explained that staff should not mistake his intentions as total transparency. 'This does not mean that we are going to throw open the front doors and unlock the files,' he underlined: 'Legitimate secrets must be protected as vigorously as ever.'[76] As he announced to an audience at the Beverly Wilshire Hotel in Los Angeles on 12 August 1977, he desired a 'new, distinctly American model of intelligence' that safeguarded vital national security secrets but also helped to promote a citizenry that was informed about intelligence.[77]

The individuals most opposed to Turner's progressive strategy were typically those who had been recruited during the early days of the Cold War. No matter how hard Turner tried to convince these seasoned cold warriors that greater openness was in the CIA's best interests, they were never likely to get on board with the programme. However, they were a declining force, and their days were numbered. Running parallel with his promise of institutionalising PR at the CIA, Turner launched a high-level purge of the Agency, with the clandestine services targeted for major housecleaning. In 1977 alone, he summarily dismissed 820 officers from the clandestine services, which amounted to an 8 per cent reduction in the CIA's workforce.[78] Angry at the purge but also at the manner of the firings (unlucky souls were selected by computer and received terse pink slips instructing them to leave by the close of play), several senior officers resigned in protest. In summer 1977, on successive Fridays, there were retirement parties for three of the CIA's longest-serving officers: Ted Shackley, George Carver and Dan Arnold. None had been dismissed; Shackley and Carver choose retirement in preference to accepting a job that would have represented a *de facto* demotion, while Arnold left because he had lost all respect for the new chief.[79]

Turner had his reasons for driving out the old guard. One, the purge was designed to provide greater opportunities for younger officers, who had long complained that the CIA had been run like a 'family business' and that the channels for promotion had been blocked for years by the old-boy network. Two, it was a chance to thin out the bloated ranks of the covert operators – the elitist Ivy League veterans who played elaborate spy games, like using depilatory cigars to deprive Castro of his 'macho' beard, and who had grown dramatically in size with the Vietnam War, hence the expression 'The Vietnam Bulge'. In their stead would be a new breed of 'analyst spy', valued more for his or her ability to think and interpret. And, finally, it allowed Turner to consolidate his own authority against badmouthing veterans, resentful of his navy background and 'hard right rudder' manner. Whatever Turner's motivation for the cuts, the knock-on effect was that the people most hostile to PR were on their way out.

In his first appointment after becoming DCI, Turner named Herbert Hetu to head a new Public Affairs Office, with a mandate to educate the American public about the role of intelligence processes.[80] A retired navy captain, Hetu knew nothing about intelligence, but everything about public relations. His career had involved twenty-one years in the field of public affairs. In 1961, he had been navy press officer in the Office of the Assistant Secretary of Defense for Public Affairs in Washington, before becoming head of the audio-visual branch of the navy's Office of Information in 1962. After a brief career break to complete an MSc in Public Relations at Boston University, he was assigned as Public Affairs Officer for the Caribbean Sea Frontier and the Tenth Naval District in San Juan, Puerto Rico. Most recently, he had directed the media operations of the American Revolution Bicentennial Administration. With good reason, Turner confidently predicted that 'Herb', as he called him, would be of 'great value to me in the PA field'.[81]

As an outsider buzzing with reformist ideas, Hetu was, unsurprisingly, not welcomed with open arms by all of his new colleagues. Indeed, some of the old-school holdovers saw him as a heretic; at one meeting, an officer turned to him and said, 'You are hurting us when potential agents read we have a PR office. They could get killed.'[82] There was also jealously that Hetu answered only to Turner and had the title of 'Assistant to the Director'. Such was the bad blood felt towards him in those early days, Hetu later joked to the *Washington Post* that every morning, before driving to work, he would check underneath his car for explosives![83] With Turner's full support, however, he would revolutionise the CIA's approach to publicity. In just over a year, the number of staff working in the Office of Public Affairs went from one (Hetu) to twenty (ten professionals, six clericals and four part-timers).[84]

Hetu produced a report – 'Suggestions for CIA Outreach to the Public' – weighing up the pros and cons of certain PR initiatives.[85] The bulk of the proposals were put into immediate effect. The most sweeping change related to the CIA's dealings with the press. Happy to talk to reporters, Colby had made a modicum of progress in this area but his grasp of media relations was limited, meaning that the job of the CIA's press person was largely to keep abreast of what was being written about the Agency and archive the clippings.[86] This contrasted starkly with the situation in other government agencies, where stories were routinely given to certain journalists and where specialists were employed to spin the scandal *du jour* and answer awkward questions in a way that satisfied the press but did not reveal too much.[87] Recognising the danger of leaving journalists to their own devices, and seeing the media as a valuable collaborator in raising the stock of the CIA, Hetu sought to put into effect similar practices at Langley.

Central to Hetu's fresh approach to the press was to abolish the traditional 'no comment' mentality, and to get the Agency responding to as many questions as possible. If a question could not be answered, the onus was put on CIA officials to explain why. 'When asked questions by the press', Turner proudly announced in August 1978, 'we still have to say "no comment" at times, but our needle is not stuck in that groove any more.'[88] For example, in April 1977, Turner received a large volume of requests from the press soliciting information about his personal life. Despite privately considering them 'nosey' and 'impertinent', he answered as many he could, revealing in the process that he slept seven to eight hours a night; kept fit with squash and tennis; enjoyed reading historical novels; earned $57,000 per annum; met his wife at Sunday School on 23 December 1953; and owned a golden retriever dog called Hornblower.[89]

Hetu greatly increased the quantity of CIA press releases. During 1979, some 139 unclassified background briefings were provided on substantive issues, while a further 100 were produced between January and September 1980.[90] While far from revelatory, they enabled the media to gain a better-rounded appreciation of contemporary security threats.

In an attempt to bolster the morale of staff and their families, stories about CIA employees receiving awards or special recognition were given to their local or home newspapers.[91] In an even bolder move, in late October 1977, the CIA briefed 100 members of the Sigma Delta Journalism Society at its headquarters at Langley. This was the first time in its thirty-year history that such an event had occurred. Guests had to submit their names to the Agency two weeks in advance, while cameras and tape recorders were forbidden. The *Baltimore Sun* was hugely impressed, reporting that guests were welcomed with smiles, handshakes and refreshments, and were given a packet containing maps, charts and a photograph of Turner. The briefing lasted for about thirty minutes, after which reporters were allowed to ask questions for nearly one hour.[92]

Thinking of journalists less as enemies and more as possible allies, Hetu worked with certain sections of the media on collaborative projects. In one of his first initiatives, he approached CBS with the idea of filming a 'Who's Who' segment inside Langley. Provided the producers were ready to accommodate certain security restrictions, he believed that such a programme was a 'good vehicle for a few selected positive points about the CIA'.[93] The suggestion raised more than a few eyebrows, especially among the old guard who were still troubled by the notion of an intelligence neophyte like Hetu meddling in their business. Paul Walsh, Associate Deputy Director for Intelligence, called on Turner to 'think long and hard' before agreeing to the venture.[94] His main concern was CBS's intrepid broadcast journalist Dan Rather – then correspondent for the Sunday evening news show *60 Minutes*. 'I have no confidence', feared Walsh, 'that he would not use the show to air his own personal views about the CIA and the Intelligence Community.'[95] Another objection, raised by the CIA's Director of Security Robert Gambino, was that by cooperating with CBS the CIA would set a precedent that might compel it to work with the other TV networks.[96] Hetu was not blind to the risks involved, but put it to Turner that it was better for the CIA to open up, on its own terms, than be forced to do so by external forces such as Congress. 'I think it is better to move in the direction of openness voluntarily and in an orderly fashion,' he wrote. 'We may as well get credit for opening our doors and enjoy the credibility that goes with such a decision.'[97] Turner agreed. On 24 July 1977, CBS's *60 Minutes* aired 'Report on the CIA', marking the first time that television cameras had been allowed into the headquarters building.

No sooner was the CBS programme a wrap, Hetu sunk his teeth into an even bigger project, this time with ABC's *Good Morning America*. With the thirtieth anniversary of the CIA approaching on Saturday 17 September 1977, he proposed to celebrate on the day with a one-hour programme illustrating 'what the CIA does and how it operates'.[98] The hour would be divided into four pre-recorded segments, each lasting roughly eight minutes, filmed at CIA headquarters. It would also include a live interview with Turner at ABC's Washington studio. In a bid to leave nothing to chance, Hetu provided the producers with a list of possible subjects for them to cover. Subjects included: the automated cartography programme; the HQ Library; recruitment; security procedures (burn bags, safes and vaults); and the preparation of analytical materials on issues such as the Soviet economy, oil, weather and ecology.[99] Although there was no expectation from the CIA for these to be used, Hetu was 'confident' that ABC would not screw them and that 'the product will sell itself'.[100]

Hetu's optimism was not misplaced; ABC stuck pretty much to the plan. Scheduling issues meant that the show had to be aired on Friday 16 September, twenty-four hours before the actual anniversary, but this hardly qualified as a disaster. At the last minute, ABC also decided to move the location of Turner's live interview to the city's Foggy Bottom neighbourhood at 2430 E Street, the yellow-brick building that housed the OSS and then the CIA from 1947 to 1961. Again, this was not a disaster. Indeed, there was a nice symmetry in Turner proselytising the CIA from the very same location where both Donovan and Dulles, the two great 'salesmen' of US intelligence, cut their cloth.

As predicted, the CIA's willingness to work with CBS and then ABC was interpreted by other sections of the media as a sign that they too would be entitled to privileges. Unsurprisingly, the CIA remained selective about what projects they involved themselves in, with each case being scrupulously judged on its own merits. For example, in April 1978, Hetu was approached by Richard Reeves of the *National Editor* asking if he could spend a week with a CIA officer stationed overseas. While acknowledging that the proposal was 'certainly imaginative and intriguing', Hetu rejected it on security grounds.[101]

Among the lucky beneficiaries was John Wilhelm, associate producer for the PBS television show *In Search of the Real America*, who was given permission for an eight-person crew to film at headquarters on 15 April 1978.[102] Another was Evert Clark of *Newsweek* who was allowed to interview Turner in August 1977, but only after Hetu had considered every possible angle, from *Newsweek*'s circulation ('3,000,000') to Clark's manner ('softly spoken'). Hetu ultimately concluded that Clark was 'generally a friend of the CIA' who wanted to 'project our point of view'.[103] In June 1977, good working relations were also established with *Time* – a laudable triumph on Hetu's part when we remember that only three years earlier the bestselling weekly had famously pictured Colby on its front cover with the menacing headline, 'The CIA: Has It Gone Too Far?' To the magazine's delight, Hetu arranged for diplomatic correspondent Strobe Talbott to interview Turner, as well as Robert Bowie, Director of the CIA's National Foreign Assessment Center, and his Deputy, Sayre Stevens. Talbott thanked Hetu for 'the extraordinary cooperation you extended to us', revealing that the interviews had provided him with enough material to 'draw on for months to come'.[104]

In a move that delighted Atlee Phillips, Turner established a Speaker's Bureau at CIA. Operating out of the Public Affairs Office, the Bureau was responsible for coordinating a regular schedule of travel and speaking engagements for 'well-qualified public speakers to represent the Agency', especially at the grassroots level in places like schools, universities and professional groups.[105] At first, the majority of appearances were performed by Turner and Hetu, who took to the task with great alacrity. 'The Turners and the Hetus will always be there,' stated Hetu passionately in one memo.[106] In his talks, Turner emphasised that, simply by being there, he showed how far the Agency had come in the openness stakes. 'As little as five to eight years ago, this talk probably would not have taken place,' he declared to an audience of 650 people at a joint luncheon of the San Diego Kiwanis Club and Chamber of Commerce in August 1978.[107] So ubiquitous did Turner become on the speaking circuit that the *Detroit News* even joked that he was 'getting to be a bore'.[108] Yet, there was no shortage of invitations. As early as 5 April 1977, Hetu lamented that it had become impossible for the Admiral and himself to keep pace with the sheer volume of requests.[109] In time, thankfully, a host of alternative speakers came forward. In 1979, therefore, the CIA could boast that the DCI and the DD/CIA had carried the CIA's message to some thirty major audiences, while other officers had addressed some thirty individual groups locally and outside of the DC metropolitan area.[110]

Hetu and his team provided in-house training for 'volunteer' speakers and even considered employing Carl Byoir & Associates, one of the three largest PR firms in the country, at a rate of $1,000 a day.[111] It is unclear from documentary evidence whether this was pursued, but it is probably safe to assume that Turner was warned off. If word had got out that the CIA was using taxpayer's dollars to instruct its staff in the dark art of media manipulation, there would have been outrage. This did not stop seasoned speakers from imparting words of wisdom based on their own public encounters. Scott Breckinridge, a one-time Deputy Inspector General of the CIA who spent many hours in his retirement fighting the Agency's corner in public, sent the Public Affairs Office a document distilling 'lessons learned'. It emphasised that 'the image one portrays is in the final analysis just about as important as the message itself'.[112] Breckinridge's experience was that audiences often liked or disliked a person based on their mannerisms, thus rendering a 'sense of humour absolutely essential'. The more earnest and sombre the individual, the more disengaged the listener. In a panel situation, involving two or more speakers, Breckinridge recommended a 'little sparring', provided it was always done with a smile and gave the impression of 'liking the other person'.[113] 'If the audience likes you as a person', he underlined, 'they will want to believe you and find the best in what you say.' Above all, Breckinridge implored speakers never to forget the 'three Ps' that must be observed for a speech to be effective – 'be PRINCIPLED, be PREPARED, and be PLEASANT'.[114]

The Speaker's Bureau arranged talks that centred upon certain key issues, including the continuing need for good intelligence; the difficult ethical and moral choices faced by the CIA in its daily operations;

the checks and balances of the oversight process; the continuing and indispensable contribution of human intelligence; and the high quality of the intelligence professional.[115] As a public speaker, Turner was especially keen to emphasise that, while he was committed to demystifying the CIA, secrecy was not a 'dirty word' and there would always be sensitive matters that must be safeguarded. 'Secrecy of itself is not bad,' he underlined in one speech: 'It permits personnel the freedom to provide their views and ideas to their seniors in confidence. It permits us to deal with nations which would not speak with us if we could not assure them of the confidentiality of their thoughts.'[116] Speaking before the Greater Los Angeles Press Club in April 1979, he tried to turn the tables on reporters by stressing that, just like the press, the CIA had a responsibility to protect its sources: 'When we have an "exclusive", we try to hold on to it as long as we can.'[117]

The biggest problem for any speaker was how to respond to tough questions without stonewalling. No speaker wanted to get into a heated debate about covert action – nor did they want to swim in the murky waters of the Kennedy assassination, the Phoenix Program in Vietnam, Chile, Watergate, or the charge that the CIA had violated the civil rights of US citizens. Yet, these were matters that interested many Americans. Thus, defensive lines were needed to avoid giving the much-maligned standing order of 'no comment'. In his 'lessons learned' document, Breckinridge gave advice on how to tackle sensitive subjects. On the issue of covert action, he recommended taking the line that it was in accordance with a long-standing principle of successive US administrations to use the minimum amount of force necessary to protect US security. In short, it was a valuable 'third option' between doing nothing and sending in the troops, which was anathema to many Americans. 'In discussing para-military efforts', he coached, 'it must be shown that ... we could use the Marines and 5,000 guns or we use six agents and $50,000.'[118] He encouraged speakers to make the point that ethical concerns relating to covert action are never absolute; rather, they must be weighed against the seriousness of the threat and the viability of other policy options, including the likelihood of a diplomatic resolution and the wisdom of a military response. Above all, when asked anything about covert action, the golden rule was to highlight 'where the marching orders came from' – 1600 Pennsylvania Avenue.[119]

When faced with controversial questions, Breckinridge's advice to speakers was to deftly and quickly move the conversation on to safer ground. Engineering a shift in the discussion, without being brusque or evasive, was not, he argued, as difficult as it sounded. At the core of every tricky question was a suspicion that the CIA was either immoral or incompetent. The trick, therefore, was to turn the question on its head by providing concrete instances of where that was not the case. 'Cite some intelligence successes,' he urged. 'We are not without ammunition to refute arguments that American intelligence is inept.'[120] Every speaker, he advocated, should have at their fingertips a success story capable of sidestepping a contentious issue. His favourite was the fact that the CIA had 'spotted Soviet nuclear missiles being delivered into Cuba in 1962'. Also in his locker, ready to use if caught under fire, was the fact that the CIA had given 'seven years' warning on the development of the Moscow anti-ballistic missile system'.[121]

Revamping media relations and launching a speaker's programme were only two elements of Hetu's grand strategy of revolutionising CIA engagement with the public. Another major development was the introduction of visits to CIA headquarters. 'Having the public see, hear and talk to Agency employees is at the heart of the programme to restore and sustain public confidence,' underlined one internal document.[122] The idea of 'CIA Tours' had originally been put forward by E. Henry Knoche, acting DCI in early 1977. His suggestion was to invite Congressmen to Langley and allow them to be photographed so that they 'could look good in front of their constituents'.[123] Copying similar tours that were used by the White House, the FBI and

Department of Defense for a number of years, he proposed setting up a walk-through display area and giving guests the chance to watch 'old Agency PR films'.[124] Turner thought it a brilliant idea, so brilliant in fact that he wanted to invite more than just politicians. His enthusiasm is evidenced by the handwritten notes he scribbled on Knoche's report. Next to the suggestion of showing a short PR film, he wrote: 'Let's get a new one'; in the left-hand marginalia of the page, he scrawled the word 'great' with a big exclamation mark.[125]

To test the feasibility of opening its doors to visitors, the CIA established a working group and organised eight trial tours over eight weeks in summer 1977, involving no fewer than 3,700 participants (3,500 of these were family members of Agency employees; the rest were navy officers' wives). Each tour began in the auditorium, nicknamed the 'bubble', with a few introductory remarks by Turner. This was followed by a slide presentation on the history of intelligence. Visitors were then given a walking tour of the facility (ground and first floors only), before being taken to the ground-floor passageway between the main building and the auditorium, where a range of exhibits had been set up, including photographs from the Cuban Missile Crisis and a camera from a U-2.[126] Coffee and doughnuts were available in the cafeteria. Feedback was extremely positive; Turner's opening address was 'very favourably received', while over two-thirds of participants claimed that the public would enjoy the tour. In terms of constructive criticism, there was a general consensus that pre-school children made too much noise and should be left at home, while some visitors recommended that security should be less visible, since at times they had felt that they were being 'monitored'.[127]

The working group made several recommendations based on the eight weeks of testing. Unsurprisingly, it considered 'open house' days for the general public as wholly unsuitable. In the interests of security, it was calculated that a five-hour open house from 10 a.m. to 3 p.m. would require an additional forty-five Federal Protective Service officers, ten CIA security officers, as well as five audio countermeasure engineers to perform a sweep of the area opened to the public. This would cost $5,800. Tour guides and cleaning personnel would also be needed, bringing the total cost of additional staffing to approximately $7,500.[128] No amount of extra security could fully protect against a 'staged incident', and it was unclear how undercovers would be able to access headquarters undetected while large numbers of the public were milling around. (It had been suggested that they assemble at somewhere remote in Northern Virginia and be bussed into a rear loading dock area, but this was rejected.)

Beyond the logistical and financial problems, the working party had other concerns. It worried that visitors might misunderstand, and be put off by, the increased security that would have to occur, and by the bag checks necessary to guard against possible 'bomb or audio endeavours'.[129] At a time when the CIA was stressing the importance of safekeeping its secrets to Congress, they feared that an open house would be read as an unnecessary security risk. They also had doubts about how it might be perceived by the press. An open house was hardly a subtle approach to image-building. Journalists might see it as 'huckstering' – a flashy attempt to sell the CIA like 'Disneyland'.[130] For his part, Hetu thought it a 'bit too "gimmicky"'. He also wondered if people would not come away from the experience disappointed.[131] Langley, after all, was a 'grey' office building.

Having ruled out the open house idea, the working party agreed that the best option was controlled visits handled on a case-by-case basis. To minimise disruption and security problems, they would be scheduled for the evenings or on weekends, while potential visitors would have to write to the Public Affairs Office at least two months prior to their proposed visit date. It was emphasised that parts of the complex would have to be 'sanitised' before the visitors arrived, including the employees' bulletin board where staff posted notices about homes to rent or cars for sale. It was also recommended that the CIA produce an improved, 28-minute version of the multimedia show on intelligence history in the bubble.[132]

Turner enthusiastically endorsed the suggestions on 19 October 1977, believing that CIA visitations would make a positive contribution to 'lifting the mystique' that surrounded the institution. As he opined to a group of reporters a few months earlier, tours of Langley would 'dispel the myth that people here are running around with cloak and daggers and long fangs and black hats', revealing instead that they were 'serious students who enjoy reading and writing'.[133] Unthinkable to a previous generation of spooks, in 1979 forty-one groups, totalling several thousand people, visited Langley for tours, briefings or presentations by the DCI.[134] Visitors included the National Newspaper Association; the Young Presidents' Organisation; Boy Scout troops; citizens groups; grade school classes; as well as alumni from Princeton, Cornell, MIT, Amherst and Vassar.[135] Hetu reported that 'special' visits for 'selected' groups were 'well worth the effort', while an internal communication claimed that they had 'resulted in a greatly enlightened and supportive segment of the American public'.[136]

Academic dignitaries and university presidents were also among the visitors to Langley, with some even being cleared for Secret briefings.[137] With good reason, the CIA had been nervous about meeting with academics. The scholarly community was generally believed to be hostile or critical of the CIA. Holding academia to be an independent free spirit, many universities had been horrified by claims during the Church Committee that a number of professors and administrators had secretly worked for the Agency, recruiting prospective agents among students and faculty, gathering intelligence while abroad and spying on radical elements. As a result of these hearings, some universities created guidelines banning the CIA from their campuses. In 1977, a public spat broke out between Turner and Harvard President Derek Bok when the latter drew up a code of professional conduct to govern contractual arrangements between Harvard employees and the CIA.

Bok's guidelines required both parties to notify the university of any contractual relations, a condition Turner flatly refused to accept. In assessing the value of reaching out to academia, officials also worried that intractable critics in the press would misinterpret the CIA's intentions as an attempt to co-opt a new generation of academic collaborators; the headlines would be 'CIA TRIES TO SEDUCE UNIVERSITY PRESIDENTS'.[138] On reflection, however, they decided that it was a risk worth taking. 'The target academics', enthused Knoche, 'are among the most prestigious and influential regional experts in the United States, and in each instance where we succeed in improving their understanding and appreciation of the intelligence process there would be a "multiplier effect" among both faculty and students'.[139]

The final piece in Hetu's PR jigsaw was memoirs. Both he and Turner had been mystified by the CIA's unwillingness to support the writings of loyal ex-spies. As a popular form of literature, memoirs, in their opinion, played an important role in shaping the CIA's image with the broad-based American public. An internal correspondence from the period (sadly the exact date is unknown) shared this view, suggesting that if the CIA wanted to enhance 'attitudinal acceptance by the "grass roots"', it should support 'first person spy memoirs of a colourful nature'.[140] With the likes of Agee spreading poison, Hetu and Turner found it counterproductive that the CIA should have made life so difficult for Atlee Phillips and his AFIO followers. 'Memoirs', emphasised the above correspondence, 'would be a counterforce to destructive, uncontrolled leaks by former employees'.[141] Accordingly, on 5 April 1977, Turner wrote to Hetu and instructed him to 'move as rapidly as we can with declassifying and publishing as many things as possible'.[142] 'I would particularly like to get some public impact', he went on, 'by issuing a spate of publications in the next few months'.[143]

Turner's directive came with certain conditions. The CIA was to be 'highly selective' about which memoirists it agreed to support.[144] The aforementioned correspondence spoke of helping only those who were 'favourably orientated toward the Agency'.[145] Memoirs would be 'sterilised as necessary, even fabricated in sensitive areas'.[146] Moreover, the CIA would not be involved in the actual sale or distribution of the book, other than 'making purchases of it in reasonable bulk quantities' to nudge it in the direction of the bestseller list!'[147]

One of the beneficiaries of this strategy was Cord Meyer. A veteran of the Pacific War, where a grenade thrown into his foxhole had cost him his left eye, Meyer had joined the CIA in 1951 and spent most of his career involved in covert operations. He remains the only CIA officer to receive three times the CIA's highest award, the Distinguished Service Medal. Yet his final years with the Agency had been mired in controversy. He drew criticism from many liberals when he was exposed as a key figure behind the CIA's programme of covertly subsidising and managing student and labour groups. He made unwelcome headlines again in 1972 when it was revealed that he had asked an old friend, then working for Harper & Row publishers, to send him the galley proofs of a book by Alfred McCoy that linked the CIA to the trafficking of heroin in South-east Asia.[148] Partly because of these scandals, he was put out to grass as the CIA's Station Chief in London in 1973. After retiring four years later, he became a nationally syndicated columnist and self-declared 'town crier of rusticated spooks'.[149] When his former bosses discovered that he was writing a book, pursuant to Turner's orders, they could not have been more helpful, inviting him to Langley to discuss how the Agency could be of assistance and allowing him to refresh his memory by granting him privileged access to files. The following, an extract from a letter by CIA General Counsel Anthony Lapham, was emblematic of the congenial working relationship: 'Why don't you get back in touch with me so that we can exchange views. Or better yet why don't you come out to lunch, or invite me for lunch downtown. Either way we can shoot the breeze a bit.'[150] Published in 1980, *Facing Reality* was precisely the sort of book Hetu and Turner had hoped for.[151] Part autobiography, part political analysis, it touted some CIA achievements and argued that the only bulwark against a relentlessly growing Soviet threat was a well-funded and unshackled intelligence force.

Of course, the $64,000 question is to what extent public relations actually changed attitudes towards the CIA. Was it all worth it? Turner certainly thought so. In a letter to AFIO on 10 September 1977, he claimed that he was 'enthusiastic' about the benefits accruing from the CIA's new openness. 'I believe we are gaining greater public acceptance of the need for intelligence', he declared, 'and also gaining greater credibility and understanding.'[152] In late 1980, acting CIA Director Frank Carlucci nominated Hetu and his office for a Congressional public service award, in recognition of their efforts to promote a 'well-informed and supportive public'. Carlucci rhapsodised that the office had 'successfully met the unique and difficult challenge of representing a secret organisation so as to foster public confidence in the nation's vital intelligence agencies'.[153]

Opinion polls provide a revealing, if problematic, assessment of whether PR had made a difference. In December 1975, the Harris Polling Station asked 1,394 adults whether the CIA was right or wrong to spy on US citizens; 61 per cent believed that it represented a 'violation of basic rights'.[154] In 1981, by contrast, 55 per cent of respondents to a Merit Survey called on Congress to pass legislation *allowing* for the CIA to operate within the homeland.[155] Ostensibly, therefore, it might be argued that there was a considerable shift in public attitudes, although whether this was a result of the phrasing of the questions, good PR or broader currents which underlie and shape society is hard to say with confidence.

It is interesting to note that Atlee Phillips came to the depressing conclusion later in his life that PR did not make a blind bit of difference. In a private note, he remarked:

The memoirs of the Old Boys had little impact on the intelligence controversy. They pleased most conservatives and they soothed readers who already agreed with the writers, but to the sceptical they were as biased and suspect as the authors of the whistle-blowing school. Who was to believe expiation written by apologists, men who had learned as an essential of their trade to lie?[156]

On the lecture circuit, he had encountered a much chillier reception than even he could have anticipated, as hordes of protestors often turned up to express their anger. His sad abiding memory of his 'Last Assignment' was being told by a literary agent in New York that he could earn '$5,000 to $10,000 a year' defending the CIA, but '$100,000 per year' attacking it.[157]

In the final analysis, the CIA's image was and remains determined by the quality of its work, not the quality of its public relations. No amount of carefully managed publicity can prevent or fully offset the harm caused by unflattering disclosures of poorly conceived operations, lousy analysis or other failings. Moreover, public relations can be a double-edged sword if it is not judged to be sincere, or if people suspect that it is being used as a cover for what goes on in the back shop. As we shall now see, this is what happened under Turner because, at the very moment he claimed to be making the CIA more open, he also made headlines as an enemy of free speech by fighting tooth and nail to stop ex-officers from publishing books critical of the Agency.

Chapter 5

The Snepp Problem

I. The PRB

I have sacrificed everything since I started writing the book. I have no friends now. I have no honor. I have no credibility.
Frank Snepp, January 1978.[1]

Marchetti and Agee had put the CIA on red alert for intelligence officers who wanted to publicise unpleasant truths about the company. As we saw in the previous chapter, part of the Agency's strategy for dealing with the revelations of renegades and whistle-blowers was to counterbalance them with a carefully coordinated PR programme that, *inter alia*, involved more press briefings and Langley 'pow-wows' for journalists and other key opinion-formers. However, the ideal solution was to stop people from washing their dirty linen in public in the first place. To this end, on 19 June 1976, CIA Director George H. W. Bush established the Publications Review Board (PRB), originally with seven members, to 'review the non-official writings of current employees'. Hitherto, the CIA's Office of Security had largely administered the vetting of manuscripts in an *ad hoc* fashion without any ground rules to inform the process. Indeed, there was no record of how many texts had been cleared over the years or what secrets had been officially approved for release.[2] This undisciplined arrangement had sufficed when memoirs were few and far between, but was clearly unsuitable in an era where more staff were looking to get into print. When Turner took over as CIA Director in 1977, he broadened the Board's reach by giving it the authority to examine the writings of former, as well as serving, intelligence officers.

At the heart of the CIA's decision to create the PRB was a desire to have more control over what authors disclosed – something that had obviously been lacking in recent years. The declared purpose of pre-publication review was to prevent authors from making inadvertent disclosures of classified information that would be damaging to national security. The Board was especially concerned with material that would undermine sources and methods; betray the identities of Agency employees; and impair US foreign relations.[3] An internal investigation into the PRB, carried out in summer 1981, emphasised that 'even supportive books about the Agency and intelligence operations have proved damaging'.[4] Without giving precise details, it referred to a former operations officer who had revealed in his book that he was a Chief of Station in a particular country. This revelation, explained the inquiry, 'could be of assistance to hostile counter-intelligence elements, could embarrass the country's government, and certainly could be exploited in anti-American propaganda'.[5] Even the most seemingly innocent disclosure, it went on, could hamper vital liaison relationships since many cooperating intelligence services regarded books by former officers as 'astonishing breaches of official discipline'.[6]

As Angus Mackenzie has argued, a formal review process was a necessary compensation for the CIA's fragile legal position in the courts with respect to memoirs.[7] In the Marchetti case, many of the deletions asked for by the CIA had been thrown out by the presiding judge, who castigated the vetting procedure as arbitrary and haphazard. By introducing a more systematic process, the CIA could claim that it had acted impartially, orderly and in accordance with the guidelines. In the words of CIA Associate General John Greaney, the Board was a 'bureaucratic cover-your-ass'.[8]

It is nevertheless hard to escape the conclusion that the CIA, in setting up the PRB, also had one eye firmly fixed on trying to stop embarrassing revelations. If the Board's sole responsibility was to safeguard classified information, it surely would have made sense to have put a seasoned career CIA officer in charge, someone with an instinctive feel for potentially harmful material based on years of experience. Instead, the first chairman of the PRB was none other than Herbert Hetu, the head of Public Affairs. The PRB staff were located in the Office of Public Affairs, which itself was within the domain of the DCI. The timing of Turner's decision to extend the Board's mandate also hints at an underlying rationale to manage negative representations. At the very moment that Turner granted the PRB the power to inspect the writings of ex-employees, he was in the process of firing 800 intelligence officers that were, in his felicitous phrase, 'clogging the system'. The PRB conveniently ensured that the CIA had advance warning of any 'surplus' officers who were tempted to take up the pen in anger.

The CIA strenuously denied that the PRB was designed to stop books that painted the Agency in a bad light. In an interview with *Washington Monthly*, Hetu stressed that the job of the Board was to sit down with authors and determine the absolute minimum number of deletions to protect national security: 'We are not censors, but a "service-orientated board" that respect the fact that people, whether loyalists or critics, have a right to their opinions.' 'Approval', he emphasised, 'will not be denied solely because the subject matter may be embarrassing or critical of the Agency.'[9] Of course, one would expect nothing less from the CIA's main PR man.

The CIA's concern about disgruntled employees penning books was not misplaced. No sooner had the PRB been established than the Agency became embroiled in perhaps the most significant secrecy battle in twentieth-century US history. It was waged against a decorated and patriotic former analyst who, the government itself acknowledged, had not revealed any secrets, but who had written a book about American overstretch in Vietnam that served as a perfect metaphor for the rise and fall of the CIA. It is this landmark case, which culminated in a far-reaching ruling by the Supreme Court on First Amendment rights, to which this book now turns.

II. Institutional Disgrace

The fall of Saigon was one of the most shameful
moments I've ever lived through.
Frank Snepp, 2013.[10]

Frank Snepp was born into a well-educated, conservative southern household in Kingston, North Carolina. In an interview, he would later state: 'I had a very traditional, almost *Gone with the Wind* upbringing.'[11] After majoring in Elizabethan literature at Columbia University, he spent a year at CBS News as a desk assistant to legendary broadcast journalists Walter Cronkite and Mike Wallace. To avoid the draft, he then returned to Columbia to study at the School of International Affairs, graduating in 1968. Snepp's upbringing and academic specialisation made him an attractive target for CIA recruitment. One of his lawyers later described him as 'poster boy' for the Agency: 'Quietly handsome in a West Point way, polite almost to a fault (he even called *me* "sir"), [and] fiercely loyal to his country.'[12] It was not long before he was recruited. The approach came from the Associate Dean of the School, Philip Moseley, who had advised President Franklin D. Roosevelt at Yalta and was a world-leading authority on the Soviet Union: 'Mosley said to me, "Frank, you should be a spy because you're not smart enough for the State Department."'[13] Brimming with love of country, Snepp agreed, and so began his career as a Company man.

After a year spent working on European strategic affairs, Snepp was detailed to Vietnam in 1969, where he served two tours of duty at the US embassy in Saigon. Like many young men at the time, the idea of being sent to South-east Asia did not instantly appeal to him. However, after being told that his 'career would be in the dumpster if he refused', he knuckled down and, in a meteoric rise, became the CIA's chief analyst of North Vietnamese politics and strategy before his thirtieth birthday. 'I was terrifically gung ho', he declared in a recent interview.[14] Rather uniquely for the CIA, he doubled as a desk analyst and a counter-intelligence officer in the field. On his final tour, from 1972 to 1975, he was truly in the thick of it, running a key informant network in the north; preparing estimates; debriefing the CIA's best spies; writing segments of the President's Daily Brief; and interrogating high-ranking prisoners and defectors, including Nguyen Van Tai, a colonel in the North Vietnamese security service who had come to the south to run assassination and terrorist operations. By his own admission, he was no saint, and advanced his career by turning a blind eye to abuses by US forces and by producing politically expedient intelligence for policymakers in Washington. The darling of Thomas Polgar, the CIA Station Chief, and Graham Martin, the US ambassador (whose daughter he briefly dated), Snepp received the CIA's coveted Medal of Merit for turning in a performance that, in Polgar's words, 'had never been equalled'.

However, the longer Snepp stayed in Vietnam, the more troubled he became with not only America's involvement, but also the moral ambiguities of intelligence work. At the embassy, he watched as nerves became frayed and emotions erupted. Many of his fellow staffers fell hopelessly into drink and drugs, and while he loved the South Vietnamese people, he had grown exasperated with the rampant corruption of their rulers. His disillusionment was finally confirmed by the US government's botched handling of the fall of Saigon on 30 April 1975, resulting in hundreds, maybe thousands, of indigenous CIA 'assets' being left behind, to the mercy of the victorious communists from the north.

As the premier analyst *in situ*, Snepp had long warned his superiors of an imminent communist takeover, and repeatedly called for intensified evacuating planning of the loyal Vietnamese nationals, and their families, who had risked their lives by working for the Americans during the war. All the intelligence in his possession pointed to an imminent end to the ceasefire with Hanoi negotiated by National Security Adviser Henry Kissinger two years earlier, which had brought the last American ground troops home, but left 140,000 North Vietnamese forces in the south.

In early 1975, to test Saigon's resiliency and Washington's resolve, the communists had encroached on territory close to the capital, emboldened by the fact that Richard Nixon, whom they regarded as a madman capable of using nuclear weapons, was no longer President. Two weeks prior to the collapse, at a CIA safe house, Snepp met with his best informant who confirmed to him that the communists had no desire for a political solution and planned to take Saigon before the birthday of the North's late revolutionary leader Hồ Chí Minh, on 19 May. Sipping a Budweiser and smoking his favourite brand of cigarettes, the first-rate source said that the final assault would begin by May Day. Snepp's predictions about the endgame, however, were dismissed, as were his calls for accelerated evacuation. Ambassador Martin had lost a son in Vietnam and was determined not to lose Saigon. 'Intellectual whore' was his favourite term for every reporter, official or wilted flower child that he felt undermined American support for Vietnam. Even as reports came in that many South Vietnamese soldiers were fleeing, shedding their uniforms as they ran, he believed that the government forces of President Nguyen Van Thieu would stand and fight before the offensive reached Saigon. Hopeful of securing a new negotiated settlement, he stressed the importance of the US not to be seen 'bugging out' and reprimanded Snepp when he discovered that the analyst and a handful of junior CIA officers were secretly burning documents. 'You're sending the wrong signal,' he bleated. Martin also complained that ashes were gathering on the roof of his limousine and soiling the embassy swimming pool.[15]

On mid-morning of 29 April, after a night of heavy bombing from communist aircraft on the edges of Saigon, and with 140,000 North Vietnamese troops within an hour's drive of downtown, the evacuation order finally came from the White House. Operation 'Frequent Wind', the largest helicopter evacuation in history, officially commenced with a radio broadcast announcing it was '112 degrees and rising', followed by a repeat playing of Bing Crosby's 'White Christmas'.

By this point, it was far too late to pull everyone out. What Snepp witnessed over the next few hours would stay with him for the rest of his life. As the enemy moved in, it was not long before thousands of panic-stricken Vietnamese were clamouring in vain at the embassy gates, begging to get out of the country. With the air toxic with smoke from enemy shelling, mothers cradled crying children while marine sentries scrapped with desperate Vietnamese who tried to climb the embassy walls, which were lined with barbed wire. Dressed in a flak jacket and packing an M-16, Snepp raced to the courtyard and pulled as many of his South Vietnamese friends to safety as he could. By mid-afternoon, he had retreated to the CIA's operations room on the sixth floor of the compound, where he listened in horror as radio calls came in from stranded Vietnamese agents, who knew they were dead men if they did not escape the besieged capital. By nightfall, the embassy was almost overrun. In the car park, the mob played demolition derby with ambassadorial limousines, while looters cracked open bottles of pinot noir from the wine cellar.[16] With this, Snepp took the last CIA chopper off the embassy roof, racked with guilt that he was abandoning loyal allies to be tortured, incarcerated or killed. From the porthole, he saw thousands of people packed in the streets below, looking upward for help that would never arrive.[17]

Snepp was scandalised by the ignominious and ill-conceived American withdrawal from Saigon. He was furious that Martin, as well as key officials in the State Department and the CIA (including Polgar), had refused to see the writing on the wall and dragged their feet on the crucial issue of contingency planning.[18] 'As a matter of honor', he emphasised in a recent interview, 'you do not leave your friends behind on the battlefield.'[19] The betrayal was made worse by the fact that many secret documents had not been destroyed. When the communist invaders examined this material, as they surely would, they would quickly discover the members of the local population who had collaborated with the Americans against the North. Snepp's guilty conscience had a personal edge to it. Hours before he boarded the chopper, he had received a phone call from a one-time mistress, called Mai Ly, begging for safe passage out of the country. Snepp had not seen the woman in two years, but they had been close and she claimed to have borne his son, a fact Snepp later acknowledged. Mai Ly made it clear to him that she would not be taken alive, and would kill herself and the child unless exit visas were arranged. Snepp promised to help, but asked her to call him back in one hour as he was busy typing another (pointless) intelligence report for the ambassador. That would be the last time he heard from her. When the call came, Snepp was away from his desk. She left him a chilling message that read: 'I would have expected better of you.'[20] A friend later told a heartbroken Snepp that Mai Ly had made good on her promise and was found, along with the baby boy, dead on a blood-drenched mattress.

Back stateside, Snepp urged the CIA to investigate what he considered to be an 'institutional disgrace'. However, just as his pleas had fallen on deaf ears in Saigon, no one was prepared to listen to him at Langley. His immediate superiors refused to sanction an 'after-action' report. The Inspector General turned him away, as did the Agency's Office of Political Research. 'The CIA', Snepp recollected, 'wanted to shut Vietnam down and be done with it.'[21] Snepp's blood really began to boil when, in the coming weeks and months, he believed some of the key personalities put out self-serving statements to absolve themselves of blame. Secretary of State Kissinger was quoted as saying that Hanoi had continually promised a negotiated settlement, only to change its mind abruptly two days before moving into Saigon, meaning that there was no time for an orderly evacuation. In a press conference, Polgar repeated the same charge about the fickleness of the North Vietnamese, and claimed that all the intelligence coming into the station had pointed to a renewed ceasefire. Snepp was appalled when he discovered that Ted Shackley, head of the CIA's East Asia Division, was seemingly leaking information to the press to save face. Purportedly, Shackley had even promised a friendly journalist access to classified CIA files if, in return, he penned a 'favourable' book about Saigon's fall.[22] In a final bid to force a true post-mortem, Snepp wrote a short paper on the foul-up, which he distributed around headquarters, arguing that his warnings had been ignored and that many friends and colleagues had needlessly died as a result. Those who cared to read it treated it like a 'skunk's carcass'.[23]

After trying unsuccessfully to blow the whistle from the inside, Snepp decided to try his luck from the outside by writing a book. 'I thought it was a matter of honor,' he later told the press:

> I tried to go through the system. I tried to prompt an internal report
> … and I had been turned away. The only thing that distinguishes
> the CIA from the Mafia or any criminal outlet is its commitment to
> getting the truth to Washington and to acknowledging the truth
> to itself. In the wake of Saigon's collapse, the CIA tried to cover reality with a lie.[24]

Snepp did not take this decision lightly. His southern establishment background had instilled in him a profound respect for authority. He was a firm believer in the CIA's mission and had taken no pleasure from seeing the national security state put on trial earlier in the decade: 'I'm not a flaming liberal … and I don't want to be in the demolition business of destroying the Agency.'[25] He subscribed to a consequentialist mentality of 'the end justifies the means', and had no scruples with the CIA getting its hands dirty to defeat legitimate threats to national security. In an interview for PBS in February 1982, he declared: 'I cannot fault the Agency for having a covert action arm or even running certain covert actions that we've seen in the past.'[26] Moreover, he despised intelligence apostates like Marchetti and Agee. In the case of Marchetti, he had 'relished the author's discomfort when the CIA, with the judge's blessing, had sliced great divots out of the text'.[27] In his opinion, Agee was a 'turncoat', 'traitor' and 'coward' who did not deserve the title of whistle-blower, which in the US has positive connotations.[28] Why? Because Agee had fingered colleagues by name with little apparent regard for the ramifications; and because he had fled the country, instead of facing the consequences of his actions in a court of law. What Snepp wanted was redemption. He wanted to atone for the CIA's mistakes, as well as his own, in the hope that lessons would be learned to stop such a tragedy from ever occurring again.

The idea of a book was discussed with Bob Loomis, senior editor at the publishing giant Random House. Loomis had a reputation for successfully shepherding 'hot' stories into print, having worked with Seymour Hersh on the journalist's historic report on the My Lai massacre. The two men met for the first time in a crowded and noisy restaurant on Manhattan's East Side, the 'perpetual clatter of dishes providing a perfect mask for confidential tête-à-têtes'.[29] Loomis agreed to support the project, but on two conditions. Firstly, the book must not disclose secrets. Snepp assured him that the last thing he wanted to do was compound the damage caused by the clumsy evacuation. Secondly, the book would be written in complete secrecy. Experience had taught Loomis that any publisher who dared to print negative material about the Agency was playing with fire. As discussed in Chapter 2, in 1964 Random House had published Thomas Ross and David Wise's groundbreaking account of the CIA, *The Invisible Government*, but not

before the Agency had stolen galleys and threatened Loomis with espionage offences. Loomis was also aware of the fact that someone from
the CIA had stolen Marchetti's book proposal from the Knopf offices
in New York. Accordingly, it was agreed that Snepp would never step
foot inside Random House headquarters. Much like a spy operation,
meetings would take place in city parks, dark alleys and restaurants.
Moreover, there would be no correspondence or drafts containing the
author's real name. Until the book went into production, Snepp would
have a cover identity – 'Virgil Black'.[30]

Snepp's efforts to keep the CIA in the dark were ultimately undone
by two individuals he trusted as friends. Since returning from
Vietnam, he had found a modicum of solace at a weekly 'open house'
for fellow mourners from Saigon. The organisers, Bill Johnson and his
wife Pam, were career CIA officers and had served with Snepp in the
Saigon embassy. Snepp became close with the couple; indeed, every
Saturday night, for twelve months, they would weep together over the
loss of Vietnamese comrades. As the friendship blossomed, he told
them about his book, but kept the Loomis connection to himself. The
Johnsons encouraged him, and even offered him classified documents.
However, his 'friends' were in fact reporting back to the CIA's counter-intelligence office. Wearing a secret wire, the Johnsons recorded
their conversations with Snepp and forwarded the tapes to Langley.
The CIA, therefore, knew chapter and verse about the progress of his
manuscript. The 'generous' offer to provide him with classified information had been a cunning ploy to get him to publish secrets and thus break
the law; fortunately, he had declined. By inciting him to publish secrets,
the Johnsons could be seen as being guilty of entrapment. Moreover,
they were in violation of the rule that the CIA does not spy at home.

Tipped off about Snepp's intentions, on 26 January 1976 the CIA
ordered him into the Office of the General Counsel (OGC) to take
a lie-detector test, to determine whether he had a manuscript and
whether he had a publishing contract. Snepp considered this an

indignity, stormed out and tendered his immediate resignation. For the next eighteen months, he worked tirelessly on the text, taking every precaution to ensure that the Agency did not get their hands on a copy. Drafts of the book were stashed at various spots around Washington, DC. Dead drops were used to get material to Random House. Ingeniously, one of Snepp's 'true' friends at CIA stored chapters in a safe at Langley, based on the theory that 'the pit bulls would never go snuffling around their own sandbox'.[31] As the publication date neared, to throw potential CIA tailgaters off the scent, Snepp met with Random House representatives outside the offices of rival publishers. Taking security to the extreme, he even carried a loaded .38 automatic. Although the possibility of some hot-headed patriot performing a hit on him was slim, Snepp took no chances; after all, this was the era when CIA assassination attempts were headline news.

In summer 1976, with its eyes fixed on Snepp, not to mention Agee, the CIA was caught completely cold by Joseph Burkholder Smith, a former Station Chief in Caracas, with a 400-plus-page tome called *Portrait of a Cold Warrior*. 'Little Joe', as he was known, had worked in such silence that the first the CIA heard of the book was when it appeared in DC bookstores. The Operations Directorate was up in arms as a damage assessment indicated that it had blown the cover of several field agents.[32] Controversially, the book touched on the sensitive issue of intelligence liaison by revealing that in the early 1960s the CIA, with London's backing, had fomented labour unrest and race riots in the then-British colony of Guiana (now Guyana), in an effort to prevent the left-wing Cheddi Jagan from being the first leader of the country after independence from the British had been achieved. Anthony Lapham, the CIA's new General Counsel, flew to New York to ask Smith's publisher, Putnam, to pull the book so that the PRB could carry out a review. Putnam agreed, but by then too many copies were in circulation and the request was scrapped. Lapham then gave serious thought to suing Smith for breaching his secrecy contract to teach him and others a lesson that the PRB was obligatory, not optional. It was decided, however, that doing so would simply draw more attention to the book. Little Joe, who had exposed actual secrets, was a lucky man.[33]

Determined not to be blindsided again, and with the credibility of the PRB at stake, on 8 October 1976, CIA attorney John Greaney, a veteran of the legal tussle with Marchetti, sent the less fortunate Snepp an ultimatum, demanding that he submit his book for pre-publication review in compliance with the secrecy agreement he had signed when he joined the CIA in 1968. Snepp knew that he might be tickling the dragon's tail if he refused, since that particular agreement clearly stated that he was obliged to seek CIA approval before publishing anything about intelligence. However, after consulting with Random House lawyers, he concluded that the dragon had no bite. Since signing his first agreement, he had signed a further five contracts, all of which required pre-publication review only in the case of *classified* writings. Crucially, when leaving the Agency, he had been told that his sixth and final agreement superseded his original contract. Provided, therefore, that he did not reveal any secrets, which he did not intend to do, he should be safe. Furthermore, the original contract emphasised that the Inspector General would investigate any employee grievance. Since this had not happened in Snepp's case, the view was taken that the CIA did not have a legal leg to stand on.

On 17 May 1977, CIA Director Turner cleared his diary to meet with Snepp in the hope of personally convincing him to submit his manuscript prior to publication. What happened at this meeting, which took place in the Admiral's office, is bitterly contested by the two men. Turner would later testify in court that Snepp promised him unequivocally that he would have the book cleared by the PRB. Snepp, he said, looked him 'right in the eye' when giving that assurance. 'I, and the CIA, accepted Mr Snepp at his word,' he said.[34] Snepp flatly rejects this version of events, suggesting that he made it perfectly clear to Turner that he had no intention of submitting his manuscript because it contained no secrets and was based entirely on unclassified materials: 'I said to him, "I'm not going to reveal any secrets, I know my obligations."'[35] Reportedly, Turner accepted this. With no recorded minutes of the conversation, it is impossible to say for certain who is telling the truth. Either way, Turner had failed to deal with the 'Snepp problem'.

III. Irreparable Harm

If Snepp is able to get away with this, it will appear to other people that we have no control.
CIA Director Stansfield Turner.[36]

In November 1977, Snepp published the hard-hitting and redemptive memoir, *Decent Interval*, without the CIA having read a word of it.[37] The CIA bought up all the copies in DC, but it quickly became a bestseller and generated a whirlwind of publicity, with front-page coverage in the *New York Times* and a *60 Minutes* exclusive with Mike Wallace. The book was a classic piece of Cold War revisionism, questioning the wisdom and morality of US foreign policy. Vietnam was presented as an old man's war and a young man's tragedy, while the fall of Saigon was portrayed as one of the most shameful episodes in US history. Snepp repeated what many critics of Nixon and Kissinger had said of the Vietnam peace settlement in January 1973; that instead of amounting to Nixon's 'peace with honor', it merely constituted a 'decent interval' before the inevitable communist takeover – hence the title of the book. Key personalities – including Martin, Polgar and Kissinger – were accused of ignoring overwhelming intelligence showing that the North Vietnamese were making haste for Saigon. Kissinger was singled out for constantly deceiving the American people about the prospects for victory in Vietnam. The CIA came out of the book particularly badly. The Agency was pilloried for ignoring its own

The Snepp Problem   193

intelligence product, and heartlessly deserting its South Vietnamese allies to the mercy of any angry enemy. Beyond the evacuation failure, Snepp gave a devastating portrait of CIA operations and management. He described how intelligence reports were routinely fabricated and distorted and then given to visiting delegations of Congressmen. Moreover, he gave examples of the CIA playing God; for example, rejecting a prisoner exchange because the American POW in question was too junior, thus condemning the man to seven years in captivity. Snepp was also brutally honest, to the point of self-flagellation, about his own mistakes. *Decent Interval* was his long-awaited attempt to tell the truth – the *unclassified* truth.

The important messages the book carried were nevertheless lost in the controversy that followed. Nothing could have prepared Snepp for the fury that was brought down upon his head. Turner reacted with outrage, and confirmed that the CIA was going to take him to court for breach of contract. In a piece for the *Washington Post*, he accused Snepp of being a war profiteer and violating an alleged oral promise to 'surrender the manuscript'.[38] He rejected the suggestion that there had been a 'cover-up' or 'cosmeticizing' of events by officials, and disputed the claim that Snepp had been unable to induce the CIA to investigate its own failings. The picture he painted was of Snepp riding a hobby-horse about Saigon from which nobody could bring him to dismount. Most seriously of all, he suggested that the unsanctioned book had caused as much damage to national security as the Pentagon Papers in 1971. What was at stake, he argued, was the integrity of the classification system. This system, he believed, was seriously jeopardised when anyone entrusted with sensitive information could subjectively decide what is secret or not secret: 'The logical conclusion of the Ellsberg-Snepp syndrome is that any one of our 210 million citizens is entitled to decide what should or should not be classified.'[39]

In a rebuttal that the *Washington Post* declined to publish, Random House President Bob Bernstein reproached Turner for starting a witch-hunt and for ignoring the fact that Snepp was by no means the first former operative to write about their experiences without prior clearance. Burkholder Smith had clearly bypassed pre-publication review; so too had Miles Copeland with his 1974 book, *Without Cloak or Dagger*. To hound Snepp, when others had gone unpunished for the same 'crime', surely gave the lie to Turner's position that no individual officer was allowed to determine what information might be safely disclosed. In short, there had to be other factors.

In trying to fathom other possible motives for the CIA's selective prosecution of Snepp, it is impossible to ignore the larger political context. There is a strong case to be made that Snepp was a victim of circumstance. With *Decent Interval*, he was poking the CIA in the eye at a time when the public image and private morale of the Agency was still recovering from its 'time of troubles'. Having had its legitimacy fiercely questioned from all angles, the last thing the CIA wanted was someone like Snepp causing further embarrassment and providing new ammunition to its critics. As intelligence authority James Bamford has written, Snepp's timing was all wrong. By publishing his exposé in such a charged atmosphere, he was effectively lighting a match 'standing near leaking gas pipes'.[40]

Snepp believes that he was targeted partly to pay the dues of Agee. One of the driving forces behind the prosecution was Deputy Director of Covert Operations Ted Shackley. Nicknamed the 'Blond Ghost' due to his hatred of being photographed, Shackley had been Polgar's predecessor as Chief of Station in Saigon. Shackley's hatred for Agee was unparalleled. In 1972, then Chief of the Western Hemisphere Division, he had been forced to discontinue productive operations in Latin America when it became apparent that Agee was intent on exposing them. In order to 'cauterise' the wound, as he described it, good agents were jettisoned and case officers uprooted from their billets.[41] Shackley, the argument goes, jumped at the chance to hang Snepp in payback for the real enemy, Agee.

Snepp also believes that he was singled out to send a warning to other employees who might be tempted to publish in vengeance: 'They were concerned about the next Agee … In fact, they were terrified of not one or two Agees, but many Agees. Turner didn't want anybody opening the floodgates.'[42] Turner's concern about 'future Agees' was arguably exacerbated by the fact that he was in the process of purging the Agency of what he labelled 'deadwood', a ghastly slur for men and women who had served the Agency with devotion. The 'Halloween Massacre', as it became known, had been carried out in the most cut-throat manner possible, and had left many of those forced out thirsting for Turner's professional blood. At the stroke of a pen, pink slips saying 'Your services are no longer necessary' were issued to hundreds of sea-soned and loyal officers, quite literally asking them to clear their desks by the end of the working day. When they protested, Turner called them 'cry-babies'.[43] At Langley, bulletin boards sprouted with anti-Turner messages and caricatures, while there was talk of the victims filing a class-action suit against their former employer. One officer told the *Chicago Daily News* that he considered Turner an 'SOB'.[44] If Snepp was allowed to get away with flouting the rules, what was to stop those who had been fired from doing the same, and perhaps even compro-mising actual secrets? 'The fear', argues Snepp, 'was that I would be some kind of wayward Pied Piper who would lead everyone off to publishing houses.'[45]

At Turner's insistence, Attorney General Griffin Bell filed a civil suit against Snepp in the Federal Court of Virginia. Based in the district in which the CIA is headquartered, the Virginia Federal Court had been the site of the Agency's victorious legal contest against Marchetti. Importantly, the Justice Department did not prosecute Snepp crimi-nally, and did not accuse him of compromising secrets. A criminal trial would have meant intelligence officers being put on the stand and being obliged to tell 'the truth, the whole truth, and nothing but the truth'. Far too risky. Instead, they sued him for breaching a 'fiduciary' obligation not to publish without pre-publication clearance. This obligation, they charged, was stipulated in a clause in his original 1968 secrecy agreement. Despite acknowledging that the book did not contain classified information, government lawyers claimed that *Decent Interval* had 'irreparably harmed' national security by creating the impression, both at home and abroad, that there had been a breakdown in internal CIA discipline. Its unauthorised release, they argued, had damaged intelligence operations because it gave the 'appearance' that the CIA cannot control its officers and thus the information to which they become privy. 'People who have been associated with us overseas have severed their association as a result of the book,' declared Turner, speaking at the Naval Education Training Center's change-of-command ceremony in 1978.[46]

A test case in the struggle between the public's right to know and the legitimate need of government for secrecy, the trial attracted considerable national and international interest. In the press, Snepp took a fair amount of criticism from friends of the CIA who, hunting in packs, gave interviews lumping him together with Agee, as well as traitors like the Rosenbergs. Herbert Hetu, the CIA's 'king of spin', accused Snepp of having no honour: 'It's a matter of honor. There's some sort of personal moral obligations – you either have personal integrity or you don't.'[47] Snepp nevertheless had plenty of supporters. Hersh applauded him for having the courage and integrity to sacrifice his career to ensure that the truth came out about the cowardly, bumbling and reprehensible end to the American involvement in Vietnam. An unlikely ally came in the shape of former CIA operative and sesquipedalian champion of conservatism William F. Buckley. Buckley, who had written books and articles for years without submitting them for clearance, argued that the shocking events described in *Decent Interval* could have been avoided if his hero, Nixon, had not been forced to resign over Watergate. The air, charged Snepp's supporters, was thick with irony: at the same time as allowing the prosecution, President Jimmy Carter was recommending a Civil Service Reform Act that would create an Office of Special Counsel to protect whistle-blowers who expose gross management errors and abuses. At a news conference, Carter was made to look foolish when he claimed that Snepp did not qualify as a whistle-blower because he had 'revealed our nation's utmost secrets'. Why then, inquired one journalist, was the government not charging him with breaking any secrecy laws?

For Snepp, the trial was a disaster from start to finish. Assigned to the case was an aged and cantankerous judge called Oren R. Lewis. Nicknamed 'Roarin Oren', Lewis was a staunch Republican and, in the words of one attorney, 'made Gengis Khan look like a civil libertarian'.[48] Rated by lawyers interviewed for a monthly law magazine as the worst federal judge in the Fourth Circuit, he had gained notoriety for handing out draconian punishments to anti-war activists, even suggesting that they should 'sample life' in North Vietnam.[49] One of his most famous victims was the outspoken man of letters Norman Mailer, who he jailed and fined following his arrest at an anti-war protest at the Pentagon. Less than thirty minutes into the trial, the writing was on the wall for Snepp. After refusing a request for a jury trial, Lewis implied that a guilty verdict was a foregone conclusion by giving Snepp directions to the appeals court in Richmond: 'You just take I-95 and go south.'[50] Throughout the proceedings, the judge went against Snepp at every turn. He turned down a request by the defence to submit evidence showing that the CIA had taken no action against other officers who had published without prior review.[51] When Turner testified that books about the CIA had prompted 'very strong complaints' from intelligence allies, the judge rejected an attempt by Snepp's lawyer to enquire, on cross-examination, whether *Decent Interval* had drawn such criticism. Lewis's political bias was on full display when, during a summation by one of the defence attorneys, he scoffed: 'You sound like someone from the ACLU.'[52] Snepp compared the experience to 'being present at your own execution; you're watching the people put the bullets in the weapons and sight down the barrel.'[53]

Fighting what appeared to be a losing battle with Lewis, Snepp could ill-afford any further setbacks. To his dismay, however, with the trial in full swing, his name was dragged through the mud in popular discourse by the antics of another disillusioned officer – John Stockwell. A blunt, hard-as-nails, moustachioed, double black belt in judo, Stockwell had been with the Agency for twelve years, serving enthusiastically in Vietnam before being appointed to lead a CIA task force in the former Portuguese colony of Angola, where a civil war had erupted. His mission was to prevent the victory of the MPLA, the most pro-Marxist of the three guerrilla groups jockeying for power in the political vacuum left by the Portuguese. He became disillusioned as the crisis escalated into a bloody Cold War battleground, with each superpower and their allies sending arms to rival factions. He resigned in disgust in December 1976, convinced that Washington was more concerned about striking a blow against Moscow, and proving that Vietnam had not diminished US power, than ending the blood-letting. With the worst possible timing, he aired his grievances in an un-cleared memoir, just as Snepp was in the firing line. Suddenly, Turner's concern about the floodgates being opened gained credibility. Worse, when Stockwell appeared on *60 Minutes*, he presented Agee as a hero and claimed that the two of them, plus Snepp, were going to blow the CIA apart. By blurring the lines between Agee, a true renegade, and Snepp, an institutional rebel, Stockwell queered the defence's pitch. Moreover, it did not help that *Covert Action Information Bulletin*, the magazine set up by Agee to 'destabilise' the CIA, openly declared itself an 'admirer' of Snepp.[54]

It came as no surprise, then, when Lewis ruled in favour of the CIA. The crotchety old judge dismissed the argument of Snepp's lawyers that the secrecy agreement only applied to disclosures of a classified nature. 'I would have no difficulty speculating', he declared, 'that the US government and the people suffered a loss by giving away this infor-mation. It doesn't have to be about the atomic bomb. I don't think the government has to show it lost $2.'[55] In the same way that a banker has a responsibility to protect the bank's money, Lewis argued that Snepp was a fiduciary, or trustee, of the CIA. As punishment for abusing that trust by publishing without clearance, he ordered that Snepp surrender all his profits from the book to the federal government, calling them 'ill-gotten gains'. He also imposed a lifetime gag order on Snepp, demanding – on pain of criminal contempt – that all his future writings, even fiction, be submitted to the CIA for prior review. John Warner, who retired as the Agency's General Counsel in 1976, later called it a 'tremendous victory' for the CIA's 'little old lawyers'.[56]

Snepp had lost the battle, but was not prepared to lose the war. As he saw it, he was the victim of a technicality, mercilessly exploited by the CIA to even the score. Accordingly, he appealed to the Appeals Court in Richmond. When that failed, he took the case all the way to the Supreme Court. Once again, circumstances seemingly conspired to work against him. In November 1979, with the Court still deliberating, the American embassy in Tehran was seized by an angry mob of militant Islamic students. More than sixty Americans were taken hostage, including several CIA officers, causing a public outcry. Against this background, claims Snepp, the 'Court had a real "hard on" for national security' and made it difficult for an alleged radical like himself to attract sympathy.[57]

There is also a case to be made that the composition of the Court meant that the scales of Lady Justice were tipped against Snepp. Justice William Rehnquist was a rock-solid conservative with a track record of penalising rebelliousness. As Assistant US Attorney General in the Nixon administration, he had defended the government's hard-knuckle programme of surveillance, wire-tapping and incarceration of Vietnam War protesters, whom he described as the 'new barbarians'. He also fired off the first volley in the Pentagon Papers dispute by unsuccessfully seeking an injunction to block their publication in the *Washington Post*. Newly discovered documents show that Justice Lewis Powell had a hidden bias towards those who ran the intelligence shop. A World War Two army intelligence officer, he was in regular private correspondence with Helms. On 15 September 1977, he wrote a letter to the former CIA Director in which he expressed his 'total contempt' for revisionist writers of the Cold War, which, of course, Snepp was.[58] Snepp later discovered from private papers in the archive of the Supreme Court that Powell had written a confidential memorandum in 1971 advocating a judicial crackdown on critics of American institutions. Documents also showed Powell imploring the other justices to recognise that Snepp had 'wilfully, deliberately, and surreptitiously' broken his secrecy contract and jeopardised CIA relations with 'intelligence services of friendly nations'. Steeped in sheer naked partisanship, Powell's private notes read like the ramblings of a CIA spokesman, not a judge.[59]

In February 1980, in a milestone ruling, the Supreme Court decreed, by a vote of six to three, not to grant Snepp's petition that they hear the case. Snepp's legal team were denied the chance to make oral arguments or submit full briefs. The view of the Court was that Snepp had violated his contract and, in doing so, had inflicted irreversible damage on intelligence activities vital to national security. As a result, the gag order was allowed to stand, as was the garnishment of earnings. Snepp was immediately reduced to penury. Stripped of every cent he had made in the nearly two years taken to write the book, and faced with a mountain of unpaid legal expenses totalling $100,000, it would take him years to recover: 'One day I had $300,000 in the bank; the next day I was flat broke.'[60] Washington lawyers subsequently began referring to litigants who had been dealt a bad hand by the Supreme Court as having been 'snepped'.[61]

One for the law textbooks, the Court's ruling had profound implications that stretched well beyond Snepp's financial plight, provoking howls of protest from First Amendment purists. Nat Hentoff of the *Los Angeles Times* exclaimed: 'No court decision in history has so imperilled whistle-blowers, and thereby, the ability of citizens to find out about rampant ineptitude and corruption in the agencies purportedly serving them.'[62] In the *Washington Monthly*, Jonathan Alter wrote that the 'decision may have been the most absurd and intellectually shoddy performance in the last twelve years of the [Warren] Burger Court'.[63] The *Washington Post* criticised the Court for disposing of the case in a 'casual, even cavalier manner', seemingly oblivious to the power it extended to the federal government to stifle free speech.[64] The Snepp precedent effectively heralded an American Official Secrets Act. Just as in Britain, it was now a criminal offence for an intelligence officer to publish any information, learned in the course of his duties, without permission. It did not matter how harmless, trivial or old the material; by winning the case, the CIA now had the authority to enforce a secrecy agreement against non-secrets and only had to silence its critics by arguing that the 'appearance' of security had been imperilled.

In the wake of the decision, President Ronald Reagan passed National Security Decision Directive 84 (NSDD-84) giving departmental heads the right to polygraph employees suspected of leaking secrets and requiring lifelong pre-publication review for every government employee, not just CIA personnel, with access to highly classified information. Reagan tried to make light of the order at a press conference, announcing, 'What we're trying to control is what seems to be the favourite game of Washington, even more popular than the Redskins, and that is leaks.'[65] But the alarming 'ripple effect' from Snepp was obvious. Every American in federal employment was now required to follow their contract, not their conscience.

Lamentably, as James Bamford has written, while the government was busy institutionalising secrecy pacts and throwing the book at Snepp for an unclassified history of an old war, it was haemorrhaging highly sensitive secrets from under its nose.[66] In late 1977, William Kampiles, a 23-year-old James Bond wannabe, decided that his talents were going to waste as a trainee watch officer and decided to steal a manual on a super-secret spy satellite. After quitting his job, he flew to Athens where he sold the invaluable compendium to a Soviet agent. Meanwhile, working in another part of Langley, translator Larry Wu-Tai Chin was being lavishly compensated by the People's Republic of China for passing them classified documents.

The seeming injustice inherent in the punishment meted out to Snepp was compounded by the fact that, over the same period, the CIA refused to punish other employees who had broken the same rules. In summer 1977, having completed the draft of his memoir *Honorable Men*, Colby gave a copy to his publisher, Simon & Schuster, two weeks *before* he sent it to the PRB.[67] A year later, his agent passed a revised version to a French publisher, again before it had been reviewed and approved by the PRB. Remarkably, the French edition went to press without any clearance whatsoever. Moreover, it was published with real classified information, including details about 'Operation Azorian', the audacious attempt by the CIA in 1974 to salvage a sunken Soviet submarine three miles beneath the surface of the Pacific Ocean. The revelation in the French edition that the vessel *Glomar Explorer* had failed in its bid to retrieve nuclear missiles, transmission devices and codes had been removed by the PRB from the American edition. Colby could easily have been prosecuted and gone to jail for either the technical offence of not submitting the manuscript for prior review or the crime of disclosing actual secrets. However, in a lenient out-of-court settlement, he escaped with a $10,000 fine. In August 1981, a CIA report into whether the PRB was fair, or whether it was prone to impartial dealing, admitted that Colby was 'an instance of the Agency allowing greater latitude to an author because of his former status and presumed pro-Agency bias'.[68]

Colby was not the only one apparently exempt from the rules. The same report confirmed that retired Agency loyalist Cord Meyer, now a columnist, steadfastly refused to submit his articles to the PRB, despite repeated requests by Hetu to get him to do so.[69] In June 1982, Meyer appeared on the BBC's *Newsnight* programme and, to quote PRB legal

Herbert Yardley headed America's cryptographic bureau, the Black Chamber. In 1931, out of work and short of money, he told his story in a bestselling memoir, outraging the US government.

Between 1945 and 1947, many of the 'glorious amateurs' recruited by OSS head William Donovan (*centre*) went public about their wartime adventures to champion the need for a strong intelligence capability as a gathering storm with the Soviet Union threatened the peace.

Dapper OSS veteran Michael Burke worked on the 1946 film *Cloak and Dagger*, starring Gary Cooper, which was loosely based on his exploits behind enemy lines.

In the 1970s, many CIA officers were constitutionally dragooned to the witness stand. Here, Lyman Kirkpatrick prepares to testify to the Rockefeller Commission.

ABOVE The 1960 U-2 incident was the first major breach in the CIA's wall of secrecy. In 1955, to demonstrate the aircraft's capability, CIA officials had given President Eisenhower a photograph of him playing golf, taken at 55,000 feet. Here, Eisenhower (*left*) watches his grandson hole out on the lawn at Camp David.

ABOVE Stylish, witty and privileged, Joseph Alsop was one of several journalists with close links to the CIA.

RIGHT CIA Director Allen Dulles, with a grinning Richard Helms in tow, is all smiles as he emerges from testifying on Capitol Hill.

LEFT In 1962, journalist Andrew Tully published the first comprehensive history of the CIA. Tully drew heavily from overseas books about the Agency, including translations of texts by communist authors writing on the orders of the KGB.

The children of CIA propaganda specialist E. Howard Hunt watch as the Senate Watergate Committee questions their father about his part in the infamous burglary. Earlier, Allen Dulles had asked Hunt to come up with America's answer to James Bond.

Students at the University of Minnesota protest against the appearance of a CIA recruiter on campus.

ABOVE CIA officer Victor Marchetti (*right*) and State Department employee John Marks (*left*), authors of the first book in US history that the federal government ever went to court to censor before its publication.

LEFT Marchetti's legal battle with the CIA left him devastated. Pictured during happier times, with his two sons, he later said: 'I shoulda kept my mouth shut and never taken on the CIA.'

ABOVE DCI James Schlesinger (*right*) ordered for CIA road signs to be erected along the George Washington Memorial Parkway and Route 123. College students evidently thought they looked better in their dorm rooms, since no fewer than nine went missing.

RIGHT Daniel Ellsberg, of Pentagon Papers fame, protests against William Colby's appearance at the Harvard University Faculty Club.

LEFT In the eyes of many at Langley, DCI William Colby was far too open with congressional investigators. Here, in August 1975, he is primed to continue with his policy of controlled cooperation.

ABOVE As CIA Director, George H. W. Bush (*left*) considered it his duty to 'get the CIA off the front pages and at some point out of the papers altogether'.

LEFT Dedicated company man David Atlee Phillips knew that the CIA had an image problem when he told his fifteen-year-old daughter, pictured here, what he did for a living and she replied, 'But, Daddy, that's dirty.'

RIGHT Philip Agee's unauthorised disclosures horrified the CIA. Indeed, one officer allegedly said, 'If I can get him with my bare hands, I'll kill, I'll kill him.'

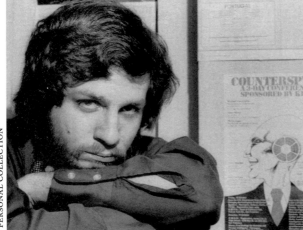

LEFT Days after CIA Station Chief Richard Welch was murdered by terrorists outside his home in Athens, Doug Porter, co-editor of the magazine *Counterspy*, announced that it would continue printing the names of CIA officers and sources.

LEFT Public sympathy for Philip Agee plummeted with the death of Richard Welch. Here, the flag-draped casket carrying the slain CIA officer is carried to its final resting place, in Arlington National Cemetery.

LEFT Senator Frank Church accused the CIA of using Welch's death as a rod to discredit the proposed reforms of congressional investigators. Pictured with Welch's widow, Kiki, President Ford authorised for the body to be buried at Arlington, a privilege normally reserved for fallen military heroes.

RIGHT After a cause célèbre, both Philip Agee and Mark Hosenball (pictured), a young US journalist, were ordered by the British government to leave the UK on national security grounds.

ABOVE President Jimmy Carter (*right*) gave Stansfield Turner (*left*) a directive to make the CIA more open. Here, both men face the cameras as Turner is sworn in as CIA Director.

RIGHT In 1977, Cord Meyer left the CIA for a career as a columnist. Controversially, he refused to submit his articles for pre-publication review, but was never punished for breaking the rules.

William Colby allowed the French-language edition of his memoirs to be published *before* it had been cleared by the CIA. He was fined $10,000, but the punishment could have been much more severe.

Frank Snepp was sued by the CIA for not submitting for pre-publication review his book *Decent Interval*. A judge ordered that Snepp turn over to the government all the profits from the book, calling them 'ill-gotten gains'.

CIA Director William Casey (*left*), a veteran of the 'Oh So Secret' OSS, had little time for public affairs.

© NARA

© PERSONAL COLLECTION

LEFT Victory in the Cold War, while a cause for celebration at the CIA, raised the spectre of reduced funding. One of the loudest advocates of budget cuts was four-term US Senator Daniel P. Moynihan.

RIGHT Popularly known by the epithet 'The Man Who Kept the Secrets', Richard Helms took everyone by surprise when he decided to write a memoir. The book tried to convey the friendlier side to his personality – something he felt historians had ignored.

© CORBIS

LEFT President Nixon greets CIA employees during a visit to Langley on 7 March 1969. In his memoirs, Richard Helms had wanted to reveal that Nixon shook the hands of over 400 staff, but his coadjutor, William Hood, felt that this would undermine the book's thesis that Nixon was cold and distrustful of the Agency.

© ALEX WONG / GETTY IMAGESS

LEFT 'If Agent Mulder ever needed a lawyer, Zaid would be his man.' Mark Zaid (*right*) has handled many cases involving memoirists and the CIA's Publications Review Board.

adviser Paul Schilling, 'made various statements concerning the intelligence capabilities of the United States'.[70] Yet, no action was taken. It
was the same story with another hard-core CIA man, former Director
George H. W. Bush. Between 1977 and 1983, he wrote extensively on
intelligence matters but submitted only one item to the PRB, a 98-page
chapter of his memoir *Looking Forward*.[71] Out on the hustings as a
vice-presidential and presidential candidate in 1980, 1984 and 1988, he
made countless statements about CIA work, again without consulting
the PRB. Recognising the double standard, Romano Louis Mazzoli
of Kentucky, a member of the House Permanent Select Intelligence
Committee, remarked cuttingly: 'Ambassador Bush has been saying a
great many things about the CIA as part of his presidential campaign'.[72]
Colby, Meyer and Bush were clear cases of there being one rule for the
high and mighty who write laudatory accounts, and quite another for
smaller fry who cause embarrassment.

The final insult for Snepp came when Graham Martin, the diplomat he
held most responsible for refusing to accept the blindingly obvious defeat
of Thieu's government, escaped punishment for what seemed an incredible breach of security. At 2 a.m. on 22 December 1977, after a long drive
through the snow from Washington to his retirement home in Winston-
Salem, North Carolina, Martin pulled his car into the driveway. Cold,
exhausted and struggling with a hernia, he decided to leave removing the
contents of the trunk until the morning. He left the keys in the ignition.
Later that night, four teenagers skulked up the drive and stole the vehicle.
On Christmas Day, the car was found abandoned in a clearing by a lake.
The trunk was empty. Martin informed police that it contained some innocuous personal papers, useless to anyone but himself. A few days later,
a stack of Top Secret documents, a foot high, was found in a bush. The
FBI took possession of the material and asked Martin if everything was
accounted for; he assured the G-men that that was the case.

Shortly thereafter, however, an even greater cache of classified
documents was discovered in a deserted house just north-east of

Winston-Salem. The FBI soon realised that the contents of Martin's trunk had been embassy files he had secretly 'squirreled away' and shipped to the US on the eve of Saigon's collapse, perhaps with the intention of one day writing his own memoir. The sensitivity of the material was beyond question. It included National Security Council cables to the embassy; maps of US missile and submarine deployments; briefings on the progress of the Paris Peace talks; private letters between Nixon and Thieu; and, most sensitively of all, messages sent strictly through 'back channels'. As one Justice Department official commented: 'The documents were a piece-by-piece record of every secret communication on strategic matters from the White House to the ambassadors in Saigon from the early '60s to Martin.'[73] 'The Russians would have paid millions for them,' he estimated.[74]

The Justice Department considered prosecuting Martin for mishandling of classified material. The loss of documents relating to national defence violated Title 18, Section 739, of the US Code, and carried a maximum $10,000 fine and ten years in prison. Although Martin claimed that as an ambassador he was authorised to declassify documents from Saigon as he saw fit (an argument dismissed by a State Department lawyer as 'utter bullshit'), he had signed an affidavit upon returning to Washington swearing that he had surrendered all classified documents to the authorities. Moreover, he had clearly lied to the police and the FBI about the true contents of the car's boot. Nevertheless, no legal action was taken. No explanation was given, but Beltway gossips hazarded a guess that he was spared because officials worried that, if charged, he would 'turn up a lot of skeletons' and implicate senior figures in US foreign policy circles. It was also speculated that officials felt sorry for Martin, recently diagnosed with lung cancer, and did not want to give him more grief. Of course, none of these reasons were of any comfort to Snepp, a lesser mortal and clearly more 'expendable' in the eyes of the authorities.[75]

IV. Double Standards

I conclude that the CIA, reacting as any bureaucracy, uses pre-publication review and spurious claims of national security to prevent the American people from learning of its illegal and embarrassing operations.
CIA Officer Ralph McGehee, 18 January 1984.[76]

In the aftermath of the Snepp ruling, the PRB was kept extremely busy, as most authors took no chances with violating their secrecy agreements. In 1977, it received forty-two submissions, comprising books, articles, novels, scripts, book reviews, speeches and letters to editors.[77] In 1978, the number had grown to sixty-two. In 1979, there were ninety-four and, in 1980, 148.[78] The proliferation of submissions put considerable strain on the PRB. An internal investigation calculated that, between April 1980 and April 1981, the equivalent of five man-years were spent on reviews. As the investigation saw it, 'This is a high expenditure of resources for an activity unconnected to intelligence collection and analysis.'[79]

Beyond the increased workload, there were other problems. The same investigation highlighted major disagreements between PRB members on what was validly classifiable. Typically, the DO wanted to delete 'substantially more' than the Office of General Counsel.[80] Moreover, when confronted with a particularly problematic manuscript, the DO preferred to ban it in total whereas the General Counsel favoured rewording only the most objectionable passages. It is not surprising that the left and the right hands of the Board struggled to work together. As former field operative Melissa Boyle Mahle wrote in *Denial and Deception* (2005), 'While the CIA is a secret organisation, the Directorate of Operations is the heart of secrecy.'[81] For the operations officer to tell anyone anything is an unnatural act. Indeed, for a long time they were forbidden from telling their spouses who they worked for.

Another problem was keeping track of what intelligence-related information existed in the public domain. Without a comprehensive institutional record of disclosed material, the PRB risked being embarrassed, or even sued, if it denied an author the right to publish something already publicly available. Since the Board was formed, it had relied heavily on the memory of old hands and time-consuming, manual file searches. However, it had been caught out on several occasions, much to the disgust of the author in question. The probability of future slips was increased by the fact that the CIA's human memory was a fast-declining commodity, owing to retirements and Turner's 'purge'.

Putting these difficulties to one side, the PRB's decision-making in the years immediately following the Snepp verdict was highly questionable, with defenders and critics seldom receiving equal treatment. Two cases, in particular, cast a long shadow over the Board's reputation for even-handedness. The first involved Ralph McGehee. Disenchanted after twenty-five years with the Agency, in 1977 he took early retirement and decided to write a book setting forth his criticisms. Like Snepp, he tried to keep his project a secret, but the CIA soon discovered his intentions and (according to McGehee) placed him under 'close, intimidating, and multiple types of surveillance'.[82] On 26 February 1980, like a good soldier, he submitted his draft to the PRB. A month later, the Board notified him that it required 397 deletions, varying in length from one word to several pages. Over the next few weeks, he liaised with a PRB representative, whom the CIA identified only as 'Bob', to prove that the forbidden items had already appeared elsewhere. During their first meeting, McGehee recalled, Bob said to him: 'It's too bad you don't work for the Israeli intelligence service. They know how to deal with people like you. They'd take you out and shoot you.'[83] Charming.

The source of the dispute was the book's discussion of McGehee's six years in Thailand, where he had worked on joint operations between the CIA and the Thai government.[84] The PRB argued that the CIA–Thai collaboration was still secret and demanded that all references to it be removed, a request that would have rendered the book worthless. McGehee successfully defeated the claim by demonstrating not only that pictures of the Bangkok Station Chief had appeared in Thai newspapers, but also that the liaison relationship had been discussed in other cleared writings, principally by pro-Agency authors. Remarkably, the PRB then reversed its earlier assessment of the manuscript and began reclassifying information it had previously judged to be safe for release. For example, it suddenly ruled that McGehee could not discuss his training at Camp Peary; nor was he now allowed to mention details of the personality assessment given to new recruits, even though a proprietary company had copyrighted and published the test. Eventually, after two years of getting nowhere with the PRB, McGehee appealed directly to CIA Deputy Director Bobby Ray Inman. Agreeing that the censorship had been arbitrary, slow and cumbersome, Inman ruled in his favour in every instance. *Deadly Deceits* was finally published in April 1983. In the media, McGehee launched a series of stinging diatribes against the PRB. 'Any officer who's writing a negative book about the CIA is going to receive the same treatment,' he said in one radio interview. 'The Agency made no bones about it. They just weren't going to let me write my book. If any information is embarrassing, shows them doing immoral things, they'll classify it.'[85]

The second high-profile case to throw into doubt the fairmindedness of the PRB concerned the flamboyant intelligence veteran Wilbur Crane Eveland. During the 1950s, bewitched by Kiplingesque myths and the legend of Lawrence of Arabia, Eveland believed passionately in the democratisation of the Arab world and had been a leading figure behind the CIA's clandestine operations in the Middle East – where he always wore top hat and tails, even in soaring desert heat. He knew the Egyptian leader Gamal Abdel Nasser, as well as the Shah of Iran, and worked closely with top Middle East operatives Miles Copeland and the cousins Archibald and Kermit Roosevelt – the

CIA's so-called 'three musketeers'.[86] In his book *The Game Player*, Copeland wrote that, 'I still think of the period 1957–60 as the Eveland Era of Arab-American politics'.[87] Eveland was never a permanent CIA employee and, accordingly, received no formal training or security briefing. An NSC staff member, he was loaned to the Agency at the personal request of Allen Dulles, contracted as a temporary consultant to provide the CIA with deniability for his actions.[88]

By 1976, a series of bad business choices and dubious professional contacts had left him languishing, destitute, in a Singapore prison. From the jailhouse, he experienced an epiphany that led him to question the US government's overt and covert interventions in the Middle East. He arrived at the view that many of the current troubles in the region – from the Palestinian issue and oil dependence to Soviet adventurism and the reluctance of Israel to accept its borders – had stemmed from thirty years of narrow-minded and ultimately self-defeating US policies. After his release, therefore, he decided to write an account showing how past mistakes had caused present problems – possibly beyond any hope of repair.

Eveland was anxious to ensure that he would not be thwarted by any CIA chicanery designed to quash his First Amendment right to inform the public about the Agency's mistakes. He watched and studied developments with the Snepp case assiduously, determined to find a loophole or some nifty way that would prevent him from being silenced. In the hope of catching the CIA off guard, he wrote the book in secret and only planned to notify them at the eleventh hour before publication. Beginning in May 1976, he also began submitting Freedom of Information and Privacy Act requests to the CIA, soliciting copies of his personnel records – performance reviews; medical and psychological reports; and most importantly, from the perspective of his authorial aspirations, secrecy contracts.[89] By January 1977, the CIA had acknowledged the existence of 226 relevant documents in the Agency's files, but, with fatiguing insistence, agreed to release to him only six.[90] Crucially, he was refused a copy of his secrecy agreement, leading him to doubt whether one in fact existed. Over the next three years, he tried repeatedly to acquire a copy of his purported contract, but to no avail. There was nothing unreasonable about his request: if the contract existed, he would be obliged to submit his manuscript for pre-publication review. Clearly, he did not want to suffer the same fate as Snepp.

On 20 February 1980, shortly after the Supreme Court ruled against Snepp, Eveland wrote to Turner outlining that he urgently needed to see his secrecy contract – to determine his contractual obligations – because he had finished a book on American failure in the Middle East and approximately fifty bound galley proofs were being circulated to commercially interested parties.[91] Believing he had shut the door on memoirs being published without clearance, Turner was taken by surprise. A comical situation followed in which the CIA continued to withhold the contract, yet insisted that prior review was compulsory. In the press, it was ridiculed for invoking a secrecy clause that was apparently too secret to disclose to the man who had signed it! 'All I want is the date of a piece of paper and the operative clause and my signature on the bottom of it,' Eveland protested.[92] On 4 April, the CIA finally relented and provided him with three contracts, the first of which was executed on 3 June 1955. With this, Eveland sprung his trap, arguing that the 'deplorable' and 'inexcusable' delay in receiving his contract exempted him from pre-publication review.[93] The CIA could hardly claim that he had wilfully, deliberately or surreptitiously breached a fiduciary duty when, acting in good faith, he had continually urged for a copy of his contract. Recognising this, and also aware of the fact that proofs were in the hands of journalists and publishers, the PRB agreed not to review the manuscript. In effect, the CIA had been hoist by its own earlier petard.

Published in June 1980, *Ropes of Sand* was a devastating first-hand indictment of US foreign policy in the era of Eisenhower. With forceful candour, Eveland argued that the recent history of the Middle East was a succession of American capitulations to oil companies, Arab 'wild men', and Israeli provocations and rapacity. The Dulles brothers were presented as fanatical ideologues who viewed the world only in Cold War terms and had no grasp of the politics and psychology of Arab nationalism. According to Eveland, their obsession with clandestine operations aimed at preventing the spread of communism had not only made the Middle East a tinderbox, but also opened the oil-rich region to Soviet penetration. 'It is impossible to understand America's continuing failure in the Middle East', he wrote, 'without taking into account the misapplication of the CIA's responsibilities and functions in that area: the extent to which presidents have ignored its intelligence estimates; the degree to which its clandestine political action capabilities have been employed as substitutes for sound foreign policy and conventional diplomacy.'[94]

At the heart of the story was the CIA's tragicomic attempt to stage an anti-communist coup in Syria in 1957. Following the previous year's disastrous attempt by the colluding powers of Britain, France and Israel to invade Egypt and remove Nasser from power, Syria had grown increasingly close to the Soviet Union, not out of an ideological affinity with communism, but to preserve and promote Arab nationalism, which Moscow endorsed. Western policymakers were deeply concerned by Syria's drift leftward, since the country contained arterial pipelines that transported oil from the pro-Western Iraq to Turkey and the Mediterranean. Flush with success after restoring the Shah of Iran to his throne in 1953, the CIA was confident that it could bring about a secret regime change in the country. The plan was hatched by Kermit Roosevelt, the leader of the coup that overthrew Mossadegh, alongside several key covert action specialists in the Lebanese capital of Beirut. So obvious was their presence that the Egyptian ambassador in Lebanon took bets on when and where the next coup would take place. Roosevelt and his team did not help themselves by using cover names drawn randomly from an old Australian telephone directory. As Eveland wryly remarked, since there were no Australians in Beirut, they might as well have worn nametags announcing, 'Hello, I'm with the CIA'.[95] Roosevelt sent Howard 'Rocky' Stone, another who had earned his spurs in Iran, to engineer the takeover from the ground in Damascus. Accredited as a second secretary at the US embassy, he passed cash-filled suitcases to right-wing Syrian Army officers, with the promise of more riches if they pulled off the coup.

However, the plot failed when some of the officers handed the kickbacks to the authorities and identified the CIA bagman who had tendered them. Stone was declared *persona non grata* and expelled from the country. Washington's tunnel-vision view of Arab nationalists being *a priori* pro-Soviet became a self-fulfilling prophecy: disgusted with the scheming Americans, the Syrian leadership became even more entrenched within the Soviet camp, signing new agreements for economic aid and military hardware.

Not long after the book's publication, Eveland was shocked to discover that the CIA had approached the Justice Department to discover if they could file a suit against him under the Snepp precedent.[96] Since the PRB had passed up the opportunity to review the manuscript, this was interpreted as the CIA once again seeking payback for someone bold enough to bruise its ego. On this occasion, however, government officials decided against any legal action. The odds of a successful conviction were stacked against them. As discussed, the Snepp decision required a *knowing* violation of a pre-publication review requirement, something that the CIA would find hard to demonstrate since it had been unreasonably dilatory in declassifying the relevant secrecy agreements. Moreover, the informal nature of Eveland's association with the CIA and the circumstances of his recruitment were such that it was not obvious that he incurred the same duty as a regular employee. Denied the opportunity to drag the old Arab adventurer through the courts, the CIA, Eveland alleged, found other ways to get its revenge. He believed that the CIA was responsible for leaking documents that implied that he had handed secrets to the British intelligence officer and traitor Kim Philby, whom he befriended when the latter was posted to Beirut in 1956. When his wife Daisy passed away of cancer in 1982, he charged that an intelligence officer coldly confessed to him in the hospital that he had switched off her respirator. Shortly after this, he nearly died in a hit-and-run car accident, which he claimed was an attempt on his life. There is no evidence to support these accusations.

Ironically, a further victim of the post-Snepp crackdown on memoirs was none other than Turner, the person who had toughened up the PRB and put respectful dissenters like Snepp, McGehee and Eveland through the wringer. After leaving the CIA in January 1981, he had become a commentator and writer. In 1983, he completed his first book, *Secrecy and Democracy: The CIA in Transition*.

In the two years since Turner had retired, there had been much change at CIA, to the extent that many historians now consider this period the Agency's 'second golden age'. Arguably, relations between Langley and the White House had never been so good. William Casey, who had been the 'Gipper's' campaign manager, and was the first CIA Director to hold a place in the Cabinet, enjoyed a close friendship with Reagan, even calling him 'Ron'.[97] As the Cold War heated up, Reagan spoke in cavalier terms of 'unleashing the CIA' and, in December 1981, he signed Executive Order 12333 giving the CIA extended powers with regard to covert action. As part of the Reagan Doctrine of opposing the global influence of the Soviet Union, and evoking the spirit of 'Wild Bill', Casey, a veteran of the OSS, armed mujahedeen forces fighting the Russian Army in Afghanistan and supported the contras in their battle against the left-wing Sandinista regime in Nicaragua.[98]

The second golden age saw a return to increased levels of secrecy. Casey had no time for public affairs. Believing that the CIA's survival and budget were no longer at stake, and true to his 'Oh So Secret' roots, he abolished the Office of Public Affairs and replaced it with an Office of External Affairs, operating further down the bureaucratic flow chart with a third fewer staff. Furious, Hetu left to set up his own PR firm. His job passed to William Doswell, an affable former statehouse lobbyist, but his brief was that of damage limitation rather than public education. On his first day, Casey told him: 'Billy, we're going to be a no-profile agency.'[99] Doswell swiftly pulled the plug on many of Hetu's initiatives, suspending press briefings and terminating outsider visits to Langley. In a memo, Casey wrote: 'It was hard for me to justify having the Rockville Rotary Club come into the CIA. I don't see how that would benefit the Agency.'[100] Public speaking by CIA officers was cut back. On 15 October 1981, Casey was given a rough ride by organised hecklers during a talk at Brown University. The school begged his forgiveness, and hoped that the behaviour of a 'malevolent minority' would not 'colour his opinion' of the university.[101] Casey accepted the apology, but his willingness to venture onto college campuses was shattered.

Casey also earned a reputation for making threatening phone calls to publishers whose authors he thought to be anti-CIA. In June 1986, Random House chairman Robert Bernstein complained to the press that Casey, in his inimitably gruff and partially unintelligible New York accent, had made numerous 'disturbing' calls in which he threatened federal prosecution if the publisher went ahead with a book by Seymour Hersh that might contain sensitive information about the downing of a Korean Air Lines jetliner in 1983. 'The idea of the head of the CIA cruising around making phone calls – I hate to use a cliché such as a "chilling effect" – but it certainly does that,' Bernstein protested.[102]

Against this background, in early 1983 Turner submitted his book to the PRB. As an author now on the receiving end of the process, he found the experience capricious and cold-blooded. Working at tortoise-like speed, the PRB spent two years haggling with him, insisting on redactions that he considered 'unreasonable', 'unnecessary' and 'nitpicking'.[103] In the case of one chapter, the clearance process lasted an excruciating five months.[104] The board's chairman, Charles Wilson, censored information that was widely available in the public domain, including quotations from unclassified speeches Turner had given as DCI. Turner later remarked that the proposed cuts 'ranged from borderline to the ridiculous'.[105] Taught from his navy days that a smooth sea never made a skilful sailor, the retired Admiral challenged many of the deletions, in some cases appealing to the higher levels of the CIA. At one point, he was even prepared to litigate.[106]

The PRB was in no mood for compromise. Trapped in a maze of his own making, Turner obtained a measly three minor concessions. By the time the book was eventually published in 1985, it had been gutted. 'The CIA's censors shredded more than 100 passages from this book,' declared the publisher on the back cover. One of the encomiums referred to the 'CIA's literary butchers'. Ludicrous pettifoggery dictated that even the colour and style of a person's hair was treated as classified information.

When asked by journalists, Turner refused to be drawn on the motives of the CIA's censors, gracefully accepting that it was a case of *c'est la vie*. The PRB's conduct was certainly consistent with Casey's broader efforts to have more secrecy back at CIA. Yet, it is also tempting to conclude that there was an element of revenge behind the way Turner was treated. Since leaving the CIA, he had been extremely vocal in his criticism of Casey, suggesting that he was too close to partisan politics. He publicly deplored Casey's indifference to oversight, and found it laughable that Casey had appointed an operations officer as the CIA's chief congressional liaison who – *quelle surprise* – was seldom forthcoming with the legislative branch. Then, of course, there was the fact that Turner was still remembered at CIA for his hugely controversial decision to decimate the undercover rank-and-file. Whatever the PRB's reason for being tough on Turner, the irony was thick: he had been snared by the very rules that he created. Snepp could not hide his delight. Speaking to the press, he said: 'I think Turner deserves everything the censors visit on him because he failed to recognise just how dangerous censorship was in the first place.'[107] Poetic justice had been served.

Chapter 6

The Helms Experiment: Righting and Writing the Record

I. Midlife Crisis

New world out there. Adjust or die.
DCI Robert Gates, handwritten notation, November 1991.[1]

The Berlin Wall was the literal and symbolic epicentre of the Cold War, an imposing concrete edifice, nearly four metres high in places, with large segments enveloped in barbed wire and patrolled by grim-faced border guards with machine guns and attack dogs. Its destruction ranks as one of the most important political events of the second half of the twentieth century. As the wall came crashing down in a cloud of dust caused by chisels, sledgehammers and bulldozers, the mood in Berlin was euphoric. On the historic night of 9 November 1989, enormous crowds gathered to celebrate and watch as thousands of East Germans surged freely through the open gates, shouting and cheering as they went, to be greeted by friends and family on the other side. With each passing day, more sections of the wall were dismantled. With the world's media capturing every moment, joyous Berliners honked car horns at each other, hugged and kissed total strangers, and danced and drank from wine bottles atop the divide. *Mauerspechte* – 'Wall Woodpeckers' – chipped away at the bricks to take home as souvenirs. A city that had been devastated by the worst conflict in human history, and then divided by the victors, separating loved ones for a generation, could at last look forward to a brighter, unified future.

Out of public view, over 4,000 miles away on the rural outskirts of Washington, the CIA had a party of its own to rival the scenes on the streets of Berlin. Former CIA officer Melissa Boyle Mahle has written that the atmosphere at Langley on the night when the first people spilled across the border was 'downright festive'.[2] 'The corridors were alive with people, talking, laughing, and swapping war stories … There was champagne and a sense of camaraderie among the Cold War warriors. The good guys had won.'[3] For the CIA, the wall's demolition was just the beginning of a two-year orgy of celebration and self-congratulation. In December 1991, the Soviet Union fragmented into fifteen separate countries, bringing the Cold War to an end. The collapse of the formidable 'Evil Empire' was hailed by the West as a victory for freedom, the ultimate triumph of capitalism and liberal democracy over socialism and authoritarian regimes. The Agency gloried in the role it had played in bringing about the end game with the Soviet Union. Milton 'Milt' Bearden, the tall, big-boned Texan who managed the CIA's covert programme of delivering Stinger missiles to flagging mujahedeen rebels battling the occupying Soviet forces in Afghanistan, was adamant that the Agency had played a decisive role in ending the Cold War. He and other celebrants pointed to the fact that within months of the beleaguered Red Army's withdrawal from Afghanistan in February 1989, countries across Eastern Europe threw off the communist yoke in a series of stunning revolutions, fortified by a belief that Russian tanks would not roll after tasting defeat in the landlocked, mountainous country.

However, the good times did not last for the spooks, as people began contemplating the future of the CIA, its relevance and purpose. With the Soviet Union broken up into constituent republics and the United States no longer at war in an era Francis Fukuyama famously hailed as the 'end of history', in which secular free-market democracy reigned unchallenged, the obvious question for critics and congressional appropriators was – what was the Agency's reason for being? As Rhodri Jeffreys-Jones has argued, with the threat of the USSR now gone, it became more possible to ask tough questions about the CIA without being branded unpatriotic.[4]

The most high-profile voice in the campaign for rethinking the relevance of the CIA was Daniel Patrick Moynihan, a distinguished former ambassador, senator and White House adviser.[5] Indeed, he remains the only person to have served in the Cabinets or subcabinets of four consecutive presidents (Kennedy, Johnson, Nixon and Ford). Moynihan's beef with the CIA was twofold. Firstly, that it was dysfunctional and incompetent; to quote David Wise, a 'bunch of Maxwell Smarts who can't even make Fidel Castro's beard fall out'.[6] Although disputed by the Agency itself and a number of revisionists, it was widely held in popular discourse that the CIA had failed to predict the disintegration of the Soviet Union, adding to earlier flops such as failing to foresee the Arab–Israeli War in 1973 and missing India's first nuclear test a year later. Trying to predict world events is, of course, extremely difficult; but, according to Langley's business managers, analysis was the brightest star in its firmament. Moynihan's second criticism was that of excessive secrecy. In 1984, he had resigned in protest as the Vice Chairman of the Senate Intelligence Committee, citing the CIA's refusal to keep the committee 'fully informed' about US support for the Contras in Nicaragua. With Glasnost now sweeping across the old Eastern bloc, he considered the CIA's obsession with secrecy as outdated and dangerous.

In a move calculated to make a metaphorical point about the CIA being a dinosaur and Cold War relic, in 1991 Moynihan proposed a bill that would have disbanded the organisation and divided up its various functions among the State Department, Department of Defense and FBI.[7] This made headline news; hitherto, only leftist firebrands such as

Agee and the editor of *CounterSpy* had been bold enough to suggest actually abolishing the CIA.[8] A year later, two federal lawmakers, US Senator David Boren and US Representative David McCurdy, chairmen of the Senate and House Intelligence Committees respectively, introduced two separate bills calling for a major restructuring of the intelligence community. Under the draft legislation, all analytical programmes, including the CIA's analysis branch, would be collapsed into a single National Intelligence Center. Even more significantly, it recommended the creation of a Director of National Intelligence (DNI) with statutory authority over the activities and budgets of every US intelligence agency. Taken together, the Moynihan and Boren-McCurdy proposals encouraged every American, from the Beltway to the heartland, to think about whether, in a post-Cold War context, it was sensible to keep ploughing money into the CIA. For liberals, a reduced intelligence budget meant better healthcare. For conservatives, lower taxes.

Not since the dark days of the intelligence flap had the CIA faced a bigger crisis. Mahle remembers seeing cars garlanded with 'abolish the CIA' bumper stickers.[9] In truth, the CIA's survival was not at stake; barring the political fringes and individuals of a conspiratorial mien, people generally accepted the continued requirement for a US foreign intelligence organisation. As David Wise wrote in the *Washington Post*, 'It is difficult to imagine the United States, the world's major power, without an intelligence service, any more than it would make do without an army, navy, or air force.'[10] However, the prospect of budget cuts and downsizing was very real; even Colby was quoted as saying that it was now time to beat swords into ploughshares. As was the possibility of Beltway rivals encroaching on the CIA's territory. The emergence of transnational terrorism, international organised crime and drug trafficking heralded a new kind of threat that knew no national borders. To eradicate these dangers, national jurisdictions were required to work together in real time, meaning that the traditional distinction between foreign and domestic intelligence collection was breaking down. At

Langley, there was deep concern that it would lose the intelligence turf wars and see its budget, personnel and prestige diminished.

Notwithstanding the fact that it is the natural instinct of any bureaucracy to want more not less resources, the CIA worried about the harm across-the-board reductions could have on national security. Arguably, the New World Order was a more dangerous place than the Cold War, when the United States had the luxury of knowing who the enemy was, and when both superpowers had a mutual interest in controlling regional conflicts, for fear that they themselves came to blows. 'There was a certain safety with the Cold War,' notes Mahle. 'Each side knew its part and played it more or less consistently.'[11] In its place had emerged something more complex, with the number of threats to the US not only multiplying, but becoming harder to identify and understand than the challenge presented by a unified but fragile USSR. The splintering of the Soviet empire had sparked wars of nationalism and religious ethnic strife, which, like a cancer, could metastasise anywhere, while there was concern about the fate of 30,000 Soviet nuclear warheads.[12] The threats to the United States, its friends and its allies from drug cartels, terrorists and third-world countries seeking weapons of mass destruction was growing, as illustrated by the 1993 World Trade Center bombing. In his confirmation hearing as DCI, James 'Jim' Woolsey painted a vivid image of the US having successfully slain a dragon, but now living 'in a jungle filled with a bewildering variety of poisonous snakes'. With justification, the CIA feared having to do more with less.

Senior Agency hands wrote to Congress and to the White House cautioning about the dangers of austerity. 'We as a nation must be committed to a strong intelligence capability,' urged DD/CIA William Studeman in a letter to Moynihan on 6 August 1992: 'It is our first line of defense.'[13] Early warning by the CIA, he argued, was more critical now than ever, owing to the fact that the 'peace dividend' was reducing America's military muscle. Put another way, intelligence was a force multiplier. A month later, it was the turn of the CIA's top man, DCI Robert Gates, to fire a shot across Moynihan's bow. Taking a different approach, Gates claimed that anyone who held that the dissolution of the USSR justified deep cuts was labouring under a 'troubling mis-apprehension' of the CIA's mission over the past fifty years.[14] Since its creation, he emphasised, it had been expected to provide intelligence on a range of military, economic and political threats and had never solely focused on Moscow. In 1980, at the height of its commitment to the Cold War, only 58 per cent of its resources were dedicated to the Soviet Union – 'a far smaller share than many may suppose'.[15] 'I believe it would be irresponsible to put the nation's intelligence capabilities in jeopardy by making a hasty decision on the floor to invoke further reductions,' Gates stressed:

> While the danger of a global holocaust has receded dramatically with the demise of the Soviet Union, in its wake we are seeing a dra-matic multiplication of civil and regional wars, dozens of countries developing weapons of mass destruction, and other problems of in-terest to you, your colleagues, the Administration and this country.[16]

In other words, protecting national security had become a major un-dertaking, and major undertakings do not come cheap.

Attempts by the CIA to convince policymakers, especially the White House, not to slash its budget too quickly or too deeply was never going to be easy. As we saw in Chapter 5, under Reagan the CIA enjoyed cosy relations with the Executive Branch, a situation that continued under George H. W. Bush (1989–93). A former CIA Director of course, Bush invited senior intelligence officers to lavish summer picnics at the White House, as well as weekends at his country retreat, Camp David. However, Bill Clinton did not share the same love for the CIA as these two predecessors, and gave conflicting public statements about his plans for intelligence spending, Out on the political hustings he had pledged to reduce spending on intelligence by $7 billion *below* the budget suggested by Bush for the fiscal years 1993–97, but at the same time compared cutting intelligence budgets in peacetime to a person cancelling their health insurance when they are fit and healthy.[17] At the CIA, there was confusion and uncertainty: would the real Clinton please stand up!

After assuming the Oval Office, Clinton kept the CIA very much at arm's length. He never visited Langley, even when there was a memorial for someone killed in the line of duty, and seldom had CIA officers to the White House.[18] Indeed, when a mentally unhinged truck driver from Maryland crashed a stolen propeller-driven Cessna airplane on to the South Lawn in 1994, staff members joked that they expected to see DCI Jim Woolsey emerge from the wreckage, desperate for an audience with the president. In a private letter to Moynihan on 31 August 1993 that would have horrified the CIA, bringing back memories of Turner's Halloween Massacre, he stated that he was coming round to the view that wholesale personnel reductions were the way to go, and was even open to other government departments annexing some of the CIA's responsibilities. 'If our global eyes have failed us in the past', he wrote, 'the answer is not to gouge them out, but to get new glasses'.[19]

In this context, the CIA realised that it would take a lot more than doom-laden letters to appropriators to persuade them that it was worth the candle. Much of the political reluctance to bankroll intelligence activity in a post-Cold War environment stemmed from ignorance of not only the CIA's operational record, but of the widening and troubling threats to national security. The very label 'post-Cold War' was emblematic of this; people knew that an era of superpower rivalry was over, but had no clue what had replaced it.[20] Under Casey in the 1980s, the CIA had retreated into its shell, cutting back on many of the PR initiatives achieved under Hetu and Turner. In consequence, it again became the devil that nobody knew. One person who saw the danger of this antediluvian approach was Robert Gates, a career CIA officer who, in November 1991, became the first analyst to be appointed as Director. During his Senate confirmation hearings, Gates promised 'better popular understanding and support' through 'greater openness'. The CIA and its sister intelligence agencies, he testified, 'must change and be seen to change, or confront irrelevance and growing sentiment for their dismemberment'.[21] Less than two weeks after being sworn in as DCI, he sent a personal memo to the Director of Public Affairs, Joseph R. DeTrani, requesting the creation of a 'Task Force on Greater CIA Openness' to explore ways of 'making more information about the Agency available to the American people ... *to the extent possible* [emphasis added]'.[22] In keeping with his broader efforts to stamp his authority on the CIA and implement as many reforms as quickly as possible – the 'hundred days' approach to leadership – he gave DeTrani a month.[23]

Based on interviews conducted with CIA employees, but also senior individuals from the media, academia, private sector, and the Executive and Legislative branches, the final report bore more than a passing resemblance to the 'Telling the Intelligence Story' document of the mid-1970s. 'We have an important story to tell, a story that bears repeating,' it proudly declared.[24] Confirming what Gates already knew, it lamented that the American people and key constituencies, like Congress, 'do not understand the intelligence process and the role of intelligence in national security policymaking'.[25] Many Americans, it went on, 'still operate with a romanticised or erroneous view of intelligence from the movies, books and newspapers'.[26] The report emphasised that too much secrecy was not helping. When the CIA was silent about what it does, people interpreted this as arrogance; worse, they assumed that it was doing something wrong or not doing anything at all. 'The CIA will have to work harder at explaining the need for intelligence in a post-Cold War world,' the report concluded. 'We need to take initiatives to share our history ... [and] explain our mission and functions in a changing world.'[27] Of course, since the Office of Public Affairs was itself a fiefdom, facing an estimated 33 per cent cuts if noisy senators had their way, its findings were hardly surprising.

Gates naturally wanted to make a big show of his commitment to opening up the Agency, and planned to go public with the recommendations of his task force on 1 April 1992 – perhaps somewhat ill-timed scheduling, what with it being April Fool's Day.[28] Gates had his thunder stolen when, in true Washington fashion, the existence of DeTrani's report was leaked on 12 January. Greater embarrassment followed when the Center for National Security Studies in Washington, DC submitted a Freedom of Information request for a copy of the report, only to have it rejected by the CIA's Information and Privacy Coordinator. In the press, the CIA was ridiculed for failing to recognise the incongruity of classifying a document on openness. 'Even openness remains a secret at the CIA,' mocked the *New York Times*.[29] Old habits, it appeared, much like the CIA's imperviousness to irony, die hard.[30]

Gates formally introduced the outcomes of DeTrani's panel with a speech to the Oklahoma Press Association on 21 February 1992, in which he admitted that 'CIA Openness' was an oxymoron, but promised to change this. Over the next few years, he and his successor, Woolsey (dubbed by Mahle the 'first prime-time DCI' owing to his appearance on *Larry King Live*), oversaw a range of initiatives designed to make the CIA more visible and understandable, although whether these qualified as genuine openness, or PR dressed up as transparency in a bid to safeguard budgets, is up for debate.[31]

With great fanfare, the Agency's Center for the Study of Intelligence released a string of glossy, expensively bound volumes of declassified documents on some of the CIA's oldest operations. *Studies in Intelligence*, the CIA's journal founded by Sherman Kent in the 1950s, had many of its articles declassified, while Agency historians, hitherto strictly in-house, were encouraged to reach out by publishing unclassified essays and speaking at academic conferences. Although the CIA was keen to stress that its declassification programme was (to use

Woolsey's expression) 'warts and all', generally speaking, the material portrayed the Agency in a favourable light and avoided 'flap' potential. Batches of documents were released on the Cuban Missile Crisis and the Venona Project, both undoubtedly 'feel good' cases for the Agency, but nothing was volunteered on embarrassing episodes such as the Bay of Pigs, Chile or Angola. Critics lambasted this as a form of 'targeted declassification' and called on the CIA to demonstrate its dedication to openness by creating and sticking to an agreed timetable for putting historical materials into the public domain.[32] This was rejected.

The CIA's bid to give itself a makeover led to the creation of a new position within the Office of Public Affairs – 'Entertainment Industry Liaison' – responsible for giving guidance and support to filmmakers looking to incorporate the Agency into their celluloid projects. There was nothing out of the ordinary about this. Quite the opposite: among Beltway partners, the CIA was very much a latecomer to Hollywood liaison. The FBI established an entertainment liaison office in the 1930s. The Department of Defense did so in 1947, and since then the army, navy and air force had all followed suit. To gain leverage over filmmakers, the Pentagon loaned priceless equipment and props such as submarines, helicopters, tanks and even aircraft carriers. In return, it was given the opportunity to make scripts more to its liking.

The first person hired for the belated CIA equivalent was Chase Brandon, a 25-year DO veteran who had good connections in Hollywood (one of his cousins was the actor Tommy Lee Jones). The logic behind his appointment was that spy fiction had a real, if intangible, impact upon public perceptions of intelligence. The alarming reality for Langley was that most filmmakers either demonised the CIA, with plots involving emotionless assassins roaming the globe, or likened them to a bunch of Keystone Kops. 'Year after year,' lamented Brandon, 'as movie goers and TV watchers, we've seen our image and our reputation constantly sullied with egregious, ugly representations of who were are and what we stand for. We've been imbued with these extraordinary

Machiavellian conspiratorial capabilities.'[33] Negative cinematic treatments started in the 1970s, at the height of the Agency's troubles, with films like *Three Days of the Condor* (1975). In his inaugural address as DCI, delivered in the 'bubble' on 4 March 1976, George H. W. Bush said that, over Christmas, his daughter – 'madly and passionately in love with Robert Redford' – had dragged him to watch *Three Days of the Condor*. This, he said, was a 'mistake'. 'It's fairly good shoot 'em up and, if I were totally untutored in this business, I might have got a yak out of it; but it was to lay at the CIA's doorstep all kinds of outrageous things that the CIA by its severest critics has never been accused of.'[34]

Tired of such negative on-screen depictions, and keen for films to give an 'accurate' and 'authentic' portrayal of the CIA, the Agency collaborated on several film and television projects, including *Enemy of the State* (1998), *Bad Company* (2002), *The Sum of All Fears* (2002) and *Alias* (2001–06). In each case, Brandon was heavily involved. He worked with scriptwriters to develop more credible storylines and characters, and advised on the Agency's technological capabilities to help with verisimilitude. He made certain intelligence officers available to interview and arranged visits for cast and crew to CIA headquarters. For 'special' projects, such as the television show *The Agency* (2001–03), he even allowed the filmmakers to bring their cameras to Langley and film the main building, plus office staff as extras. The collaboration worked because it was mutually advantageous. The studios could market their films as realistic, while the CIA was able to prevent negative characterisations at the source. Unsurprisingly, filmmakers who desired to present the CIA as an evil rogue entity, toppling governments and killing people, were given the cold shoulder. Take Doug Liman's *Bourne Identity*, starring Matt Damon. 'By page twenty-five [of the script]', recollected Brandon in an interview, 'I lost track of how many rogue operatives had assassinated people … I chucked the thing in the burn bag.'[35]

Declassification and film liaison were important for the CIA in trying to spread its gospel in light of the New World Order. But something was missing. In the past, whenever it had faced a crisis, someone from its ranks had always come forward with a book designed to shape public perceptions or set the record straight. After the Bay of Pigs, which had critics bloodlessly crucifying the CIA, Allen Dulles wrote *The Craft of Intelligence*; during the turbulent mid-1970s, David Atlee Phillips published *The Night Watch*. The predicament faced by the Agency as it sought to re-establish its footing in the post-Cold War world required someone to step up and do the same. The CIA needed a salesman and, as unlikely as it sounds, that person was Richard Helms.

II. 'The Man Who Kept the Secrets'

Dick believed for most of his life that nobody from CIA should write a memoir, especially former Directors.
Cynthia Helms, interview 2011.[36]

The first generation of CIA men and women had its fair share of colourful characters and soldiers of fortune. Take William Harvey – a covert operator who claimed to have slept with a woman every day since he was twelve years old, and who was often spotted at his desk and in meetings toying with a loaded revolver, spinning the chamber and squinting down the barrel. Known as 'America's real James Bond', and famed for his four-martini lunches, he once visited the Oval Office with a gun in the pocket of his pants and a holstered Colt Detective Special .38 attached to his belt in the small of his back.[37] Unsurprisingly, the Secret Service was not amused when they found out. Then there was Miles Copeland, a one-time Alabama jazz musician and trumpet player for the Glenn Miller orchestra who handed Egyptian leader Gamal Abdel Nasser a suitcase filled with $3 million without asking for a receipt.[38] Led by the freewheeling Frank Wisner, who suffered a tragic breakdown and committed suicide with his son's shotgun, the Operations Directorate in the 1950s was largely made up of Eastern Establishment 'cowboys' who had been together since Groton and then Harvard, Yale or Princeton. FBI Director J. Edgar Hoover described them as a 'gang of weirdos', although, given his own lifestyle, this might be seen as a case of the pot calling the kettle black.[39]

Amid the eccentrics and Ivy League patricians was Richard Helms. Neither moneyed nor well-born, he had graduated from Williams College. Although he was a familiar face on the capital social scene, he had no airs or graces. During a dinner party in April 1965, Senator Eugene McCarthy asked him if he knew the wine being served. He did not. He was then asked if he could identify the sauce on one of the courses, or the name of the flower in the table centrepiece. When he replied that he had no idea, McCarthy commented that James Bond would have done better.[40]

Helms buckled no swashes. He was not an adventurer. While it would be unfair to describe him as the classic man in an empty suit (not least because his suits were exquisite), he was a dyed-in-the-wool intelligence bureaucrat, laconic and reserved. In the early 1970s, few public servants enjoyed higher standing than Helms, even though little was actually known about him. He received favourable, sometimes fawning attention from the press, who commented on his quick mind, integrity, devotion to duty and – the highest honour in a town of dilettantes – consummate professionalism. In 1971, *Newsweek* called him a 'bureaucrat of cool competence', and claimed that he was second only to Henry Kissinger, DC player par excellence, on the party circuit – 'partly because it's chic to have a master spy to dinner and partly because he is such an attentive companion for the ladies'.[41] *Time* magazine, which featured Helms on its front cover on 24 February 1967, even admired his good looks, comparing him to the Italian actor and sex symbol Rudolph Valentino, known for his tall, dark and lean frame, and combed-back, pomaded hair.[42] Those who did know him thought him the very soul of the intelligence community – 'a professional among professionals'[43] – who kept the game honest and spoke truth unto power. Helms's stock in official circles soared when it emerged that President Nixon had asked him, unsuccessfully, to have the CIA pay bail for the Watergate burglars and to block the FBI's investigation into the scandal. By refusing to enmesh the Agency in the cover-up, Helms was seen as an official with a sense of honour, unmoved by political pressure.

By 1975, however, his reputation had taken a battering. The various inquiries into the CIA discovered his name on documents relating to virtually every misdeed performed by the Agency since its founding. Helms had never been one to lose sleep over the morals of intelligence work; he used to say that, 'If we wanted to be in the boy scouts, we would have *joined* the boy scouts.'[44] Yet, many of the revelations made him out to be a monster. He was linked with plots to assassinate Patrice Lumumba in the Congo, and was said to have approved the transfer of sniper rifles to Dominicans who wanted to kill Rafael Trujillo. His fingers were all over efforts in the early 1960s to hire the Mafia to poison Fidel Castro. (The mobster in question, 'Handsome Johnny' Roselli of the Chicago crime syndicate, was found dead in 1976, dismembered and stuffed into a 55-gallon steel fuel drum off the Miami coast.) Helms's signature authorised the invasive prying into over 200,000 items of first-class mail. Under Presidents Johnson and Nixon, he was revealed to have sanctioned Operation CHAOS, which involved CIA officers growing their hair, learning the language of the New Left and infiltrating anti-war movements. He oversaw the CIA's notorious programme of mind-control and drug testing, and was at the heart of the cover-up into the death of Frank Olson, the 43-year-old germ warfare specialist who was given LSD in a spiked glass of Cointreau and nine days later hurled himself through a closed window from the tenth floor of a New York hotel room. Helms was also criticised by the Rockefeller Commission for authorising the destruction of key evidence, including files relating to drug testing and Watergate.

As far as the court of public opinion was concerned, the final nail in Helms's coffin came in 1977 when federal prosecutors moved to indict him for perjury. The legal action stemmed from Helms's testimony before the Senate Foreign Relations Committee in 1973, where he was quizzed on whether the CIA had taken any part in the overthrow of Salvador Allende, the Marxist President of Chile, or passed any money to opposition groups in the country. In both cases, he gave an unequivocal 'No, sir'. It subsequently came to light that he had in fact run a major secret operation in the country, funnelling millions of dollars to enemies of the Allende government in a bid to destabilise it. In keeping with his policy of confessing the Agency's sins, DCI Colby turned the Helms matter over to the Justice Department, a decision that was regarded by the army of Helms's supporters as a shocking betrayal. Legendary counter-intelligence chief James Jesus Angleton told friends that he wondered if Colby might be working for the 'other side'.[45]

Helms ultimately cut a deal with the Justice Department whereby he pleaded 'no contest' to a lesser charge of misdemeanour and escaped with a two-year suspended sentence and a $2,000 fine. Outside the courtroom, he declared proudly that he wore his conviction 'like a badge of honor'. For his refusal to reveal secrets to democracy's watchdogs, he was a hero to the hard-core traditionalists at Langley. After the trial, he attended a reunion of former colleagues who gave him a standing ovation and raised his fine by passing the hat. For critics, however, he was a symbol of everything that was wrong about the CIA. Whatever good this charming and dedicated spook may have done was suddenly forgotten. Seen through the prism of dirty tricks, and through the splenetics of his opponents, he was reconstituted as a ruthless master of the dark arts, someone who had waged US foreign policy in the gutter. In the eyes of many, to quote James Bamford, he became the 'CIA's Darth Vader'.[46]

One of the most scathing attacks came from John le Carré, master of the cerebral spy novel. A critic of American espionage in his fiction (his CIA officers typically lacked the style, patience and manners of their British counterparts, and were obsessed with saving the world), le Carré described Helms in the *New York Times* as a boot-licker of the presidency, so in awe, and so desperate to serve and advance his career, that he rode roughshod over civil liberties, not to mention his own purist professional instincts. 'As Helms drew nearer and nearer to the Presidential sun', the acclaimed novelist wrote, 'the wax on his own wings began to get distinctly tacky.'[47] Retired senior CIA man John Bross suggested that le Carré's criticism was born out of 'personal interest in making the real world intelligence services as wicked, perfidious and sinister as possible in order to enhance the plausibility of his own macabre improvisations'.[48] Unsurprisingly, Helms had no time for le Carré. He was quoted as not just disliking *The Spy Who Came in From the Cold*, arguably the writer's best work, but 'detesting' it.[49] Le Carré's portrayal of the Soviet bloc and the West as equally cynical and equally corrupt – two sides of the same grubby coin – was anathema to him.

As we have seen, the intelligence 'flap' of the 1970s convinced many old hands to publish memoirs in rebuttal, contributing to what Rhodri Jeffreys-Jones has called 'the embryonic historiography of the CIA'.[50] One person nevertheless remained conspicuously absent from this burgeoning literature. In spite of all the bad press, and despite the blandishments of dollar-hungry publishers and agents, Helms resisted the temptation to write a book.

Why? Firstly, he was exhausted, both physically and mentally. Congressional subpoenas had required him to fly to Washington from Tehran, where he was ambassador to Iran, no fewer than sixteen times in four years. He testified on forty occasions, for a total of more than 100 hours. After returning home from Iran permanently in 1977, he was keen to take an extended holiday and, in his own earlier words, 'let it all shake out of me – Colby's sickening behaviour, Church's fraud about opening letters to his mother-in-law, President Ford's appalling handling over the assassination issue, the drive of zealots like Anthony Lewis to nail me for perjury'.[51] These things, he told friend and legendary foreign affairs adviser William P. Bundy, 'have to get washed out of one's craw'.[52]

Secondly, he was not seduced by the prospect of padding his bank balance. As DCI, he earned $42,000 a year but lived frugally in a rented high-rise apartment costing $220 per month.[53] 'He didn't give a damn about money,' claimed Cynthia, his British-born second wife, in a 2011 interview: 'He didn't know the difference between a nickel and dime. He drove an old car, didn't care what he wore, and would not pay more than $2.50 for a bottle of wine.'[54]

However, his main reason for not going into print was because it went against his deepest personal instinct. Aptly described by Thomas Powers as 'The Man Who Kept the Secrets', he believed that intelligence service demanded a lifetime obligation to absolute secrecy, much in the same way as the Mafia committed its members to a code of *omertà*.[55] In all aspects of his life, both professional and personal, secrecy was the bedrock of his personality; it became second nature to him. As DCI, he made only one speech to a non-governmental audience.[56] On the night before she married him, Cynthia was told by a friend, half in the spirit of jest, 'not to marry Dick Helms because he doesn't say anything!'[57] According to Cameron LaClair, a 21-year veteran of the CIA, he was 'absolutely first class at not answering questions'.[58] Helms's devotion to secrecy was perfectly encapsulated by his entry in the American edition of *Who's Who*. Less than an inch long, it identified him as 'govt. official', and included the prosaic detail that he was a member of the City Tavern Association.

In testament to Helms's lack of interest in writing an autobiography, he made no effort to generate or preserve personal records that might be of value to him as an author in the future. His final days at the CIA occasioned wholesale destruction of documents. 'When Helms was about to leave', recollected Ken Knaus (Deputy Inspector General from 1969 to 1973), 'he called me to his office.'[59] Here, the two men discussed what to do with the 'Dulles Material', perhaps the most sensitive collection of documents held in the vaults at Langley. Beyond Top Secret, the 'Dulles Material' included five bulky copies of the Bay of Pigs Report, as well as the only copy of an 'Assassination Report', which was sealed in a manila envelope and identified a range of CIA plots against Castro.[60] According to Knaus, the majority of the papers Helms 'simply tore up and tossed into his burn bag without comment'.[61] Among the items for destruction included a set of 'eight x ten glossies of Ted Kennedy cavorting naked in a Rome whorehouse'.[62] 'We don't need in Agency files dirty pictures of a US Senator who one day may be President,' Helms reportedly quipped.[63] One of the few documents to survive the cull was the 'Assassination Report', something he later regretted when the Agency was required by court order to surrender it to Church and Rockefeller. Looking back, CIA alumnus Scott Breckinridge could never understand why Helms had not destroyed this 'ticking time bomb'.[64]

This is not to say that Helms's reluctance to write a memoir was indicative of someone immune to criticism. On 28 April 1975, standing directly outside the Vice President's office, he erupted at Daniel Schorr, the reporter who broke the story about CIA assassination plots, calling him a 'cocksucker', 'killer' and 'son-of-a-bitch' right to his face.[65] In retirement, Helms often proved extremely sensitive to the way his career was depicted, and could react with anger when he felt that his name had been impugned. When John Taylor, head of the Nixon Presidential Library, leaked to him a pre-release version of Oliver Stone's film *Nixon*, the former CIA chief threatened to sue the Hollywood director for libel. Helms objected to two scenes. The first included a shot of Helms (played by Sam Waterston) with all-black devil eyes and chillingly reciting William Yeats's 'The Second Coming'. The second featured Helms verbally assaulting Nixon while wearing his tennis clothes. He interpreted this as an attempt to link him – falsely – to the cave-dwelling clique of CIA officials who enjoyed hobnobbing around Georgetown, the epicentre of Washington high society during the Cold War, and who had a reputation for being beholden to no one and living by their own rules. Following a letter from Helms's lawyers – warning 'my client will take you for everything you've got' – Stone deleted the scenes from the theatrical release, albeit the director would claim that he had done so for 'artistic reasons'.[66] When interviewed on 22 May 1978 by fleet-footed British journalist David Frost (fresh from eliciting his televised *mea culpa* from Nixon), Helms argued with theological intensity that he had done nothing more than execute the wishes of the President. Moreover, in December 1993, when he learned that CIA veteran Sam Halpern was gossiping to the press about CIA botched attempts to kill Castro, Helms promised, ominously, to 'straighten him out'.[67]

III. Fighting Back

The word is that you have taken Hood and quill in hand.
Angus Thuermer, ex-CIA Public Affairs official, February 1998.[68]

Twenty-six years no less passed between Helms's retirement as US ambassador to Iran in 1977 and the publication of his autobiography *A Look Over My Shoulder* in 2003. 'This is a memoir I never expected to write,' he explained in the book's preface.[69] So, what prompted Helms – this most secret of human beings – to finally write a memoir? His public justification was that the end of the Cold War had given him far greater latitude to disclose information.[70] As borders opened and free elections ousted Communist regimes across Eastern Europe, so the secrets of the conflict (the secrets of which Helms had been the custodian) were thought to be decidedly *passé*, immaterial to a New World Order in which global intelligence services were placing greater emphasis on accountability and transparency. Privately, however, he was motivated by other factors. Stories that he had organised secret wars, planned assassination and played court procurer for White House dirty tricks had failed to go away in the two decades since the time of troubles. Like a pressure cooker slowly building up steam before blowing its top, Helms read everything that was published and grew increasingly resentful and bitter. According to his widow, 'The more he read, the more he became upset and his views [about memoirs] changed.'[71] Having been diagnosed with multiple myeloma in 1995 (a condition he kept a secret, even from his son), he was struck with a dawning realisation that the window for correcting these accounts was closing fast.[72]

Three books, in particular, caused him great distress. The first was *War of Numbers* (1994) by former CIA analyst Sam Adams.[73] Published six years after the death of Adams, the book reopened old wounds by accusing Helms of 'spinning' intelligence on the Vietnam War to suit the political objectives of the White House. The book, which included reproductions of documents that Adams had secretly taken from the CIA and buried for safe keeping in the woods near his 250-acre Virginian farm, showed in shocking detail how the Agency under Helms had conspired to minimise enemy troop strength to maintain public support for the war. In doing so, charged Adams, the CIA fatally misjudged the ferocity of the Tet Offensive in 1968.

The second book to anger Helms was *The Very Best Men* by Evan Thomas, assistant managing editor of *Newsweek* magazine.[74] Published in 1995, the book assumed as a thesis that the Agency was run by a privileged Ivy League clique, possessing a swagger and hubris totally disproportionate to its achievements. Thomas had benefited from Executive Order 12356, allowing him to examine certain classified documents, on the proviso that he signed a secrecy agreement and submitted his work to pre-publication review. To Helms's fury, it transpired that the work had not been properly vetted, and that Thomas had been given far greater access to documentation than should have been the case. He immediately blamed Robert Gates, who had been

DCI when Thomas had begun writing. Gates made his own enquiries and informed Helms that, when he left the Agency in January 1993, the bureaucratic turmoil that followed his departure had led 'lower level people' to assist Thomas without prior approval. He wrote apologetically: 'I hope [this] persuades you that I had not taken leave of my senses … I deeply regret the embarrassment this has caused you.'[75] Of course, it may be unwise to take Gates at face value in this correspondence. It is quite possible that he was to blame. Regardless, Helms was aggrieved and his motivation for writing increased.

The third book to trouble Helms was one that was first published in 1979. Surprisingly, he had long refused to do more than skim-read *The Man Who Kept the Secrets: Richard Helms and the CIA* (1979) by Pulitzer Prize-winning journalist Thomas Powers, despite the fact that it was and remains the only biography of the CIA spymaster. According to Cynthia, he believed he knew the book pretty well. The broad brush strokes had been widely reported by the press, while he and Powers had talked at length during its production.[76] Indeed, when he first discovered that Powers was writing the book, he actively sought out the author to offer him the opportunity of an interview.[77] However, when he finally subjected it to a closer inspection, he found that the devil was in the detail. Although Powers was generally sympathetic towards Helms, presenting him as a patriotic good soldier who took orders from one president at a time, there were many aspects of the book that distressed him.

By his own admission, Helms did not possess a winningly exotic personality; but Powers had made it look like he did not have a personality at all. The Helms described – to quote intelligence veteran Walter Pforzheimer – was 'flat and humourless, as if made of bureaucratic cardboard'.[78] From the first page to the last, remarked le Carré, Powers had given readers 'a man of determined plainness', 'a blank face moving through a crowded room'.[79] This was not how Helms viewed himself; nor was it how his closest companions knew him. David Atlee Phillips

wrote privately that there was a human side that Powers had failed
to acknowledge. The Helms he remembered was an accomplished
dancer, partial to getting 'slightly tipsy', and who had engaged in an
'audacious New Year's Eve frolic in Havana'. [80] During Helms's time of
travail, Phillips recollected, he was invited to a Sunday night soirée,
a Georgetown ritual, where Kissinger and journalist Barbara Walters,
among other luminaries, had raised champagne to him with eulogies
and best wishes. 'That kind of crowd', claimed Phillips, 'does not con-
gregate in Georgetown to toast a plastic man.'[81]

As much as Helms disliked being cast as stiff and prosaic, the
greater anguish came from the book's core proposition: CIA operations
represented a 'record of crime, blunder, embarrassment and failure', conducted on behalf of power-hungry presidents hell-bent on 'intervening
callously and recklessly around the world'.[82] Powers put great emphasis
on Helms 'cooking' intelligence estimates at the request of Nixon. He
accused him not only of acquiescing to grossly erroneous assessments
of Viet Cong and North Vietnamese forces in South Vietnam, but of
inflating the strategic threat posed by a Soviet first-strike capability. As
a professional who prided himself on never succumbing to politicisa-
tion, this was an impossible pill for Helms to swallow. Moreover, the
book ended on what he regarded as a needlessly insulting and lugubri-
ous note, with him being given a stern lecture by the District Judge in
1977 for bringing shame on his oath to tell the truth. Protecting secrets,
Helms believed, was not automatically a sign of having no honour.

Concerned, therefore, at the way he and the Agency were being
represented, Helms took pen in hand. With his health deteriorating,
he enlisted the help of his friend and former trusted aide William
Hood to work as a research assistant and co-author. Although others
were considered for the job, Hood was the standout candidate. Like
Helms, he had been there at the creation, serving with the OSS before
transferring to the CIA, where he rose through the ranks to become
Chief of Latin American Operations in 1962. As a major figure in the

clandestine services for over three decades, he knew the intelligence world from the inside out. According to Cynthia, 'Dick did not want to waste his time bringing someone up to speed on the fundamentals of the business. He wanted someone who needed no tutoring on tradecraft.'[83] As the author of several books, including three spy novels, Hood possessed strong literary credentials. Importantly, he was liked and trusted by the CIA. His 1982 book *Mole*, the story of the first Soviet agent to be successfully turned by the CIA in the early Cold War, had been adopted in training courses for new recruits.[84] He had always co-operated with the PRB, even though it had caused him problems. The board shilly-shallied for eighteen months before clearing *Mole*, and insisted that he use pseudonyms for almost all the book's protagonists, including himself (hence, in the text he is disguised as 'Amos Booth').

A convert to the view that the CIA should play an increasingly influential role as a purveyor of public memory, Hood was delighted to be teaming up with Helms once again, in what amounted to one last mission for two ageing spies. A man of lavish tastes (he drove Jaguar cars and dressed in bespoke suits from Anderson & Sheppard Haberdashery on Savile Row), the remuneration helped to fund his latest automotive and sartorial extravagances. From the outset, he was heavily involved in all areas of the book. He convinced Helms to sign with a literary agent: 'The conventional wisdom is that publishers prefer to deal with agents – to whom they can speak freely without shattering the fragile persona of the exquisites who write the stuff. I think 10 per cent is well spent.'[85] Thanks to Hood's connections in the publishing world, Helms secured the services of Sterling Lord, who counted as clients such literary icons as Jack Kerouac and John Irving. Hood chose the book's title – *A Look Over My Shoulder: A Life in the Central Intelligence Agency* – overruling Helms's preference for *The Second Oldest Profession*, which had already been used by noted intelligence writer Phillip Knightley.[86] Hood gave Helms 'assigned reading'. By far the most important text was *For the President's Eyes Only* by

Cambridge historian Christopher Andrew, a meticulously researched study of the uses and abuses to which presidents have put intelligence. Professors Andrew's book was regarded as the perfect model for Helms since it argued that, far from being a 'rogue elephant' or out of control, the CIA in the Cold War had simply done its job – namely, follow the dictates of the White House.[87] On Hood's advice, Helms contracted his memoirs with Bob Loomis at Random House, no stranger of course to spy books. How ironic: Helms, the shy night animal of espionage, had entered into a working relationship with the publishing daredevil who had escorted the inflammatory accounts of Wise and Ross, and then Snepp into print.

Hood was instrumental in shaping the memoir's style. Helms had initially favoured an 'informal, conversational' approach, simply describing 'what I did and what I saw'.[88] Instead, Hood encouraged him to nail opponents to the wall: 'As topics come up, you should comment on some of the nonsense and poisons that have been strewn by the likes of [Tom] Mangold, Hersh and company, and drive a stake through the heart of some of the nonsense that may otherwise come to pass as history.'[89] (Mangold was the author of a book on CIA counterintelligence chief James Jesus Angleton, claiming that the infamous spy's relentless and single-minded hunt for a Soviet 'mole' had tied the CIA in knots, virtually paralysing operations against the USSR.)[90]

Hood was particularly keen for Helms to attack Richard Nixon and reinforce the popular conventional wisdom that the thirty-seventh president was a crook, wholly without morals or any bedrock of human decency. At first, Helms was uncomfortable with the idea, believing that there was a sacred bond between DCI and President that should never be broken. Dulles had been of the same mind when writing *The Craft of Intelligence*, and indeed resisted the temptation to detract from the grand redwood forest of JFK's life by revealing the detritus underfoot. Hood, however, was very persuasive. So much mud had already been thrown at Nixon, a little more wouldn't make any difference.

Accordingly, Hood was adamant that the book exposed every sordid twist and turn of the embattled President's attempts to suck the CIA into the cover-up of the Watergate burglary.[91] It would reveal that Nixon had instructed H. R. 'Bob' Haldeman, White House Chief of Staff, to strong-arm Helms into blocking the FBI's investigation into the affair. It would reveal that Haldeman tried to blackmail Helms by claiming that, unless the investigation was stopped, it would lead ineluctably to the unravelling of sensitive CIA operations, including the abortive Bay of Pigs invasion in 1961. It would also detail how Nixon, brazen even by his standards, then asked White House lawyer John Dean to pressurise Helms to pay the bail money to spring the jailed burglars.

Hood dissuaded Helms from saying anything that might generate sympathy for Nixon. For example, Helms had wanted to include a complimentary anecdote about Nixon's first visit to Langley. Warned that the president did not like to meet with individuals, Helms had arranged it so that Nixon did not have many hands to shake. However, as the two men passed through the atrium, Nixon asked him: 'How many people does this hall accommodate?' After Helms had replied, 'Slightly more than four hundred', Nixon unexpectedly climbed onto the stage and shook the hand of everybody in the room.[92] This rare moment of affection from Nixon was clearly at odds with the bigger picture Hood was trying to paint; accordingly, he deleted it.

Determined to give Nixon no quarter, Hood convinced Helms to describe in detail the moment, in February 1973, when the president 'invited' him to Camp David, only to demand his resignation and send him packing, to Tehran, as ambassador to Iran. As Hood saw it, readers would be irresistibly drawn to the high drama of a status-obsessed, insecure President, privately smarting at Helms's intransigence over Watergate, abruptly firing America's top spy.[93] The episode was highly revealing of Nixon's dark side. It showed a man who never forgave a brush-off or criticism; who could shake your hand but stab you in the back at the same time; and who harboured a deep-seated hatred of the Eastern Establishment that coagulated into an undiscriminating suspicion of all elites. Hood encouraged Helms to paint a scene reminiscent of the infamous television debate in 1960, when a tired, edgy and pallid Nixon squared up against the athletic and poised John F. Kennedy: 'I like to think of him perspiring and furtively blotting away a bit of sweat.'[94]

Hood's influence was perhaps most keenly felt when it came to the book's treatment of covert action. No aspect of CIA activity attracted more public interest or induced more heated debate. Revelations had done much to construct a popular image of the Agency straying beyond its traditional mandate of collection and analysis, seduced by the allure of manipulating the domestic politics of foreign countries by sleight of hand. Unsurprisingly, Helms was nervous about how the subject was to be handled. 'What in the hell are we going to do?' he asked his reliable coadjutor.[95]

Hood had a solution. As he saw it, three arguments had to be made. One, covert action was 'as old as secret intelligence', and certainly did not originate with the CIA.[96] He provided Helms with examples dating back as far as the days of George Washington, including the fact that, in 1790, senators had granted the President a 'Contingency Fund for Foreign Intercourse' (then a less suggestive expression), money that was neither accounted for nor audited by Congress.[97] The implication was that if covert action was acceptable to the father and selfless leader of the new republic, it should be palatable to every contemporary American. Two, covert action was only ever carried out at the explicit request of the President. To illustrate this crucial point, Hood advised Helms to show that, while he had favoured a 'slow burn' approach with Castro, the White House had put 'relentless pressure' on the CIA to remove the Cuban revolutionary by any means necessary. What was Camelot, the Kennedy brothers doggedly believed, if it could not defeat a heathen so close to its lands? Three, covert action was hugely important in containing Soviet expansionism. As an example, Hood called on Helms to spread on thick the CIA's role in swinging the Italian elections in 1948, which kept a pro-Stalinist government out of power and paved the way for a vital NATO presence in the Mediterranean.

On the subject of covert action, Hood saved Helms from potential embarrassment. In a draft chapter, Helms had made the astonishing claim that the CIA had conducted 'thousands' of covert actions in its early days, a revelation that was hardly likely to placate Americans who worried that the Agency was an enormous squid-like meddler in global affairs. Hood – 'so as not to frighten anyone' – changed this to 'hundreds'.[98] He also quashed Helms's suggestion of discussing how the 'law of unintended consequences' had come back to haunt a number of 'successful' covert actions. For example, Helms had written a chapter in which he argued that a communist Afghanistan was in retrospect preferable to the repressive Taliban ideology that had since engulfed the country. Probably true, counselled Hood, but to tell readers this would 'simply succeed in giving the Agency a black eye'.[99]

As well as guiding Helms on what to write, there is strong evidence that Hood actually wrote a great deal of the book himself. Eagle-eyed readers will spot that several passages from *A Look Over My Shoulder* are paraphrased from Hood's previous books. Early on in the book's production, Hood warned Helms, 'I'm putting a lot of words and opinions in your name, and you must be sure that you agree.'[100] There is no evidence in the Helms papers that the master spy objected to any of the 'ghosted' material.

That Hood toiled away on his companion's manuscript was partly a consequence of Helms's poor health. His illness prevented lengthy sessions in front of the computer. It also sadly deprived him of his intuitive feel for what was classified and what was not, and thus made him fearful of the potential for inadvertent disclosure.[101] Cameron LaClair met him at a symposium on Vietnam in the late 1990s, but his friend of fifty years scarcely remembered who he was.[102] Moreover, Hood took on the lion's share of the writing because Helms, by his own admission, was not a naturally accomplished writer. His style was that of obfuscating 'bureaucratese', with all the verve of an office flow chart. It was humourless, technical and clannish, accessible only to a small band of informed, mutually acquainted intelligence specialists. In a damning assessment of one of Helms's draft chapters, Hood likened it to 'blinding the reader in a blizzard of acronyms'.[103] Worried that the narrative made few concessions to the general reader, and was 'not as vivid and enlightening as it should be', in January 1998 Loomis intervened and asked Hood to ensure that it had a 'more intimate and inside feeling' to it.[104] From this moment, Helms's role was reduced to providing anecdotes and character sketches that Hood might then use to bring the book to life. Many of these did not make the final cut. They included such curious details as former Secretary of State Dean Rusk being fond of watching football and drinking whisky highballs as he ploughed through his paperwork, and President Johnson having large ears and large hands, walking with the pace of a countryman, and not being circumcised.[105]

IV. Quasi-Official History

I believe you can count on me not to abuse any privileges I might receive.
Richard Helms to CIA Information and Privacy Coordinator,
21 January 1997.[106]

James Bamford, the bestselling writer on US intelligence, has claimed that Helms was hampered not only by a 'lack of access to still-classified documents', but also by a 'rigid Agency review process'.[107] This assessment needs revisiting. After Helms decided to write a memoir, he approached the CIA for assistance in getting access to records about his directorship, and the Agency was cooperative. Helms had the luxury of being given his own office in the Center for the Study of Intelligence at CIA headquarters, where he could make use of the

Agency's vast archive and internal histories, as well as speak to serving personnel.[108] He initially was provided with a CIA officer as a research assistant. Later, Dr David Robarge, formerly a political analyst who joined the CIA's History Staff in 1996, was given that role in addition to his other historian responsibilities. He helped Helms identify relevant archival collections, read draft chapters, and put forward suggestions in the service of accuracy and style. According to Cynthia Helms, Robarge – a graduate of Columbia University, with a PhD in modern American history – was 'enormously helpful, talking to Dick all the time and accompanying him on research trips'.[109]

As a former officer 'engaged in a historical research project', Helms was entitled under Section 4.5 of Executive Order 12958 to inspect any CIA record generated during the period in which he had served. He immediately availed himself of this right. Bending the rules, the Agency acquiesced to his request that Hood be granted the same privilege.[110] The CIA also helped Helms gain access to information to which technically he was not entitled. For example, in spring 1998 he applied to the Lyndon B. Johnson Presidential Library in Austin, Texas, asking for permission to inspect classified records relating to LBJ's time in the Oval Office. When this approach was rejected, John Hollister Hedley, Chairman of the PRB, appealed to Harry Middleton, Director of the Library, requesting that Helms be afforded 'every courtesy and accommodation'.[111] Hedley – acknowledged as the most enlightened and accommodating PRB chairman in CIA history – explained that, 'We [the CIA] are excited about the undertaking.' 'We feel certain', he continued, 'that when all his research and writing comes to fruition, he will make a unique and valuable contribution to intelligence literature and to the history of the Cold War.'[112] Hedley's deft personal touch had the desired effect: Helms subsequently had no access difficulties with the Johnson library.

So often the bane of the spy memoirist, the pre-publication review process was no impediment to Helms. The PRB was punctual in returning material, and there was no protracted 'back and forth' process on what could be disclosed. Cuts to the manuscript were minimal, and none were regarded by Helms as being unreasonable. In each case, there was a legitimate reason for the deletion. For example, Helms had identified two officers – 'Jerry D' and 'John P' – whose widows, fearing reprisals from a hostile intelligence service, had explicitly asked the Agency in writing for the names not to be disclosed until they themselves had passed away.[113] Justifiably, the PRB asked that all references be removed to equipment that was still being used in the field. Redactions were also made, again with good reason, to protect US foreign relations. For example, Helms had mentioned a 'friendly nation' who, in the recent past, had successfully spied against the United States.[114] Clearly, policymakers did not want to embarrass this country or jeopardise present relations. Moreover, in Helms's case, the PRB showed a much greater willingness to reword objectionable items instead of taking the red pen to the entire section. For example, Helms had several pages on Israel's controversial intelligence agency, Mossad, but the Board did not want any acknowledgement that the CIA had formal ties with the organisation. Rather than prohibit the whole discussion, the PRB offered Helms rephrased alternatives. Thus, 'Jim Angleton ... handled liaison with the Israeli intelligence services' became 'Jim Angleton ... handled some matters with Israel'.[115] Similarly, 'Jim's liaison with the Israeli services was of exceptional value' became 'Jim's interest in Israel was of exceptional value'.[116]

It is fascinating to note that the real 'censor' in Helms's case was not the CIA, but the publisher, Random House. The PRB had happily turned a blind eye to the inclusion of several secret code names, but Random House regarded them as obfuscating and removed them, prioritising instead 'personal observations, gossip [and] anecdotes'.[117] The publisher sent to the cutting room floor an absorbing chapter on 'Agency Families', where Helms had discussed the unsung heroes of intelligence work – the devoted wives and girlfriends. Required to live in diverse and remote locations, the 'ladies', as Helms called them, provided the essential 'stability and continuity' of family life. Examples were given of women organising and participating in social activities such as lunches, brunches, dinners and film showings – 'to maintain individual and unit morale'. Helms also provided instances where women had bravely assisted their husbands in an operational capacity, including one occasion where a wife had made a dead drop and another where a wife had made a 'brush contact' with an agent-in-place on a 'busy street in Warsaw'.[118] Such material – caviar to the scholar of intelligence – was strangely dismissed as being boring.

How do we explain the fact that the CIA was so accommodating with Helms? To some extent, officials were probably making a virtue out of necessity. Stubborn, determined and not easily intimidated, Helms was going to publish whether the Agency liked it or not. No one had the nerve to threaten him, let alone frogmarch him off to court. This, after all, was perhaps the most revered figure in the US intelligence community. Another explanation could be that Helms benefited from the particularly special regard in which he was held by George Tenet, CIA Director during the years when the book was being prepared. Tenet made no secret of his admiration for Helms. When he became DCI in July 1997, his first decision was to take the oil portrait of Helms, located in the first-floor hallway at Langley, and hang it on his office wall as a sign of respect and source of inspiration.[119] One only has to look at Tenet's reaction to Helms's death on 23 October 2002 to realise just how far he would have gone to help his predecessor. 'The men and women of American intelligence have lost a great teacher and true friend,' he lamented in a staff circular.[120] At the memorial service at Fort Myer, Virginia, it was Tenet who led the tributes. 'In Richard Helms, intelligence in service to liberty found an unsurpassed champion,' he eulogised before the group of mourners.[121] At Arlington, it was Tenet who presented the flag to Helms's widow. It is often said that the

CIA is a reflection of its Director. If so, Helms could not have wished for a better DCI than Tenet as he made his way into print.

The Tenet connection, however, tells only half the story. Evidence tantalisingly suggests that the CIA was in fact trying to mould the book as a surrogate official history with the aim of improving public understanding. As we discussed at the beginning of this chapter, since the end of the Cold War, the CIA had become deeply concerned about how it was perceived by the American people. In a world where the historic enemy had ceased to exist, with the prospect of big reductions in the congressional intelligence appropriation and increased competition with other government agencies, the CIA realised that simply circling the wagons was no longer a viable approach. Ways had to be found to communicate to taxpayers and their representatives that the singular overt threat of the Soviet dragon had been replaced, as Woolsey had noted, by a myriad of dangerous reptiles hidden in the long grass. In addition, the public needed to know that the CIA was not the inept or unethical organisation so often portrayed in the history books, press headlines and popular culture. As Scott Breckinridge wrote in December 1993, 'Things had changed ... Denial wasn't the way to handle it, but an effort to balance things seemed appropriate.'[122] Put another way, the time had come for the CIA to right – as well as write – the record.

Few individuals fitted the bill better as a producer of official history by proxy than Helms. He was the perfect messenger with the perfect message. To quote his widow, 'intelligence was his whole life'.[123] He was the ultimate defender of the intelligence faith, and described working for the CIA as not merely 'a job', but rather 'a calling'.[124] There was absolutely no question of him wanting to embarrass the Agency or disclose secrets. 'The CIA knew he wouldn't screw them,' noted Cynthia, 'its reputation meant everything to him.'[125] As far as the CIA was concerned, *A Look Over My Shoulder* hit all the right notes. 'It is my intention ... to introduce the reader to the remarkable men and women I knew,' he explained in the proposal. 'The history of the Agency', he continued, 'is made up of many intensely personal and human stories, of small results painfully achieved, tragic consequences and comic interludes.'[126] The core message he looked to convey about the importance of a strong human intelligence capability was precisely what the CIA wanted the American people to hear. While Helms valued the contribution of advanced technical methods of collection, he was sceptical of gadgeteers who said, 'Give us the money and leave it to us', and was adamant that billion-dollar satellites would never supplant HUMINT as the best way to 'know your enemy'.[127] During his acceptance speech for the OSS Donovan Medal in 1983, he had warned that so-called 'spies in the sky' were incapable of divining a person's intentions. 'There is no substitute', he declared, 'for old-fashioned analysis performed by old-fashioned brain power.' [128] The only thing he disliked about HUMINT was the term itself, which he felt sounded like a type of fertiliser.[129]

Helms, who passed away aged eighty-nine on 23 October 2002, sadly did not live to see the publication of his memoirs. Guided over the finishing line by Hood in the spring of 2003, the book was everything Gates's Openness Task Force could have hoped for when, a decade earlier, it had recommended that the CIA 'share our history'. Much was made of the CIA's ability to 'make a difference', from its discovery of Soviet missiles in Cuba, which afforded Kennedy a critical advantage in the ensuing crisis, to the successful tapping of underground telephone lines in Berlin and Vienna, which gave policymakers access to over 360,000 Soviet conversations over eleven months. Much was made of the CIA's pride in doing credible, unbiased analysis, keeping out of policymaking and sticking to the facts, even when this was not what officials necessarily wanted. For example, it revealed Helms's dogged determination to deliver unwelcome forecasts about Vietnam to President Nixon.

In discussing some of the CIA's most controversial programmes, Helms argued that the Agency had suffered unwarranted opprobrium for errors of the Executive. Responding to the allegation that the CIA had been too subservient to forceful presidents and their aides (such as the Kennedy brothers who constantly called for the CIA to 'get off its ass' and 'do something' about Castro), he reminded readers that it is the job of the CIA to serve the president and, like it or not, do what it is told. On the specific accusation that the CIA had gone too far by spying on anti-war protestors – whom Johnson and Nixon feared might be beneficiaries of foreign backing – he claimed that, while certain mistakes had been made, it was at least sensible for the CIA to run the programme with a degree of control. If he had declined, the job would have gone to an outfit like the fabled 'plumbers', operating with no moral compass or restraint whatsoever. In short, one of the main themes of the Helms memoir was that if the CIA was guilty of anything, it was professionalism. Indeed, so dedicated was Helms to his work and serving the presidency, he revealed that he had even asked permission from Johnson to divorce his wife of twenty-nine years, Julia Bretzman Shields, in 1968. He also recollected that when she was having potentially life-threatening surgery in New York, he stayed in DC to do paperwork!

As reviewers pointed out, there was nothing in the Helms memoir that undermined the epithet 'The Man Who Kept the Secrets'.[130] Helms had adhered regimentally to Gates's instruction letter of 18 November 1991, in which he asked DeTrani to find ways to improve 'openness … to the extent possible' – the operative words being 'extent possible'. The book disclosed no new operations; added no names to the list of known spies; and revealed nothing in the way of material that could be exploited by critics to attack the Agency.[131] Having stomached federal prosecution and risked prison to protect secrets, Helms was never going break the habit of a lifetime and suddenly start singing.

The fact that someone who knew so much clearly said so little nevertheless took nothing away from the book. Published eighteen months after the surprise attack of 9/11, there was a timeliness and added significance to his discussion of the need for accurate intelligence. His repeated references to Pearl Harbor as an example of the failure to predict disaster had a painful resonance for every American haunted by the image of commercial jet liners crashing into the Twin Towers, New York's seemingly indestructible towering pillars of aluminium and steel. His retelling of old, almost forgotten battles between the CIA and key constituencies such as the White House, Congress and the media were highly relevant as the Agency embarked on combating a new enemy in Islamic terrorism. In retracing the peregrinations of the quintessential Cold War spymaster, *A Look Over My Shoulder* posited important questions about US intelligence that were as timely as when Helms had entered the spook factory, with OSS, in 1942. How broad a mandate should the CIA have to protect national security? What powers should the country give the CIA to safeguard national defence, but not undermine the very liberties it is defending? Who is the CIA responsible to? How can the need for secrecy be balanced against the public's constitutional right to hold government to account? Helms had given his answers; now it was the time for a new generation of spy memoirists to give theirs.

Epilogue:
21st-Century Disputes

I. The Honest Broker

Think twice about a cover-up: a budding author
may be standing under the cloak next to you.
James Bamford, intelligence historian, July 1999.[1]

Upon becoming Chairman of the PRB in 1996, John Hollister Hedley took over a process that had a reputation for pulling authors from pillar to post, and for scrubbing manuscripts of innocuous material based on the flimsiest of grounds. Moreover, accusations were repeatedly levelled against the PRB for seldom treating a negative book about the CIA with the same respect and objectivity it afforded to accounts that glorified the Agency. The experience of Scott Breckinridge – author of *CIA and the Cold War: A Memoir* (1993) – is highly revealing of the state of affairs prior to Hedley's arrival. Breckinridge's dealings with the Board deteriorated to such an extent that he felt compelled to write to the CIA's Inspector General, Frederick Hitz, in protest. 'The fact is', he complained,

that the current PRB reveals repeatedly incredible unfamiliarity
with the published materials, on which they are supposed to judge

responsibly. I suggest that someone check through the literature with which these people are so unfamiliar and draw up a source on what is in the public domain. The clumsy and weak performance of PRB had added months to my own scheduled completion of my book. While I acceded to most of their requests (even when I thought them in error) there were some that simply were offensive and to which I took exception. They ought to get their act together, for they represent the Agency poorly in dealing with past employees who want to write about it all.[2]

Clearly, some housecleaning was required.

Under Hedley, thankfully, considerable progress was made. In spring 1998, he published an article in the CIA's journal *Studies in Intelligence* claiming that the Board had put the dark days described by Breckinridge behind it and moved on. In the article, he suggested that the Board's interpretation of what damages national security was no longer absolute or fixed, thus opening the door to the disclosure of some of the Agency's older secrets. Calling himself an 'honest broker', he emphasised that the role of the Chairman was not to raise problems for authors, but to help them find solutions. 'Small changes can often do the job,' he wrote encouragingly.[3] He underlined that the Board did not exist to censor opinions or correct mistakes; indeed, he has written elsewhere that he once approved a manuscript of an officer who served under CIA Director Bob Gates, but who referred in the text to Bill Gates, of Microsoft fame.[4] Ultimately, the article presented Hedley as someone who prided himself on what he left *in*, not what he took *out*, and who recognised that new realities demanded new ways of thinking. 'What we are seeing', he explained,

is a new era based on two indisputable facts: the Cold War is over, and this is a free country. Ours is a robust democracy in which people want and deserve to know more about an organisation, even a secret one, that exists to serve them. We have to respond to that interest even as we are responsible to our statutory obligation to keep certain sensitive matters secret.[5]

A few years later, in another article for *Studies in Intelligence*, he made the frank admission that 'this reviewer does not know of a single recruitment pitch, operational plan, or liaison relationship that was ruined or precluded by the publication of a book.'[6] Thinking back to when Marchetti *et al* received sharp tongue-lashings from CIA officials for their alleged damages to national security, Hedley's comment was not just reassuring, it was revolutionary.

To illustrate just how far the PRB had come under the avuncular Hedley, take *A Spy for All Seasons: My Life in the CIA* by Duane R. Clarridge, published in 1997.[7] Clarridge – known to almost everyone by his childhood nickname 'Dewey' – had the sort of background that would have provoked a neuralgic twinge in previous PRB Chairmen. Possessing the right combination of brain and brawn, he had spent the bulk of his career out in the field, always operating (as one retired intelligence official put it) 'on the edge of his skis'.[8] Significantly, he had been knee-deep in the biggest political scandal of the 1980s: Iran–Contra. As Chief of the Latin America Division of the Directorate of Operations between 1981 and 1984, he directed Agency efforts in support of the right-wing Nicaraguan Contras against Marxist guerrillas, and planned the clandestine mining of Nicaragua's harbours, an act for which the United States was convicted in 1986 at the International Court of Justice at the Hague. He was later indicted by a federal grand jury for giving false statements to Congress to cover up the Reagan administration's secret shipments of arms to Iran. As a general rule, operations people like Clarridge did not write books; they retired, without a fuss, and lived somewhere remote in Northern Virginia. Accordingly, he was pushing the envelope.

Fully anticipating a rough ride with the PRB, Clarridge tried to be his own self-censor; indeed, when reviewers read the draft, they were bewildered by some of the content, before discovering that he had, for security reasons, invented operational scenarios and falsified places, dates and participants.[9] To his surprise, he found the Board in a generous mood. Relaxing old rules, Hedley permitted him to reveal where and when he had served overseas, and give broad brush-strokes about what he had done there. Allowing former operatives to discuss their operational career, assignment by assignment, without recourse to sweeping generalisations like 'a job in Latin America', was a huge step. According to former CIA Counterterrorism Chief Vincent Cannistraro, 'Clarridge raised eyebrows … People realised you could write books and retire overtly … rather than maintain lifelong cover.'[10] To be sure, not everyone was happy about the introduction of this new standard. Hedley has written that 'Some CIA retirees were aghast when Clarridge's book came out, contending that he was allowed to say anything and everything.'[11] This, of course, was not true. The noose had been loosened, but the CIA still held the rope. The 'Clarridge Precedent', as it became known, did not give authors the freedom to reveal sources and methods; cover arrangements; or liaison relationships.

Hedley knew that, in granting unprecedented latitude to Clarridge, he was opening up a new chapter in the development of CIA memoir writing. 'Whatever its sales outside Washington', he wrote a year after the book's release, 'the book seems to have been snapped up by former Agency officers interested in writing their own books, and they use it as a ready reference and guide!'[12] After Clarridge, there was a noticeable spike in the number of memoirs being written, including more accounts by former operations officers about operational matters. On the eve of the new millennium, the volume of book manuscripts appearing before the PRB had grown to 18,000 pages a year.[13]

A further boost to memoir production came with the publication of another book Hedley had shepherded into print, albeit in its early stages: the Helms memoir. Discussed in Chapter 6, *A Look Over My Shoulder* had the effect of convincing many old hands that perhaps it wasn't wholly inappropriate to write a book, and that greater openness through memoir writing was a valuable mechanism to dispel falsehoods and thus build the Agency's reputation and credibility. It clearly spoke volumes that the super-secretive Helms – of all people – had concluded that it was time for the CIA to educate and inform.

One of those to follow in Helms's footsteps was Dick Holm, author of two memoirs – *The American Agent* (2004) and *The Craft We Chose: My Life in the CIA* (2011).[14] In a thrilling, if occasionally hazardous, 35-year career, Holm had been a paramilitary adviser, operations officer and Station Chief, serving, among other places, in Laos, Hong Kong, Brussels and Paris. In 1965, he suffered near fatal injuries in a harrowing plane crash in central Africa's Congo. Temporarily blinded and covered in gasoline, his life was saved by a local tribesman, who cleaned off his burned skin with a knife and treated his wounds with tree bark and snake oil. Rescued after ten days in the jungle, he spent the next two years at Walter Reed Army Medical Center, where he underwent dozens of operations and eventually regained his eyesight and use of his hands. One evening, alone in the darkness, Helms brought him a Thermos flask filled with martinis. 'Like many', Holm remarked in a 2011 interview, 'I objected to operations officers publishing memoirs.'[15] However, he changed his mind after speaking to Helms, who convinced him that stonewalling was no longer the right approach and that it was necessary to drop the veil a little to ease public fears. 'At first I baulked at the idea but then he explained to me that if we don't write about the Cold War period, it will be written by journalists and academics, and they will get it wrong.'[16]

II. Tightening the Noose, Again

I have reluctantly made the changes, because
I am well aware you can wield a big stick.
Bayard Stockton to C. Bruce Wells (acting Chairman of PRB),
14 July 2003.[17]

The Hedley era proved to be a false dawn in terms of authors receiving a fair hearing from the PRB. No sooner had Hedley retired in 1998 than memoirists began complaining that old habits had started to creep back in, from the Board taking too long to review manuscripts to material being redacted either for nonsensical reasons or because it painted the CIA in an embarrassing light. In the twenty-first century, running the gauntlet of the PRB has become so disputatious that many memoirists are taking their complaints to court, suing the Agency in a bid to get redactions overturned. The sheer volume of memoirs being published should not automatically be interpreted as a sign that the CIA is more open, any more than the mass of information and news available at the click of a button on the internet should be read that society is necessarily better informed, especially about the way it is governed. Lots of books include page after page of blacked-out text. Others are replete with so many falsehoods about people, places and dates that it would be more accurate to describe them as spy fiction than spy memoirs.

One of the first to discover that the PRB had gone backwards after Hedley's retirement was Bayard Stockton, who had been with the CIA between 1951 and 1957, before moving on to become *Newsweek*'s Bureau Chief in Bonn and a career in journalism. In early 2003, now in his seventies, he finished a biography of legendary CIA figure William Harvey, which he had been encouraged to write by Harvey's widow.[18] Stockton had served with the pistol-packing operative for two years in Berlin when the latter had been the CIA's Berlin Station Chief. By

Stockton's own admission, he was an old man writing about an old subject. Harvey, who died in 1976, had plied his trade during the early Cold War and had been discussed in countless books.

In April 2003, the PRB returned Stockton's manuscript riddled with deletions, the majority of which he considered 'picayune, irrelevant, even immature'.[19] Hedley's promise that the Board would be sensitive to the passage of time had clearly been abandoned. The PRB deleted the names of people who had been dead for decades – forty-five years in the case of a certain Siegfried Hoxter.[20] It removed the names of officers, such as Ted Shackley, which had been in the public domain for years.[21] In some instances, it even deleted pseudonyms that Stockton had 'dreamed up' to satisfy the DO's 'skittishness' about names.[22] Stockton found it 'absurd' that he was forbidden from mentioning that the IG Farben building in Frankfurt had been the headquarters of the CIA's German mission in the 1950s. 'The equivalent', he protested, 'would be a prohibition on a former officer identifying a building at Langley-McLean in which he had worked as CIA.'[23] Like many memoirists, he was baffled by the Board's embargo on the phrase 'Chief of Station', and pointed out that this rule had been broken by at least four authors that he knew of – David Atlee Phillips (*The Night Watch*), William Hood (*Mole*), Peer de Silva (*Sub Rosa*), and Milt Bearden (*The Main Enemy*).[24] In a letter to C. Bruce Wells, the PRB's acting Chairman, he wrote: 'If official concern is that terrorists might have figured out from reading [my book] that CIA officers actually are permanently located in American embassies abroad, I find the concern slightly naïve, indeed worrisomely so.'[25]

Stockton challenged the deletions, claiming that the excised material amounted to 'ancient history', and complained about the 'tedious, bureaucratic pace' of the review process.[26] By July, however, his patience had run out and he informed Wells that he would yield to the 'inscrutable rules'.[27] The Hedley era was a now distant memory; so much for the PRB turning over a new leaf.

It was a similar story of frustration for Bob Wallace, a retired Director of the CIA's Office of Technical Service (OTS), the Agency's real-life 'Q-Branch'. On 6 September 2005, he and Keith Melton, a collector of spy paraphernalia and intelligence historian, submitted a co-authored 774-page manuscript to the PRB on the history of the CIA's spy gadgets and the operations in which they were used. The text was a love letter to the distinctive world of the CIA engineer, with absolutely no dirty tricks and plenty of feel-good stories about technological wizardry, from the invention of the 'Insectothopter', a small unmanned aircraft in the shape of a dragonfly fitted with cameras and audio sensors, to the development of a robotic catfish called 'Charlie', so realistic that it was likely to be eaten by larger sea predators.

Having heard nothing for six months, they eventually received a letter, on 13 March 2006, decreeing that only chapters one to three, the first thirty-four pages, which dealt with OSS and equipment from World War Two, could be published. No effort was made, as Hedley had done in the past, to write around objectionable passages or words; a blanket was thrown over all the remaining 740 pages. In a controversial move – known as the 'mosaic theory' of redaction – the Board acknowledged that there was little classified information in these pages, but justified red-flagging them on the grounds that pieces of banal unclassified information, when aggregated, might provide an enemy with enough emergent detail to learn something that is classified. Wallace was dumbfounded by the apparent chicanery. 'There seems to be no awareness', he later wrote, 'that adversaries read English and have the same internet access and Google tools we used in our research.'[28] The ruling was particularly galling for him because, during his time with the OTS, he had vetted several books by ex-officers and thought he knew where the line should be drawn in terms of permissible disclosures. Moreover, the Board had previously cleared a detailed outline and several sample chapters.

To appeal the ruling, Wallace hired attorney Mark S. Zaid, a specialist in national security law, government accountability and free speech constitutional claims. In the twenty-first century, Zaid has become a go-to person for federal employees, intelligence officers and whistle-blowers with a grievance against agencies of the US government. In the words of the *National Law Journal*, 'If Agent Mulder ever needed a lawyer, Zaid would be his man.'[29] According to Agency regulations, the CIA's Executive Director should adjudicate appeals within thirty days of receipt. Once again, however, the CIA dragged its feet. Eight months passed with no word from the Agency, which Wallace interpreted as an attempt to induce the publisher, Dutton, a boutique imprint of Penguin USA, to throw in the towel. Wallace planned to take the case to federal court, but before doing so, in December 2006, he made a last-ditch plea to the CIA's Associate Deputy Director. The personal touch had the desired effect; on 8 February 2007, the PRB suddenly informed Wallace that he could publish all but fifty pages. By July, permission had been given to publish almost all of the original manuscript, plus more than 100 photographs of OTS gadgets and gizmos. 'The best that can be said of the experience', wrote Wallace in the book's preface, 'is that Agency management eventually recognised a need to reform its pre-publication policy and repair the broken review process.'[30] Like all ex-officers, he was required to include a disclaimer stating that the book had been reviewed by the PRB and that all statements of fact, opinion or analysis expressed were those of the author and not the US government. Mischievously, he encrypted this disclaimer, using a one-time pad technique, and provided instructions for deciphering it in the appendix.

Looking at the evolution of CIA memoirs as a whole since the early 1960s, one of the most noticeable developments has been the gradual willingness of authors to criticise the policymaking community. For a long time, spies-turned-authors never dreamed of attacking their political masters. As the much-publicised fall guy for the Bay of Pigs disaster, Allen Dulles doubtless had many negative things he could have said about President Kennedy, yet he remained tight-lipped in

The Craft of Intelligence (1963). In the 1970s, loyalists like Atlee Phillips responded to 'rogue elephant' charges by highlighting that the Agency had acted under high-level policy directives, but stopped well short of outright condemnation of the White House. In a stark break with tradition, Richard Helms spared President Nixon no quarter in *A Look Over My Shoulder* (2003), but it was not something that came naturally to him and owed a lot to the influence of his coadjutor, William Hood. Today, however, it would be almost unusual for a CIA memoirist *not* to criticise the White House. The trigger for this transformation is the War on Terror, which has been as much a climacteric for the CIA as it has been for the American public at large.

The trend for excoriating policymakers started with *Imperial Hubris: Why the West is Losing the War on Terror* by Michael Scheuer, a counterterrorism expert who, from 1996 to November 2004, created and advised a special analytical unit at CIA tasked with tracking Osama bin Laden.[31] Scheuer had not even left the Agency when the book was released in June 2004; indeed, he had only been allowed to publish on the condition that his identity remained secret, hence his pen name 'Anonymous'. Hidden behind a curtain or with his face blurred, he made several appearances on broadcast and cable news channels, before eventually outing himself and resigning from the CIA later in the year, after the presidential election was concluded. The book criticised just about everybody associated with US foreign policy towards Muslims and the Middle East, with the exception of a handful of staff who had been with him at the sharp end. Islamist enemies, he argued, do not want to destroy the US because of its values and freedoms, as President George W. Bush and his entourage claimed. Rather, they hate the US because of its policies and actions in the Muslim world: its unqualified support for Israel; its exploitation of oil resources in the region; its armed presence in the Arabian Peninsula; its closeness to perceived apostate Muslim countries like Saudi Arabia; and its invasion of both Afghanistan and Iraq. Unless policymakers wake up to this fact, he asserted, Al Qaeda would continue plotting to attack the continental US and an all-out military confrontation against Islam might be the only option.

The venom directed at the White House was without parallel in the history of CIA memoirs. Scheuer – a sharp mind with an even sharper tongue – described the administration's decision to invade Iraq as being 'out of character for America in terms of our history, sense of morality, and basic decency'.[32] Not pulling his punches, he claimed that Iraq was 'an avaricious, premeditated, unprovoked war against a foe who posed no immediate threat but whose defeat did offer economic advantages'.[33] As he saw it, the invasion was a grave strategic error that made the menace of jihadi terrorism 'geometrically worse'. From Osama bin Laden's perspective, he likened it to a 'Christmas present you long for but never expected to receive' – a gift that made Iraq a breeding ground for Al Qaeda and more broadly radicalised new parts of the Islamic world. Such stupidity, he claimed, would 'haunt, hurt, and hound Americans for years to come'.[34] Scheuer was especially critical of Secretary of Defense Donald Rumsfeld, whom he accused of misleading the American people about the situation in Afghanistan. He pilloried Rumsfeld for telling reporters in Kabul, in May 2003, that the bulk of Afghanistan was 'permissive and secure', and that children were again playing in the streets. The reality, he claimed, was that Rumsfeld's obsession for lightning-fast operations, with minimal boots on the ground, had resulted in tens of thousands of Taliban insurgents escaping across the border, where they were primed for a renewed assault. 'Mr Rumsfeld, to be charitable, is ill-informed; America's Afghan war is still in its infancy', he wrote cuttingly.[35] And, of course, he was right.

It was widely reported that senior administration officials were furious that the CIA had allowed the book to be published, and interpreted this as the Agency getting revenge for what it perceived as years of ideologically motivated interference by the White House, especially when it came to flawed intelligence on Iraq, for which it had borne the brunt of public ire. In an election year, the last thing the already-embattled administration needed was a respected senior intelligence officer like Scheuer using his status as a bully pulpit to expound negative views about how the War on Terror was being waged. The political storm caused by the book soon led the press to speculate that a crackdown on memoirists was imminent, with the White House regarding them as political liabilities that had to be stopped. Bush was quoted as saying to new CIA Director Porter Goss, who assumed office on 24 September 2004, 'I don't want anything to come out of the Agency. Shut this down.'[36] Within two months of arriving at Langley, Goss had sent a memo to all CIA employees promising to 'clarify beyond doubt the rules of the road' as far as memoir writing was concerned, and emphasising 'We remain a secret agency.'[37] In January 2005, details of Goss's memo were leaked, and an anonymous Agency spokesman confirmed that the PRB was indeed re-evaluating its procedures. From the outside looking in, it appeared as if the window for publishing was closing fast. 'The feeling is that Goss is going to put the kibosh on people writing articles or books or talking to the press in any form,' said former clandestine service officer Lindsay Moran, who had her memoir *Blowing My Cover* (2005) cleared before the stink over *Imperial Hubris*.[38] 'It is going to be very difficult to publish a book on anything except cooking or civil war history,' predicted Scheuer.[39]

T. J. Waters, who worked for the CIA between 2002 and 2004, walked straight into the eye of the storm with his book *Class 11: Inside the CIA's First Post-9/11 Spy Class*.[40] Waters had been a member of the first post-9/11 class of recruits for the national clandestine service, joining a mishmash of patriotic individuals desperate to serve their country in the wake of the terrorist attacks – a professional football player, a comedian, a chef, a single mother, and the fiancée of a World Trade Center victim. His book took readers on a journey from his first day at Langley to his graduation from the 'Farm', the CIA's legendary training facility near Williamsburg, Virginia, where trainees practise surveillance detection, learn how to withstand interrogation, rehearse servicing dead drops, and master the art of glad-handing and gathering scuttlebutt at cocktail parties. An unflinching cheerleader for the CIA, Waters believed the book would be a terrific recruiting tool, since it dispelled the notion that to be a spy, a person had to be a 'corn fed Aryan' or tapped on the shoulder by an Ivy League professor.[41] The CIA clearly felt this way too, for the book was approved by the PRB in early September 2004, just before Goss's arrival, with only small tweaks required. However, after submitting a revised version two months later, Waters then heard nothing until February 2006 when the PRB returned it with almost half the content suddenly designated as classified. Waters immediately teamed up with Zaid to sue the Agency for violating his constitutional right to free speech. 'There's literally been a reinstitution [under Goss] of the 1950s attitude that what happens at CIA stays at CIA,' said Zaid.[42] In court the judge leaned particularly hard on the Agency to review its decisions again, and after some negotiation Waters was allowed to publish with much of the manuscript intact.

Another to fall foul of the Goss regime was Gary Berntsen. A throwback to the freewheeling days of the 1950s, experienced in the John Rambo type of marauding that generates CIA legends, Berntsen was a 225-pound, six-feet-tall, aggressive field operative who led a team of intelligence and Special Forces personnel into the mountains of southern Afghanistan after 9/11 in a no-holds-barred pursuit of Al Qaeda and Osama bin Laden. 'I don't want bin Laden and his thugs captured, I want them dead,' instructed his boss Cofer Black (head of the CIA's Counterterrorism Center). 'I want bin Laden's head shipped back in a box filled with dry ice. I want to be able to show bin Laden's head to the president.'[43] Berntsen submitted his manuscript in May 2005, the same month that he retired after twenty-three years in the NCS. He did not anticipate any problems with the PRB. Like most operations people who risk their lives in the field, he poked fun at the desk-jockeys and paper-pushers back at Langley, and was critical of their inability to fully grasp the threat of Al Qaeda in the 1990s. But this hardly made him a renegade. Moreover, he was encouraged by the fact that his predecessor in leading the Jawbreaker team, Gary Schroen, had published his own account – *First In* – earlier in the year. Tellingly, however, Schroen's permission to publish had come *before* Goss's arrival.

Berntsen waited until mid-July for a response from the PRB, which never came, at which point he did what beforehand would have been unthinkable for him and filed a lawsuit against his former employer. He later called this the 'most surreal and frustrating experience in my life'.[44] A federal judge ordered the CIA to release the manuscript in late August. It came back with over forty pages of material redacted, including absurd deletions such as the distance between cities in Afghanistan – available at the click of a button on Google Maps – and the name of murdered CIA Station Chief William Buckley, whose identity had been widely reported since he had been snatched off the streets by Muslim extremists in Beirut in 1984 and who died in captivity, apparently after torture and prolonged medical neglect, the next year. Indeed, in May 1988, the CIA had symbolically laid him to rest with a public memorial service with full military honours at Arlington National Cemetery. To Berntsen's annoyance, the PRB even deleted material that it had permitted Schroen to publish. To fathom the PRB's position, he met with the CIA's Executive Director, Kyle 'Dusty' Foggo, who told him flatly that Goss had given an order for no more books to be published.[45] According to Berntsen, the CIA was so determined to stop his memoir that Foggo 'offered me any job I wanted', even a university position as a placeholder until Goss could fix the bureaucratic pathologies that had led him to leave the Agency in the first place.[46] When he replied that he wasn't interested, Foggo allegedly said to him, 'I will redact the ****' out of your book so no one will want to read it.'[47]

It is easy to see why Berntsen's book might have failed a political 'appropriateness' test, and why therefore the PRB tried to redact it to the point of rendering it unreadable. By Berntsen's telling, he could have captured and killed Osama bin Laden if only Washington had given him more resources and time. In particular, he recounted how he had Bin Laden trapped like a scared rabbit in the caves of Tora Bora and how he begged the military, to no avail, to prevent his escape by sealing the border into Pakistan with a battalion of US Army Rangers. However, the view from the Pentagon (Rumsfeld) was that ground troops would alienate Afghan allies. With this short-sightedness, argued Berntsen, the US lost its best chance (at the time) to kill the world's most notorious terrorist. Moreover, the book featured an encomium, written by Scheuer, perfectly calculated to rile the administration: 'Read this heartbreaking book, keep it safe, and reread it after al-Qaeda detonates a nuclear device in America. You will then know who signed the death warrant for tens of thousands of your countrymen.'

After the disastrous meeting with Foggo, Berntsen felt that he had no option but to file a second suit against the CIA, this time for violating his First Amendment rights. 'Didn't they read my psychological profile,' he joked to the *Washington Post*, before spelling out what it would say: 'This guy is a risk-taker. And if he believes he's right, he's not gonna walk away.'[48] Berntsen succeeded in getting about two-thirds of the deletions restored, but remained angry that many significant details had been denied to the American people. In the text, which came out in December 2005, he took a small measure of revenge by inserting stinging 'Notes to the reader' next to some of the blacked-out passages. For example, there is a farcical point at which he says that if readers want to know the name of an Afghan warlord, forbidden in his account, they should simply open page 117 of Schroen's book.[49]

Goss resigned as Director of the CIA on 5 May 2006, leaving behind him a review process where secrecy had again become a habit, not a matter of practical security concerns or common sense, and where political forces, with their own agendas, could seemingly impose restrictions and influence judgements. The 'presence' of the White House in PRB decision-making was almost certainly in evidence with *Fair*

Game: My Life as a Spy, My Betrayal by the White House (2007), the heavily redacted memoir of former clandestine service officer Valerie Plame (Wilson).[50] When Plame submitted her manuscript in the summer of 2006, she did so off the back of three years of bitter fighting with senior figures in the Bush White House, which, she argues, made them determined to stop her book and crush her once and for all.

Plame's story – or 'Plamegate', as it came to be known – has been written about at length in the context of the decision to invade Iraq, and will only be summarised here. The trouble started in February 2002 when Plame, an undercover CIA operative, suggested that her husband, Joseph Wilson, a former ambassador and expert on Niger, be sent to the country to investigate the allegation of then Vice President Dick Cheney that Saddam Hussein had tried to purchase yellowcake uranium to build Weapons of Mass Destruction (WMDs). Wilson debunked it, but this did not stop President Bush and his security apparatchiks filling political discourse with apocalyptic stories about Iraqi WMDs. Almost a year later, during his 2003 State of the Union address, Bush spoke forebodingly of Hussein seeking 'significant quantities of uranium from Africa', directly contradicting Wilson's findings. On 6 July 2003, with the war four months old, and with no sign of the weapons about which Bush had ominously warned and used to justify the invasion, Wilson decided to go public about his trip to Niger with an op-ed in the *New York Times*. Entitled 'What I Didn't Find in Africa', the article contained the explosive claim that his intelligence report had been either ignored or twisted by the administration to sell the war on a false premise. To discredit Wilson, senior officials leaked Plame's identity to several reporters, pushing the story that she had sent her husband to Niger not on a fact-finding mission, but to advance his career as a business consultant. Eight days later, Plame was 'outed' by *Washington Post* columnist Robert Novak.

The fallout was huge. Novak's column effectively ended Plame's CIA career. With her cover blown, she eventually resigned in December

2005. In July 2006, she and her husband filed a civil lawsuit against the Beltway protagonists who, for purely political reasons, had, she argued, conspired to destroy her career. These included Vice President Cheney; the President's trusted *consigliere* and chief political strategist Karl Rove; Deputy Secretary of State Richard Armitage; and vice-presidential adviser I. Lewis 'Scooter' Libby. In a protracted melodrama, played out before a grand jury, Rove and Armitage escaped prosecution, despite confessing to leaking Plame's classified identity (Rove, the architect of the leak, reportedly told MSNBC hardballer Chris Matthews that Wilson's wife was 'fair game'). Libby was less fortunate. On 6 March 2007, he was convicted of obstruction of justice, making false statements and two counts of perjury. In a move described by Plame as 'disappointing', but 'not surprising', Bush later commuted Libby's thirty-month prison sentence (although he was still ordered to pay a $250,000 fine). By the time it was over, the controversy had caused untold damage to the administration. Key officials had been exposed for being so obsessed with selling the war in Iraq that they had been willing to go to any lengths to protect their untruths, including unmasking and smearing an undercover CIA officer. 'The administration', Plame has written, 'had plenty of reasons to be angry at the Wilsons.'[51] It should also be said that the CIA was none too pleased with Plame either. In January 2004, while still an Agency employee, she appeared in *Vanity Fair*, photographed in Wilson's vintage Jaguar, wearing a headscarf and sunglasses, *à la* Grace Kelly. Many of her colleagues at Langley took this as evidence that she was out to cash in on her newfound fame.

Against this background, she entered the fun house of pre-publication review. The manuscript came back heavily expurgated. Remarkably, the PRB refused her clearance to acknowledge that she worked for the CIA at any time prior to her involuntary outing in 2002. Reneging on the 'Clarridge Precedent', it redacted all dates and places of service, information that had been widely reported by the press since she became famous. Naturally, she was furious. How could she write about a 21-year career if the first seventeen years were redacted? The level of sabotage was illustrated by the fact that she could not even disclose what she had eaten for lunch at the 'Farm', save that it was a 'throwback to traditional southern cooking ... dipped in batter and deep-fried'.[52] According to Plame, even the PRB itself felt sheepish about the deletions, with the Chairman using words to her like 'absurd' and 'ludicrous' to describe certain decisions made by unnamed senior managers within the Agency.[53]

In May 2007, believing that the CIA was treading on her First Amendment rights, and convinced that the Agency's position had more to do with punitive action at the behest of the administration than with protecting classified information, Plame sued the CIA in an effort to get the redactions overturned. After a Federal District Court ruled in the CIA's favour, she was left with no choice but to publish a version containing long swathes of redacted text. 'Although the CIA vigorously denied that there was any "outside interference" in its decision making', she wrote in the book's introduction, 'I never had any doubt that there was a connection and influence by the White House.'[54]

It certainly made for a surreal read. For example, there are seven and three-quarter lines of nothing but black bars between Plame meeting her future husband for the first time and him popping up again as the father of the couple's twins. At certain points, Plame plays a guessing game with the reader about where she was at a particular moment in time with remarks like, 'Which country has this proverb, "The goat's hair needs a fine-tooth comb"?'[55] Ironically, the section of the book where she discusses the redactions is itself filled with redactions! In a clever move to circumvent the CIA's strictures, her publisher, Simon & Schuster, commissioned journalist Laura Rozen to pen a lengthy 'Afterword', drawn from open sources, filling in many of the blacked-out details removed from the main manuscript. As John Prados has advised, 'Readers would be smart to turn to the afterword first, before tackling [Plame] Wilson's disjointed narrative.'[56]

III. Confessions in the Digital Age

A couple of colleagues came to me and said, 'Glenn, why are
you writing this book? You should not air our dirty laundry.'
Glenn Carle, former CIA officer and author of *The Interrogator*.[57]

Today, the credibility of the pre-publication review process is
at an all-time low. Negative headlines abound, such as: 'The
CIA's Censorship Machine'; 'Strangled to Death'; 'The CIA's Shark-
Jumping Censorship of Former Agents'; and 'CIA Publications Review
Board Accused of Politically Motivated Censorship'.[58] In the ever-
expanding blogosphere, where people are free to indulge and express
their thoughts, the criticism is particularly stinging. 'The heavy hand
of censorship has never been wielded more clumsily by the nation's
intelligence community than it is being wielded right now,' fumed one
angry blogger, writing for *Harper's Magazine* online, on 29 August
2011.[59] The biggest complaint is by no means a new one, and relates to
the CIA's perceived discriminatory enforcement of its own edicts on
secrecy. As this book has shown, the CIA has long played favourites
in clearing submissions, with different standards being applied de-
pending on the status of the author and whether he or she is critical
or supportive of the Agency. In the last five years, however, the selective application of the rulebook seems to have grown to new levels –
something that has not gone unnoticed by overseers on Capitol Hill. In
spring 2012, the *Washington Post* reported that members of the Senate
Select Committee on Intelligence had written to CIA Director David
Petraeus expressing their concern at the apparent disparities and fa-
vouritism inherent in the review process.[60] In a bid, perhaps, to ward
off more penetrating outsider scrutiny, the CIA agreed to launch an
internal investigation into the matter.

The trigger for this investigation appears to have been the contrasting
fortunes of three individuals who wrote about the CIA's controversial

detention and interrogation programme after 9/11 – Glenn Carle and John Kiriakou on the one hand, and Jose Rodriguez on the other. Let us turn firstly to Carle, author of *The Interrogator: An Education* (2011).[61] Carle's story was a shocking one. In the months after 9/11, he was given the task of prying information out of a prisoner who was believed to be a high-ranking Al Qaeda kingpin, with ties to Osama bin Laden and knowledge of his whereabouts. Uncomfortable with the CIA's re-laxed rules for questioning, which permitted torture, he opted instead to build a rapport with the suspect, whom he referred to in his book as CAPTUS. Over the course of the interrogation, he determined that the man was not who the CIA thought he was, and communicated this to his bosses. According to Carle, they refused to listen and ordered him to press harder. At Langley, the fact that the detainee could not answer questions was interpreted as proof of guilt. Despite Carle's protests, the suspect was rendered to a 'blacksite' known as 'Hotel California', an off-the-books prison beyond the reach of the Red Cross and interna-tional law, where he was tortured. The suspect, who was never charged, endured eight years of incarceration before being freed in 2010 with a muted apology from the US government.

Carle, who retired in 2007, was haunted by the experience: 'We had destroyed the man's life based on an error.'[62] Outraged by the immoral-ity and illegality of what had occurred, he decided to write a tell-it-all book, pointing the finger of blame firmly in the direction of Bush and Cheney. The PRB gutted it. The 250-page manuscript came back with 100 pages redacted – roughly 40,000 words. It was immediately appar-ent to Carle that the reviewing officials had looked for far more than just classified information, and were using the guise of national secu-rity to eliminate or soften harsh facts about US policies of rendition, detention and coercive interrogation. 'Their goal was to intimidate me,' he later told the press. 'That was quite clear.'[63] He was not allowed to confirm the language in which he is fluent (French), a fact that was obvious to the reader since he had discussed, elsewhere in the text, that he had lived in France for twelve years, was schooled there, and met his wife there.[64] His opinion that someone was a 'gibbering fool' was suppressed, as was his view that somewhere he visited was a 'shithole'.[65] He was not permitted to say that someone spoke 'with authority', nor was he allowed to make the 'explosive' revelation that on one occasion he and his colleagues had 'disagreed'.[66] Quotations from T. S. Eliot and Rudyard Kipling were redacted, so too was his description of fog being 'brown'. He could not use the word 'kidnap' in a certain sentence, despite the fact that he was directly quoting from a book cleared by the Agency.[67] For months he argued with the Board over whether he could mention that the prison urinals were five feet off the ground, and thus too high for men to use.[68] Another lengthy spat concerned the inclusion of the phrase 'football-size stones', which the PRB claimed could reveal the location of a blacksite in Afghanistan. 'But the whole world is made out of rocks!' he protested, incredulous.[69]

In total, Carle spent two years fighting the redactions. Allegedly, the PRB told him: 'We will not allow you to take the reader into the interrogation room. We will not allow you to make the prisoner a human being. To the extent that we can, we will take out anything that gives him a personality.'[70] Accordingly, he was prevented from saying that he 'saw fear' in a person's eyes, or that the detainee was a 'middle-aged man'. [71] After more than a dozen rewrites, trying to meet the CIA's professed sources and methods concerns, he eventually elected to publish with the redactions in place, albeit with the occasional withering footnote such as: 'Apparently the CIA fears that the redacted passage would either humiliate the organisation for incompetence or expose its officers to ridicule; unless the Agency considers obtuse incompetence a secret intelligence method.'[72] In the book's Afterword, he lamented: 'The CAPTUS tale is darker than I have been allowed to tell.'[73]

The PRB was similarly unforgiving in the case of John Kiriakou, a self-declared 'torture whistle-blower', who in recent years has become a rallying point for critics of the CIA's role in the War on Terror. Kiriakou, who served in the CIA from 1990 until March 2004, first as an analyst and then as a counterterrorism operations officer, submitted a sixty-page proposal, plus sample chapter, in early 2007. 'They redacted every single word,' he later recalled, despite it being what he believed was a 'pro-Agency book'. Indeed, at this stage, it contained no mention of torture. 'They said, "You can't say any of this stuff, it's all classified."'[74] Like others before him, he girded his loins for the battle that lay ahead, but even he could not have anticipated how tough that battle would be.

In December 2007, his struggle with the PRB ongoing, Kiriakou proceeded to add oil to the fire. For a good while, the CIA had successfully managed to hide the extent of its harsh interrogation methods, which had been authorised by the Justice Department under President Bush. Gradually, however, cracks in the wall of secrecy started to appear amid FOIA requests by the ACLU and sleuthing by press hounds. In September 2006, in a televised address, Bush officially confirmed the existence of CIA secret prisons overseas, adding that they had been a vital tool for holding and questioning high-value suspects and had led to intelligence that had saved lives. With the whiff of scandal in the air, journalists continued to investigate and, on 6 December 2007, *New York Times* reporter Mark Mazzetti revealed that the CIA had videotaped abusive interrogations of at least two high-ranking Al Qaeda operatives, including Abu Zubaydah, said to be one of Bin Laden's top lieutenants and the first terror suspect in CIA custody after 9/11. He also wrote that in 2005 senior CIA man Jose Rodriguez had ordered the destruction of the tapes. With this, the press went looking for CIA officers to comment. A few days later, in a taped interview for ABC News, Kiriakou became the first CIA officer to acknowledge publicly the use of the simulated drowning technique known as waterboarding. In the interview, he claimed that Zubaydah had cracked after thirty seconds, after one application of the waterlogged cloth, and that his coerced confessions prevented potentially dozens of terrorist attacks. In the following weeks and months, he spoke freely to reporters, repeatedly insisting that the programme had adhered to the rule of law and had kept Americans safe.[75]

The CIA was furious. His wife Heather, a CIA analyst at the time, told him that officials at Langley were incandescent and considered him a traitor.[76] It did not matter that, during the interview, Kiriakou had defended the 'gloves-off' approach to terror suspects as 'something that we really needed to do'.[77] It also did not matter that he insisted that the CIA had meticulously followed the rules established by its own lawyers and by the Justice Department. What mattered was that he had spoken at all. 'I broke the code,' he later declared. 'You don't ever talk to the press and you don't talk about dirty laundry, and I did.'[78] Interestingly, Kiriakou had in fact got the Zubaydah story wrong, something his bosses doubtless knew and were terrified about being revealed. Released by order of Barack Obama during the first year of his presidency, a legal memo revealed that Zubaydah had actually been water-boarded at least eighty-three times, in August 2002 alone. In December 2014, the Senate Intelligence Committee 'Torture Report' claimed that he was nothing more than a low-level foot soldier in the Al Qaeda hierarchy, and that no substantive intelligence about plots or the structure of terrorist networks was gleaned from him. More shockingly, it suggested that he had been used as a guinea pig, to test the limits of human endurance and provide administration officials with legal guidelines for interrogating future suspects. His stark ordeal included sleep deprivation, grinding white noise, being body-slammed by his captors, and being hooded for long periods before being un-masked and ominously shown a coffin-like box. Water-boarded as often as twice a day – to the point where he would be 'completely unresponsive, with bubbles rising through his open, full mouth' – his torment horrified even some of his interrogators. According to a cable sent from a prison in Thailand, cited in the report, 'Several on the team [were] profoundly affected ... to the point of tears and choking up.'[79]

There is little doubt that events on the outside intensified Kiriakou's internal struggle with the PRB. In October 2008, after a meeting to discuss the book at CIA headquarters, a Board member walked him to his car and, alluding to his willingness to talk to journalists about the CIA's secret and sensitive interrogation programme, said flatly that no matter what changes were made to the manuscript, it would never be published. 'You still have a lot of very powerful enemies here,' the man said, threateningly.[80] Kiriakou continued to appeal the redactions, but got nowhere. He later told the press: 'When they mail it [the manuscript] back to you, if you've got a thick envelope, you know you're screwed because it's all of the redacted material, page after page, blacked-out sentences. I have a stack probably two feet tall of just blacked-out pages.'[81] Eventually, he decided not to resubmit the manuscript until after the results of the presidential election, in the hope that a new President, and presumably a new Director of the CIA, would take a different view. The tactic worked. After Obama replaced Bush in the White House, and installed Leon Panetta at the CIA, the book was finally cleared, albeit with some names and locations changed, and with some true events obscured.[82]

Published in March 2010, *The Reluctant Spy: My Secret Life in the CIA's War on Terror* was a different animal to the proposal Kiriakou had sent the PRB in early 2007.[83] Three years was a long time, in which much had been revealed about the scores of suspects that were held in the CIA's secret detention centres; clearly, it would have been remiss of him not to discuss the subject. By 2010, his views on the techniques used by the CIA had also changed, and publicly he had begun pouring cold water on his previously held belief that torture produced actionable intelligence. 'But even if torture works', he said in the book, 'it cannot be tolerated – not in one case or a thousand or a million.'[84] 'Torture', he went on, quoting President Obama, 'corrodes the character of a country.'[85]

Unfortunately for Kiriakou, the battle did not end with the publication of his book. Within twenty-four hours of his ABC interview, and without his knowledge, the CIA had filed a crimes report with the Justice Department, claiming that he had broken federal secrecy laws.[86] The more interviews he gave, the more reports the Agency filed. No evidence of wrongdoing was found, but he was a marked man and prosecutors kept digging. Meanwhile, in 2008, he abruptly lost his job as a consultant with Deloitte, the Big Four accountancy firm he joined after leaving the Agency. In January 2012, while on maternity leave, his wife resigned from the CIA amid reports that she had been leaned on to step down.[87] To survive until she could secure a job in the private sector, they went on food stamps, leased their family home in Arlington, Virginia, and moved, with their three young children, to a small rented bungalow.[88] The IRS has audited Kiriakou every year since 2007. During this time, prosecutors eventually stumbled upon something they could use against him. In 2009, in connection with an unrelated investigation into the allegation that defence lawyers for Guantanamo Bay detainees had obtained names and photographs of undercover CIA interrogators, the Justice Department discovered emails between Kiriakou and several journalists, including Scott Shane of the *New York Times* and freelancer Matthew Cole. In one email, to Cole, Kiriakou had confirmed the name of a covert CIA officer involved in the rendition programme. Although Cole never printed the name, Kiriakou was charged with disclosing classified information to journalists. In October 2012, facing thirty-five years in jail if found guilty of all the charges, including three counts of breaking the First-World-War-era Espionage Act, he copped a plea bargain and pleaded guilty to violating the Intelligence Identities Protection Act, making him the first CIA officer ever to be convicted of disclosing classified information to the press and only the second person ever convicted in the history of the Act. On 25 January 2013, he was sentenced to thirty months at the Federal Correctional Institute in Loretto, Pennsylvania.

In the long history of CIA officers telling tales out of school, few have been more divisive than Kiriakou; he walks a fine line. Judged strictly on its own terms, there is a strong argument to be made that the indictment was correct. Leaking the name of a covert CIA officer is a serious offence, deserving of punishment. The memorial wall at Langley would include many more stars if the identities of undercover intelligence officers were revealed in real-time. Had Cole printed the name, or if his emails had been hacked or fallen into the wrong hands, Al Qaeda and its sympathisers might well have sought to retaliate against the officer in question. Perhaps unprepared for the media attention, Kiriakou has admitted that he became too loquacious with reporters, foolishly letting his guard down when he should have known better. 'I should never have provided the name ... I made a mistake,' he has said, repentantly.[89]

Put into a larger context, however, his punishment seems harsh. Speaking for those who believe that he was really targeted because he dared to speak on the record about government-sanctioned torture, former CIA officer Bruce Riedel, now at the Brookings Institution, told the New York Times that the prosecution appeared 'disproportionate and more like persecution'.[90] He continued: 'There appears to be a vindictiveness about this.'[91] It is staggering to think that, until Kiriakou took a plea deal, the federal government was looking to put him under lock and key for thirty-five years. This was the same government that only a decade earlier had asked him to risk his life in pursuit of Al Qaeda. It is also a sobering thought that not one person involved in creating and administering the Bush-era interrogation programme has gone to prison – save Kiriakou, the individual who helped to expose it. To quote Riedel: 'The irony of this whole thing is, very simply, that Kiriakou's going to be the only CIA officer to go to jail over torture.'[92] In short, is Kiriakou any more a 'criminal' than the people who approved of and participated in torture, and whom the Obama administration has thus far eschewed prosecution?

Yet, by far the biggest protest relates to an egregious double standard. Despite leaking Valerie Plame's name to reporters, effectively ending her career and putting her at risk of reprisal, Karl Rove and Richard

Armitage were never indicted, while 'Scooter' Libby has never spent one night in a correctional facility. It has not gone unnoticed that while the CIA has raised 'holy hell' over the actions of lesser mortals and critics such as Carle and Kiriakou, Agency loyalists and high-flyers, especially those from the executive ranks, have seemingly traded their insider knowledge with impunity.

Among those believed to have been looked upon favourably is Jose Rodriguez, a former Chief of the CIA's Counterterrorism Center and, before his retirement in September 2007, Director of the NCS. The tough-talking Rodriguez has been a vigorous defender of the CIA's widely condemned 'enhanced' interrogation techniques, suggesting that they worked like magic on Zubaydah, among others; provided critical information about terrorist plots; and boasting that torture is an expression of American strength. 'We needed to get everybody in government to put their big boy pants on,' he declared during a *60 Minutes* interview in April 2012. He added: 'The objective is to let them know [Al Qaeda] there's a new sheriff in town.'[93] Co-authored with former CIA chief spokesman Bill Harlow, his 2012 memoir *Harsh Measures: How Aggressive CIA Actions After 9/11 Saved American Lives* appears to have sailed through the PRB.[94] Controversially, he has never been reprimanded for apparently sanctioning the destruction of the videotapes that documented the torture of terror suspects in 2002. According to an internal CIA email, his calculation was that, 'The heat from destroying is nothing compared with what it would be if the tapes ever got into public domain ... they would make us look terrible.'[95] Critics, including Virginia Democratic Representative Jim Moran, find this unacceptable, especially in the light of what Moran calls Kiriakou's 'selective prosecution'. 'Rodriguez ... admits to deciding without any legal authorisation to erase videotapes of torture sessions so they could never be used in US courts but has never been forced to answer for this destruction of evidence,' he admonished on the floor of the House on 17 November 2014.[96]

Former CIA Director Leon Panetta is another the naysayers can point to as evidence of there not being a level playing field. In October 2014, it was revealed that he had allowed his publisher to edit and begin distributing review copies of his memoir, *Worthy Fights*, before it had been cleared by the PRB. A bound copy provided to the *Washington Post* had the date '11 August' stamped on each page, but final approval from the Agency did not arrive until early September.[97] As we know, for publishing without permission, authors, such as Frank Snepp, had been sued for breach of contract and forced to hand over every cent of their so-called 'ill-gotten gains' to the US Treasury. Yet, lending weight to the belief that there is one rule for the high and mighty and another for lesser mortals, no action was taken against Panetta. 'If he doesn't follow the specific protocols, then why should there be any expectation for anybody underneath him to do so?' commented Zaid.[98] In Panetta's case, the air is particularly thick with irony because, in his final government position as Defense Secretary (July 2011 to February 2013), he publicly reprimanded former SEAL Team Six member Matt Bissonnette for his eyewitness account of the raid that killed Osama bin Laden, which had gone to press without clearance from the Pentagon. Authorising a criminal probe by the Justice Department, Panetta declared at the time: 'I cannot, as secretary, send a signal to SEALs who conduct these operations – "Oh, you can conduct these operations and then go out and write a book about it".'[99]

Then there is Petraeus. When Kiriakou pleaded guilty on 23 October 2012, the decorated four-star army general, then the CIA Director, issued a statement praising the conviction as 'an important victory for our Agency, for our intelligence community, and for our country'.[100] 'Oaths do matter', he emphasised, 'and there are indeed consequences for those who believe they are above the laws that protect our fellow officers and enable American intelligence agencies to operate with the requisite degree of secrecy'.[101] Less than three weeks later, he resigned under a cloud after the FBI discovered, upon delving into his private email account in relation to a separate investigation, that he had had an extramarital affair with a woman later identified as his biographer, Army Reserve officer and fellow West Point graduate Paula Broadwell. With all the elements of a classic Washington scandal, it was alleged that Petraeus had passed classified information to his mistress. Prosecutors subsequently established that he had shared eight five-by-eight-inch 'black books' with Broadwell, containing notes from his consultations with President Obama; quotes from National Security Council meetings; and material pertaining to war strategy, intelligence capabilities and the identities of CIA officers.[102] In March 2015, Petraeus pleaded guilty to the charge of mishandling classified documents, an offence that carried with it a potential prison sentence. However, under the terms of a generous plea deal, his punishment was two years' probation and a $100,000 fine. Compared to what happened to Kiriakou, it barely qualified as a slap on the wrist. As one commentator noted sarcastically, given Petraeus's CV – war hero, spy chief, disgraced adulterer – he will pay his fine with two hours' work on the lucrative rubber chicken circuit.[103] As a yardstick, ex-CIA Directors Gates, Woolsey and Tenet command $20,000, $42,500 and $50,000 per talk, respectively, plus first-class airfare.[104]

At the time of writing, the results of the CIA's internal investigation into the PRB are unknown, but it is clear that it has some work to do if it wants to shake off the prevailing wisdom that its review procedure is inconsistent and unfair. The danger of failing to reform is severe. Congress or the Executive Branch could intervene. For example, a law or Executive Order could be passed that puts power in the hands of independent classified review experts to adjudicate on disputed pre-publication reviews. One solution would be to establish a body analogous to the International Security Classifications Appeals Panel (ISCAP), which handles mandatory declassification review requests. Comprised of senior representatives from the principal national security agencies, and administered through the National Archives'

Information Security Oversight Office, ISCAP has the authority to overturn, modify or affirm the objection of the classifying agency. At Langley, having to justify its pre-publication review decisions to an audience of Beltway rivals, especially if the offending material is an open secret already in the public domain, would be a scary proposition.

A second danger is that authors might become so disillusioned with what they regard as a broken system, that they elect simply to 'publish and be damned', and take their chances in court. Today, authors can enjoy strong legal representation, with an ever-growing array of well-pedigreed national security attorneys to choose from, and can offset the costs not only by bumper book deals and serialisation, but by the riches on offer as a television pundit. 'The Government will always employ a team of lawyers to protect its interests and is guaranteed to be a formidable opponent. There is no reason why the same cannot be said for you,' underlines Zaid's website.[105] While politically expedient at the time, the leniency shown to Petraeus could well come back to haunt US authorities further down the line. As Zaid has said, in future classification disputes, defence attorneys are likely to use it as leverage in arguing for mercy: '"I want the Petraeus deal." That is now our catchphrase.'[106]

Over the coming years, the PRB is likely to be kept extremely busy. The public appetite for spy memoirs shows no sign of diminishing, hardly surprising given that scarcely a day goes by without the CIA being in the news. The ongoing struggle against Al Qaeda, its affiliates and now ISIS (the so-called Islamic State) will provide a steady stream of interesting and controversial material for CIA officers to recycle into books, from drones to cyber operations. As John Prados has written, there will doubtlessly be bad secrets or 'Family Jewels';[107] but there will also be good secrets like 'Argo' that intelligence officers will be keen to narrate, especially for profit, and which the public will delight in knowing.

The increased size, but more importantly the transmogrified demographic and culture of the CIA's workforce, also points to a heightened workload for the PRB. Since 9/11, to meet the threat of international terrorism, the CIA has taken on people, including private contractors to cut costs and bureaucratic red tape, that see the Agency as a job, just like any other, not a career, and certainly not a 'calling'. Many of the millennial generation of CIA officers will remain with the Agency for just a few years, a hockey season by the standard of the seasoned cold warriors discussed in this book. Infamous computer engineer Edward Snowden, who spent less than three years with the CIA between mid-2006 and February 2009, before joining the NSA for a similarly short period of service, is testament to this. Of course, this does not mean that all CIA employees are wired like Snowden, waiting for the opportunity to reveal what they know on the internet, and unilaterally decide what is secret and what is not. But what it does mean is that there is a growing pool of officers who may not have quite the same level of deference to secrecy. Significantly, they are also a generation that has been accustomed to CIA officers writing books; it is no longer taboo.

Finally, the workload of the PRB will continue to grow as new mediums are developed for officers to tell their stories. When Herbert Yardley planted the seed that eventually germinated into a whole new genre, he could turn to just a handful of publishers brave enough to print what he had to say. Today, officers can type wikis, blogs and tweets, in an ever-enlarging digital emporium of outlets. While languishing in jail, Kiriakou maintained a blog, 'Letters from Loretto', documenting his time in the federal penitentiary, to the chagrin of the Bureau of Prisons. Upon completing his sentence, his first instinct was to tell the world, in no more than 140 characters, 'Free at last. Free at last. Thank God Almighty. I'm free at last.' As even newer tools of communication are advanced, the wave of company confessions will become a flood, and at least one person will be waiting to enjoy it – the lawyer.

Bibliography

Major Repositories of Unpublished Government Documents

FBI Files, http://www.fbi.gov/foia/

National Archives of Japan, Tokyo.

US National Archives II, College Park, Maryland, USA (NARA).

Newspapers

Baltimore Sun

Christian Science Monitor

Daily Mail (UK)

Dallas Texas Herald

Detroit News

The Guardian (UK)

The Independent (UK)

Life

Los Angeles Times

National Observer

New Yorker

New York Herald

People Magazine

San Francisco Examiner

St Louis Post-Dispatch
Texas Observer
New York Review of Books
New York Times
USA Today
Washington Star
Washington Post

Private Papers

I. United States

Agee, Phillip. Tamiment Library and Robert F. Wagner Labor Archives, New York University, New York, NY.

Atlee Phillips, David. Manuscript Division, Library of Congress, Washington, DC.

Bancroft, Mary. Arthur and Elizabeth Schlesinger Library on the History of Women in America, Radcliffe Institute, Harvard University, Cambridge, MA.

Breckinridge, Jr, Scott D. Wendell H. Ford Public Policy Research Center, University of Kentucky, Lexington, KY.

Brown Associates Records. Rare Book and Manuscript Library, Columbia University, NY.

Casey, William. Hoover Institution, Stanford University, CA.

Castle, William R. Houghton Library, Harvard University, Cambridge, MA.

Cline, Ray. Manuscript Division, Library of Congress, Washington, DC.

Colby, William. Seeley G. Mudd Manuscript Library, Princeton University, NJ.

Deuel, Wallace Rankin. Manuscript Division, Library of Congress, Washington, DC.

Donovan, William J. US Army Military History Institute, Carlisle, PA.

Dulles, Allen. Seeley G. Mudd Manuscript Library, Princeton University, NJ.

Eisenhower, Dwight. Eisenhower Presidential Library, Abilene, KS.

Eveland, Wilbur Crane. Hoover Institution, Stanford University, CA.

Farago, Ladislas. Howard Gotlieb Archival Research Center, Boston University, MS.

Ford, Corey. Rauner Special Collections Library, Dartmouth College, NH.

Forgan, J. Russell. Hoover Institution, Stanford University, CA.

Friedman, William F. George C. Marshall Research Library, Lexington, VA.

Helms, Richard. Georgetown University Special Collections Research Center, Georgetown University, Washington, DC.

Hood, William. Georgetown University Special Collections Research Center, Georgetown University, Washington, DC.

Kent, Sherman. Manuscript Collections, Yale University Library, Yale University, New Haven, CT.

Kirkpatrick, Lyman. Seeley G. Mudd Manuscript Library, Princeton University, NJ.

Knopf, Alfred. Harry Ransom Center, Austin TX.

Krock, Arthur. Seeley G. Mudd Manuscript Library, Princeton University, NJ.

McCone, John. Bancroft Library, University of Berkeley, CA.

Meyer, Cord. Manuscript Division, Library of Congress, Washington, DC.

Moynihan, Daniel P. Manuscript Division, Library of Congress, Washington, DC.

NBC Collection. State Historical Society of Wisconsin, Madison, WI.

Stockton, Bayard. Davidson Library, Department of Special Collections, University of California, Santa Barbara, CA.

Swanson, H. N. Margaret Herrick Library, Academy of Motion Picture Arts and Sciences, Los Angeles, CA.

Turner/MGM Scripts. Margaret Herrick Library, Academy of Motion Picture Arts and Sciences, Los Angeles, CA.

Wear, Robert. Milne Special Collections and Archives Department, University of New Hampshire Library, Durham, NH.

Weingarten, Lawrence. Edward L. Doheny Jr Memorial Library, University of Southern California, Los Angeles, CA.

II. United Kingdom

Lewin, Ronald. Churchill College, Cambridge University.

Diaries and Memoirs

Adams, Sam. *War of Numbers: An Intelligence Memoir*. Hanover, NH: Steerforth, 1994.

Agee, Phillip. *Inside the Company: CIA Diary*. London: Harmondsworth, 1975.

— *On the Run*. London: Bloomsbury, 1987.

Atlee Phillips, David. *The Night Watch: Twenty-Five Years of Peculiar Service*. New York: Atheneum, 1977.

Berntsen, Gary. *Jawbreaker: The Attack on Bin Laden and Al-Qaeda: A Personal Account by the CIA's Key Field Commander*. New York: Three Rivers Press, 2005.

Bush, Barbara. *Barbara Bush: A Memoir*. New York: Scribners, 1994.

Carle, Glenn. *The Interrogator: An Education*. New York: Nation Book, 2011.

Clarridge, Duane R. *A Spy for All Seasons: My Life in the CIA*. New York: Scribner's, 1997.

Colby, William and Forbath, Peter. *Honorable Men: My Life in the CIA*. Simon & Schuster: New York, 1978.

Copeland, Miles. *The Game Player: Confessions of the CIA's Original Political Operative*. London: Aurum Press, 1989.

Cooper, Chester. *The Lion's Last Roar*. New York: Harper & Row, 1978.

Downes, Donald. *The Scarlet Thread: Adventures in Wartime Espionage*. London: Derek Verschoyle, 1953.

Dulles, Allen. *Germany's Underground*. New York: Macmillan, 1947.

Eveland, Wilbur Crane. *Ropes of Sand: America's Failure in the Middle East*. New York: Norton, 1980.

Gates, Robert M. *From the Shadows: The Ultimate Insider's Story of Five Presidents and How They Won the Cold War*. New York: Simon & Schuster, 1996.

Goodall Jr, H. L. *A Need to Know: The Clandestine History of a CIA Family*. Walnut Creek, CA: Left Coast Press, 2008.

Hall, Roger. *You're Stepping on My Cloak and Dagger*. New York: Norton, 1957. Annapolis, MD: Naval Institute Press, 2004.

Helms, Richard with Hood, William. *A Look Over My Shoulder: A Life in the Central Intelligence Agency*. New York: Random House, 2003.

Holm, Richard L. *The American Agent: My Life in the CIA*. London: St Ermin's, 2003.

— *The Craft We Chose: My Life in the CIA*. Mountain Lake Park, MD: Mountain Lake Press, 2011.

Kalugin, Oleg. *Spymaster: My Thirty-Two Years in Intelligence and Espionage against the West*. New York: Basic Books, 2009.

Kiriakou, John with Ruby, Michael. *The Reluctant Spy: My Secret Life in the War on Terror*. New York: Bantam Books, 2010.

Macdonald, Elizabeth. *Undercover Girl*. New York: Macmillan, 1947.

Mahle, Melissa Boyle. *Denial and Deception: An Insider's View of the CIA*. New York: Nation Books, 2006.

Marchetti, Victor and Marks, John D. *The CIA and the Cult of Intelligence*. New York: Alfred A. Knopf, 1974.

McGarvey, Patrick. *CIA: The Myth and the Madness*. Baltimore: Penguin, 1972.

Meyer, Cord. *Facing Reality: From World Federalism to the CIA*. New York: Harper & Row, 1980.

Moran, Lindsay. *Blowing My Cover: My Life as a CIA Spy*. New York: Putnam, 2005.

Nelson, Kay Shaw. *The Cloak and Dagger Cook: A CIA Memoir*. Gretna, LA: Pelican, 2009.

Panetta, Leon with Newton, Jim. *Worthy Fights: A Memoir of Leadership in War and Peace*. New York: Penguin, 2014.

Paseman, Floyd L. *A Spy's Journey: A CIA Memoir*. Minneapolis, MN: Zenith Press, 2004.

Powers, Francis Gary. *Operation Overflight: A Memoir of the U-2 Incident*. Washington, DC: Potomac Books, 2004.

Press, Sylvia. *The Care of Devils*. London: Constable & Company, 1958.

Rodriguez Jr, Jose with Harlow, Bill. *Hard Measures: How Aggressive CIA Actions After 9/11 Saved American Lives*. New York: Simon & Schuster, 2012.

Scheuer, Michael. *Imperial Hubris: Why the West is Losing the War on Terror*. Dulles, VA: Brassey's, 2004.

Schroen, Gary C. *First In: An Insider's Account of How the CIA Spearheaded the War on Terror in Afghanistan*. New York: Ballantine Books, 2005.

Shackley, Ted. *Spymaster: My Life in the CIA*. Washington, DC: Potomac Books, 2006.

Smith, Joseph Burkholder. *Portrait of a Cold Warrior*. New York: Ballantine Books, 1976.

Smith, Russell Jack. *The Unknown CIA: My Three Decades with the Agency*. McLean, VA: Berkeley Books, 1989.

Snepp, Frank. *Decent Interval*. New York: Random House, 1977.

— *Irreparable Harm: A Firsthand Account of How One Agent Took on the CIA in an Epic Battle over Free Speech*. Lawrence: University Press of Kansas, 1999.

Tenet, George with Harlow, Bill. *At the Center of the Storm: My Years at the CIA*. New York: Harper Collins, 2007.

Turner, Stansfield. *Secrecy and Democracy: The CIA in Transition*. New York: Harper & Row, 1985.

Wallace, Robert and Melton, Keith. *Spycraft: The Secret History of the CIA's Spytechs From Communism to Al Qaeda*. New York: Dutton, 2008.

Waters, T. J. *Class 11: Inside the CIA's First Post-9/11 Spy Class*. New York: Dutton, 2006.

Wilson, Valerie Plame. *Fair Game: My Life as a Spy, My Betrayal by the White House*. New York: Simon & Schuster, 2007.

Yardley, Herbert O. *The American Black Chamber*. Indianapolis, IN: Bobbs-Merrill, 1931; Reprint Edition, Annapolis: Naval Institute Press, 2004.

— *The Chinese Black Chamber: An Adventure in Espionage*. Boston: Houghton Mifflin, 1983.

Secondary Literature

Aftergood, Steven. 'Secrecy and Accountability in U.S. Intelligence.' 9 October 1996, http://www.fas.org/sgp/cipsecr.html.

Aid, Matthew. *The Secret Sentry: The Untold History of the National Security Agency*. New York: Bloomsbury Press, 2009.

Aldrich, Richard J. *The Hidden Hand: Britain, America and Cold War Secret Intelligence*. London: John Murray, 2001.

— 'Regulation by Revelation? Intelligence, Transparency, and the Media', in *Spinning Intelligence: Why Intelligence Needs the Media, Why the Media Needs Intelligence*, edited by Michael Goodman and Rob Dover. New York: Columbia University Press, 2009: Chapters 13–37.

— *GCHQ: The Uncensored Story of Britain's Most Secret Intelligence Agency*. London: Harper Press, 2010.

— 'CIA History as a Cold War Battleground: The Forgotten First Wave of Agency Narratives', in *Intelligence Studies in Britain and the US: Historiography since 1945*, edited by Christopher Moran and Christopher Murphy. Edinburgh: Edinburgh University Press, 2013: Chapters 19–46.

— 'American Journalism and the Landscape of Secrecy: Tad Szulc, the CIA and Cuba.' *History: The Journal of the Historical Association* 100: 340 (April 2015): 189–209.

Andrew, Christopher. *For the President's Eyes: Secret Intelligence and the American Presidency from Washington to Bush*. New York: Harper, 1995.

— and Vasili Mitrokhin. *The KGB in Europe and the West*. London: Penguin, 1999.

Arnold, Jonathan P. 'Herbert O. Yardley, Gangster.' *Cryptologia* 12:1 (1988): 62–4.

Axelrod, Alan. *The Real History of the Cold War: A New Look at the Past*. New York: Sterling, 2009.

Bacevich, Andrew. *Washington Rules: America's Path to Permanent War*. New York: Metropolitan Books, 2010.

Barrett, David M. *CIA and Congress: The Untold Story from Truman to Kennedy*. Lawrence: University Press of Kansas, 2005.

Barron, John. *KGB Today: The Hidden Hand*. London: Hodder & Stoughton, 1984.

Carter, D. and Clifton, R. (eds). *War and Cold War in American Foreign Policy 1942–62*. Basingstoke: Palgrave, 2002.

Cockburn, Alexander. *Corruptions of Empire: Life Studies and the Reagan Era*. London: Verso, 1987.

— and Jeffrey St Clair. *Whiteout: The CIA, Drugs and the Press*. London: Verso, 1998.

Coll, Steve. *Ghost Wars: The Secret History of the CIA, Afghanistan and Bin Laden, From the Soviet Invasion to September 10, 2001*. New York: Penguin, 2004.

Corke, Sarah-Jane. *US Covert Operations and Cold War Strategy: Truman, Secret Warfare and the CIA, 1947–53*. London: Routledge, 2008.

Cullather, Nick. *Secret History: The CIA's Classified Account of its Operations in Guatemala, 1952–1954*. Stanford: Stanford University Press, 1999.

Dearborn, Mary Von. *Mailer: A Biography*. New York: Houghton Mifflin Company, 1999.

DeLillo, Don. *Libra*. New York: Penguin, 1986.

Denniston, Robin. 'Yardley's Diplomatic Secrets.' *Cryptologia* 18:2 (1994): 81–127.

Dershowitz, Alan M. *The Best Defense: The Courtroom Confrontations of America's Most Outspoken Lawyer of Last Resort – the Lawyer Who Won the Claus von Bülow Appeal*. New York: Random House, 1982.

Deutsch, James I. '"I was a Hollywood Agent": Cinematic Representations of the Office of Strategic Services in 1946.' *Intelligence and National Security* 13:2 (1998): 85–99.

Dick, Bernard F. *The Star Spangled Screen: The American World War II Film*. Lexington, KY: The University Press of Kentucky, 1996.

Dooley, John F. 'Was Herbert Yardley a Traitor?' *Cryptologia* 35:1 (2010): 1–15.

— 'Who Wrote the Blonde Countess? A Stylometric Analysis of Herbert O. Yardley's Fiction.' *Cryptologia* 33:2 (2009): 108–17.

Egerton, George. 'The Lloyd George *War Memoirs*: A Study in the Politics of Memory.' *The Journal of Modern History* 60:1 (March 1988): 55–94.

— (ed.) *Political Memoir: Essays on the Politics of Memory*. London: Frank Cass, 1994.

Eisendrath, Craig (ed.). *National Insecurity: US Intelligence after the Cold War*. Philadelphia: Temple University Press, 2000.

Escalante, F. *CIA Targets Fidel: The Secret Assassination Report*. New York: Ocean Press, 1996.

Farago, Ladislas. *The Broken Seal: 'Operation Magic' and the Secret Road to Pearl Harbor*. London: Arthur Barker, 1967.

Fleming, Ian. *You Only Live Twice*. London: Jonathan Cape, 1964.

Ford, Corey and MacBain, Alastair. *Cloak and Dagger: The Secret Story of the OSS*. New York: Grosset & Dunlap, 1945.

Frank, Jeffrey. *Ike and Dick: Portrait of a Strange Political Marriage*. New York: Simon & Schuster, 2013.

Garthoff, Douglas F. *Directors of Central Intelligence as Leaders of the Intelligence Community 1946–2005*. Washington, DC: Center for the Study of Intelligence, 2007.

Gill, Peter. 'Reasserting Control: Recent Changes in the Oversight of the UK Intelligence Community.' *Intelligence and National Security* 11:2 (1996): 313–31.

Gleijeses, Piero. *Shattered Hope: The Guatemalan Revolt and the United States, 1944–1954*. Princeton: Princeton University Press, 1991.

Greene, John Robert. *The Presidency of Gerald R. Ford*. Lawrence: University Press of Kansas, 1995.

Gup, Ted. *Nation of Secrets: The Threat to Democracy and the American Way of Life*. New York: Doubleday, 2007.

Hagerty, Alexander. 'An Unpublished Yardley Manuscript.' *Cryptologia* 23:4 (1999): 289–97.

Hammond, Andrew. 'Through a Glass, Darkly: The CIA and Oral History.' *History: The Journal of the Historical Association* 100:340 (April 2015): 311–26.

— *Struggles for Freedom: Afghanistan and US Foreign Policy since 1979*. Edinburgh: Edinburgh University Press, 2016.

Hassan, Oz. *Constructing America's Freedom Agenda for the Middle East: Democracy or Domination*. Abingdon: Routledge, 2013.

Hatonn, Gyeorgos C. *Silent Blood Suckers of the Tangled Webs*. Carson City: America West Publishers, 1992.

Hedley, John Hollister. 'Reviewing the Work of CIA Authors: Secrets, Free Speech, and Fig Leaves.' *Studies in Intelligence* (Spring 1998): 75–83.

— 'Three Memoirs by Former CIA Officers.' *Studies in Intelligence* 49:3 (2005): 79–83.

Helms, Richard. 'Intelligence in American Society.' *Studies in Intelligence* 11:3 (Summer 1967): 1–16.

Herman, Michael. *Intelligence and Power in Peace and War*. Cambridge: Cambridge University Press, 1996.

Holzman, Michael Howard. *James Jesus Angleton, the CIA, and the Craft of Counterintelligence*. Amherst: University of Massachusetts Press, 2008.

Hood, William. *Mole: The True Story of the First Russian Spy to Become an American Counterspy*. New York: Norton, 1983.

Hulnick, Arthur S. *Fixing the Spy Machine*. Westport, CT: Praeger, 1999.

— 'Openness: Being Public about Secret Intelligence.' *International Journal of Intelligence and Counterintelligence* 12:4 (1999): 463–83.

Immerman, Richard. *The CIA in Guatemala: The Foreign Policy of Intervention*. Austin: University of Texas Press, 1983.

— *The Hidden Hand: A Brief History of the CIA*. Malden, MA: John Wiley & Sons, 2014.

Jeffreys-Jones, Rhodri. 'The Historiography of the CIA.' *The Historical Journal* 23:2 (June 1980): 489–96.

— *The CIA and American Democracy*. New Haven: Yale University, 1989.

— 'Why was the CIA Established in 1947?' *Intelligence and National Security* 12:1 (January 1997): 21–40.

— *Cloak and Dollar: A History of American Secret Intelligence*. New Haven: Yale, 2002.

— *In Spies We Trust: The Story of Western Intelligence*. Oxford: Oxford University Press, 2013.

Jenkins, Tricia. *The CIA in Hollywood: How the Agency Shapes Film and Television*. Austin, TX: University of Texas Press, 2012.

Johnson, Loch K. *America's Secret Power: The CIA in a Democratic Society*. New York: Oxford University Press, 1989.

— 'The Church Committee Investigation of 1975 and the Evolution of Modern Intelligence Accountability.' *Intelligence and National Security* 23:2 (April 2008): 198–225.

Jones, Matthew. '"The Preferred Plan": The Anglo-American Working Group Report on Covert Action in Syria, 1957.' *Intelligence and National Security* 19:3 (2004): 401–15.

— 'Journalism, Intelligence and the New York Times: Cyrus L. Sulzberger, Harrison E. Salisbury and the CIA.' *History: The Journal of the Historical Association* 100:340 (April 2015): 229–50.

Kackman, Michael. *Citizen Spy: Television, Espionage, and Cold War Culture.* Minneapolis: University of Minnesota Press, 2005.

Kahn, David. *The Reader of Gentlemen's Mail: Herbert O. Yardley and the Birth of American Codebreaking.* New Haven: Yale University Press, 2004.

Kessler, Ronald. *Inside the CIA.* New York: Pocket Books, 1992.

Kimball, Warren F. 'Arguing for Accountability: Openness and the CIA.' *Studies in Intelligence* 10 (Winter–Spring 2001): 63–7.

Kinzer, Stephen. *All the Shah's Men: The Hidden Story of the CIA's Coup in Iran.* New Jersey: Wiley, 2003.

— *The Brothers: John Foster Dulles, Allen Dulles, and their Secret World War.* New York: Times Books, 2013.

Knightley, Phillip. *The Second Oldest Profession: Spies and Spying in the Twentieth Century.* London: Deutsch, 1986.

Knott, Stephen F. *Secret and Sanctioned: Covert Operations and the American Presidency.* New York: Oxford University Press, 1996.

Kolko, G. and Kolko, J. *The Limits of Power: The World and United States Foreign Policy 1945–1954.* New York: Harper & Row, 1972.

Kruh, Louis. 'Stimson, The Black Chamber, and the "Gentlemen's Mail" Quote.' *Cryptologia* 12:2 (1988): 65–89.

— 'Tales of Yardley: Some Sidelights to His Career.' *Cryptologia* 13:4 (2010): 327–57.

LaFeber, W. *America, Russia and the Cold War.* New York: John Wiley & Sons, 1967.

Lemmon, J. Michael. *Norman Mailer: A Double Life.* New York: Simon & Schuster, 2013.

Lucas, Scott. *Freedom's War: The Crusade against the Soviet Union*. Manchester: Manchester University Press, 1999.

Lycett, Andrew. *Ian Fleming*. London: Weidenfeld & Nicolson, 1995.

Mackenzie, Angus. *Secrets: The CIA's War at Home*. Berkeley: University of California Press, 1997.

Mangold, Tom. *Cold Warrior: James Jesus Angleton, The CIA's Master Spy Hunter*. New York: Simon & Schuster, 1991.

Mascaro, Tom. *Into the Fray: How NBC's Washington Documentary Unit Reinvented the News*. Dulles, VA: Potomac Books, 2012.

McCarthy, David Shamus. 'The CIA and the Cult of Secrecy'. Unpub. PhD thesis, The College of William and Mary, 2008.

McCrisken, Trevor, 'The Housewife, the Vigilante and the Cigarette-Smoking Man: The CIA and Television, 1975–2001'. *History: The Journal of the Historical Association* 100:340 (April 2015): 293–310.

Melley, Timothy. *The Covert Sphere: Secrecy, Fiction, and the National Security State*. Ithaca: Cornell University Press, 2012.

Mistry, Kaeten. *The United States, Italy and the Origins of the Cold War: Waging Political Warfare 1945–1950*. Cambridge: Cambridge University Press, 2014.

Moran, Christopher. *Classified: Secrecy and the State in Modern Britain*. Cambridge: Cambridge University Press, 2013.

— 'Ian Fleming and the Early Public Profile of the Central Intelligence Agency'. *Journal of Cold War Studies* 15:1 (Winter 2013): 119–47.

— and Christopher Murphy (eds). *Intelligence Studies in Britain and the US: Historiography since 1945*. Edinburgh: Edinburgh University Press, 2013.

Nolan, Cynthia. 'Seymour Hersh's Impact on the CIA'. *International Journal of Intelligence and Counterintelligence* 12:1 (1999): 18–34.

Olmsted, Kathryn. *Challenging the Secret Government: the Post-Watergate Investigations of the CIA and FBI*. Chapel Hill: University of North Carolina Press, 1996.

Paglen, Trevor. *Blank Spots on the Map: The Dark Geography of the Pentagon's Secret World*. New York: Penguin, 2009.

Paterson, Thomas G. *Soviet-American Confrontation: Postwar Reconstruction and the Origins of the Cold War*. Baltimore: Johns Hopkins Press, 1973.

— *Meeting the Communist Threat: Truman to Reagan*. New York: Oxford University Press, 1988.

Peake, Hayden. 'SIGINT Literature: World War 1 to Present.' *American Intelligence Journal* 15.1 (Spring–Summer 1994): 88–92.

Polsgrove, Carol. *It Wasn't Pretty, Folks, But Didn't We Have Fun? Surviving the '60s with Esquire's Harold Hayes*. Oakland, CA: RDR Books, 1995.

Powers, Thomas. *The Man Who Kept the Secrets: Richard Helms and the CIA*. London: Weidenfeld & Nicolson, 1979.

Prados, John. *Presidents' Secret Wars: CIA and Pentagon Covert Operations Since World War II*. New York: William Morrow, 1986.

— *Lost Crusader: The Secret Wars of CIA Director William Colby*. New York: Oxford University Press, 2003.

— *Safe for Democracy: The Secret Wars of the CIA*. Chicago: Ivan R. Dee, 2006.

— *Family Jewels: The CIA, Secrecy and Presidential Power*. Austin: University of Texas Press, 2013.

Ranelagh, John. *The Agency: The Rise and Decline of the CIA*. New York: Simon & Schuster, 1986.

Rappaport, Helen. *Conspirator: Lenin in Exile*. London: Basic Books, 2012.

Richardson, Peter. *A Bomb in Every Issue: How the Short, Unruly Life of Ramparts Changed America*. New York: The New Press, 2009.

Robarge, David S. 'Richard Helms: The Intelligence Professional Personified.' *Studies in Intelligence* 46:4 (2002): 35–43.

Rogers, J. N. and Clevenger Jr, T. '"The Selling of the Pentagon": Was CBS the Fulbright Propaganda Machine?' *Quarterly Journal of Speech* 57:3 (1971): 266–73.

Salisbury, Harrison E. *Without Fear or Favour: The New York Times and its Times*. New York: Times Books, 1980.

Sayle, Edward F. 'George Washington: Manager of Intelligence.' *Studies in Intelligence* 27:4 (Winter 1983): 1–10.

Schmitz, Dave and Jespersen, Chris (eds). *Architects of the American Century: Individuals and Institutions in 20th Century US Foreign Policymaking*. Indiana: Imprint Publications, 2000.

Schoenfeld, Gabriel. *Necessary Secrets: National Security, The Media, and the Rule of Law*. New York: Norton, 2010.

Scott, Peter Dale. *The Road to 9/11: Wealth, Empire, and the Future of America*. Berkeley: University of California Press, 2007.

Shanahan, William O. 'Review: *Germany's Underground* by Allen Dulles.' *The Review of Politics* 9:4 (October 1947): 510–17.

Sheehan, Susan and Means, Howard. *The Banana Sculptor, the Purple Lady, and the All-Night Swimmer: Hobbies, Collecting, and Other Passionate Pursuits*. New York: Simon & Schuster, 2002.

Smist, Frank John. *Congress Oversees the United States Intelligence Community, 1947–1994*. Knoxville: The University of Tennessee Press, 1994.

Smith, Bradley. *Shadow Warriors: OSS and the Origins of the CIA*. New York: Basic Books, 1983.

Smith, Richard H. *OSS: The Secret History of America's First Central Intelligence Agency*. Berkeley: University of California Press, 1972.

Smith, W. Thomas. *Encyclopaedia of the Central Intelligence Agency*. New York: Facts on File, 2003.

Srodes, James. *Allen Dulles: Master of Spies*. Washington, DC: Regnery, 1999.

Stockton, Bayard. *Flawed Patriot: The Rise and Fall of CIA Legend Bill Harvey*. Washington, DC: Potomac Books, 2006.

Tenet, George. 'Eulogy for Former DCI Richard McGarrah Helms.' *Studies in Intelligence* 46:4 (2002).

Thomas, Evan. *The Very Best Men: Four Who Dared: The Early Years of the CIA*. New York: Simon & Schuster, 1995.

Tully, Andrew. *CIA: The Inside Story*. New York: Crest Books, 1962.

Turner, Stansfield. 'Intelligence for a New World Order.' *Foreign Affairs* 70:4 (Autumn 1991): 150–66.

Waller, Douglas. *Wild Bill Donovan: The Spymaster Who Created the OSS and Modern American Espionage*. New York: Free Press, 2011.

Weiner, Tim. *Legacy of Ashes: The History of the CIA*. New York: Random House, 2007.

Wilford, Hugh. *The Mighty Wurlitzer: How the CIA Played America*. Cambridge, MS: Harvard University Press, 2008.

— *America's Great Game: The CIA's Secret Arabists and the Shaping of the Modern Middle East*. New York: Basic Books, 2013.

Williams, William Appleman. *The Tragedy of American Diplomacy*. First published in 1959; 50th anniversary edition, New York: W. W. Norton, 2009.

Willmetts, Simon. 'Quiet Americans: The CIA in Early Cold War Culture.' *Journal of American Studies* 47:1 (2013): 127–47.

— 'The Burgeoning Fissures of Dissent: Allen Dulles and the Selling of the CIA in the Aftermath of the Bay of Pigs.' *History: The Journal of the Historical Association* 100:340 (April 2015): 167–88.

— *In Secrecy's Shadow: The OSS and the CIA in Hollywood Cinema, 1941–1979*. Edinburgh: Edinburgh University Press, 2016.

Winks, Robin. 'The Wise Man of Intelligence: Uncovering the Life of Allen Dulles.' *Foreign Affairs* 73:6 (November/December 1994): 144–9.

Wise, David. *The American Police State: The Government against the People*. New York: Random House, 1976.

— and Ross, David. *The Invisible Government*. New York: Random House, 1964.

Woodward, Bob. *Veil: The Secret Wars of the CIA, 1981–1987*. New York: Simon & Schuster, 1988.

Zegart, Amy. *Flawed by Design: The Evolution of the CIA, JCS, and NSC*. Stanford: Stanford University Press, 1999.

— *Eyes on Spies: Congress and the United States Intelligence Community*. Stanford, CA: Hoover Institution Press, 2011.

Endnotes

Introduction

1   Arthur S. Hulnick, 'Openness: Being Public about Secret Intelligence', *International Journal of Intelligence and Counterintelligence* 12:4 (1999): 463.

2   *Memorial Wall Publication* (CIA: Office of Public Affairs, June 2010), https://www.cia.gov/library/publications/additional-publications/cia-memorial-wall-publication/MemWall%20WebVrsn%20June2010b.pdf.

3   Melissa Boyle Mahle, *Denial and Deception: An Insider's View of the CIA* (New York: Nation Books, 2006), 48.

4   Ted Gup, 'Star Agents', *Washington Post*, 7 September 1997.

5   Ibid.

6   Susan Sheehan and Howard Means, *The Banana Sculptor, the Purple Lady, and the All-Night Swimmer: Hobbies, Collecting, and Other Passionate Pursuits* (New York: Simon & Schuster, 2002), 203.

7   'The Demystification of Intelligence: Remarks by Admiral Stansfield Turner at the Commonwealth Club of California, 5 August 1977', CIA Records Search Tool (hereafter CREST), National Archives II (hereafter NARA), College Park, MD, USA.

8   Steven Aftergood, 'Secrecy and Accountability in U.S. Intelligence', 9 October 1996, http://www.fas.org/sgp/cipsecr.html.

9   Readers interested in the broader history of the CIA might wish to consult one of the following excellent overviews: John Ranelagh, *The Agency: The Rise and Decline of the CIA* (New York: Simon & Schuster, 1986); John Prados, *Presidents' Secret Wars: CIA and Pentagon Covert Operations Since World War II* (New York: William Morrow, 1986); Loch K. Johnson, *America's Secret Power: The CIA in a Democratic Society* (New York: Oxford University Press, 1989); Christopher Andrew, *For the President's Eyes Only: Secret Intelligence and the American Presidency from Washington to Bush* (New York: Harper Collins, 1995); John Prados, *Safe for Democracy: The Secret Wars of the CIA* (Chicago: Ivan R. Dee, 2006); Richard H. Immerman, *The Hidden Hand: A Brief History of the CIA* (Malden, MA: John Wiley & Sons, 2014). For a comparative examination of British and American secret services see: Richard J. Aldrich, *The Hidden Hand: Britain, America and Cold War Secret Intelligence* (London: John Murray, 2001).

10   Warren F. Kimball, 'Arguing for Accountability: Openness and the CIA,' *Studies in Intelligence* 10 (Winter–Spring 2001): 63.

11   Sheehan and Means, *Banana Sculptor*, 202–8.

12   Richard Williams, 'Spy Books Strain CIA Review Board', *USA Today*, 30 April 2007.

13   Tim Weiner, 'Chronicle/CIA Memoirs', *New York Times*, 10 April 2005.

14   John Hollister Hedley, 'Reviewing the Work of CIA Authors: Secrets, Free Speech, and Fig Leaves', *Studies in Intelligence* (Spring 1998): 75–83.

15   'New Rules to Govern Publications by CIA Officers', *USA Today*, 11 January 2005.

16   Williams, 'Spy Books Strain CIA Review Board'.

17   Anon., 'CIA Prepublication Review in the Information Age', *Studies in Intelligence* 55:3 (September 2011): 11. Available at: http://nsarchive.gwu.edu/NSAEBB/NSAEBB493/docs/intell_ebb_024.PDF.

18   Greg Miller, 'Panetta Clashed with CIA over Memoir, Tested Agency Review Process', *Washington Post*, 21 October 2014; Leon Panetta with Jim Newton, *Worthy Fights: A Memoir of Leadership in War and Peace* (New York: Penguin, 2014).

19   George Tenet with Bill Harlow, *At the Center of the Storm: My Years at the CIA* (New York: Harper Collins, 2007).

20   Interview with Tony Mendez. For an interesting look at the value of oral history for scholars of the CIA please see: Andrew Hammond, 'Through a Glass, Darkly: The CIA and Oral History', *History: The Journal of the Historical Association* 100:340 (April 2015): 311-326.

21   Joseph Burkholder Smith, *Portrait of a Cold Warrior* (New York: Ballantine Books, 1976).

22   Russell Jack Smith, *The Unknown CIA: My Three Decades with the Agency* (McLean, VA: Berkeley Books, 1989).

23   H. L. Goodall Jr, *A Need to Know: The Clandestine History of a CIA Family* (Left Coast Press, 2008); Lindsay Moran, *Blowing My Cover: My Life as a CIA Spy* (New York: Putnam, 2005).

24   Arthur S. Hulnick, *Fixing the Spy Machine* (Westport, CT: Praeger, 1999).

25   John Hollister Hedley, 'Three Memoirs by Former CIA Officers', *Studies in Intelligence* 49:3 (2005): 79–83.

26   George Egerton, 'The Politics of Memory: Form and Function in the History of Political Memoir from Antiquity to Modernity', in *Political Memoir: Essays on the Politics of Memory*, ed. George Egerton (London: Frank Cass, 1994), 2.

27   Ibid.

28   Ken Knaus to Scott Breckinridge, 2007MS063, Box 34, Scott J. Breckinridge, Jr Papers (hereafter SB), Wendell H. Ford Public Policy Research Center (hereafter WHF), University of Kentucky, Lexington, KY, USA.

29   George Egerton, 'The Lloyd George *War Memoirs*: A Study in the Politics of Memory', *The Journal of Modern History* 60:1 (March 1988): 89–90.

30   David Atlee Phillips, undated correspondence, MMC 3579, Box 4, David Atlee Phillips Papers (hereafter DAP), Manuscripts Division, Library of Congress (hereafter LOC), Washington, DC, USA.

31   Scott Shane, 'Ex-Spies Tell It All', *New York Times*, 15 March 2006; Floyd L. Paseman, *A Spy's Journey: A CIA Memoir* (Minneapolis, MN: Zenith Press, 2004).

32   James E. Flannery, 'Thoughts on the Craft of Intelligence', SB, Box 1, WHF.

33   Lawrence R. Houston, 'Espionage Act', 5 May 1947, CREST.

34   Walter Pforzheimer to DD/P, Chief I&R, 'Proposed Legislation', 12 November 1953, CREST.

35   'Preliminary Investigation Report for the Publications Review Board', 27 August 1981, CREST.

36   Ibid.

37   Edward F. Sayle, 'George Washington: Manager of Intelligence', *Studies in Intelligence* 27:4 (Winter 1983): 3.

38   Hedley, 'Reviewing the Work of CIA Authors', 75–83.

39   'Helping Safeguard Our Nation's Secrets – The Publication Review Board', 4 April 2014, https://www.cia.gov/news-information/featured-story-archive/2014-featured-story-archive/helping-safeguard-our-nations-secrets-the-publication-review-board.html.

40   Ibid.

41   Ann Gerhart and Annie Groer, 'Richard Helms: From Spycraft to Wordcraft', *Washington Post*, 6 January 1998.

42   Stansfield Turner, 'Intelligence for a New World Order', *Foreign Affairs* 70:4 (Fall 1991): 166.

43   Kimball, 'Arguing for Accountability', 63.

44   Scott Breckinridge to Michael Turner, 7 December 1995, SB, Box 11, WHF.

45   Scott Breckinridge to Frederick Hitz, June 1991, SB, Box 34, WHF.

46   SB, Box 20, WHF.

47   Interview with Joseph Wippl.

48   Ibid.

49   Ibid.

50   Richard Helms, 'Intelligence in American Society', *Studies in Intelligence* 11:3 (Summer 1967): 1–16.

51   Lyman Kirkpatrick to Roy E. Porter, 13 July 1966, MC209, Box 6, Lyman Kirkpatrick Papers (hereafter LK), Seeley G. Mudd Manuscript Library (hereafter SGM), Princeton University, NJ, USA.

52   'Lyman Kirkpatrick Interviewed: WWDC Radio, 4 December 1969', CREST.

53   Hulnick, 'Openness', 463.

54   'Opening Statement of William Casey Before the Senate Select Committee on Intelligence', 13 January 1981, MS 99003, Box 302, William Casey Papers (hereafter WC), Hoover Institution (hereafter HI), Stanford University, CA, USA.

55   Hedley, 'Three Memoirs'.

Chapter 1

1   Herbert Yardley, 4 March 1931, Series III, Author File, Box 391, Brown Associates Records 1927–1992 (hereafter BAR), Rare Books and Manuscripts Library, Columbia University (hereafter RBML), NY, USA.

2   Herbert Yardley to George T. Bye, 14 June 1931, Box 391, BAR, RBML.

3   Ibid.

4   Ibid.

5   Ibid.

6   David Kahn, *The Reader of Gentlemen's Mail: Herbert O. Yardley and the Birth of American Codebreaking* (New Haven: Yale University Press, 2004), 105.

7   Ibid., 106.

8   Herbert O. Yardley, *The American Black Chamber* (Indianapolis, IN: Bobbs-Merrill, 1931; Reprint Edition, Annapolis: Naval Institute Press, 2004).

9   Theodore M. Hannah, 'The Many Lives of Herbert O. Yardley', *NSA Cryptologic Spectrum*

11:4: 5–29, RLEW 5/41, Ronald Lewin Papers (hereafter RLEW), Churchill College, Cambridge University (hereafter CCC), UK.

10   Wesley Wark, 'Struggle in the Spy House: Memoirs of US Intelligence', in *Political Memoir: Essays on the Politics of Memory*, ed. George Egerton (London: Frank Cass, 1994), 315.

11   Herbert Yardley to George T. Bye, 14 June 1931, Box 391, BAR, RBML.

12   Hannah, 'Many Lives', RLEW 5/41, CCC.

13   Kahn, *Gentlemen's Mail*, 21.

14   Ibid., 45.

15   Hannah, 'Many Lives', RLEW 5/41, CCC.

16   Ibid.

17   Kahn, *Gentlemen's Mail*, 55.

18   Hannah, 'Many Lives', RLEW 5/41, CCC.

19   Louis Kruh, 'Tales of Yardley: Some Sidelights to His Career', *Cryptologia* 13:4 (2010): 333.

20   'Annotated Version of *The American Black Chamber*', William F. Friedman Collection (hereafter WFF), George C. Marshall Foundation (hereafter GCMF), http://marshallfoundation.org/library/wp-content/uploads/sites/16/2014/06/American-Black-Chamber_II_watermark.pdf.

21   Yardley, *Black Chamber*, 312.

22   Hannah, 'Many Lives', RLEW 5/41, CCC.

23   Kahn, *Gentlemen's Mail*, 83.

24   Ibid., 101.

25   Louis Kruh, 'Stimson, The Black Chamber, and the "Gentlemen's Mail" Quote', *Cryptologia* 12:2 (1988): 70.

26   There is some debate about whether Stimson actually uttered his now famous dictum at the time, in 1929, or later – or even at all. The precise wording of his pronouncement is also disputed. See Louis Kruh, 'Stimson, The Black Chamber, and the "Gentlemen's Mail" Quote', *Cryptologia* 12:2 (1988): 65-89.

27   Jonathan P. Arnold, 'Herbert O. Yardley, Gangster', *Cryptologia* 12:1 (1988): 62–4.

28   'Annotated Version of *The American Black Chamber*', WFF, GCMF.

29   Ibid.

30   Hannah, 'Many Lives', RLEW 5/41, CCC.

31   Ibid.

32   Kahn, *Gentlemen's Mail*, 46.

33   Ibid., 107.

34   Herbert Yardley, 4 March 1931, Box 391, BAR, RBML.

35   Ibid.

36   Ibid.

37   Kahn, *Gentlemen's Mail*, 106.

38   Ibid., 109.

39   Ibid.

40   Hayden Peake, 'SIGINT Literature: World War 1 to Present', *American Intelligence Journal* 15.1 (Spring-Summer 1994): 88.

41   Kahn, *Gentlemen's Mail*, 117.

42   Ibid., 123.

43   Ibid., 147–8.

44 William F. Friedman quoted in William R. Castle Diaries, 23 December 1931, MS Am 2021 (22), William R. Castle Diaries (hereafter WRC), Houghton Library (hereafter HL), Harvard University , Cambridge, MA, USA.

45 'Annotated Version of *The American Black Chamber*', WFF, GCMF.

46 Ibid.

47 Ibid.

48 Kahn, *Gentlemen's Mail*, 125.

49 Gabriel Schoenfeld, *Necessary Secrets: National Security, The Media, and the Rule of Law* (New York: Norton, 2010), 119.

50 Hannah, 'Many Lives', RLEW 5/41, CCC.

51 Kahn, *Gentlemen's Mail*, 131.

52 Schoenfeld, *Necessary Secrets*, 120.

53 Kahn, *Gentlemen's Mail*, 131.

54 Ibid., 136.

55 Hannah, 'Many Lives', RLEW 5/41, CCC.

56 Rhodri Jeffreys-Jones, *Cloak and Dollar: A History of American Secret Intelligence* (New Haven: Yale, 2002), 111.

57 Herbert Yardley to George T. Bye, 11 December 1940, Box 391, BAR, RBML.

58 Kahn, *Gentlemen's Mail*, 138.

59 Herbert Yardley to George T. Bye, April 1935, Box 391, BAR, RBML.

60 Herbert Yardley to George Bye, 1932 [exact date unknown], Box 391, BAR, RBML.

61 From the introduction to Herbert O. Yardley, *The American Black Chamber* (New York: Ballantine Books, 1981), xiv.

62 Kahn, *Gentlemen's Mail*, 159.

63 William Castle Diaries, 20 February 1933, MS Am 2021 (22), WRC, HL.

64 Ibid.

65 Ibid.

66 Robin Denniston, 'Yardley's Diplomatic Secrets', *Cryptologia* 18:2 (1994): 117.

67 William Castle Diaries, 20 February 1933, MS Am 2021 (22), WRC, HL.

68 George T. Bye to Eleanor Roosevelt, 5 December 1941, Box 391, BAR, RBML.

69 Kruh, 'Tales of Yardley', 343.

70 William Castle Diaries, 20 February 1933, MS Am 2021 (22),WRC, HL.

71 Herbert Yardley to George T. Bye, 9 May 1934, Box 391, BAR, RBML.

72 John F. Dooley, 'Who Wrote the Blonde Countess? A Stylometric Analysis of Herbert O. Yardley's Fiction', *Cryptologia* 33:2 (2009): 108–17.

73 Kahn, *Gentlemen's Mail*, 174.

74 Herbert Yardley to George T. Bye, April 1935, Box 391, BAR, RBML.

75 Denniston, 'Diplomatic Secrets', 120.

76 H. O. Yardley, 'Notes on Treatment', 21 May 1934, Turner/MGM Scripts (hereafter MGM), *Rendezvous*, 1935, File R-400, Margaret Herrick Library, Academy of Motion Picture Arts and Sciences (AMPAS), Los Angeles, CA, USA.

77 Ibid.

78 'Rendezvous: Review', *New York Post*, Lawrence Weingarten Collection (hereafter LWC), Edward L. Doheny Jr Memorial Library, University of Southern California (hereafter ELD), Los Angeles, CA, USA.

79   Ibid.

80   'Advertising Approach and Box Office Analysis', File R-423, MGM, AMPAS.

81   Ibid.

82   H. N. Swanson to David Selznick, Samuel Goldwyn, Samuel Marx et al, 8 March 1938, H. N. Swanson Collection (hereafter HNS), AMPAS.

83   Ibid.

84   H. N. Swanson to Fritz Lang, 1 November 1938, HNS, AMPAS.

85   Herbert Yardley to George T. Bye, [unknown date], Box 391, BAR, RBML.

86   George T. Bye to Eleanor Roosevelt, 5 December 1941, Box 391, BAR, RBML.

87   Herbert O. Yardley, *The Chinese Black Chamber: An Adventure in Espionage* (Boston: Houghton Mifflin, 1983).

88   George T. Bye to Eleanor Roosevelt, 5 December 1941, Box 391, BAR, RBML.

89   Denniston, 'Diplomatic Secrets', 118.

90   Kruh, 'Tales of Yardley', 346.

91   Ibid.

92   Ibid., 354.

93   D. M. Ladd to J. Edgar Hoover, 2 January 1942, FBI Files (hereafter) FBI, http://www.fbi.gov/foia/.

94   Herbert Yardley to George T. Bye, [date unknown], Box 391, BAR, RBML.

95   Ladislas Farago, *The Broken Seal: 'Operation Magic' and the Secret Road to Pearl Harbor* (London: Arthur Barker, 1967).

96   Ibid., 57–8.

97   John F. Dooley, 'Was Herbert Yardley a Traitor?', *Cryptologia* 35:1 (2010): 3.

98   Kahn, *Gentlemen's Mail*, 273.

99   A. J. P. Taylor, 'Through the Key Hole', *New York Review of Books*, 10 February 1972.

100 Dooley, 'Traitor', 13.

101 Hannah, 'Lives of Yardley', RLEW 5/41, CCC.

102 Fred Woodrough, 'Comments on the Sakuma Memorandum', Record Group 457, NARA.

103 Walter Pforzheimer to Rufus Taylor, 12 December 1967, CREST.

104 Ibid.

105 Ibid.

106 Ibid.

107 My enormous thanks to Dr Ken Kotani of the Japanese National Institute of Defense Studies for locating this.

108 Robert Craigie to Anthony Eden, 4:20 a.m., 30 September 1941, REEL No. A-0289, National Archives of Japan (hereafter NAJ), Tokyo.

109 Alexander Hagerty, 'An Unpublished Yardley Manuscript', *Cryptologia* 23:4 (1999): 289.

110 'CIC Agent Surveillance Reports: 6 August 1942; 11 August 1942; 13 August 1942; 20 August 1942; 21 August 1942; 22 August 1942; 25 August 1942; 28 August 1942', FBI, http://www.fbi.gov/foia/.

111 'MID Report on Yardley', 7 September 1942, FBI, http://www.fbi.gov/foia/.

112 Ibid.

113 Ibid.

114 Dooley, 'Traitor', 9.

115 Ibid., 10.

Chapter 2

1   'WRC Radio, Capital Byline, Author of *CIA: The Inside Story*', 15 January 1962, CREST.

2   Richard H. Smith, *OSS: The Secret History of America's First Central Intelligence Agency* (Berkeley: University of California Press, 1972), 341.

3   Sylvia Press, *The Care of Devils* (London: Constable & Company, 1958).

4   Carol Polsgrove, *It Wasn't Pretty, Folks, But Didn't We Have Fun? Surviving the '60s with Esquire's Harold Hayes* (Oakland, CA: RDR Books, 1995), 126.

5   Kay Shaw Nelson, *The Cloak and Dagger Cook: A CIA Memoir* (Gretna, LA: Pelican, 2009), 58.

6   Thomas Powers, *The Man Who Kept the Secrets: Richard Helms and the CIA* (London: Weidenfeld & Nicolson, 1979), 65.

7   'An Address by William Colby at Santa Clara University', 3 May 1976, CREST.

8   For a useful discussion about the 'myth' of the CIA see Timothy Melley, *The Covert Sphere: Secrecy, Fiction, and the National Security State* (Ithaca: Cornell University Press, 2012), esp. 118–20. Jonathan Nashel, an outstanding scholar from Indiana University South Bend, is also writing on this topic. The working title for his book is *Darkness Visible: A Cultural History of the CIA*.

9   Ibid., 119.

10 Don DeLillo, *Libra*, New York: Penguin, 1986, 260.

11 Robert Wear, 'Unpublished Memoir: Snooping and Scooping with the CIA', MC 177, Box 1, Folder 9, Robert Wear Collection (hereafter RW), Milne Special Collections and Archives, University of New Hampshire Library (MSC), Durham, NH, USA.

12 John Chamberlain, 'OSS', *Life* magazine, 19 December 1945.

13 W. Thomas Smith, *Encyclopaedia of the Central Intelligence Agency* (New York: Facts on File, 2003), 74.

14 Wallace Deuel, 'Memorandum on a Public Information Policy for OSS', 4 August 1945, MSS75905, Wallace Rankin Deuel Papers (hereafter WRD), LOC.

15 Ibid.

16 Douglas Waller, *Wild Bill Donovan: The Spymaster Who Created the OSS and Modern American Espionage* (New York: Free Press, 2011).

17 Wallace Deuel, 'Memorandum on a Public Information Policy for OSS', 4 August 1945, MSS75905, WRD, LOC.

18 Wallace Deuel to General Donovan, 'Outline of Suggested Remarks at a Press Conference', 13 August 1945, MSS75905, WRD, LOC.

19 Tim Weiner, *Legacy of Ashes: The History of the CIA* (New York: Random House, 2007), 4.

20 Ibid.

21 'OSS Part in Victory is Disclosed', *Michigan News*, 15 September 1945; 'OSS Played Major Role in Allied Victory', *Michigan Gazette*, 17 September 1945.

22 Waller, *Wild Bill*, 333.

23 Wallace Deuel, 'Memorandum on a Public Information Policy for OSS', 4 August 1945, MSS75905, WRD, LOC.

24 Wallace Deuel to William Donovan, 'Outline of Suggested Remarks at a Press Conference', 13 August 1945, MSS75905, WRD, LOC.

25 Ibid.

26 Christopher Moran, *Classified: Secrecy and the State in Modern Britain* (Cambridge: Cambridge University Press, 2013), 283–89.

27 H. Arnold to William Donovan, 19 September 1944, ML-30, Box 36, Folder 44, Corey Ford Papers (hereafter CF), Rauner Special Collections Library (RSC), Courtesy of Dartmouth College Library, NH, USA.

28 'By Wallace R. Deuel of Our Washington Bureau', 17 August 1945, MSS75905, WRD, LOC.

29 Ibid.

30 Ibid.

31 Ibid.

32 Charles T. Pinck and Don Pinck, 'The Best Spies Didn't Wear Suits', *New York Times*, 10 December 2004.

33 Wallace Deuel, 'People's Reactions to Him', 17 August 1945, WRD, LOC.

34 Waller, *Wild Bill*, 4.

35 Ibid.

36 Interview with Frederick P. Hitz.

37 'Motion Pictures of OSS Activities', [unknown date], Box 67, William J. Donovan Papers (hereafter WJD), US Army Heritage and Education Center (hereafter USAHEC), Carlisle, PA, USA.

38 Ibid.

39 James I. Deutsch, '"I was a Hollywood Agent": Cinematic Representations of the Office of Strategic Services in 1946', *Intelligence and National Security* 13:2 (1998): 85–99.

40 Alexander Cockburn, *Corruptions of Empire: Life Studies and the Reagan Era* (London: Verso, 1987), 50.

41 Deutsch, 'Hollywood Agent', 89.

42 Tom Mascaro, *Into the Fray: How NBC's Washington Documentary Unit Reinvented the News* (Dulles, VA: Potomac Books, 2012), 7.

43 Michael Burke to Corey Ford, 2 February 1946, ML-30, Box 36, Folder 44, CF, RSC. After the film was wrapped up, he was kept on as a writer at $600 per week.

44 Ibid.

45 Cockburn, *Corruptions of Empire*, 50.

46 Corey Ford and Alastair MacBain, *Cloak and Dagger: The Secret Story of the OSS* (New York: Grosset & Dunlap, 1945).

47 Michael Burke to Corey Ford, 5 December 1945, ML-30, Box 36, Folder 44, CF, RSC.

48 Dennis Drabelle, 'The Spy Who Owned the Yankees', *UPenn Gazette*, May/June 2013, http://www.upenn.edu/gazette/0513/feature3_1.html.

49 Bernard F. Dick, *The Star Spangled Screen: The American World War II Film* (Lexington, KY: The University Press of Kentucky, 1996), 120.

50 'Memorandum of Comments', 13 May 1946, 73089-8.36, Box 1, J. Russell Forgan Papers (hereafter JRF), HI.

51 Ibid.

52 J. Russell Forgan to William Donovan, 1 March 1946, 73089-8.36, Box 1, JRF, HI.

53 Ibid.

54 'Memorandum of Comments', 13 May 1946, 73089-8.36, Box 1, JRF, HI.

55 Ibid.

56 [Anon] to William Casey, 19 March 1946, 73089-8.36, Box 1, JRF, HI.

57 William Donovan to Louis De Rochement, 3 July 1946, 73089-8.36, Box 1, JRF, HI.

58 Ibid.

59 Ibid.

60   Deutsch, 'Hollywood Agent', 85–99.

61   Elizabeth Macdonald, *Undercover Girl* (New York: Macmillan, 1947).

62   Ibid., Preface by William Donovan.

63   Elizabeth Macdonald to Russell Forgan, 31 May 1946, 73089-8.36, Box 1, JRF, HI.

64   Allen Dulles, *Germany's Underground* (New York: Macmillan, 1947). See William O. Shanahan, 'Review: Germany's Underground by Allen Dulles', *The Review of Politics* 9:4 (October 1947): 510–17.

65   Robin Winks, 'The Wise Man of Intelligence: Uncovering the Life of Allen Dulles', *Foreign Affairs* 73:6 (November/December 1994): 144–9.

66   Rhodri Jeffreys-Jones, *Cloak and Dollar: A History of American Secret Intelligence* (New Haven: Yale University Press, 2002), 155.

67   Helen Rappaport, *Conspirator: Lenin in Exile* (London: Basic Books, 2012), 288.

68   Dulles, *Germany's Underground*, 196.

69   Readers interested in learning more about the origins of the CIA might wish to consult: Bradley Smith, *Shadow Warriors: OSS and the Origins of the CIA* (New York: Basic Books, 1983); Stephen F. Knott, *Secret and Sanctioned: Covert Operations and the American Presidency* (New York: Oxford University Press, 1996); Rhodri Jeffreys-Jones, 'Why was the CIA Established in 1947?', *Intelligence and National Security* 12:1 (January 1997): 21-40; Amy Zegart, *Flawed by Design: The Evolution of the CIA, JCS, and NSC* (Stanford: Stanford University Press, 1999); Sarah-Jane Corke, *US Covert Operations and Cold War Strategy: Truman, Secret Warfare and the CIA, 1947-53* (London: Routledge, 2008).

70   Waller, *Wild Bill*, 353.

71   Interview with Joseph Wippl.

72   'History of CIA Public Affairs', unknown date, CREST.

73   Ronald Kessler, *Inside the CIA* (New York: Pocket Books, 1992), 213.

74   Stansfield Turner, *Secrecy and Democracy: The CIA in Transition* (New York: Harper & Row, 1985), 104.

75   For more information about the subject of the CIA and Hollywood see: Tricia Jenkins, *The CIA in Hollywood: How the Agency Shapes Film and Television* (Austin, TX: University of Texas Press, 2012); Simon Willmetts, 'Quiet Americans: The CIA in Early Cold War Culture', *Journal of American Studies* 47:1 (2013), 127–47; Simon Willmetts, *In Secrecy's Shadow: The OSS and the CIA in Hollywood Cinema, 1941-1979* (Edinburgh: Edinburgh University Press, 2016); Trevor McCrisken, 'The Housewife, the Vigilante and the Cigarette-Smoking Man: The CIA and Television, 1975–2001', *History: The Journal of the Historical Association* 100:340 (April 2015), 293–310.

76   'CART Report', June 1951, M95–101, NBC Collection, State Historical Society of Wisconsin, Madison, WI, USA; See also Michael Kackman, *Citizen Spy: Television, Espionage, and Cold War Culture* (Minneapolis: University of Minnesota Press, 2005), 11.

77   'CIA Executive Management Daily Meeting', 6 February 1952, CREST.

78   Robert Wear, 'Unpublished Memoir: Snooping and Scooping with the CIA', MC 177, Box 1, Folder 9, RW, MSC.

79   S. W. Souers, 'Avoidance of Publicity Concerning the Intelligence Agencies of the US Government', 6 January 1950, http://cryptome.org/0005/spy-brag-ban.pdf.

80   Kessler, *Inside the CIA*, 214.

81   Michael Herman, *Intelligence and Power in Peace and War* (Cambridge: Cambridge University Press, 1996), 211.

82   Jeffreys-Jones, *Cloak and Dollar*, 180.

83   Amy Zegart, *Eyes on Spies: Congress and the United States Intelligence Community* (Stanford, CA: Hoover Institution Press, 2011), 20–21.

84   Ibid., 21.

85   Ibid.

86   Mary Bancroft to Tom Powers, 10 August 1979, MC 454.163, Mary Bancroft Papers, 1862–1997 (hereafter MB), Arthur and Elizabeth Schlesinger Library on the History of Women in America (hereafter AES), Radcliffe Institute, Harvard University, Cambridge, MA.

87   Thomas G. Paterson, *Meeting the Communist Threat: Truman to Reagan* (New York: Oxford University Press, 1988), 240.

88   'The Oral History Program: An Interview with Former General Counsel John S. Warner (U)', http://www.foia.cia.gov/sites/default/files/DOC_0000872669.pdf.

89   Excellent accounts of this 'golden age' include: Piero Gleijeses, *Shattered Hope: The Guatemalan Revolt and the United States, 1944-1954* (Princeton: Princeton University Press, 1991); Nick Cullather, *Secret History: The CIA's Classified Account of its Operations in Guatemala, 1952-1954* (Stanford: Stanford University Press, 1999); Matthew Jones, '"The Preferred Plan': The Anglo-American Working Group Report on Covert Action in Syria, 1957,' *Intelligence and National Security* 19:3 (2004): 401-15; Stephen Kinzer, *All the Shah's Men: The Hidden Story of the CIA's Coup in Iran* (New Jersey: Wiley, 2003); Kaeten Mistry, *The United States, Italy and the Origins of the Cold War: Waging Political Warfare 1945-1950* (Cambridge: Cambridge University Press, 2014).

90   Zegart, *Eyes on Spies*, 21.

91   Ibid., 21.

92   Harrison E. Salisbury, *Without Fear or Favour: The New York Times and its Times* (NY: Times Books, 1980), 479.

93   Hugh Wilford, *The Mighty Wurlitzer: How the CIA Played America* (Cambridge, MS: Harvard University Press, 2008), 226.

94   Ibid., 226.

95   Evan Thomas, *The Very Best Men: Four Who Dared: The Early Years of the CIA* (New York: Simon & Schuster, 1995), 106.

96   Ibid., 106.

97   Louis Menand, 'Table Talk: How the Cold War Made Georgetown Hot', *New Yorker*, 10 November 2014.

98   Lyman Kirkpatrick, 'Draft Manuscript: Newsworld, Intelligence, Academia', MC205, Box 1, Folder 2, Series 1, LK, SGM.

99   Interview with Frederick P. Hitz.

100 'CIA Library: The Office of Strategic Services', 24 July 1958, MSS75905, WRD, LOC.

101 Adam Bernstein, 'Roger Hall: Memoirist of World War II Espionage', *Washington Post*, 22 July 2008.

102 Chester Cooper, *The Lion's Last Roar* (New York: Harper & Row, 1978), 170.

103 Loose note by Deuel, unknown date, MSS75905, WRD, LOC.

104 Donald Downes, *The Scarlet Thread: Adventures in Wartime Espionage* (London: Derek Verschoyle, 1953).

105 Ibid., 155–56.

106 Wark, 'Struggle in the Spy House', 317.

107 Downes, *Scarlet Thread*, 25.

108 Wark, 'Struggle in the Spy House', 317.

109 Downes, *Scarlet Thread*, 27.

110 Sherman Kent, 'Unpublished Memoir', Group 854, Series N, Box 15, Sherman Kent Papers (hereafter SK), Yale University Library (hereafter YUL), Yale University, New Haven, CT, USA.

111 Loose Note by Wallace Deuel, 29 July 1954, MSS75905, WRD, LOC.

112 Thomas, *Very Best Men*, 73.

113 Jeffrey Frank, *Ike and Dick: Portrait of a Strange Political Marriage* (Simon & Schuster, 2013), 88.

114 Sherman Kent, 'Unpublished Memoir', Group 854, Series N, Box 15, SK, YUL.

115 James Srodes, *Allen Dulles: Master of Spies* (Washington, DC: Regnery, 1999), 451.

116 See Allen Dulles Papers (hereafter AD), MC019, Series 3, 'Speeches, 1926–68', SGM.

117 Jeffreys-Jones, *Cloak and Dollar*, 161.

118 Sherman Kent, 'Unpublished Memoir', Group 854, Series N, Box 15, SK, YUL.

119 Wallace Deuel to Allen Dulles, 22 January 1954, MSS75905, WRD, LOC.

120 'Portrait of a Top Operator: Man Behind US Spies', *Associated Press*, 8 August 1954, CREST.

121 Andrew Bacevich, *Washington Rules: America's Path to Permanent War* (New York: Metropolitan Books, 2010), 37.

122 Ibid.

123 Stephen Kizner, 'When a CIA Director Had Scores of Affairs', *New York Times*, 10 November 2012; Godfrey Hodgson, 'Obituary: Mary Bancroft', *Independent*, 17 February 1997.

124 Kizner, 'When a CIA Director Had Scores of Affairs'.

125 Mary Bancroft to Robert Lantz, 11 January 1956, MC 454.163, MB, AES.

126 Mary Bancroft, 'Possible Prologue', MC 454.163, MB, AES.

127 Robert Lantz, 'CIA – TV Project', 10 April 1957, MC 454.163, MB, AES.

128 Mary Bancroft, 'General Outline', MC 454.163, MB, AES.

129 Richard Helms, 15 November 1961, 4/22/37, Richard Helms Papers (hereafter RH), Georgetown University Special Collections Research Center (hereafter GUSC), Georgetown University, Washington, DC, USA.

130 'CIA report on U-2 Vulnerability Tests', April 1960, Office of the Staff Secretary, Subject Series, Alphabetical Subseries, Box 15, Intelligence Matters (9), Eisenhower Presidential Library (EPL), Abilene, KS, USA.

131 John Ranelagh, *The Agency: The Rise and Decline of the CIA*, 315.

132 'Statement by Mr Allen Dulles, Director of Central Intelligence, to the Senate Foreign Relations Committee on 31 May 1960', http://www.foia.cia.gov/sites/default/files/document_conversions/5829/CIA-RDP80B01676R004100180002-8.pdf.

133 Francis Gary Powers, *Operation Overflight: A Memoir of the U-2 Incident* (Potomac Books: Washington, DC, 2004), 61.

134 Ibid.

135 'The 1 May U-2 Incident and Powers's Fate: Source – A reliable Soviet source who was in an excellent position to acquire this information', www.foia.cia.gov, Doc No. 0000012388.

136 Gary Powers's account of his fateful flight has recently been questioned by Matthew Aid, a widely admired authority on the NSA. According to Aid, the NSA produced a report suggesting that Soviet air traffic controllers had detected the plane flying at 34,000 feet, contradicting Powers's claim that the plane had been hit at 70,000 feet. See Matthew Aid, *The*

Secret Sentry: The Untold History of the National Security Agency (New York: Bloomsbury Press, 2009).

137   'Cover plan to be used for downed U-2 flight', 2 May 1960, Office of the Staff Secretary, Subject Series, Alphabetical Subseries, Box 15, Intelligence Matters (14), EPL.

138   'State Department press release concerning U-2 incident', 6 May 1960, Christian Herter Papers, Box 20, U-2 (1), EPL.

139   Thomas, *Very Best Men*, 219.

140   Kinzer, *Brothers*, 256–7.

141   Eisenhower's aspirations for the summit are captured in 'Memorandum for Ann Whitman', 11 May 1960, Dwight D. Eisenhower Papers, Diary Series, Box 50, Staff Notes May 1960 (2), EPL.

142   Rhodri Jeffreys-Jones, *The CIA and American Democracy* (New Haven: Yale University, 1989), 99.

143   David. M. Barrett, *CIA and Congress: The Untold Story from Truman to Kennedy* (Lawrence: University Press of Kansas, 2005), 395.

144   'Interview with Drew Pearson: Patty Cavin at 12.15 p.m. over WRC (Washington)', 23 August 1960, Office of Staff Secretary, Subject Series, Alphabetical Subseries, Box 15, Intelligence Matters (17), EPL.

145   For a more detailed examination of press reporting of CIA activities see: Richard J. Aldrich, 'American Journalism and the Landscape of Secrecy: Tad Szulc, the CIA and Cuba', *History: The Journal of the Historical Association* 100: 340 (April 2015): 189-209; Richard J. Aldrich, 'Regulation by Revelation? Intelligence, Transparency, and the Media', in *Spinning Intelligence: Why Intelligence Needs the Media, Why the Media Needs Intelligence*, edited by Michael Goodman and Rob Dover (New York, NY: Columbia University Press, 2009), 13-37; Matthew Jones, 'Journalism, Intelligence and the *New York Times*: Cyrus L. Sulzberger, Harrison E. Salisbury and the CIA', *History: The Journal of the Historical Association* 100: 340 (April 2015): 229-250.

146   Kinzer, *Brothers*, 302.

147   Jeffreys-Jones, *Cloak and Dollar*, 184.

148   Kinzer, *Brothers*, 298–9.

149   Ibid.

150   Richard J. Aldrich, 'CIA History as a Cold War Battleground: The Forgotten First Wave of Agency Narratives', in *Intelligence Studies in Britain and the US: Historiography since 1945*, edited by Christopher Moran and Christopher Murphy (Edinburgh: Edinburgh University Press, 2013), 19–46.

151   Andrew Tully, *CIA: The Inside Story* (New York, NY: Crest Books, 1962).

152   William Stringer, 'From the Bookshelf: Probing the Probers', *Christian Science Monitor*, 19 January 1962.

153   Aldrich, 'CIA History as a Cold War Battleground', 40.

154   Stringer, 'From the Bookshelf'.

155   'A Bad Book by Andrew Tully: A Review by Sherman Kent, 1962', Group 854, Series 11, Box 20, SK, YUL.

156   Ibid.

157   Ibid.

158   David Wise and Thomas Ross, *The Invisible Government* (New York: Random House, 1964).

159   Kessler, *Inside the CIA*, 216–17.

160 Richard Helms to Stewart Alsop, 22 May 1965, 5/3/338, RH, GUSC.

161 'David Wise and Thomas B. Ross, The Invisible Government', Group 854, Series 11, Box 20, SK, YUL.

162 Ibid.

163 Richard Helms to Stewart Alsop, 22 May 1965, 5/3/338, RH, GUSC.

164 'Reader's Roundup', *Denver Post*, 28 June 1964; Gyeorgos C. Hatonn, *Silent Blood Suckers of the Tangled Webs* (Carson City: America West Publishers, 1992), 111.

165 David Wise, *The American Police State: The Government against the People* (New York: Random House, 1976), 198.

166 'On the Right by W. F. Buckley Jr', Box 33, MC 019, AD, SGM.

167 John McCone to J. Finney, 21 October 1965, BANC/MSS 95/20, John McCone Papers (hereafter JM), Bancroft Library (hereafter BL), University of Berkeley, CA, USA.

168 'New Book on the CIA', *Journal Standard* (Freeport, IL), 27 June 1964.

169 Dulles, *Craft of Intelligence*, 42.

170 Ibid., 39.

171 Ibid., 42.

172 Kinzer, *Brothers*, 302.

173 'Interview with Ray Cline conducted by Roger W. Fontaine and William E. Ratliff, March 28, 29, 30, 1993', 99023, HI.

174 David Wise, 'A Patrician for the CIA', *New York Times*, 11 December 1994. 175 S r o d e s, *Dulles*, 551–53; See also: Simon Willmetts, 'The Burgeoning Fissures of Dissent: Allen Dulles and the Selling of the CIA in the Aftermath of the Bay of Pigs', *History: The Journal of the Historical Association* 100:340 (April 2015): 167-188.

176 See Jonathan Nashel, 'The Rise of the CIA and American Popular Culture', in *Architects of the American Century: Individuals and Institutions in 20th Century US Foreign Policymaking*, edited by Dave Schmitz and Chris Jespersen (Indiana: Imprint Publications, 2000), 65–80.

177 Christopher Moran, 'Ian Fleming and the Early Public Profile of the Central Intelligence Agency', *Journal of Cold War Studies* 15:1 (Winter 2013): 119–47.

178 Andrew Lycett, *Ian Fleming* (London: Weidenfeld & Nicolson, 1995), 418.

179 Ian Fleming to Arthur Krock, 12 July 1961, Box 25, The Arthur Krock Papers (hereafter AK), SGM.

180 Ian Fleming, *You Only Live Twice* (London: Jonathan Cape, 1964), 30.

181 Srodes, *Master of Spies*, 552; Walter Pforzheimer, 'Proposed Anthology by Mr. Dulles', 19 July 1965, CREST. The public was oblivious to the involvement of Hunt and Roman as ghostwriters. Former British intelligence officer Malcom Muggeridge even wrote in a review: 'Everything suggests that *The Craft of Intelligence* is his own unaided work'. Malcolm Muggeridge, 'Secret Agent', *New York Review of Books*, November 1963.

182 Maurice Dolbier, 'The Cloak and Dagger Set', *New York Herald*, 9 October 1963.

183 R. R. Bowie, 'Lifting the Cloak But Only a Bit', *Washington Post*, 13 October 1963.

184 Jeffreys-Jones, *Cloak and Dollar*, 184.

185 Lyman Kirkpatrick to Allen Dulles, 4 November 1963, MC209, Box 4, LK, SGM.

186 Lyman Kirkpatrick to Allen Dulles, 23 December 1963, MC209, Box 4, LK, SGM; Kirkpatrick to Allen Dulles, 4 November 1963, MC209, Box 4, LK, SGM.

187 Roger Hollis to Allen Dulles, 29 November 1963, MC019, Box 71, Folder 1, AD, SGM.

188 Dick White to Allen Dulles, 14 November 1963, MC019, Box 57, Folder 30, AD, SGM.

189 Management Advisory Group to the Executive Director-Controller, 'The Agency's Image', 18 November 1970, CREST.

190 Allen Dulles, 'Memorandum for the Record: Conversation with Mr Robert Saudek', 16 April 1965, MC019, Box 71, Folder 14, AD, SGM.

191 William Raborn to Clark Clifford, 'The Soviet and Communist Bloc Defamation Campaign', 20 September 1965, CREST.

192 For the CIA's reaction to the book see Walter Pforzheimer, 'Memorandum for the Executive Director. Subject: *Oswald: Assassin or Fall Guy* by Joachim Joesten', 28 August 1964, CREST.

Chapter 3

1 Jeff Rosenzweig to William Colby, MCC 113, Box 7, William Colby Papers (hereafter WCP), SGM.

2 Kathryn Olmsted, *Challenging the Secret Government: The Post-Watergate Investigations of the CIA and FBI* (Chapel Hill: University of North Carolina Press, 1996), 17.

3 Peter Richardson, *A Bomb in Every Issue: How the Short, Unruly Life of Ramparts Changed America* (New York: The New Press, 2009).

4 'The University on the Run: Ramparts v. MSU v The CIA', *The Paper* 1:12 (21 April 1966): 1.

5 Angus Mackenzie, *Secrets: The CIA's War at Home* (Berkeley: University of California Press, 1997), 17.

6 Ibid.

7 Neil Sheehan, 'A Student Group Concedes It Took Funds from CIA', *New York Times*, 14 February 1967.

8 Philip Agee, 'The National Student Association Scandal', *Campus Watch* (Fall 1991): 12.

9 Thomas, *Very Best Men: Four Who Dared*, 330.

10 Richard Helms to D. A. Woodruf, 12 August 1972, 8/30/438, RH, GUSC.

11 Rhodri Jeffreys-Jones, *In Spies We Trust: The Story of Western Intelligence* (Oxford: Oxford University Press, 2013), 160.

12 William Colby, 'Lecture: Intelligence and the Press. Associated Press Annual Meeting', 7 April 1975, 2007MS063, Box 1, SB, WHF.

13 Robert M. Gates, *From the Shadows: The Ultimate Insider's Story of Five Presidents and How They Won the Cold War* (New York: Simon & Schuster, 1996), 60.

14 Amy B. Zegart, *Eyes on Spies: Congress and the United States Intelligence Community* (Hoover Institution Press: Stanford CA, 2011), 23. For further analysis of the Church investigation see: Loch K. Johnson, 'The Church Committee Investigation of 1975 and the Evolution of Modern Intelligence Accountability', *Intelligence and National Security* 23:2 (April 2008): 198-225.

15 John Robert Greene, *The Presidency of Gerald R. Ford* (Lawrence: University Press of Kansas, 1995), 101.

16 Richard Nixon to Richard Helms, 24 October 1983, 2/83/204, RH, GUSC.

17 David Atlee Phillips, *The Night Watch: 25 Years Inside the CIA* (London: Robert Hale, 1977), vii.

18 Turner, *Secrecy and Democracy*, 6.

19 Gates, *From the Shadows*, 61.

20 Eleanor French to J. Nakamura, 19 April 1974, KNOPF 942.3, Alfred Knopf Papers, Harry Ransom Center (hereafter HRC), Austin TX, USA.

21   Alan Barth, 'Free Speech, Security and the CIA', *Washington Post*, 16 June 1972.

22   'John McCone: Speech to the Association of Former Intelligence Officers, San Diego, Hotel del Coronado', 2 October 1978, BANC/MSS 95/20, Container 27, Folder 63, JM, BL.

23   Ibid.

24   'The CIA, Secrecy, and Books', *Stanford Daily*, 7 February 1978.

25   David Atlee Phillips, 'The CIA Story – Irresponsible Critics and Suspect Sources', Box 1, SB, WHF.

26   William Appleman Williams, *The Tragedy of American Diplomacy* (1959; 50th anniversary edition, New York: W. W. Norton, 2009).

27   Seminal 'revisionist' works include W. LaFeber, *America, Russia and the Cold War* (New York: John Wiley & Sons, 1967); G. Kolko & J. Kolko, *The Limits of Power: The World and United States Foreign Policy 1945–1954* (New York: Harper & Row, 1972); Thomas G. Paterson, *Soviet-American Confrontation: Postwar Reconstruction and the Origins of the Cold War* (Baltimore: Johns Hopkins Press, 1973).

28   Ralph Novak, 'Victor Marchetti: A "Spook" Who Haunts the CIA', *People Magazine* 2:11, 9 September 1974.

29   Henry Allen, 'Quitting the CIA: And Living to Tell About it, More or Less', *Washington Post*, October 1972.

30   'Interview with Victor Marchetti: Station WBAI', 21 February 1972, CREST.

31   Henry Allen, 'Quitting the CIA'.

32   'Interview with Victor Marchetti: Station WBAI', 21 February 1972, CREST.

33   'The Whistle Blowers', *Nation*, 6 November 1972.

34   Mackenzie, *Secrets*, 43.

35   Michael T. Malloy, 'Spook Turns Writer', *National Observer*, 6 May 1972.

36   'CIA's "Family Jewels" Report', 16 May 1973. Declassified in June 2007 and available as a PDF file on the National Security Archive website. http://www.gwu.edu/~nsarchiv/NSAEBB/NSAEBB222/family_jewels_full_ocr.pdf.

37   'CIA Spied on Spook Author', 9 April 1979, http://jfk.hood.edu/Collection/Weisberg%20Subject%20Index%20Files/M%20Disk/Marchetti%20Victor%20CIA/Item%2027.pdf.

38   Ibid.

39   Ibid.

40   John Marks, 'On Being Censored', *Foreign Policy* 15 (Summer 1974), CREST.

41   Patrick McGarvey, *CIA: The Myth and the Madness* (Baltimore: Penguin, 1972).

42   Ibid., 61.

43   'CBS Evening News', 19 October 1972, CREST.

44   Mackenzie, *Secrets*, 42.

45   Powers, *Man Who Kept the Secrets*, 244–5.

46   Mackenzie, *Secrets*, 44.

47   Alan Birth, 'Free Speech, Security and the CIA', *Washington Post*, 16 June 1972.

48   Ibid.

49   'The Whistle Blowers', *Nation*, 6 November 1972.

50   Jim Manu, 'CIA Says It Won't Prosecute Ex-Agent for Revealing Secrets', *Washington Post*, 20 April 1972.

51   Ibid.

52   Novak, 'Victor Marchetti'.

53   David E. Rosenbaum, 'Ex-Boss Says Writer Has Not Revealed Any Secrets', *New York Times*, 20 April 1972.

54   Anthony M. Schulte to Victor Marchetti, 12 February 1974, KNOPF 796.1, Alfred Knopf Papers, HRC.

55   'CIA as White-Collar Mafia', *Village Voice*, 16 June 1975.

56   '$6 Billion a Year Spent on Spying, Authors Say', *Los Angeles Times*, 19 June 1974.

57   Marks, 'On Being Censored'.

58   Frank Snepp, *Irreparable Harm: A Firsthand Account of How One Agent Took on the CIA in an Epic Battle over Free Speech* (Lawrence: University Press of Kansas, 1999), 172.

59   Mackenzie, *Secrets*, 51.

60   'Spy Story', *New Republic*, 22 June 1974, 8.

61   Victor Marchetti and John D. Marks, *The CIA and the Cult of Intelligence* (New York: Alfred A. Knopf, 1974), 46.

62   Kessler, *Inside the CIA*, 217.

63   'Spy Story', *New Republic*, 22 June 1974, 8.

64   Anthony M. Schulte to David Obst, 16 May 1975, KNOPF 796.1, Alfred A. Knopf Inc. Papers, HRC.

65   Mackenzie, *Secrets*, 52.

66   Snepp, *Irreparable Harm*, 173.

67   Ibid., 171.

68   'CIA Whistleblower', *The Washington*, 15 December 1980; Snepp, *Irreparable Harm*, 171.

69   Snepp, *Irreparable Harm*, 171.

70   Ibid., 170.

71   Ibid., 173.

72   'The CIA vs. Philip Agee', *Covert Action Information Bulletin* 8 (March–April 1980), CREST.

73   Philip Agee, *Inside the Company: CIA Diary* (London: Harmondsworth, 1975), entry for 28 October 1968.

74   Duncan Campbell, 'The Spy Who Stayed Out in the Cold', *The Guardian*, 10 January 2007.

75   Agee, *Inside the Company*, entry for 28 October 1968.

76   [Anon.], 'Phillip B. P. Agee', TAM 517, Box 5, Philip Agee Papers (hereafter PA), Tamiment Library and Robert F. Wagner Labor Archives (hereafter TAM), New York University, New York, NY, USA.

77   [Anon.], 'Agee's Character', TAM 517, Box 5,PA, TAM.

78   John Barron, *KGB Today: The Hidden Hand* (London: Hodder & Stoughton, 1984), 227–30.

79   [Anon.], 'Personal Problems', TAM 517, Box 5, PA, TAM.

80   [Anon.] to Deputy Director for Plans, 'Mr. Phillip B. F. Agee and the CIA Exposé in the Uruguayan Press', TAM 517, Box 5, PA, TAM.

81   Oleg Kalugin, *Spymaster: My Thirty-Two Years in Intelligence and Espionage against the West* (New York: Basic Books, 2009), 93, 220.

82   Ibid., 220.

83   Philip Agee to James Risen, 4 October 1997, TAM 517, Box 2, PA, TAM.

84   Ibid.

85   Christopher Andrew and Vasili Mitrokhin, *The KGB in Europe and the West* (London: Penguin, 1999), 269.

86   Interview with Cameron LaClair.

87   'RENDEZVOUS IN GENEVA: MY SPY EXPOSED', *CounterSpy* 3:2.

88   'Affidavit: Agee', TAM 517, Box 7, PA, TAM.

89   Turner, *Secrecy and Democracy*, 62.

90   Andrew and Mitrokhin, *Mitrokhin Archive*, 300.

91   David Atlee Phillips, 'The CIA Story – Irresponsible Critics and Suspect Sources', Box 1, SB, WHF.

92   John Greaney to Anthony P. Brown, 15 November 1974, TAM 517, Box 2, PA, TAM.

93   Philip Agee, *On the Run* (London: Bloomsbury, 1987), 56.

94   'Affidavit: Agee', TAM 517, Box 7, PA, TAM.

95   Agee, *On the Run*, 84.

96   'CIA Diary on Sale', *Washington Post*, 11 April 1975.

97   Walter Pincus, 'Review: Inside the Company', *New York Times*, 3 August 1975,

98   Andrew, *Mitrokhin*, 301.

99   Sayle, 'George Washington', 4.

100   Ibid.

101   'Affidavit: Stansfield Turner', TAM 517, Box 7, PA, TAM.

102   'Book Review of *Inside the Company*', *Studies in Intelligence*, https://www.cia.gov/library/center-for-the-study-of-intelligence/kent-csi/vol19no2.

103   Ibid.

104   David Atlee Phillips, 'The CIA Story – Irresponsible Critics and Suspect Sources', Box 1, SB, WHF.

105   [Anon.], 'Inside the Company: CIA diary by Philip Agee', TAM 517, Box 5, PA, TAM.

106   Ibid.

107   Pincus, 'Review: Inside the Company'.

108   Ladislas Farago to the editors of *Publishers Weekly*, 7 May 1975, MS 807, Box 25, Ladislas Farago Papers (hereafter LF), Howard Gotlieb Archival Research Center (hereafter HGARC), Boston University, MS, USA.

109   'Agee Book Draws Retaliation', *National Guardian*, 1 May 1975.

110   Ladislas Farago to the editors of *Publishers Weekly*, 7 May 1975, MS 807, Box 25, LF, HGARC, Boston University, MS, USA.

111   J. Michael Lemmon, *Norman Mailer: A Double Life* (New York: Simon & Schuster, 2013), 460.

112   Ibid.

113   'US Electronic Espionage: A Memoir', *Ramparts* 11:2 (August 1972): 35–50.

114   David Atlee Phillips, 'The CIA Story – Irresponsible Critics and Suspect Sources', Box 1, SB, WHF.

115   Ibid.

116   'Chiefs of Station: Who's Who, What they Do', *CounterSpy* 2:2 (Winter 1975): 23.

117   Interview with Peter Earnest.

118   Agee, *On the Run*, 132.

119   Mary Von Dearborn, *Mailer: A Biography* (New York: Houghton Mifflin Company, 1999), 394.

120   'CIA Blamed for Greek Death', *New York Times*, 25 December 1975.

121   Jeffreys-Jones, *In Spies We Trust*, 167.

122   Melvin Wulf, 'Remembering Philip Agee', *Socialism and Democracy Online*, 6 March 2011, http://sdonline.org/51/remembering-philip-agee.

123   Von Dearborn, *Mailer*, 394.

124   'The Fifth Estate and a CIA Agent's Death', *National Observer*, 19 January 1976.

125   Olmsted, *Secret Government*, 153.

126   Mike Ackerman, 'Lessons in Death of Richard Welch', *Evening Independent*, 31 December 1975.

127   Frank John Smist, *Congress Oversees the United States Intelligence Community, 1947–1994* (Knoxville: The University of Tennessee Press, 1994), 64.

128   Michael Howard Holzman, *James Jesus Angleton, the CIA, and the Craft of Counterintelligence* (Amherst: University of Massachusetts Press, 2008), 313.

129   Olmsted, *Secret Government*, 153.

130   Agee, *On the Run*, 132.

131   Mackenzie, *Secrets*, 65.

132   Barbara Bush, *Barbara Bush: A Memoir* (New York: Scribners, 1994), 134; 'Press Conference, National Press Club, DC, 5 September 1995: Former CIA Officer Filing Lawsuit Against Former First Lady Barbara Bush', TAM 517, Box 5, PA, TAM.

133   Cord Meyer, *Facing Reality: From World Federalism to the CIA* (New York: Harper & Row, 1980), 222.

134   Campbell, 'Spy Who Stayed Out in the Cold'.

135   Jeffreys-Jones, *In Spies We Trust*, 164.

136   'Scourge of the US Spymen is ordered to clear out of GB.' *Daily Mail*, 18 November 1976.

137   Campbell, 'Spy Who Stayed Out in the Cold'.

138   Richard J. Aldrich, *GCHQ: The Uncensored Story of Britain's Most Secret Intelligence Agency* (London: Harper Press, 2010), 288–90. Heath got his own back a few months later when, during the Yom Kippur War, he imposed heavy overflight restrictions on US aircraft from bases in Britain and Cyprus.

139   Andrew, *Mitrokhin*, 301.

140   'The CIA vs. Philip Agee', *Covert Action Information Bulletin* 8 (March–April 1980), CREST.

141   Melvin Wulf to CIA 'Claim for Damage, Injury, or Death', 3 December 1981, PA, TAM.

142   'Affidivit June 1980: Agee', TAM 517, Box 7, PA, TAM.

143   Ibid.

144   Ibid.

145   Wulf, 'Remembering Philip Agee'.

146   'Lives of CIA Agents Deliberately Imperiled', *Human Events*, 19 August 1978.

147   'Anti-CIA Magazine Readied', *Philadelphia Inquirer*, 6 August 1978.

148   Richard G. Stilwell to Griffen Bell, 10 August 1978, CREST.

149   Andrew, *Mitrokhin*, 303.

150   Ibid., 305.

151   Oliver Stone to Philip Agee, 3 March 1988, TAM 517, Box 2, PA, TAM.

152   'Request by Senator Lloyd Bentsen for Information on Agee', 7 September 1978, CREST.

153   Stansfield Turner to The Editor of the *Washington Post*, 28 December 1977, CREST.

154   'Request by Senator Lloyd Bentsen for Information on Agee', 7 September 1978, CREST.

155   Ibid.

156   Stansfield Turner to The Editor of the *Washington Post*, 28 December 1977, CREST.

Chapter 4

1 David Atlee Phillips, 'Resignation Letter', May 1975, MMC 3579, Box 1, DAP, LOC.

2 Gates, *From the Shadows*, 60.

3 Peter Dale Scott, *The Road to 9/11: Wealth, Empire, and the Future of America* (Berkeley: University of California Press, 2007), 299.

4 Kessler, *Inside the CIA*, 215.

5 Ibid.

6 Michael Lopez, 'Turners Tells of New Era of CIA Openness during Visit Here', *San Diego Union*, 9 August 1978.

7 William Colby and Peter Forbath, *Honorable Men: My Life in the CIA* (New York: Simon & Schuster, 1978), 21.

8 John Blake to Scott Breckinridge, exact date unknown, 2007MS063, Box 1, SB, WHF.

9 'Congressional Award for Exemplary Service to the Public. Nomination: Herbert E. Hetu', CREST.

10 Richard Dudman, 'CIA to Shed Cloaks and Daggers in Quest for Polished Public Image', *St Louis Post-Dispatch*, 19 May 1977.

11 M. Kennedy, 'With Speeches, Spy Comes in Out of the Cold', *Dallas Texas Herald*, 4 November 1976.

12 Dudman, 'CIA to Shed Cloaks and Daggers'.

13 Scott Lucas, *Freedom's War: The Crusade against the Soviet Union* (Manchester: Manchester University Press, 1999).

14 Peter Gill, 'Reasserting Control: Recent Changes in the Oversight of the UK Intelligence Community', *Intelligence and National Security* 11:2 (1996): 313–31.

15 C. Adams, 'CIA Sends Its Spooks into the Cold', MMC 3579, Box 5, DAP, LOC.

16 'Intelligence Gathering: Insiders Meet on the Outside', *Washington Post*, 18 September 1976.

17 M. Kennedy, 'With Speeches, Spy Comes in Out of the Cold', *Dallas Texas Herald*, 4 November 1976.

18 John Blake to Scott Breckinridge, exact date unknown, 1981, 2007MS063, Box 1, SB, WHF.

19 Jeffreys-Jones, *Cloak and Dollar*, 212.

20 Thomas Powers, 'Spy Stories', *New York Times*, 21 May 1978. Readers interested in learning more about William Colby or the CIA in the 1970s should consult the publications of eminent historian of the CIA John Prados.

21 'Presidential Publicity for CIA's Twenty-Fifth Anniversary', exact date unknown, 1971, CREST.

22 'Should the Agency concern itself with the public understanding of the role of intelligence?', exact date unknown, 1971, CREST.

23 Ibid.

24 Ibid.

25 CIA Public Affairs, 'The Ups and Downs of CIA's Roadsigns', unknown date, CREST.

26 Ibid.

27 Tim Weiner, 'William Colby, 76, Head of CIA in a Time of Upheaval', *New York Times*, 7 May 1996.

28 Colby, *Honorable Men*, 376.

29 Ibid.

30 Ibid., 378.

31 Powers, 'Spy Stories'.

32 Ibid.

33 Richard Helms to Charles Murphy, 19 March 1975, 9/9/452, RH, GUSC.

34 Trevor Paglen, *Blank Spots on the Map: The Dark Geography of the Pentagon's Secret World* (New York: Penguin, 2009): 193.

35 Colby, *Honorable Men*, 15.

36 Ibid., 21.

37 John Prados, *The Secret Wars of CIA Director William Colby* (Oxford: Oxford University Press, 2003), 311.

38 'The Oral History Program: An Interview with Former General Counsel John S. Warner (U)', http://www.foia.cia.gov/sites/default/files/DOC_0000872669.pdf.

39 Ibid., 321.

40 Ibid, 327.

41 This task force has also been discussed in an excellent PhD thesis by David Shamus McCarthy. See David Shamus McCarthy, 'The CIA and the Cult of Secrecy' (unpub. PhD thesis, The College of William and Mary, 2008), especially pages 98-131.

42 Samuel Wilson, 'Telling the Intelligence Story', 30 October 1975, CREST.

43 Ibid.

44 J. N. Rogers and T. Clevenger Jr, '"The Selling of the Pentagon": Was CBS the Fulbright Propaganda Machine?', *Quarterly Journal of Speech* 57: 3 (1971): 266–73.

45 Phillips, *Night Watch*, 269.

46 W. Lowther, 'When it's time to hand up the cloak and hand in the dagger, what on earth does a spy do?', *Daily Mail*, 3 October 1975.

47 John F. Blake to Director of Central Intelligence, 'Employee Perceptions', 16 October 1975, CREST.

48 Ibid.

49 Phillips, *Night Watch*, 270.

50 Ibid.

51 'Ex-Spy David Phillips Preaches The CIA Story, But Can't Convince his own Daughter', *People*, 23 June 1975.

52 See Richard Immerman, *The CIA in Guatemala: The Foreign Policy of Intervention* (Austin: University of Texas Press, 1983).

53 John Blake to Scott Breckinridge, exact date unknown, 1981, 2007MS063, Box 1, SB, WHF; AFIO Newsletter, 2007MS063, Box 1, SB, WHF.

54 'The CIA: Can it Survive? Library of Congress, News Broadcast', MSS79313, Box 1, Ray Cline Papers (hereafter RC), LOC.

55 O. B. Patton to Ray Cline, 28 June 1974, MSS79313, Box 1, RC, LOC.

56 Cord Meyer to Ray Cline, 17 July 1974, MSS79313, Box 1, RC, LOC.

57 Ray Cline to David Atlee Phillips, 27 March 1975, MSS79313, Part I, Box 7, Folder 3, RC, LOC. See also McCarthy, 'The CIA and the Cult of Secrecy', 111.

58 C. Adams, 'CIA Sends its Spooks into the Cold', MMC 3579, Box 1, DAP, LOC.

59 Colby, *Honorable Men*, 412.

60 'Memorandum for the Record: Staff Meeting Minutes of 6 June 1980', CREST.

61 J. Coakley to John McCone, BANC/MSS 95/20, Container 1, Folder 12, JM, BL.

62 J. McCone, 16 October 1978, BANC/MSS 95/20, Container 1, Folder 12, JM, BL.

63   'Intelligence Gathering: Insiders Meet on the Outside', *Washington Post*, 18 September 1976.

64   Olmsted, *Challenging the Secret Government*, 147.

65   T. Bates to Mrs David Atlee Phillips, 20 July 1988, MMC 3579, Box 6, DAP, LOC.

66   Ibid.

67   Phillips, *Night Watch*, 271.

68   Ibid., 67; McCarthy, 'The CIA and the Cult of Secrecy', 115.

69   David Atlee Phillips, Undated Correspondence, MMC 3579, Box 4, DAP, LOC.

70   Ibid.

71   'The Demystification of Intelligence: Remarks by Admiral Stansfield Turner at the Commonwealth Club of California', 5 August 1977, CREST.

72   'The CIA: An Old Salt Opens Up the Pickle Factory', *Time*, 29 June 1977.

73   'The Demystification of Intelligence: Remarks by Admiral Stansfield Turner at the Commonwealth Club of California', 5 August 1977, CREST.

74   'CIA lets sun in but holds on to shade', *Detroit News*, 12 August 1977.

75   Stansfield Turner, 'Director's Note: Communicating with the Public', March 1977, CREST.

76   Ibid.

77   'Secrecy in American Society: Remarks by Admiral Stansfield Turner', 12 August 1977, CREST.

78   Tad Szulc, 'Good-Bye, James Bond', *New York Magazine*, 13 February 1978.

79   'Tinker, Turner, Sailor, Spy', *New York Magazine*, 3 March 1980.

80   The Director of Central Intelligence, 'Note to the Media', 28 March 1977, CREST; R. Green, 'New CIA Image', *Manilla Bulletin*, 27 October 1977.

81   Stansfield Turner to Robin W. Goodenough, 3 May 1977, CREST.

82   Kessler, *Inside the CIA*, 216.

83   'They Didn't Laugh When I Invited CBS to Film the CIA', *Washington Post*, 15 July 1984; McCarthy, 'The CIA and the Cult of Secrecy', 136.

84   'Hetu, Herbert E: Nomination for the Congressional Award for Exemplary Service to the Public', CREST.

85   'Suggestions for CIA Outreach to the Public', 19 April 1977, CREST. This report is also discussed in McCarthy, 'The CIA and the Cult of Secrecy', esp. 132-35.

86   Kessler, *Inside the CIA*, 215.

87   Ibid.

88   M. D. Lopez, 'Turner Tells of New Era of CIA Openness', *San Diego Union*, 9 August 1978.

89   'Personal Questions', Herbert Hetu to Stansfield Turner, 18 April 1997, CREST.

90   'Hetu, Herbert E: Nomination for the Congressional Award for Exemplary Service to the Public', CREST.

91   'Suggestions for CIA Outreach to the Public', 19 April 1977, CREST.

92   'CIA Cracks Door at Headquarters', *Baltimore Sun*, 30 October 1977.

93   Robert Gambino to Deputy Director of Central Intelligence, 'CBS Who's Who', 21 April 1977, CREST.

94   Paul V. Walsh to Assistant to the Director (Public Affairs), 'CBS – 'Who's Who'', 14 April 1977, CREST.

95   Ibid.; McCarthy, 'The CIA and the Cult of Secrecy', 134.

96   McCarthy, 'The CIA and the Cult of Secrecy', 134; Robert Gambino to Deputy Director of Central Intelligence, 'CBS Who's Who', 21 April 1977, CREST.

97   Herbert Hetu to Stansfield Turner 'CBS – "Who's Who"', 18 April 1977, CREST.

98   Herbert Hetu to Stansfield Turner, 'ABC – "Good Morning America"', 10 August 1977, CREST.

99   'Memorandum for the Record. Subject: Second Meeting with ABC Good Morning America Representatives', 4 August 1977, CREST.

100   Ibid.

101   Herbert Hetu to Richard Reeves, 4 April 1978, CREST.

102   Office of Public Affairs to Office of Legislative Counsel, 'Agency Contacts with PBS', 3 July 1978, CREST.

103   Herbert Hetu to Stansfield Turner, 23 August 1977, CREST.

104   Strobe Talbott to Herbert Hetu, 15 June 1977, CREST.

105   'Suggestions for CIA Outreach to the Public', 19 April 1977, CREST.

106   Herbert Hetu to Barry [unknown surname], 5 May 1977, CREST.

107   Michael D. Lopez, 'Turner Tells of New Era of CIA Openness during Visit Here', *San Diego Union*, 9 August 1978.

108   'CIA lets sun in but holds on to shade', *Detroit News*, 12 August 1977.

109   Herbert Hetu to DDI, 'Public Speaking', 5 April 1977, CREST.

110   'Hetu, Herbert E: Nomination for the Congressional Award for Exemplary Service to the Public', CREST.

111   Herbert Hetu to Stansfield Turner, 16 November 1977, CREST.

112   Scott Breckinridge, 'Some Random Thoughts on Public Appearances and Debates', 2007MS063, Box 1, SB, WHF.

113   Ibid.

114   Ibid.

115   'Director's Public Speeches', 5 December 1977, CREST.

116   'Secrecy in American Society: Remarks by Admiral Stansfield Turner', 12 August 1977, CREST.

117   M. L. Stein, 'CIA Chief Says "We Are Trying to be more Open"', *Editor and Publisher*, 7 April 1979.

118   Scott Breckinridge, 'Some Random Thoughts on Public Appearances and Debates', 2007MS063, Box 1, SB, WHF.

119   Ibid.

120   Ibid.

121   Ibid.

122   'Hetu, Herbert E: Nomination for the Congressional Award for Exemplary Service to the Public', CREST.

123   'Suggestions for CIA Outreach to the Public', 19 April 1977, CREST.

124   Ibid.

125   Ibid; McCarthy, 'The CIA and the Cult of Secrecy', 133.

126   Public Affairs, 'Decision Made on CIA Tours', 4 November 1977, CREST.

127   'Navy Officers' Wives Tour', 8 October 1977, CREST; 'Family Day Questionnaire', 13 October 1977, CREST.

128   'Suggestions for CIA Outreach to the Public: Attachment Public "Visitation Day"', 19 April 1977, CREST.

129   Ibid.

130   Ibid.

131   Herbert Hetu to Stansfield Turner, 'Suggestions for CIA Outreach to the Public', 5 May 1977, CREST.; McCarthy, 'The CIA and the Cult of Secrecy', 135.

132   Herbert Hetu to Stansfield Turner, 'Recommendations for Future of CIA Tours', 17 October 1977, CREST.

133   Richard Dudman, 'CIA to Shed Cloaks and Daggers in Quest for Polished Public Image', *St Louis Post-Dispatch*, 19 May 1977.

134   'Hetu, Herbert E: Nomination for the Congressional Award for Exemplary Service to the Public', CREST.

135   Ibid.

136   Ibid.; Herbert Hetu, 'Future of CIA Tours and Visits', 19 April 1978, CREST.

137   Associate Coordinator for Academic Relations, 'University Presidents Visit, 15 February 1980', 5 February 1980, CREST.

138   Unknown to Stansfield Turner, 29 March 1977, CREST.

139   'Suggestions for CIA Outreach to the Public', 19 April 1977, CREST; McCarthy, 'The CIA and the Cult of Secrecy', 134.

140   'The Agency Vis-à-vis Academic and Opinion Maker Circles and the Broad Based Public', Date Unknown, CREST.

141   Ibid.

142   Stansfield Turner to Herbert Hetu, 5 April 1977, CREST.

143   Ibid.

144   Ibid.

145   Ibid.

146   Ibid.

147   Ibid.

148   Alexander Cockburn and Jeffrey St Clair, *Whiteout: The CIA, Drugs and the Press* (London: Verso, 1998), 249.

149   J. Roche, 'The CIA Needs a Good Amateur', *Detroit News*, 1 June 1981.

150   A. Lapham to Cord Meyer, 15 May 1978, MSS006035, Box 1, Cord Meyer Papers (hereafter CM), LOC.

151   Cord Meyer, *Facing Reality: From World Federalism to the CIA* (New York: Harper & Row, 1980).

152   Stansfield Turner to Executive Director of AFIO, 10 September 1977, CREST.

153   'Hetu, Herbert E: Nomination for the Congressional Award for Exemplary Service to the Public', CREST.

154   Cynthia Nolan, 'Seymour Hersh's Impact on the CIA', *International Journal of Intelligence and Counterintelligence* 12:1 (1999): 22.

155   Ibid., 29.

156   David Atlee Phillips, 'Miscellaneous Note', MMC 3579, Box 5, DAP, LOC.

157   Ibid.

Chapter 5

1   Gloria Emerson, 'The Spy Who Rang My Doorbell', *New York Magazine*, 23 January 1978.

2   Snepp, *Irreparable Harm*, 109.

3   Executive Secretary (PRB), 'Procedures for Submission of Manuscripts to the PRB', 6 November 1980, CREST.

4   'Preliminary Investigation Report for the PRB', 27 August 1981, CREST.

5   Ibid.

6   Ibid.

7   Mackenzie, *Secrets*, 72.

8   Ibid.

9   Jospeh Nocera, 'Le Couvert Blown: William Colby en Francais', *Washington Monthly*, November 1980.

10   Interview with Frank Snepp.

11   Dan Logan, 'What Becomes of an Ex-Agent Who Exposes the CIA', *Orange Coast Magazine* (April 1987): 45.

12   Alan M. Dershowitz, *The Best Defense: The Courtroom Confrontations of America's Most Outspoken Lawyer of Last Resort – the Lawyer Who Won the Claus von Bülow Appeal* (New York: Random House, 1982), 227.

13   Interview with Frank Snepp.

14   Ibid.

15   Evan Thomas, 'The Last Days of Saigon', *Newsweek*, 13 March 2010.

16   Ibid.

17   Snepp, *Irreparable Harm*, xvii.

18   Calling Snepp a 'liar', Polgar would strongly deny that he had been at fault, a view shared by CIA alumnus Scott Breckinridge. In a private correspondence, Breckinridge wrote: 'In fact, Polgar made repeated strong representations to the ambassador on the matter [of evacuation], and had been turned down on the grounds that evacuation of CIA employees and their families would cause panic and contribute to the already deteriorating forces at work'. (Scott Breckinridge to Paul Schilling, CIA Associate Legal Adviser, 24 October 1984, 2007MS063, Box 37, SB, WHF.)

19   Interview with Frank Snepp.

20   Snepp, *Irreparable Harm*, 4.

21   Interview with Frank Snepp.

22   Snepp, *Irreparable Harm*, 21.

23   Ibid., 30.

24   'Q & A: Snepp tells of His War with the CIA', *Washington Star*, unknown date.

25   Emerson, 'Spy Who Rang My Doorbell'.

26   'PBS Late Night, 11 February 1982: Interview with Snepp', CREST.

27   Snepp, *Irreparable Harm*, 26.

28   'PBS Late Night, 11 February 1982: Interview with Snepp', CREST.

29   Snepp, *Irreparable Harm*, 42.

30   Interview with Frank Snepp.

31   Snepp, *Irreparable Harm*, 81.

32   Acting Director of Security to Deputy Director for Administration, 'Office of Security Significant Activities', 11 October 1976, CREST.

33   Snepp, *Irreparable Harm*, 84.

34   'CIA Seeks to Improve Image', *Flat Hat: William and Mary College*, 17 March 1978; Stansfield Turner, 'Draft Article: Secrecy and Society', CREST.

35   Interview with Frank Snepp.

36   Fred Barbash, 'Ex-CIA Agent's Defenses of Viet Book Rebuffed', *Washington Post*, 21 June 1978.

37   Frank Snepp, *Decent Interval* (New York: Random House, 1977).

38   Stansfield Turner, 'Draft Article: Secrecy and Society', CREST.

39   Ibid.

40   James Bamford, 'Spy vs Spies', *New York Times*, 18 July 1999.

41   Ted Shackley, *Spymaster: My Life in the CIA* (Potomac Books: Washington, DC, 2006), xvii.

42   Interview with Frank Snepp.

43   David Binder, 'Cutbacks by CIA's New Director Creating Turmoil Within Agency', the *New York Times*, 10 December 1977.

44   Keyes Beach, 'CIA Aides Plan Suit to Win Back Jobs', *Chicago Daily News*, 11 November 1977.

45   Interview with Frank Snepp.

46   Irene Wielawski, 'Spy-and-Tell Authors Damaging CIA Efforts, says Turner', *Providence Journal*, 23 June 1978.

47   'The CIA, Secrecy, and Books', *Stanford Daily*, 7 February 1978.

48   Snepp, *Irreparable Harm*, 177.

49   Dershowitz, *Best Defense*, 228.

50   'Snepp Gets Early Directions To Appeals Court from Judge', *Washington Star*, 21 June 1978.

51   Dershowitz, *Best Defense*, 228.

52   Snepp, *Irreparable Harm*, 180.

53   'Radio TV Reports: Sunday Morning, 28 March 1982, to Public Affairs Staff', CREST.

54   'The CIA vs. Philip Agee', *Covert Action Information Bulletin* 8 (March–April 1980), CREST.

55   Fred Barbash, 'Ex-CIA Agent's Defenses of Viet Book Rebuffed', *Washington Post*, 21 June 1978.

56   'The Oral History Program: An Interview with Former General Counsel John S. Warner (U)', http://www.foia.cia.gov/sites/default/files/DOC_0000872669.pdf.

57   Interview with Frank Snepp.

58   Justice Lewis Powell to Richard Helms, 15 September 1977, 2/104/226, RH, GUSC.

59   Snepp, *Irreparable Harm*, 349.

60   Interview with Frank Snepp.

61   Dershowitz, *Best Defense*, 232.

62   Snepp, *Irreparable Harm*, 344.

63   Logan, 'What Becomes of an Ex-Agent', 48.

64   Ibid.

65   'ABC Nightline, 28 April 1983, 11:30 p.m.', CREST.

66   Bamford, 'Spy vs Spies'.

67   John Prados, *Lost Crusader: The Secret Wars of CIA Director William Colby* (New York: Oxford University Press, 2003), 338.

68   'Preliminary Investigation Report for the PRB', 27 August 1981, CREST.

69   Ibid.

70   Paul Schilling to Cord Meyer, 8 July 1982, MSS006035, Box 2, CM, LOC.

71   Mackenzie, *Secrets*, 78.

72   Ibid., 79.

73   Gregory Rose, 'The Stolen Secrets of Vietnam', *New York Magazine*, 27 November 1978, 76.

74   Ibid.

75   Ibid.

76   Ralph McGehee, 'CIA: Bane of Insider Author's Existence', 18 January 1984, CREST.

77   'Preliminary Investigation Report for the PRB', 27 August 1981, CREST.

78   Ibid.

79   Ibid.

80   Ibid.

81   Mahle, *Denial and Deception*, 45.

82   Ralph McGehee, 'CIA: Bane of Insider Author's Existence', 18 January 1984, CREST.

83   'Warning: CIA Censors at Work', *Columbia Journalism Review* (July/August 1984).

84   'WETA Radio: NPR Dateline, Disclosing Classified Information, 20 April 1983, 4:30 p.m.', CREST.

85   Ibid.

86   Hugh Wilford, *America's Great Game: The CIA's Secret Arabists and the Shaping of the Modern Middle East* (New York: Basic Books, 2013).

87   Miles Copeland, *The Game Player: Confessions of the CIA's Original Political Operative* (London: Aurum Press, 1989), 122.

88   Mark Lynch to Alice Daniel, 24 June 1980, MS 80118, Box 3, Wilbur Crane Eveland Papers (hereafter WCE), HI.

89   Wilbur Eveland to CIA Privy Act Coordinator, 4 May 1976, MS 80118, Box 3, WCE, HI.

90   Wilbur Eveland to CIA Privy Act Coordinator, 17 March 1977, MS 80118, Box 3, WCE, HI.

91   Mark Lynch to Alice Daniel, 24 June 1980, MS 80118, Box 3, WCE, HI.

92   Howard Fields, 'Former CIA Agent Finds Woe in Seeking Clearance for Book', *Publishers Weekly*, 18 April 1980.

93   Mark Lynch to Alice Daniel, 24 June 1980, MS 80118, Box 3, WCE, HI.

94   Wilbur Crane Eveland, *Ropes of Sand: America's Failure in the Middle East* (New York: Norton, 1980), 3.

95   *Washington Monthly*, June 1980.

96   Mark Lynch to Alice Daniel, 24 June 1980, MS 80118, Box 3, WCE, HI.

97   'Presidential Reflections on US Intelligence: Ronald Reagan', https://www.cia.gov/news-information/featured-story-archive/2010-featured-story-archive/presidential-reflections-reagan.html; Richard Kovar, 'Mr. Current Intelligence: An Interview with Richard Lehman', *Studies in Intelligence* 43:2 (Summer 2000), https://www.cia.gov/library/center-for-the-study-of-intelligence/csi-publications/csi-studies/studies/summer00/art05.html.

98   Excellent studies of the CIA under Reagan include: Bob Woodward, *Veil: The Secret Wars of the CIA, 1981-1987* (New York: Simon & Schuster, 1988); Andrew Hammond, *Struggles for Freedom: Afghanistan and US Foreign Policy since 1979* (Edinburgh: Edinburgh University Press, 2016).

99   Michael Isikoff, 'Keeping the Lid on Tight at the "No-Profile Agency"', *Washington Post*, 29 April 1983.

100   Ibid.

101   Brown University to William Casey, 31 October 1981, MS 99003, Box 304, WC, HI.

102   Eleanor Randolph, 'Casey Warns Writers, Publishers About Putting Secrets in Books', *Washington Post*, 26 June 1986; Edwin McDowell, 'CIA Said to Warn Publisher on Book', *New York Times*, 25 June 1986.

103 'Censors Gets Scissored Out', *Olympias Olympian*, 2 June 1983.
104 Turner, *Secrecy and Democracy*, 287.
105 Ibid., 288.
106 Seymour Hersh, 'Ex-Intel Director Disputes Censorship of His Book on CIA', *New York Times*, 18 May 1983.
107 Ibid.

Chapter 6

1   Douglas F. Garthoff, *Directors of Central Intelligence as Leaders of the Intelligence Community 1946–2005* (Washington, DC: Center for the Study of Intelligence, 2007). Available at: https://www.cia.gov/library/center-for-the-study-of-intelligence/csi-publications/books-and-monographs/directors-of-central-intelligence-as-leaders-of-the-u-s-intelligence-community/dci_leaders.pdf.
2   Mahle, *Denial and Deception*, 56.
3   Ibid.
4   Jeffreys-Jones, *In Spies We Trust*, 173.
5   For an excellent discussion of Moynihan and the CIA see: Paul McGarr, '"Do we Still Need the CIA?" Daniel Patrick Moynihan, the Central Intelligence Agency and US Foreign Policy', *History: The Journal of the Historical Association* 100:340 (April 2015): 275-292.
6   David Wise, 'The CIA's Midlife Crisis', *Washington Post*, 14 September 1997.
7   Mackenzie, *Secrets*, 181.
8   Ibid.
9   Mahle, *Denial and Deception*, 147.
10 Wise, 'CIA's Midlife Crisis'.
11 Mahle, *Denial and Deception*, 162.
12 Robert Gates to Daniel Patrick Moynihan, 16 September 1992, MSS 75913, Part II, Box 268, Daniel P. Moynihan Papers (hereafter DPM), LOC.
13 William Studeman to Patrick Moynihan, 6 August 1992, MSS 75913, Part II, Box 268, DPM, LOC.
14 Robert Gates to Daniel Patrick Moynihan, 16 September 1992, MSS 75913, Part II, Box 268, DPM, LOC.
15 Ibid.
16 Ibid.
17 President Clinton to Daniel Patrick Moynihan, 31 August 1993, MSS 75913, Part II, Box 268, DPM, LOC.
18 Steve Coll, *Ghost Wars: The Secret History of the CIA, Afghanistan and Bin Laden, From the Soviet Invasion to September 10, 2001* (New York: Penguin, 2004).
19 President Clinton to Daniel Patrick Moynihan, 31 August 1993, MSS 75913, Part II, Box 268, DPM, LOC.
20 Oz Hassan, *Constructing America's Freedom Agenda for the Middle East: Democracy or Domination* (Abingdon: Routledge, 2013), 57.
21 'Mysteries and Secrets', *Los Angeles Times*, 19 April 1992.
22 Robert Gates to Director of Public Affairs, 'Greater CIA Openness', 18 November 1991, www.cia-on-campus.org/foia/pa01.html.

23   Garthoff, *Directors of Central Intelligence*.

24   Task Force on Greater CIA Openness to DCI, 'Task Force on Greater CIA Openness', 20 December 1991, www.cia-on-campus.org/foia/pa01.html; See also McCarthy, 'The CIA and the Cult of Secrecy', 212-16.

25   Ibid.

26   Ibid.

27   Ibid.

28   Mackenzie, *Secrets*, 186.

29   'Topics of the Times: The CIA, Open and Shut', *New York Times*, 7 April 1992.

30   John Farrell, 'No End in Sight to Top Secret Paper Trail', *San Francisco Examiner*, 8 February 1992.

31   Mahle, *Denial and Deception*, 121–22.

32   Kate Doyle, 'The End of Secrecy: US National Security and the New Openness Movement', in *National Insecurity: US Intelligence after the Cold War*, ed. Craig Eisendrath (Philadelphia: Temple University Press, 2000), 108.

33   Paula Bernstein, 'Hardest Working Actor of the Season: The CIA', *New York Times*, 2 September 2001. Readers keen to know more about the CIA's post–Cold War dealings with Hollywood might wish to consult the work of Tricia Jenkins and Simon Willmetts.

34   DCI Speech to CIA, 'Today and Tomorrow: Headquarters Auditorium', 4 March 1976, CREST.

35   Josh Young, '"24", "Alias" and the New Spook Shows: Hollywood Pries Open the Lid on Normally Top-Secret CIA', 21 September 2001, *Entertainment Weekly*, http://www.ew.com/article/2001/09/21/24-alias-and-new-spook-shows.

36   Interview with Cynthia Helms.

37   David Martin, 'The CIA's "Loaded Gun"', *Washington Post*, 10 October 1976.

38   Miles Copeland, *The Game of Nations: The Amorality of Power Politics*, New York: Simon & Schuster, 1970; Miles Copeland, *Without Cloak or Dagger: The Truth About the New Espionage*, New York: Simon & Schuster, 1974; Miles Copeland, *The Game Player: Confessions of the CIA's Original Political Operative*, London: Aurum Press, 1989; Joan Cook, 'Miles Copeland, 74, Expert on Mideast, Writer and Ex-Spy', *New York Times*, 19 January 1991.

39   Alan Axelrod, *The Real History of the Cold War: A New Look at the Past* (New York: Sterling, 2009), 245.

40   Powers, *Man Who Kept the Secrets*, 168.

41   'The Cool Pro Who Runs the CIA', *Newsweek*, 22 November 1971.

42   'The Administration: The Silent Service', *Time*, 24 February 1967.

43   William Sullivan to Richard Helms, 4 December 1972, 8/34/442, RH, GUSC.

44   Priscilla Johnson, 'Helms, CIA, the Cold War', *Washington Star*, 4 November 1979.

45   Olmsted, *Challenging the Secret Government*, 92.

46   Bamford, 'Spy vs Spies'.

47   John le Carré, 'An American Spy Hero', *New York Times Book Review*, October 1979.

48   John Bross, 'Comments on *The Man Who Kept the Secrets*', 10/1/485, RH, GUSC.

49   David S. Robarge, 'Richard Helms: The Intelligence Professional Personified', *Studies in Intelligence* 46:4 (2002): 35–43.

50   Rhodri Jeffreys-Jones, 'The Historiography of the CIA', *Historical Journal* 23:2 (June 1980): 489–96.

51   Richard Helms to William P. Bundy, 28 November 1976, 422/2/453, RH, GUSC.

52   Ibid.

53   'The Cool Pro Who Runs the CIA', *Newsweek*, 22 November 1971.

54   Interview with Cynthia Helms.

55   Powers, *Man Who Kept the Secrets*.

56   Robarge, 'Richard Helms'.

57   Interview with Cynthia Helms.

58   Interview with Cameron LaClair.

59   Ken Knaus to Scott Breckinridge, 2007MS063, Box 34, SB, WHF.

60   For more information on the Assassination Report see F. Escalante, *CIA Targets Fidel: The Secret Assassination Report* (New York: Ocean Press, 1996).

61   Ken Knaus to Scott Breckinridge, 2007MS063, Box 34, SB, WHF.

62   Ibid.

63   Ibid.

64   Ibid.

65   Powers, *Man Who Kept the Secrets*, 292.

66   Interview with Cynthia Helms.

67   R. J. Smith to Scott Breckinridge, 6 December 1993, 2007MS063, Box 34, SB, WHF.

68   Angus Thuermer to Richard Helms, 8 February 1998, 9/20/464, RH, GUSC.

69   Richard Helms with William Hood, *A Look Over My Shoulder: A Life in the Central Intelligence Agency* (New York: Random House, 2003), Preface.

70   Ibid.

71   Interview with Cynthia Helms.

72   Ibid.

73   Sam Adams, *War of Numbers: An Intelligence Memoir* (Hanover, NH: Steerforth, 1994).

74   Evan Thomas, *The Very Best Men: The Early Years of the CIA* (New York: Simon & Schuster, 1996).

75   Robert Gates to Richard Helms, 1 November 1995, 9/17/461, RH, GUSC.

76   Interview with Cynthia Helms.

77   Richard Helms to William Reilly, 22 November 1976, 1/42/42, RH, GUSC.

78   Walter Pforzheimer, 'On the Intelligence Bookshelf: Thomas Powers, 1979', 4/7/104, William Hood Papers (hereafter WH), GUSC.

79   Le Carré, 'An American Spy Hero'.

80   David Atlee Phillips, 'Miscellaneous Note', MMC 3579, Box 5, DAP, LOC.

81   Ibid.

82   Powers, *Man Who Kept the Secrets*, xi.

83   Interview with Cynthia Helms.

84   William Hood, *Mole: The True Story of the First Russian Spy to Become an American Counterspy* (New York: Norton, 1983); Interview with Cameron LaClair.

85   William Hood to Richard Helms, 26 February 1996, 10/31/575, RH, GUSC.

86   William Hood to Richard Helms, 9 June 1996, 10/31/575, RH, GUSC; Phillip Knightley, *The Second Oldest Profession: Spies and Spying in the Twentieth Century* (London: Deutsch, 1986).

87   William Hood to Richard Helms, 14 June 1996, 10/31/575, RH, GUSC; Christopher Andrew, *For the President's Eyes Only: Secret Intelligence and the American Presidency from Washington to Bush* (New York: Harper Collins, 1996).

88   Richard Helms, 'Book Proposal', 20 February 1996, 10/70/554, RH, GUSC.

89   William Hood to Richard Helms, 28 April 1996, 10/70/554, RH, GUSC.

90   Tom Mangold, *Cold Warrior: James Jesus Angleton, The CIA's Master Spy Hunter* (New York: Simon & Schuster, 1991).

91   William Hood to Richard Helms, 24 June 1996, 10/31/575, RH, GUSC.

92   Richard Helms to William Hood, 'Biographical Comments', 4 January 2001, 2/20/52, WH, GUSC.

93   William Hood to Richard Helms, 29 April 1996, 10/70/554, RH, GUSC.

94   Ibid.

95   Richard Helms to William Hood, 16 March 1998, 1/28/28, WH, GUSC.

96   William Hood to Richard Helms, 9 October 1997, 10/42/526, RH, GUSC.

97   Ibid.; Helms, *Look Over My Shoulder*, 109–10.

98   William Hood to Richard Helms, 9 October 1997, 10/42/526, RH, GUSC.

99   Richard Helms to William Hood, 16 March 1998, 1/28/28, WH, GUSC.

100   'Draft Chapter: Agency Families', 10/51/535, RH, GUSC.

101   Interview with Cynthia Helms.

102   Interview with Cameron LaClair.

103   William Hood to Richard Helms, 4 October 1997, 10/43/527, RH, GUSC.

104   Robert Loomis to William Hood, 5 January 1998, 10/46, RH, GUSC.

105   Richard Helms to William Hood, 'Biographical Comments', 4 January 2001, 2/20/52, WH, GUSC.

106   Richard Helms to Lee Strickland, 21 January 1997, 17/3/657, RH, GUSC.

107   James Bamford, 'Company Man', *Washington Post*, 27 April 2003.

108   Interview with John Hollister Hedley.

109   Interview with Cynthia Helms.

110   Richard Helms to Lee Strickland, 21 January 1997, 17/3/657, RH, GUSC.

111   John Hollister Hedley to Harry Middleton, 6 May 1998, 18/4/714, RH, GUSC.

112   Ibid.

113   Scott Koch to Richard Helms, May 2000, 10/59/543, RH, GUSC.

114   Scott Koch to William Hood, 3 July 2002, 4/67/398, RH, GUSC.

115   'Chapter 30: Six Days', 4/75/406, RH, GUSC.

116   'Chapter 28: Beyond X-2', 4/73/404, RH, GUSC.

117   William Hood to Richard Helms, 27 October 1997, 10/47/531, RH, GUSC.

118   'Draft Chapter: Agency Families', 10/51/535, RH, GUSC.

119   Interview with John Hollister Hedley.

120   George Tenet, 'CIA Annuitant Mailing List', 23 October 2002, 3/42/281, RH, GUSC.

121   George Tenet, 'Eulogy for Former DCI Richard McGarrah Helms', *Studies in Intelligence* 46:4 (2002).

122   Scott Breckinridge, 'Miscellaneous Note', 31 December 1993, 2007MS063, Box 34, SB, WHF. The Cambridge historian David Reynolds has written about surrogate official histories in the British context.

123   Interview with Cynthia Helms.

124   Helms quoted in evidence to the Rockefeller Commission, 16 January 1975.

125   Interview with Cynthia Helms.

126   Richard Helms, 'Book Proposal', 20 February 1996, 10/70/554, RH, GUSC.

127   'Former DCI Richard Helms Awarded OSS Donovan Medal', *CIRA Newsletter* 8:3 (Summer 1983), CREST.

128   Ibid.

129   Robarge, 'Richard Helms'.
130   Stevan Kellman, 'Confessions of a Stonewall', *Texas Observer*, 25 April 2003.
131   Thomas Powers, 'From the Grave, Helms Tells How, Not What', *New York Times*, 14 May 2003.

Epilogue

1   Bamford, 'Spy vs Spies'.
2   Scott Breckinridge to Frederick Hitz, June 1991, 2007MS063, Box 34, SB, WHF.
3   Hedley, 'Reviewing the Work of CIA Authors', 76.
4   John Hollister Hedley, 'Giving Retired Spies Their Say', *Washington Post*, 10 June 2012.
5   Ibid., 82.
6   Hedley, 'Three Memoirs by Former CIA Officers', 82.
7   Duane R. Clarridge, *A Spy for All Seasons: My Life in the CIA* (NY: Scribner's, 1997).
8   Mark Mazzetti, 'Former Spy with Agenda Operates a Private CIA', *New York Times*, 22 January 2011.
9   Hedley, 'Reviewing the Work of CIA Authors', 80.
10   Noam Scheiber, 'The CIA Goes Public', *New Republic*, 5 June 2006.
11   Hedley, 'Reviewing the Work of CIA Authors', 81.
12   Ibid., 80.
13   Ibid., 81.
14   Richard L. Holm, *The American Agent: My Life in the CIA* (London: St Ermin's, 2003); Richard L. Holm, *The Craft We Chose: My Life in the CIA* (Mountain Lake Park, MD: Mountain Lake Press, 2011).
15   Lou Novacheck, 'Former Top CIA Officer's New Book Provides Rare, Behind-the-Scenes Look at the Life and Work of a Member of the Nation's Clandestine Service', *Blogcritics*, 30 October 2011, http://blogcritics.org/book-review-the-craft-we-chose.
16   Ibid.
17   Bayard Stockton to C. Bruce Wells, 14 July 2003, MSS174, Box 1, Bayard Stockton Papers (hereafter BS), Davidson Library (hereafter DL), Department of Special Collections, University of California, Santa Barbara, CA.
18   Bayard Stockton, *Flawed Patriot: The Rise and Fall of CIA Legend Bill Harvey* (Washington, DC: Potomac Books, 2006).
19   Bayard Stockton to C. Bruce Wells, 14 July 2003, MSS174, Box 1, BS, DL.
20   Ibid.
21   Bayard Stockton to C. Bruce Wells, 21 April 2003, MSS174, Box 1, BS, DL.
22   Stockton, *Flawed Patriot*, Preface.
23   Bayard Stockton to C. Bruce Wells, 14 July 2003, MSS174, Box 1, BS, DL.
24   Bayard Stockton to C. Bruce Wells, 15 April 2003, 21 April 2003, 14 July 2003, MSS174, Box 1, BS, DL.
25   Bayard Stockton to C. Bruce Wells, 14 July 2003, MSS174, Box 1, BS, DL.
26   Ibid.
27   Ibid.
28   Robert Wallace and Keith Melton, *Spycraft: The Secret History of the CIA's Spytechs From Communism to Al Qaeda* (New York: Dutton, 2008), xx.
29   http://www.markzaid.com/biography.php?id=1.

30   Wallace and Melton, *Spycraft,* xxi.

31   Anonymous (later revealed as Michael Scheuer), *Imperial Hubris: Why the West is Losing the War on Terror* (Brassey's: Dulles, VA: 2004).

32   Ibid., xvi.

33   Ibid, xvii.

34   Ibid., 214.

35   Ibid., 181.

36   Laura Miller, 'Censored by the CIA', 30 August 2011, *Salon,* http://www.salon.com/2011/08/31/censored_by_cia.

37   'New Rules to Govern Publications by CIA Officers', *USA Today,* 11 January 2005.

38   Ibid.

39   Ibid.

40   T. J. Waters, *Class 11: Inside the CIA's First Post-9/11 Spy Class* (New York: Dutton, 2006).

41   John Lehman, 'Get Smart', *Washington Post,* 26 November 2006.

42   Scott Shane and Mark Mazzetti, 'Moves Signal Tighter Secrecy within CIA', *New York Times,* 24 April 2006.

43   Gary C. Schroen, *First In: An Insider's Account of How the CIA Spearheaded the War on Terror in Afghanistan* (New York: Ballantine Books, 2005), 38.

44   Gary Berntsen, *Jawbreaker: The Attack on Bin Laden and Al-Qaeda: A Personal Account by the CIA's Key Field Commander* (New York: Three Rivers Press, 2005).

45   Dana Priest, 'Suing over the CIA's Red Pen', *Washington Post,* 9 October 2006.

46   Ibid.; Sean Naylor, 'Slouching Toward Tora Bora', *Washington Monthly* (May 2006).

47   Priest, 'Suing over the CIA's Red Pen'.

48   Richard Leiby, 'Knocking on Osama's Cave Door', *Washington Post,* 16 February 2006.

49   Berntsen, *Jawbreaker,* 115.

50   Valerie Plame Wilson, *Fair Game: My Life as a Spy, My Betrayal by the White House* (New York: Simon & Schuster, 2007).

51   Ibid., xiii.

52   Ibid., 12.

53   Ibid., 268.

54   Ibid., xiv.

55   Ibid., 31.

56   John Prados, *Family Jewels: The CIA, Secrecy and Presidential Power* (Austin: University of Texas Press, 2013), 270.

57   David W. Brown, 'The CIA's Shark-Jumping Censorship of Former Agents', *The Week,* 11 June 2012.

58   Scott Horton, 'The CIA's Censorship Machine', *Harper's Magazine Blog,* 29 August 2011; 'Strangled to Death', 5 June 2012, https://roundersandrogues.wordpress.com/2012/06/05/strangled-to-death; 'CIA Publication Review Board Accused of Politically Motivated Censorship', 2 June 2012, http://www.allgov.com/news/top-stories/cia-publication-review-board-accused-of-politically-motivated-censorship?news=844565.

59   Horton, 'Censorship Machine'.

60   Greg Miller and Julie Tate, 'CIA Probes Publication Review Board over Allegations of Selective Censorship', *Washington Post,* 31 May 2012.

61   Steve Meacham, 'Uncle Sam's Secrets', *Sydney Morning Herald,* 7 August 2011.

62   Glenn Carle, *The Interrogator: An Education* (New York: Nation Book, 2011), 115.

63   Miller, 'Censored by the CIA'.

64   Meacham, 'Uncle Sam's Secrets'.

65   Carle, *Interrogator*, 292.

66   Ibid.

67   Ibid.

68   Debra Black, 'A CIA Interrogator Gives Inside Look at the War on Terror and the Mysterious Hotel California', *Star World*, 19 August 2011.

69   Brown, 'Shark-Jumping Censorship'.

70   Miller, 'Censored by the CIA.'

71   Ibid.

72   Ibid.

73   Carle, *Interrogator*, 291.

74   Jordy Yager, 'Book: The Spy Who Came in from the Farm', *The Hill*, 16 March 2010.

75   Steve Coll, 'The Spy Who Said Too Much: Why the Administration Targeted a CIA Officer', *New Yorker*, 1 April 2013.

76   Ibid.

77   Ibid.

78   Ibid.

79   *The Senate Intelligence Committee Report on Torture: Committee Study of the Central Intelligence Agency's Detention and Interrogation Program* (December 2014), 44.

80   Yager, 'Spy Who Came in from the Farm'.

81   Ibid.

82   Ibid.

83   John Kiriakou with Michael Ruby, *The Reluctant Spy: My Secret Life in the CIA's War on Terror* (New York: Bantam Books, 2010).

84   Ibid., 140.

85   Ibid.

86   Coll, 'Spy Who Said Too Much'.

87   Charlie Savage, 'Ex-CIA Officer's Path from Terrorist Hunter to Defendant', *New York Times*, 24 January 2012.

88   Scott Shane, 'Ex-Officer is First from CIA to Face Prison for a Leak', *New York Times*, 5 January 2013.

89   Ibid.

90   Ibid.

91   Ibid.

92   Ibid.

93   Amy Davidson, 'Jose Rodriguez and Ninety-Two Tapes', *New Yorker*, 30 April 2012.

94   Jose Rodriguez Jr with Bill Harlow, *Hard Measures: How Aggressive CIA Actions After 9/11 Saved American Lives* (New York: Simon & Schuster, 2012).

95   Peter Finn and Julie Tate, '2005 Destruction of Interrogation Tapes Caused Concern at CIA, Emails Show', *Washington Post*, 16 April 2010.

96   Kevin Gosztola, 'Congressman Criticizes "Selective Prosecution" of CIA Whistleblower John Kiriakou, Calls for Pardon', *The Dissenter*, 20 November 2014.

97   Greg Miller, 'Panetta Clashed with CIA Over Memoir, Tested Agency Review Process', *Washington Post*, 21 October 2014.

98   Ibid.

99   David McCabe, 'Ex-Navy SEAL Under Criminal Investigation for Bin Laden Book', *The Hill*, 31 October 2014.

100   Scott Shane, 'Ex-Officer is First from CIA to Face Prison for a Leak', *New York Times*, 5 January 2013.

101   Ibid.

102   Tom McCarthy, 'David Petraeus Pleads Guilty for Passing Classified "Black Books" to Lover', *The Guardian*, 3 March 2015.

103   http://www.reuters.com/article/2015/04/24/us-usa-petraeus-idUSKBN0NE15520150424

104   Ted Gup, *Nation of Secrets: The Threat to Democracy and the American Way of Life* (New York: Doubleday, 2007), 66.

105   http://www.markzaid.com.

106   Mitch Weiss, 'Petraeus Sentenced to 2 Years' Probation for Military Leak', *Associated Press*, 24 April 2015.

107   Prados, *Family Jewels*, 274. This book also contains some interesting reflections about CIA memoirs, especially chapters 7 and 8.

Index